MIRADOR

A Novel

JAMES JENNINGS

ALSO BY JAMES JENNINGS

The Light Most Favorable
A Novel

MIRADOR

A Novel

JAMES JENNINGS

GREENPOINT PRESS
NEW YORK, NY

Mirador by James Jennings

No part of this book may be reproduced or transmitted in any form or by any electronic or mechanical means, including photocopying and recording, or by any information storage and retrieval system without the express written permission of the publisher, except where permitted by law.

ISBN 978-0-9906194-4-4

Library of Congress Cataloging-in-Publication Data

Book Designer: Robert L. Lascaro
LascaroDesign.com

Greenpoint Press
A division of New York Writers Resources
greenpointpress.org
200 Riverside Boulevard, Suite 32E
New York, NY 10069

New York Writers Resources:
· newyorkwritersresources.com
· newyorkwritersworkshop.com
· greenpointpress.org
· prisonwrites.org

Printed in the United States on acid-free paper

Mirador is a work of fiction. However, some aspects of the story it tells and some of the places, events, and persons referenced are based on historical fact. Some names have been changed; some haven't. All actual people, places, and events mentioned have been used fictitiously, for the purpose of telling a fictional tale. The rest are products of the author's imagination. Any resemblance to actual persons, living or dead, or actual businesses, places, or events is coincidental.

The village of *Mirador*, as described in the novel, does not exist. Nate Hunter is a fictional character. His role in the Zapatista uprising of 1994 springs entirely from the author's imagination. Nothing in this story is meant to suggest that any North American played any role whatsoever in the uprising, the creation of the Zapatista website, or any communiqué issued by *El Ejército Zapatista de Liberación Nacional (EZLN)*. Nothing in this story is meant to suggest that any person has actually been injured or killed on a mission trip to Mexico at any time, in any place.

For Victoria, God's best work

CONTENTS

❧

PART THREE: EL PITÓN

❧

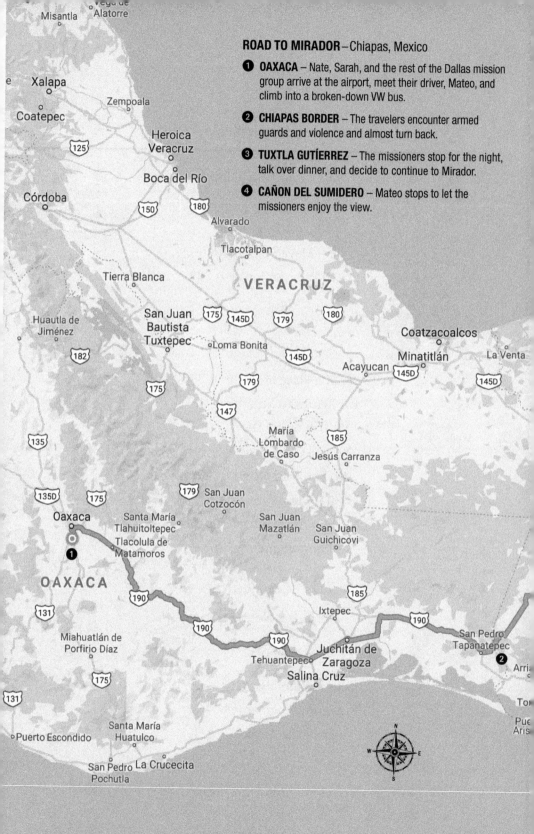

ROAD TO MIRADOR – Chiapas, Mexico

❶ OAXACA – Nate, Sarah, and the rest of the Dallas mission group arrive at the airport, meet their driver, Mateo, and climb into a broken-down VW bus.

❷ CHIAPAS BORDER – The travelers encounter armed guards and violence and almost turn back.

❸ TUXTLA GUTÍERREZ – The missioners stop for the night, talk over dinner, and decide to continue to Mirador.

❹ CAÑON DEL SUMIDERO – Mateo stops to let the missioners enjoy the view.

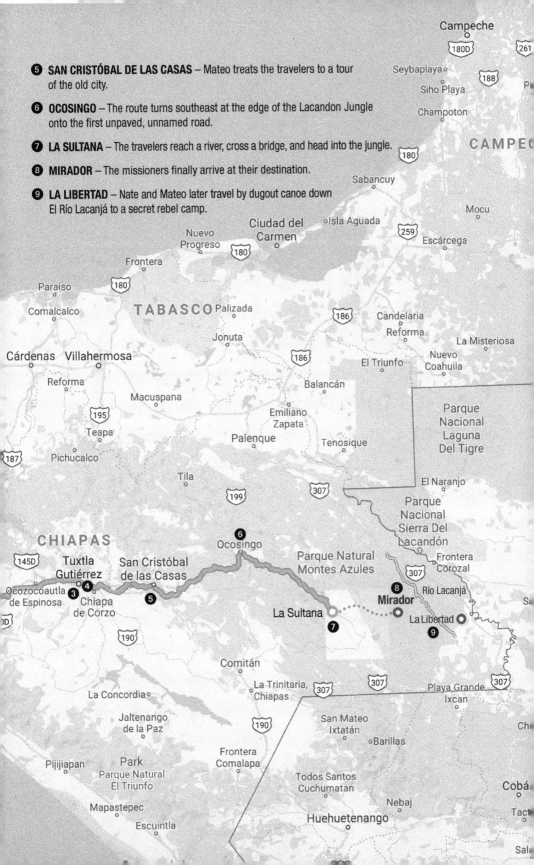

5 **SAN CRISTÓBAL DE LAS CASAS** – Mateo treats the travelers to a tour of the old city.

6 **OCOSINGO** – The route turns southeast at the edge of the Lacandon Jungle onto the first unpaved, unnamed road.

7 **LA SULTANA** – The travelers reach a river, cross a bridge, and head into the jungle.

8 **MIRADOR** – The missioners finally arrive at their destination.

9 **LA LIBERTAD** – Nate and Mateo later travel by dugout canoe down El Río Lacanjá to a secret rebel camp.

"Between the idea
And the reality
Between the motion
And the act
Falls the Shadow"

—T.S. Eliot, "The Hollow Men" (1925)

"The border means more than a customs house, a passport officer,
a man with a gun. Over there everything is going to be different;
life is never going to be quite the same again...."

—Graham Greene, *The Lawless Roads* (1939)

(The author's account of traveling by muleback
through the State of Chiapas in 1938)

Enough!

N *ew Year's Eve, 1994. San Cristóbal de Las Casas, State of Chiapas, Mexico.* Under cover of darkness, about six hundred rebel fighters moved into position on the outskirts of the city and prepared to attack. A little past midnight, as townspeople and tourists welcomed the new year in the central plaza, the rebels marched up side streets and stormed the white colonnaded *Palacio de Gobierno* located on the west side of the square. Crudely uniformed and poorly armed, they raced through a series of arches supported by Tuscan columns and broke down heavy panel doors with sledgehammers. They ransacked the government building, burned furniture and official records, dumped files onto the plaza, and freed political prisoners from their cells.

As news of the attack spread, hundreds of local residents streamed into the plaza. Finally, at around 5:00 a.m., a short, stout rebel *comandante,* clad in green fatigues and wearing a red bandana around his neck, climbed an alabaster staircase and appeared on a high-windowed, wrought iron balcony. Breath fogging in predawn chill, he brandished a printed broadside and read these words to the crowd gathered below:

> TODAY WE SAY ENOUGH IS ENOUGH!
> To the people of Mexico:
> Mexican brothers and sisters:
>
> We are a product of 500 years of struggle: first against slavery, during the War of Independence against Spain led by insurgents; then to avoid being absorbed by American imperialism; then to promulgate our

constitution and expel the French Empire from our soil; and later the dictatorship of Porfirio Diáz denied us just application of the Reform laws, and the people rebelled and leaders like Villa and Zapata emerged, poor men like us. We have been denied the most elemental preparation so they can use us as cannon fodder and pillage the wealth of our country. They don't care that we have nothing, absolutely nothing, not even a roof over our heads, no land, no work, no health care, no food, nor education. Nor are we able to freely and democratically elect our political representatives, nor is there independence from foreigners, nor is there peace nor justice for ourselves and our children.

But today we say, ENOUGH IS ENOUGH.

We are the inheritors of the true builders of our nation. The dispossessed, we are millions and we thereby call upon our brothers and sisters to join this struggle as the only path, so that we will not die of hunger. . . .

At the same time as the raid in San Cristóbal, other battalions of a rebel army consisting of no more than three thousand stouthearted men and women launched coordinated attacks in other parts of Chiapas. By noon, the insurgent forces of *El Ejército Zapatista de Liberación Nacional (EZLN)*—The National Zapatista Liberation Army—had seized four county seats, several smaller towns, and numerous ranches and plantations. Before the echo of the opening shots faded, the Zapatistas were using faxes and a new mode of communication called the Internet to enlist support for their cause, focus the world's attention on the injustices inflicted upon Mexico's forgotten indigenous people, and explain why they had chosen New Year's Day to rise up: January 1 was the day the North American Free Trade Agreement (NAFTA) went into effect. The rebels decried the treaty as a death sentence for their traditional, agrarian way of life. For them, the new era would be as bloody as the last.

The shooting war lasted twelve days. With the world watching, the Mexican government declared and immediately violated a ceasefire and demanded that the Zapatistas surrender their arms as a condition for dialogue. The Zapatistas refused. The rebels declared in one of a series of communiques to "the People of Mexico" and "the governments of the world":

> Our struggle doesn't end, nor does our cry end after the "ENOUGH" we uttered on January 1, 1994. It is still a long walk. There are different paths but one longing: Freedom! Democracy! Justice!

> We will continue to struggle until we achieve the freedom that is our right, the democracy that is our reason, and the justice that is our life!

Thus began what the Zapatistas called *The War Against Oblivion,* the first revolution in history to be fought on both the battlefield and the World Wide Web.

The known dead after a dozen days of bloodshed numbered one hundred fifty-nine, including sixteen soldiers of the Mexican Army, thirty-eight civilian security agents, sixty-seven civilians, and at least seventy Zapatistas. Some say the tally was much higher. Some say a lone American also perished in the fighting.

PART ONE

SARAH

CHAPTER 1

Going South

February 1993—one year before the uprising

Nate Hunter woke up exhausted. After packing and getting to bed late, he had hardly slept at all. He had checked the time at least hourly, risen twice when he thought he heard something. When the alarm clock sounded reveille at 4:00 a.m., he threw back the covers, swung his legs over the side of the bed, and sat, face in his hands, eyes closed, elbows on knees, feet on the cool polished-wood floor of his comfortable suburban Dallas home, feeling tortured by both the night's length and its brevity. Now came the first real test of the promise he had made to himself, and to Sarah, to stop objecting, put all reservations aside, and have a good attitude about the trip to Mexico.

Sarah, already up and dressed in her tan linen travel outfit, stood over him.

"Time to rise and shine, sweetie," she said, emerald-green eyes bright and shiny, strawberry-blond hair pulled back in a no-nonsense ponytail.

Nate groaned.

"I may be rising, but I won't be shining."

He fell back onto the bed.

"Five more minutes," he mumbled, burying his face in his pillow. "I think I just got to sleep."

"That's what happens when you're journey proud," Sarah said, tugging the pillow away.

Nate looked up at her through one squinted eye.

"Journey what?"

"Journey proud," she repeated, smiling down at him. "My grandmother used to say that. It's when you can't sleep the night before a trip because you're too excited."

"That's me, all right. Journey proud."

"Come on," Sarah said, taking his hand and pulling him upright. "We'll miss the flight."

"Okay," he said, getting to his feet. "I'm up. *Carpe diem.*"

Near first light, Nate and Sarah met their traveling companions at the Dallas/Fort Worth Airport. Six of them and, by their looks, not a seasoned traveler in the lot: a seemingly mismatched married couple in their fifties named Harold and Midge Bottomley—he was as tall and skinny as she was squat and round; a thin, gray-haired, retired schoolteacher named Wilma Trout, who was dressed in what looked like brand new camping wear; a fresh-faced, sandy-haired brother-and-sister team named Jeffrey and Stephanie Oliver, who had just graduated from college and might have been twins, Nate wasn't sure; and the slight, fair-haired, forty-something-year-old clergyman who had organized the trip.

Nate had met the clergyman before—first at a gala at the Dallas Museum of Art, then at a church function and again at a tea Sarah had arranged to sell Nate on signing up for the trip. Gentle-mannered and soft-spoken, The Reverend Thomas L. Butler—"Pastor Tom," he liked to be called—was involved with a nondenominational mission organization known as Heartland Missions that teamed up with local churches in Mexico and Guatemala to build schools, clinics and playgrounds, and restore churches. As the minister had put it, "We build bridges between people—the Haves and the Have Nots." Their accomplishments were small, he had assured Nate, but even small efforts like this next trip—two weeks deep in southern Mexico's Lacandon Jungle, restoring a crumbling old chapel in a rural village called *Mirador*—helped to make the world a better place and were pleasing in the sight of God.

Sarah had eaten it up. A registered nurse by profession and a tender-hearted do-gooder by nature, she was always ready to jump in to help others. Nate was more cautious and skeptical. Analytical by nature and a computer engineer by profession, he had questioned what a small group of gringo volunteers could accomplish in a mere two weeks. But

Sarah had been determined, and, as strong-willed as she was beautiful, what Sarah wanted she usually got. So, at the airport, on the morning of their departure, Nate kept his doubts to himself and made peace with the fact that the trip was underway.

As the members of the group filed down the ramp to board the plane, Sarah turned to Nate and said in a low voice, "I want you to know I really appreciate this. I think it will be worthwhile. And I think we'll feel good about it. I truly do."

Nate smiled, and they shared a chaste kiss.

"I love you," Sarah said.

"I know. And I love you." And in a playful tone, he added, "And I am your dutiful knight-errant, after all." He made a mock sweeping bow. "Your wish is my command."

Sarah laughed, but Nate meant every word. He loved his wife with all his heart, and he would do anything to see that she had whatever she truly wanted, pay any price to keep her happy and safe. And she truly wanted this trip. She had been waiting for it, in a way, ever since going on a medical mission trip to northeast Mexico during her last year of nursing school. She had returned with a small figurine of a jaguar that a young boy had given her and a determination to make this kind of volunteer work a bigger part of her life. It hadn't happened yet, but that first trip hadn't been that long ago, and Nate had known better than to think Sarah would lose interest. As long as that figurine remained on her dressing table—terracotta body, black spots, predatory stance—he knew she hadn't forgotten. Instead, she had started reading about Mexico and its ancient cultures. Nate remembered the night about a year earlier when she had looked up from a book she was reading while he watched TV.

"They developed the first writing system in the Americas, did you know that?"

"Who did?"

"The Maya."

"Hmm," he had grunted, half listening, caught up in an episode of *Dallas*.

"And they might have been the first culture to come up with the concept of zero."

Nate had grunted again.

"And they were astronomers and healers. And then their culture collapsed—disappeared. And now the people have what? Nothing." She had put down her book. "Nate, are you listening?"

He had turned away from the TV then, giving her his attention.

"I still want to go, Nate," she had said softly.

"Okay," he had said, nodding, knowing better than to argue.

This trip wasn't a medical mission. But it was the next best thing—a chance to help while learning firsthand about the Mayan people and their culture. Sarah would have gone with or without him. He didn't intend to let her go alone.

The 7:00 a.m. flight from Dallas/Fort Worth to Mexico City landed in time for the travelers to make their connection to *Oaxaca*. From there, the rest of the journey would be by car. They would spend the night in *Tuxtla Gutiérrez* in the neighboring state of Chiapas and continue on to Mirador the next day. The overnight stay in a four-star hotel in Tuxtla was the only part of the trip that sounded good to Nate. A direct flight from Oaxaca to somewhere near Mirador would have been preferable to almost two days on the road, but air travel in this remote corner of North America was unreliable, Pastor Tom had explained. Driving was their best bet. Nate knew the pastor was right. He had checked it out. He had checked everything out.

The ancient Zapotec city of Oaxaca lay at the base of a tall hill called *Cerro del Fortín* in a high valley surrounded on the north, south and east by *Sierra Madre* mountain chains. On the plane's final approach to Oaxaca's *Xoxocotlán* International Airport, Nate and Sarah got their first good look at the Sierra Madre, the mother mountains of Mexico— big-boned peaks, some rising as high as twelve thousand feet, their summits veiled in fog and mist. A quiltwork of green and rust-colored fields—corn, wheat, and maguey, Nate guessed—carpeted the valley floor. Scattered along roadways, Nate spotted buildings constructed out of the locally quarried, green-hued stone. He had read that the city's original name had been *Antequera* and that it had acquired the nickname *La Verde Antequeras*—the green Antequeras—as it grew. Now, he understood why.

A bull of a man approached the travelers when they emerged with their luggage from the terminal. Grinning, arms open, straw hat in hand, he embraced the minister heartily.

"This is Mateo," the minister said, smiling as he extricated himself from the man's bear hug. "He'll be taking us to Mirador."

The man smiled and nodded. "Welcome, my friends," he said in heavily accented English. "*Bienvenidos*. Thank you for coming." A dark-haired, rough-hewn fellow in his middle years, Mateo stood taller than most Mexicans, broad at the shoulders, stout through the barrel, but straight-backed, proud. A weathered face and hoary temples, along with his imposing bulk, lent him an air of authority. The minister introduced him around, and Mateo shook hands with the other members of the group. When he got to Sarah, Mateo smiled, bowed slightly and kissed her hand. "*Señora* Hunter," he said. "It is a pleasure to see you again."

"And you," Sarah said, returning the smile.

Mateo turned to Nate. "*Señor* Hunter," he said, nodding.

"Mateo." As they shook hands, Nate registered again the man's strong grip, large hands and thick wrists, the prominent veins in his muscular forearms, and his direct, penetrating gaze.

"Forgive me," Pastor Tom said. "Of course, you three have met."

"Yes, at the museum," Sarah said, smiling.

Nate had found the man intriguing then and found him equally intriguing now. He and the pastor had described themselves as old friends, and Mateo had impressed Nate by showing interest in his work. But when Nate had asked Mateo about himself, Mateo had ducked the questions, saying only that he helped restore old churches. Now, here he was, offering his services as their driver. But he was no mere driver, this Mateo. Nate didn't know who or what he was yet, but he knew intelligence and strength when he saw it, and this man had a commanding presence.

Next thing, Mateo was grinning again, apologizing for the quality of the transportation as he led the group down the walkway, sweeping his hat toward a worn-out old VW microbus parked at the curb.

"It is not much, *lo siento*," he said, "but it is the best *La Iglesia de la Ventana de Luz* has to offer at this time."

Nate gave it the once-over: 1971 model, red body, white roof, luggage rack on top. *"Not much," the man says,* he thought. *Beat to hell is more like it.* There were patches of rust along the rocker panels. The right front fender was bashed in and the headlight was missing. The rear window was cracked. The tires were far from new. *And this is supposed to get us to the Lacandon Jungle?*

Mateo was talking softly to Pastor Tom. The minister frowned, nodded and turned toward the group.

"Mateo says he is sorry, but there is no air-conditioning," the minister said.

"Are you—"

Sarah squeezed Nate's hand—their private signal for *Don't.* Nate closed his mouth and said nothing.

The minister patted the air placatingly. "Yes, I know. I apologize. It will be a little uncomfortable. But Mateo will try to get it repaired tomorrow morning in Tuxtla. Now, we must hurry if we want to get there before dark. Mateo has packed some bottled water and snacks to hold us until dinner."

After getting the luggage loaded and tied down, Mateo conferred with the pastor again, then assigned seats for optimal weight distribution—in a vehicle that apparently was also afflicted with dilapidated shocks. Nate ended up riding shotgun.

"This will give you a chance to get acquainted," Pastor Tom said as Nate climbed into the front next to Mateo. "I think you'll find Mateo interesting. And I know he will enjoy talking to you."

In the second row of seats, Sarah sat wedged in next to the Bottomleys. The pastor happily ensconced himself in the back with the teacher and the kids. The arrangement didn't make sense to Nate, but he went along, taking his seat and tucking his camera bag between his feet.

They fought their way northward through heavy urban traffic, mostly a swarm of VW bugs. Near its outer limit, the city took on an industrial look—electricity generating plants, *Pemex* gasoline stations. When they came to *Avenida Niños Héroes*, Mateo swung right onto a road that soon became Federal Highway 190—four lanes until they reached the outskirts of the city, where four resolved into two. Following signs indicating the way to *Mitla*, they struck out southeast across mostly flat terrain along roads bordered with the most luxuriant and varied tropical vegetation Nate had ever seen: from cactus and low shrubs, to palm trees, banana trees, and various kinds of towering evergreens—pines and firs. Here and there, patches of blood-red bougainvillea, wildflowers of every color, and the brilliant purple explosion of an occasional Jacaranda tree drew his attention. Every now and then, he noticed a wooden cross along the roadside inscribed with what looked like a name and a date. He pulled out his camera, attached the zoom and began taking pictures.

"Looks a little like Texas," Nate said. "Parts of it, anyway. Maybe New Mexico. All with a touch of the tropics. Very interesting."

"It is a land of great diversity," Mateo said. "And mystery. Far more to it than meets the eye... from the road, I mean."

Nate inhaled deeply.

"Now that we're out of the city, I can smell the flowers. I've been feeling the elevation since we arrived."

"*Sí*. Thin air. Over five thousand feet here. And we are climbing."

Mateo gestured toward the glove compartment. "There is a map in there. Under the binoculars."

Nate pulled it out, removed his designer sunglasses to study it, found their approximate location and looked around. Gazing out in every direction, he could see rolling hills in the middle distance. Beyond those, landmark mountains, now gunmetal gray with the advance of day, stood silhouetted against China blue sky.

"Mountains rule this kingdom," Mateo said, pointing. "*Es verdad, no?*"

Nate nodded.

"The farther we go, the more you will see what I mean."

An hour into the drive, billowing smoke off to the right side of the road caught Mateo's eye. He looked past Nate, through the side window, and pointed.

"*Mezcaleros*," he said. "Roasting maguey hearts."

Nate saw sombreroed men with machetes tending open firepits, lifted his camera and fired off a few quick shots. Mateo tilted back his head to breathe in the air scented with woodsmoke.

"Ahh..." he said. "Smell that? Oaxaca is the world capital of *mezcal*, you know. *Mezcal legítimo*. Elixir of the gods. People here say, 'For everything good, mezcal. For everything bad, mezcal.'"

"Hmm," Nate said. "A shot of mezcal sounds good to me. Five o'clock somewhere."

Mateo smiled, but he did not laugh. Nate turned and caught Sarah and the married couple frowning slightly. *Oh, right. Church mission. Those two must be teetotalers.* In the back seat, the brother of the brother-and-sister team leaned forward, grinning. "Awesome!" he said. "Is that where they dig the worms, too?" His sister giggled and elbowed him in the side.

"Ow!" Jeffrey said, laughing and ducking. "Why'd you do that?"

"Worms are, like, yucky," Stephanie said, scrunching her nose. "I hate worms."

Sitting on her right, the minister smiled and patted her hand. "It's okay, you won't have to eat any."

The road continued to climb. In the uplands, the air was cool, and Mateo stopped briefly to let the travelers stretch their legs.

"Just in time," Stephanie said, smiling wanly and holding her stomach. "Wow. Talk about a roller coaster ride!"

"How high are we now?" Nate asked Mateo, sneaking a shot of Sarah smiling and gazing out at their surroundings.

"Over six thousand feet," Mateo answered.

Walking back to the microbus hand in hand with his wife, Nate enjoyed the pleasant temperature, but he knew what was coming. Stifling heat. Back home in Dallas, February was a cool month. Not here. Nate knew that, this far south, the tropical savanna climate drove daytime temperatures into the nineties, even in winter. Once they quit the heights and descended toward the Pacific coast, steamy air would smother them like a rain-soaked blanket.

In another hour, they started down.

"I think my ears just popped," Nate said to Mateo.

"*Sí*. So it will be, most of the way. Up and down, up and down. Better fasten our seatbelts."

Nate felt around his seat.

"We don't have seatbelts."

Mateo's eyebrows went up. He shrugged.

"No problem. No problem."

On the southeastward slopes that flanked the high country, the travelers passed family-sized coffee farms, men tending goats, pigs, chickens. When they reached the lowlands, descending from more than six thousand feet nearly to sea level, Nate felt the temperature and humidity soar. Thermals rose from the pavement.

Traversing the coastal plain in their eastward advance, they passed cattle ranches and sugar plantations. From the road, the cropland had a prosperous look. Country folk toiled in fields and pastures, labored beneath raised hoods of farm vehicles, bent to all manner of agrarian tasks, seldom lifting their eyes from their work, paying no mind to the passing microbus.

"This low country, a little farther on, along the coast in Chiapas—

it was once known as the breadbasket of Mexico," Mateo said. He shook his head. "Imagine that. . . the breadbasket. And now people go hungry there."

Nate nodded. "So I've learned."

Mateo cast him an assessing glance. "It is the way of the world, my friend. The strong feed on the weak. The powerful feed on the strong. It is a question of where you are in the chain. The indigenous people of Chiapas are at the bottom."

Nate nodded but said nothing. He turned his attention back to the map in his lap, too tired to get into a discussion of global politics.

As they drove, the American traveling companions got to know one another. Sitting behind Mateo, Harold Bottomley reminded Nate of Ichabod Crane with his receding hairline, bony cheeks, outsized ears, protuberant eyes behind his black horn-rimmed glasses, pointy beak, and keen chin. He was a geologist, Harold explained in a surprisingly deep, resonant voice that Nate thought probably qualified him to sing bass in a church choir. His personalized license plates read ROCKER, he said, snorting and laughing as Nate watched his prominent Adam's Apple bob up and down. He was a talker whose favorite subject was rocks. He'd comment on the people they saw from the road, the vegetation, the architecture, the culture, the climate, but he had greatest interest in the terrain. He appeared to take much pleasure in lecturing the group on how the mountains surrounding them had been formed millions of years ago—going on and on about continental drift, subduction of tectonic plates, volcanoes rising from ruptures in the earth's crust. . . . Worse, he had a habit of peppering every mini-lecture with the phrase, "That is on it."

"These mountains are volcanic, that is on it—part of the Trans-Mexican Volcanic Belt."

What the hell? Nate thought. *Who talks like that?* After a while, Nate had to fight the urge to turn to him and ask, "What exactly does that mean, Harold? Where'd that odd phrase come from, anyway?" With some effort, he refrained.

Sitting next to her husband and making up in width for what she lacked in height, Midge Bottomley had a certain bovine quality about her. Squat, and red-faced with ginger hair she wore done up in a beehive style that made her head resemble a basketball, she had baggy jowls and a touch of puppet mouth. She also liked to talk, thought nothing of interrupting her husband, who invariably ceded the conversational ground, had an opinion on everything—the weather, the road, the people—and didn't hesitate to share it with the group.

"I don't care much for this heat. Don't like it one little bit."

Then, waving her hand before her face and manufacturing a cough: "Don't like this exhaust, either. Hadn't counted on that."

And a little later: "Road's pretty rough. I thought this was a national highway."

Nate gave Sarah a look that said, *This is going to be a long ride.* He reached back to squeeze her hand, then turned forward and gazed out the window, trying to block the ginger woman out. Forget the roller-coaster road, the hairpin turns, the potholes, the exhaust fumes, the sheer drop-offs, the lack of guardrail and center line. Listening to Midge's grousing was going to be the real challenge.

To shift the conversation without insulting Midge, Sarah turned to the thin, gray-haired woman in the back row and tried to draw her out. "So you're a teacher, Wilma?"

"Was," Wilma said, smiling nervously.

Single and childless, Wilma Trout had taught high school Spanish for more years than she cared to reveal, she said, and had promised herself an adventure when she retired. "So here I am." Tall and somewhat round-shouldered with short-cropped hair, she had outfitted herself for the first day of the trip in a blue plaid camper shirt—water-repellant and breathable—high-waisted stonewashed jeans, and a mail-order nylon explorer hat with a wide sloping brim, chinstrap and mesh band in the crown for ventilation.

Sarah—*Kind Sarah*, Nate thought—complimented Wilma on the hat. "That should be good protection against the sun and the rain."

"Oh, yes," Wilma said, nervously touching the brim. "I thought it was very sensible. It's guaranteed for life, and it was very inexpensive."

Wilma was doing her best to appear brave and adventurous on their first day away from civilization, but, in truth, Nate saw, she was a timid sort of woman who teared up over anything and everything: the colorful clothes the locals wore, the natural beauty of the countryside, the thought of the wonderful work they would do in Mirador. The serpentine road full of S curves and crazy drivers clearly terrified her. She gasped at every sharp turn and braced for impact in her corner seat every time another car passed them going either way. Nate gave her points, though, for being able to *habla español*. When introduced to Mateo, she had said *"Mucho gusto,"* and, looking impressed, he had responded *"Encantado."* Nate knew a few words, and Sarah had been brushing up on her high-school Spanish in preparation for the trip, but neither of them was anywhere near fluent. Wilma's language skills could come in handy later, Nate thought, when they were checking into their hotel and ordering dinner. Maybe she could help him order a mezcal on the sly. If she did that, it would be okay with him if she cried all the way to Mirador.

Sitting next to Wilma, the dynamic duo brother-and-sister team did a lot of smiling and peering out the windows, taking in their surroundings and pointing out new sights and saying "Wow" and "Awesome" and "Totally" and "Like." Each was quick with a lighthearted remark that often ignited a shared burst of laughter, and Stephanie Oliver was especially eager to talk about why she and her brother were there. Their dad was a rich oil man from Midland who had made "a bundle," as Stephanie put it, triggering another burst of sibling laughter, when he sold his small production company at the peak of the boom.

"He mostly plays golf now and sits on boards," Jeffrey said.

"Yeah, and Mom is all into her charity work," Stephanie added. "So we don't really have to earn a living, you know? Which is awesome. I mean, we're like totally lucky. But Mom and Dad, they make sure we know how lucky we are, right Jeff?"

Stephanie looked to her brother, who nodded. "Yeah, and they don't just give us money or anything. We always have to earn it. Doing chores and stuff."

"Yeah, and when we graduated from college, they said, 'Okay, we'll give you a year to figure out what you want to do. But then you have to commit to something, because if you think we're going to let you just sit around on your backsides'"—another burst of shared laughter—"'you better think again.'"

"So when we heard about this trip . . ." Jeffrey said.

"We both thought, like, *yes*," Stephanie said, "because it's important to, like, give something back," her intonation rising on the word "back" as if she were asking a question instead of making a declarative statement of firm purpose.

At that point, Mateo took another hairpin curve, and the siblings suddenly stopped talking and held their stomachs. Pastor Tom quickly called to Mateo, "Mateo, another rest stop, please?" It had already become part of the driving routine. From time to time, Stephanie or Jeffrey would announce, "I think I'm going to be sick" or "I don't feel well," and Mateo would have to pull over to let them exit the bus to calm their innards. The second time it had happened, Nate had offered to move to the back and let the two trade off taking his seat up front, but Mateo had frowned at the suggestion and, catching his frown, the siblings had insisted they'd be fine and the back seat was okay. They were game kids. Nate had to concede that. More dilettantes than philanthropists, he reckoned. But nice enough. And, they were people with money. As he saw it, people with money were always good to know.

It also quickly emerged that, except for Nate and Sarah, the members of this newly formed sect of sojourning gringos were all members of the church in Dallas where Pastor Tom was senior minister.

"I thought for sure more people would sign up after that talk you gave," Stephanie said, looking at the minister sitting beside her in his nonclerical traveling garb of khaki pants and short-sleeved shirt.

Pastor Tom nodded and shrugged. "Yes. Well. . . . "

Nate felt embarrassed for him. These were the only parishioners who were willing to take him up on his proposal to make this trip. Turned out, an adventure to the Lacandon Jungle, even one with a godly purpose, made a hard sell. *The dropouts were the smart ones,* Nate thought. *Anyone with an ounce of sense said no.* Once again, he kept quiet.

Along the way, Mateo acted as tour guide—naming the towns they passed through, warning about approaching turns, announcing their falling altitude as they descended into the heat of the fertile coastal flatland—but, as in Dallas, he talked little of himself. Finally, to be gracious when Stephanie kept pelting him with questions, he allowed that he hailed from Mexico City, but he did not elaborate. He said that he admired *los indígenas* of Mesoamerica—the *Tzotzil, Tzeltal, Tzoque,* and other ethnic groups—but could not claim their noble bloodlines as his own.

"I am a *mestizo,*" he said. "Half this, half that. A mixture of Spanish *conquistador* and conquered *indio*. Of course, that is true for all of us. We are all two people, I mean. At least two. Maybe more. *Verdad?*"

He shrugged affably.

"I am a mongrel, you see? Much the same as the four-legged variety you see trotting along the road here. A better driver, though."

"What exactly do you do for the church?" Nate asked. "I don't think you've said."

Mateo hesitated, then answered.

"I am what you might call *el alguacil,* a sort of manager. I assist *Tatic*—Father Javier, that is, you will meet him—with the business of the church. I do...whatever needs to be done. *Un factótum*—jack of all trades, master of none."

With the sun now at their backs, they made their way across the Isthmus of Tehuantepec, Midge complaining of the heat all the way. At the town of *San Pedro Tapanatepec,* they veered northeastward and left the flatland behind. The temperature cooled as they ascended again. Mammoth mountains closed in around them.

"And now it's chilly again," Midge said, rubbing her arms. "We go from one extreme to the other, don't we?"

Nate turned to give Sarah another look and saw Harold put an arm around his wife and rub her shoulder, which she frowningly allowed.

"How far is the border of Chiapas?" Nate asked Mateo.

"As the crow flies, only about twenty kilometers—about twelve American miles. Of course, we are not crows and we are not flying. It will not be long, though. From here, the road rises again."

Soon, they were up around fifteen hundred feet again and the road began to zigzag. Nate knew from checking the map in his lap that this meant they were nearing the State of Chiapas, which meant they were closing in on Tuxtla, their stopping point for the night. Harold asked to have a look at the map. Nate passed it to him.

"Where are we?" Harold said, Adam's apple bobbing, smoothing the map on his knees and pushing his glasses to his forehead.

Nate reached over and pointed. "Right there. See where it says 'the middle of nowhere'? That's it."

He caught Sarah's disapproving look and, with a contrite smile, attempted to blunt the sharp remark by quickly adding, "It may be terra incognita, but it's really pretty country. Lush, green forest. Mountains in all directions. Never seen anything like it."

Nate glanced at Sarah for approval, and she graced him with a forgiving, if still somewhat scolding look. He felt the gentle lash of her reproof. *Only the first day and I'm already in trouble,* he thought. *And we haven't even made it to the State of Chiapas yet.*

"You are right," Mateo said, nodding in response to Nate's comment about the beauty of the country. "But life is not easy here." He glanced at Nate. "Soon you will see. Soon, all of you will see." ▲

CHAPTER 2

A Boiling Cauldron

Following the narrow roadway through a valley that ran perpendicular to the general strike of steeply pitched peaks, the missioners finally came to the border of the state for which they were bound. Despite it being a nondescript location in the middle of nowhere, they found themselves coming up on a logjam of people and vehicles extending in both directions from a red-and-white striped, articulated barrier arm patrolled on each side of the road by soldiers in green fatigues with rifles slung over their shoulders. The sight silenced the travelers.

"You all have your passports, *sí?*" Mateo asked, glancing up at his passengers through the rearview mirror. Everyone murmured and nodded.

Nate turned to see Sarah sitting with hands clasped in her lap, eyes wide with surprise. He reached back and squeezed her hands. "It's okay," he said. "We'll be fine." But the truth was he was feeling nervous, too. This was not what Nate expected at the border of a state.

"Why so many cars and people?" he asked Mateo. "Why a barrier? Why soldiers?"

"It is nothing," Mateo said, eyes on the road. "It is just the Chiapas border. We have many borders in Mexico. Borders here. Borders there. Borders everywhere. No problem. No problem."

"Is there a town nearby?"

"*Sí, Rizo de Oro* is to the north, not very far."

"*Rizo de Oro,*" Nate said, extending a hand for Harold to return the map. "*Oro* is gold. What does *rizo* mean?"

"Curl," Wilma volunteered from the back seat.

"*Sí*, curl," Mateo said, nodding and making a twirling motion with his finger. "Curl of gold."

Mateo glanced in the rearview mirror and smiled.

"Like the hair of your lovely wife."

Nate turned to see Sarah frown and blush, and, for the millionth time since the day they met, he fell in love with her all over again. *She has no idea how beautiful she is,* he thought. He wasn't bad-looking himself, he knew—tall, fit, dark-haired. He was intelligent, hard-working, had a good job, was respected in his field. But Sarah.... Her father had made clear to Nate when Nate had asked for her hand that, as far as he was concerned, no man was really good enough for his precious only child. And he was right. Four years into married life, Nate still couldn't believe Sarah was his. He'd sworn to Trevor Blake that night that he would always love and provide for his daughter. Always protect her. He had wanted to add that he would die for her but had been afraid his future father-in-law would think that over-dramatic. He would, though. In a heartbeat.

"At one time, there was much gold in these mountains," Mateo continued, sweeping his hand through the air with a gracefulness that took Nate by surprise. "*The Treasure of the Sierra Madre*, no? But, of course, it was pillaged by Spaniards. Later, by... " He brought himself up short. "Well... by everyone. Chiapas has a long history of bleeding its natural resources from... *cómo se dice... heridas abiertas.*"

"Open wounds," Wilma said.

"*Sí*, open wounds."

Nate detected resentment in Mateo's tone. It stoked his rising sense of unease with the man. He did not quite know what to make of this fellow. Affable one moment, brooding the next. And his last remark did not help.

The rickety old microbus joined the line of vehicles stopped at the barrier. Nate welcomed the break from the rocky ride, the acrid exhaust. But as soon as the air cleared, the smell of exhaust was replaced by a hint of horse manure and garbage. Rot of something dead. Nate pinched his nose.

He didn't like what he was seeing any better. Soldiers with guns everywhere. A small, whitewashed cinder-block building that looked like a guardhouse slightly ahead on his side of the road. Weathered-looking, bronze-skinned women sitting cross-legged on the ground in brightly colored, woven skirts, trinkets displayed on blankets in front of them. Children and animals everywhere. A three-legged, piebald dog of no identifiable breed. A shirtless, barefoot kid with a bloated belly. Snarling flies. And, as they inched forward, a sign. Nate removed his sunglasses, took the binoculars from the glove compartment and focused. It was a one-word command painted in large scarlet letters on a piece of blanched plywood nailed to a post—*ALTO!*

The sign triggered a feeling of sudden dread that snapped Nate to attention. He straightened in his seat, propped an elbow on the sill of the rolled-down window, leaned forward, and took another, clearer look at the long line of vehicles, the soldiers, the barrier, the guns. Feeling his facial muscles tighten beneath a thin glaze of perspiration, he turned to the man at the wheel.

"What is this? Some kind of military checkpoint? You said it was just the border."

Mateo did not answer. His eyes remained fixed on the stern-looking soldiers up ahead as the line of vehicles inched forward. Leapfrogging each other, two teams of soldiers marched from car to car, one soldier on each side, peering in windows, demanding papers, studying documents and faces before waving cars forward as the barrier arm lifted to let them pass one by one. Watching them, Nate had a strong feeling of being off his turf. He could hear the dull thump of his heart. Feel it in his throat.

"This is just the border of a state, right?" he asked again.

Again Mateo didn't answer. He stared straight ahead.

Nate turned to study the driver now. He saw Mateo pass the back of a hand across the moist, bronze skin of his forehead.

"Is something wrong?" Nate asked.

Mateo sighed. He turned toward Nate and shook his head, but did not speak. He faced the front again and eased the bus forward one more car length. In profile, Nate could see the man's right eye narrow, the lower lid twitch.

No one in the bus made a sound. Nate twisted around to shoot a worried glance at the slight, fair-haired man of the cloth in the back seat, but Pastor Tom was staring placidly out the window. When the clergyman shifted slightly and met Nate's gaze, he only shrugged. Nate looked to Mateo again.

"Is something *wrong*?" he repeated more forcefully.

Responding to the change in tone, this time Mateo answered. "No. No. Nothing is wrong. No problem. No problem."

The mestizo smiled, but the smile faded quickly. He sighed once more, this time from the core of his being. Gone was the hearty conviviality that had marked his manner earlier in the day. His sigh sounded world-weary to Nate and... something else. Something dark. Something hard-edged.

Mateo and his passengers waited their turn in silence as the line of vehicles crept forward. The air did not stir. Still, Nate sensed in it a feverish energy that seemed to flush the skin of the place, a throbbing like a raw nerve.

Turning to check on Sarah, Nate saw her sitting like a stone effigy. She had leaned forward for more breathing room and a clearer view out the windshield, but, otherwise, she sat unmoving, her cheeks flaming. Catching her husband's gaze, she smiled, trying to appear at ease. But the upturn of her lips had no more conviction than Mateo's and faded in an instant, yielding to an expression that asked, *Was this a good idea? Have we made a mistake?*

Nate's first response was a look of silent reproach, a narrowing of the eyes that wounded Sarah, he could tell. He couldn't help it. The strangeness of this distant land in which they now found themselves, the dizzying journey through the heat and altitude in this broken-down bus, these strangers they'd been thrown in with, and this man at the wheel who had begun making Nate uneasy even before they arrived at this checkpoint. And now this. Soldiers. With guns. The sense of being out of control and in over his head set his teeth on edge. And Sarah was the one who had insisted they come. He had opposed the idea but he'd given in. *Why did I let her get us into this? What in the hell are we doing here? Why didn't I say no and stick to it?*

But Sarah was genuinely concerned. She was scared. Nate could see it. She needed him to reassure her, to be strong. Softening, he reached back and took her hand.

"It's okay. It's okay. Don't worry."

Nate studied Mateo in silence. *Exactly what does he mean, 'No problem. No problem'? Why the deep sigh and fake smile? Why the twitch?* But Nate could glean nothing from the man next to him. His questions would have to wait.

Nate returned his sunglasses to his face and the binoculars to the glove compartment. He turned and, with feigned calmness, let his gaze wander the landscape, telling himself he wouldn't speak again until they crossed the border, wouldn't utter so much as a word unless it was necessary, absolutely necessary.

At the edges of the roadway, vegetation closed in—a stand of cane grass, low shrubs, scrub trees of a dozen varieties. Everywhere he looked, Nate saw green. Green, green, and more green, a million shades of it. Some deep, almost black. Some pale as unripe limes. Some bright as jade. And teal, almost turquoise, almost the blue of the Caribbean waters that Nate knew lay only about five hundred miles to the east. Beyond the roadside sedge and thickets stretched a narrow undulating plain—short grass, scatterings of iron-gray volcanic rocks, offscourings of the restless earth. To the north and east, beyond the local relief of slump-shouldered hills, loomed ranges of thickly forested mountains. Steely silhouettes of large caliber sierras knifed through a sky of pure spectral blue, penetrating at the beltline a sash of low clouds. Above that stretched a gleaming transom of clear air. At higher altitudes, sentinel peaks vanished in an expanse of ponderous overcast, the color of slate. The layering of bands of air and light was like nothing Nate had seen in all his thirty-one years of life in the U.S. For a moment, he forgot his dread, removed his sunglasses and reached again for his camera.

Ahead, at the barrier, two soldiers approached a vehicle a few cars in front of the VW bus. Each wore a U.S. government Kevlar helmet with camouflage cover. The soldier on Nate's side carried an M-16 rifle with a thirty-round magazine slung over his shoulder and wore a .45 automatic holstered at the hip. Nate watched as they discharged their duties with aplomb, examining papers and passports with trained eyes. They were all business.

With a sharp movement of one hand and without lifting his eyes from the passport he was examining, the soldier on Nate's side of the line of cars swatted the back of his neck. Nate watched him open his hand, examine his palm, then flick something away and wipe his hand on a trouser leg.

The soldiers were taking their time with that car's papers, and the line seemed stalled. Nate's attention drifted to a gaggle of raggedy children clustered by the wall of the nearby guardhouse. The kids were inspecting something with rapt attention. Nate lifted his camera, adjusted the zoom and brought the object of the children's fascination into focus. A large black-and-yellow orb-weaver spider with tentacle appendages sat at the center of a silken web that stretched from a low bush to a corner of the building. Lustrous strands formed a complex array of geometric patterns, all studded with carcasses of the spider's insect prey. In time, they would make a fine spider's feast. He snapped a picture.

At the web, one child crouched on his heels. Another leaned forward, hands on knees. One pointed, mouth agape, eyes wide. One turned away from the others, looked purposely at the air above him and reached up suddenly, trapping an insect between cupped hands. With thumb and forefinger, he plucked the critter from the hollow of his loose fist and tossed it into the arachnoid snare. It stuck. The children stepped back and watched it squirm. When it fell still, some laughed, some shrieked, some gasped and others simply gaped as the spider glided swiftly across slender threads and, in one seamless movement, seized, rolled and spun the insect, encasing it in pale filament.

Scowling, a girl picked up a stick as long as her arm, raised it high and, with one unsparing blow, put the intricate lair asunder, sending the spider skittering.

"*Basta! Ya basta!*" she cried.

Startled and outraged, the other children turned on her, grabbed the stick away and rebuked her with sneers, shouts and angry gestures until she slunk away, passing so close, not ten feet from the bus, that Nate could see tears tracking down her cheeks.

Looking up the line of vehicles to check on their progress, Nate saw two beefy-looking men in dark uniforms—faded black, not the green of soldiers—come around the far side of the barrier arm, marching a third man at gunpoint in their direction along the ragged fringe of the two-lane road. The third man looked like a farmer, thin and brown-skinned in dusty clothes and fraying straw hat. His hands were bound behind him. One of the armed men gave him a shove, and, when he stumbled, then recovered his balance, Nate saw what looked like bailing wire cinched tight around his wrists and streaks of blood covering the backs and palms of his hands.

The children scattered as the black-uniformed men hazed their captive toward the guardhouse and pushed his back against the wall where the children had been watching the spider a moment before. The man bent forward, eyes darting, face streaming with sweat, as if preparing to flee. Above him, along the roof ridge, a perfect line of crows observed.

Nate put a hand on Mateo's elbow. Without looking in his direction, Mateo answered in a whisper.

"*La policía*. State police. Gangsters."

The men in dark uniforms commenced yelling at their captive, gesticulating wildly. Nate couldn't make out their words. One stepped closer and punched the man in the face, sending his straw hat tumbling to the ground. "No! No!" the man shouted as his second captor stepped forward and struck him another blow, this time sending the man to his knees.

"Nate," Sarah whispered learning forward, her breath in his ear, her hands on the back of his seat. He reached around without turning and squeezed her hand—their signal. She was still a moment, returned the signal, then silently sat back. No one else made a sound. The women selling trinkets along the roadside sat like statues, not looking, not moving.

The two men in dark uniforms yanked their captive upright by his bony shoulders and stood in front of him, ready to rain down more blows, when suddenly the man crouched and lunged, butting one of them hard in the chest. Then he bolted. But with his hands bound, legs weak with terror, he managed only a few clumsy steps before going down like an armless drunk. Close behind, the two policía hauled him to his feet again, threw him back against the wall and held him pinned, guns drawn and pointed.

Nate watched the policemen confer, then pull the man from the wall, spin him around so he stumbled and almost fell again, prod him forward with the barrels of their guns and march him along the margin of the road, back in the direction they had come from. The soldiers ignored them and continued checking cars. The policía marched their captive back around the barrier and kept going. Just before reaching a far bend in the road, they took a hard right and headed into the brush, raising a scud of dust from the undergrowth as they disappeared.

Nate watched the dust drift back to earth, then turned to Mateo.

"What was that about? Who was that man?"

Mateo squeezed the steering wheel and stared straight ahead. A loud crack sounded out, splitting the air, sending the crows flapping, and wrenching shouts and gasps out of everyone in the VW bus. Everyone except Mateo. Nate saw the soldier working his way toward their bus turn sharply toward the noise, then turn back, frowning and shaking his head as if disgusted.

Nate wheeled around to see Sarah sitting rigid, pressed against the back of her seat, eyes round and alive with comprehension, terror and disbelief. He grasped her knee, sought her gaze.

"Sarah, you're okay," he said firmly, more a command than a question. "Do you hear me? You're okay."

She shuddered, met his gaze, and he saw her eyes clear. She nodded. "Yes, Nate," she said, putting a cold hand atop his. "I'm okay."

Midge sat with her hands over her mouth, her husband's arms around her. Wilma Trout sat pressed into her corner seat, eyes squeezed shut, hugging herself, one hand at her throat. The siblings clutched each other's hands, eyes and mouths open wide. The minister sat frozen, looking down.

Nate turned to Mateo. "What was that?" he demanded.

Mateo didn't answer.

"I said, 'What was *that?*'"

Mateo shook his head vigorously. "*No sé. No sé.*"

Angry now, Sarah reached for the seatback and pulled herself forward. "What do you mean, you don't know? That was a gunshot! I know a gunshot when I hear it!"

Mateo shook his head again. "I do not know. I do not think so."

Sarah stared at him in disbelief. "Mateo, it was. You know it was."

"No. No. I . . . I doubt it."

Then Nate saw his wife's eyes go wide again and, turning to look out the front windshield where she was looking, he saw two men in black uniforms, the same two policía, walking back toward them down the side of the road . . . without their captive. The soldier checking passports glanced up at them and shook his head again as they passed, but said nothing.

"Oh, my God," Sarah gasped, one hand flying to her mouth. "They shot him! They shot that man! We have to do something. He may still be alive."

She looked from Nate to Mateo to her other companions. No one responded. No one moved. The bus inched forward again.

"I don't *believe* this," she said angrily. "What's wrong with all of you? We can't just sit here! We have to do something!"

Sarah leaned forward and reached for the handle to the sliding back door. Nate wheeled and seized her wrist.

"Nate! What—"

"Sarah, no. It's too dangerous."

But once the fires of compassion and determination were ignited within her, Sarah was not easily dissuaded.

"They shot that man, Nate!" she said angrily. "He may still be alive. He may need help."

"No, Sarah. This isn't Dallas. These guys aren't rent-a-cops patrolling some parking lot back home."

"I don't care!" Sarah squirmed, trying to break free from Nate's grip just as the green-clad soldiers approached their bus. One now stood at Mateo's window.

"*Licencia, pasaportes,*" the soldier said in a perfunctory manner as his partner peered in Nate's window.

Nate quickly released his wife, watched Sarah turn her glare from him to the man in green fatigues, then saw her eyes soften.

"Sir," she began. "Perhaps—"

"Sarah, don't," Nate said. "Let it go."

But she refused.

"*Señor, por favor.* We heard a shot. Someone may be hurt. I'm a nurse...."

The soldier at Nate's window walked away. The one at Mateo's window ignored her. Nate watched him quickly check his reflection in Mateo's sideview mirror, smooth one side of his mustache with a finger then resume his rigid, military bearing and extend a hand toward Mateo.

"*Pasaportes,*" he said again.

"*Sí, sí, sí, sí,*" Mateo responded, nodding rapidly. He turned to Nate and the other *norteamericanos* and flashed a smile that disappeared before it had fully formed. "Passports, everyone. Please. It will only take a minute. Then we will be on our way. Passports. *Por favor.*"

Without speaking, the travelers began digging into their pockets, purses and packs. Nate turned to see Sarah sitting with her passport already in her lap, but when he tried to catch her eye, she turned to look out the window, freezing him out.

To try to lighten the mood as his passengers gathered their passports, Mateo smiled up at the soldier.

"*Buenas tardes,*" he said.

And then he began to explain who he and his passengers were and where they were going. Nate picked up *Estados Unidos, Oaxaca, iglesia, Mirador.*

At the mention of Mirador, the soldier's eyebrows shot up. Dead silence followed. Then he smirked and turned toward a small group of other soldiers gathered on his side of the road.

"*Oye!*" he called out. "*Estos gringos van a Mirador. Van a Mirador.*"

To a man, these uniformed troops also looked surprised, and then broke into laughter. They shook their heads, exchanged inaudible remarks and guffawed. The soldier at the bus put both hands on the rim of Mateo's open window and leaned in slightly. He knitted his brow, shook his head slowly and spoke in what almost sounded like a concerned tone.

"*Mirador? Conoce a El Pitón?*" he asked, drawing a line with his thumb across his right cheek from nose to ear, as if to indicate a mark of some kind—a cut or scar.

Nate felt his stomach lurch. "El Pitón?" he said to Mateo. "Who's El Pitón?"

When Mateo shrugged, the soldier shook his head and turned back to his comrades. "*No conoce a El Pitón,*" he called to them, mimicking Mateo's shrug. "*No lo conoce.*" Again, they cackled.

The soldier turned back to Mateo.

"*No tiene miedo?*" he asked gravely.

When Mateo didn't answer, he turned to Sarah.

"You? You no have fear?"

"Fear of what?" Sarah asked sharply, her back still up.

"Sarah," Nate said in a low voice.

She ignored him and turned to gather passports from the passengers in the back seat.

The soldier turned back to Mateo. "Fear of what," he said, repeating Sarah's words and giving Mateo a cold stare. He shook his head again and chuffed. "*Qué pendejos,*" he said under his breath.

"Who's El Pitón?" Nate asked Mateo again.

Again, Mateo shrugged.

Nate wanted to press him, but the soldier's manner had become stern again. He snapped his fingers and held out his hand.

"*Pasaportes. Pasaportes.*"

Sarah handed them forward, Nate added his and passed them to Mateo, who ordered them like playing cards, fanning them out, then stacking them again. Nate watched him take a fifty-peso note from his pants pocket—worth between sixteen and seventeen U.S. dollars by Nate's math—slip it into the middle of the stack, and present the stack to the soldier with an obsequious smile. The minute the soldier accepted the documents and dropped his gaze to examine them, Mateo's smile vanished.

Taking his time, the soldier counted the passports as the Americans sat silent, hands folded in their laps. When the soldier came to the money, showing no reaction at all, he squirreled it away in a back pocket, then evened the stack of passports, opened the top one and began studying it. Mateo glanced at Nate and nodded almost imperceptibly. Nate turned and winked reassuringly at Sarah.

The soldier peered in through Mateo's window, studied Nate's face, looked down at the passport he was holding open, looked at Nate again, looked down again, flipped a few pages of the passport, closed it and put it at the bottom of the stack. *Good God*, Nate thought. *How long is this going to take?* When the soldier seemed finished with him, to calm himself, Nate turned his attention out his window again and noticed an Indian woman, a barefoot *campesina* some little distance away, walking toward him along the edge of the road, bent forward under the weight of a bundle on her back, never lifting her gaze from the earth in front of her feet. Her blue-black hair hung in two shaggy braids. She wore a faded print dress—flowers of blue, red and purple—torn at one shoulder, and a tumpline harness filled with branches that looked longer than she was tall. Firewood. Head down, plodding forward, strap across her brow, she reminded Nate of a dray horse straining against its traces. The heavy load of sideways branches on her back made Nate think of a crucifix, Jesus carrying a cross of sticks.

As she came closer, Nate saw that the woman had two children in tow in stair-step formation—a girl wearing a brilliant yellow-and-green dress, walking in the same bent-over posture and carrying a smaller bundle of firewood; and, behind her, a younger boy in a tattered t-shirt and brown trousers with a bundle of his own strapped across his chest. Nate thought of the family that lived a few houses down from him and Sarah back home in Dallas. The kids, a boy and a girl, were about the same age. They'd be home from school now, probably out in their backyard, playing. Not here. Nate had done his reading. He knew Chiapas was no Shangri-La and thought he was prepared to see poverty, but his first glimpses of it jarred him.

Moving slowly to avoid attention, Nate lifted his camera and adjusted the lens to wide angle to capture the mother and her brood as they passed. Looking through the viewfinder, he saw the woman shift her gaze in his direction. *Perfect.* He snapped a picture and watched the woman turn and charge directly toward him, hand extended, eyes angry.

"*No fotos!*" she shouted. "*No fotos sin dinero! Veinte pesos! Veinte pesos!*"

"Okay! Okay!" Nate exclaimed, recoiling. "I'm sorry!"

The soldier at Mateo's window stopped examining passports and came to attention. "*Que pasó?*" he demanded.

"*Está bien, está bien,*" Mateo assured him, then leaned across Nate to address the woman at his window.

"*Lo siento, Señora. Él no sabe. Lo hizó sin querer. Disculpelo, por favor. Disculpelo.*"

Then Mateo turned to Nate. "Give her twenty pesos."

"What? Why?"

"Pay her," Mateo said sternly. "No pictures without money."

Nate fumbled for his wallet, fingered through the money he had exchanged the week before and pulled out a note. He extended it toward the woman. "I'm sorry," he said. Frowning, she jerked the bill from his hand and walked away.

"Christ," Nate said, heart pounding. "I'm sorry. I didn't know."

"It is the custom," Mateo explained, softening his tone. "That is all. I should have told you. No problem. No problem."

Nate set the camera back in the case between his feet, put on his sunglasses, folded his arms across his chest and stared straight ahead. His cheeks burned.

The soldier checking their passports now seemed amused by the incident. He was smiling when he returned them to Mateo.

"*Está bien,*" he said. "*Todos en orden.*"

He stepped back, and, for a moment, Nate thought he saw an almost sympathetic expression cross the soldier's face.

"*Buena suerte,*" he said. Then, looking in through the window at Sarah in particular, "Good luck."

Resuming a soldier's stance and manner, he motioned Mateo forward with a curt wave of an arm.

"*Vayanse! Largo de aquí!*"

Mateo nodded and put his foot to the gas. The old engine coughed and died. Mateo turned the ignition key. The engine groaned and sputtered but did not start. Sweat rolled off Mateo's face. He glanced at the soldier, smiled a nervous smile, pumped the accelerator and tried the engine again. This time it grudgingly came to life, and the passengers in the rows of seats behind him breathed a collective sigh of relief. But as he put the bus in gear, Nate spun around to give Sarah a quick warning look, whipped off his sunglasses and seized the steering wheel.

"Hold on!" he said as Mateo surrendered the wheel in surprise. "I think we've seen enough of Chiapas. I don't think this is what we had in mind. I don't know who this El Pitón is, but I think you do, and I don't think we want to meet him. So why don't you just turn around and head back to the airport."

A wave of agreement surged forward from the back seats.

"Perhaps we should."

"I think Nate's right."

"Maybe this wasn't such a good idea."

"I'd like to go home."

Only the minister remained silent. Only Sarah protested.

"No! Wait! Wait a minute! We came here to help people! We can't just turn and run away!"

"*Señora* Hunter is right," Mateo said respectfully, regaining his composure. "We cannot go back now. We would never make it before dark and, my friends, you do not want to be on the road at night. And this vehicle... well... you know... it is not the best. We must go on to Tuxtla. You can go home in the morning if you desire."

More mutterings came from the back seats.

"Oh, dear, no, we don't want to be on the road at night."

"I could use a good night's sleep first."

"And maybe a good meal."

The soldier who had waved them forward stepped toward the bus again and peered in, frowning.

"*Vayanse! Vayanse!*" he commanded, motioning them on again.

Mateo gave Nate an imploring look.

"Please."

Nate looked at Sarah, whose eyes were also pleading. He sighed heavily, released the steering wheel, nodded with reluctance, and sat upright in his seat, jaws clenched. The barrier arm rose and the bus moved forward. They entered Chiapas.

We shouldn't be here, Nate thought. He felt it in his bones. *We shouldn't be here. Sarah shouldn't be here.* But he said nothing. Too late for that, anyway. They were here now. Nothing to do but go on. ▲

CHAPTER 3

Pressing On

From the border, Nate and his companions pushed north to Rizo de Oro, switchbacking and climbing again to over twenty-six hundred feet. There, they swung northeast along a slightly straighter roller coaster of a road toward *Lázaro Cárdenas*. No one spoke until Rizo was well behind them. Even Harold and Midge kept their own counsel.

Alone with his thoughts, Nate stared blankly at his surroundings like a sunstruck wanderer. From the shotgun seat, he could see nothing beyond the immediate prospect but cloud-capped peaks in an endless succession of parallel ranges, ridges and spurs hung with gray mist, skirtings of green. Trundling along a skinny intermontane corridor, he felt as if he had been gobbled up by some mythic beast, as if he were sliding down its gullet into its bilious belly. *Jonah and the whale. Gepetto and the Terrible Dogfish.*

After about half an hour, like a frozen lake melting, the silence within the VW bus began breaking up. A word here, a word there.

"It's chilly again. We must be climbing."

"Hmmmm."

"I'll be glad when we get to Tuxtla."

"Me, too."

Finally, Harold, the rocker, began holding forth.

"We're in the midst of a series of mountain ranges, you see—what's called a cordillera..."

"From the Spanish word for rope," Wilma added from the back seat.

Harold paused a moment, cleared his throat, resumed.

"By the way, the process of mountain building is called *orogeny*."

Nate turned to roll his eyes at Sarah and saw Harold glance down at his wife.

"Orogeny," he repeated, pronouncing the word deliberately, as if it had some special meaning. "Orogeny."

"Oh, yeah?" Jeffrey piped up from the back seat. "So we're in an erogenous zone?"

Stephanie giggled. Harold frowned.

"That's *oh*-rogeny—with an O."

His wife patted his knee.

"Harold is very smart," she sniffed to her traveling companions. "And he loves his rocks, don't you know."

In the back, Jeffrey snickered.

"Gotta like a guy who loves his rocks."

His sister giggled again and elbowed him in the side.

"Owww! Hey!"

She scorched him with a look.

"Okay! Okay!" Eyes glimmering, Jeffrey tried to make amends. "Uhh…that's really very interesting though, Harold. These mountains are awesome. I wish I'd paid more attention in my geology class."

At that moment, the road dog-legged around a cape of gray volcanic rock, jostling the passengers to their left, then back to their right when the road straightened.

"Oooh…" Stephanie groaned, one hand on her stomach, the other clutching her brother's leg. "That was not good. I'm sorry, Mateo. Can you…like…slow down a little?"

"Yes, a little slower, please," Wilma said, pressed against the window and bracing herself against the seatback in front of her with one arm.

"*Sí, sí*, no problem, no problem," Mateo said mechanically. "But we must get to Tuxtla, no?"

"Yes, of course, Mateo," the preacher said kindly. "Just a little slower, though, if you don't mind." Then, to Stephanie and Wilma, "Don't worry. Mateo is an excellent driver and he knows these roads. He'll get us there safely."

Gazing out the window, looking lost in her own thoughts, Sarah said nothing. Neither did Nate, though turning forward again to steady himself for the next bend, he did swear under his breath. He was still reeling from events at the border and he berated himself for allowing Sarah and the others to buffalo him into continuing on instead of insisting they turn back. He had done his research, had known the trip would not be without risks. *I knew better, dammit.* And yet, here he was. Here *they* were. Because he couldn't say no to Sarah. And because of his damned, deep-seated need to maintain harmony and peace, to keep everybody calm and happy and avoid arguments at any cost. *That's what got us into this mess. That's me, all right—go along to get along. And now we're paying the price.*

In the row of seats behind Nate, perhaps to cover his own anxieties, Harold was now holding forth again about every aspect of their geological surroundings, as if he were conducting a class, ending every observation with his trademark phrase. He pointed at what looked like a collapsed mountain top in the distance on the right.

"You see that kettle-shaped depression over there? I believe that might be a caldera. Yes, a caldera... that is on it."

"In English, the word would be cauldron," Wilma said in a quavering voice from the rear, bracing herself in her corner with a stiff arm against the back of Harold's seat. "You know... a large kettle... a boiler."

Harold cleared his throat and continued his dissertation.

"A caldera, you see, is a volcanic phenomenon. A violent propelling of magma from within the vent creates a sudden void. We're veritably surrounded by volcanic arcs here. That's the extinct Sierra Madre Miocenic arc to our south and the Chiapanecan arc to our north...."

"So beautiful, so beautiful," Wilma said, her voice choking with emotion.

"*El Chichón* is part of the Chiapanecan arc," Harold continued. "You've heard about El Chichón, of course."

"*Chichonal*," Wilma corrected. "I think the locals—"

"Erupted three times in nineteen eighty-two," Harold continued, talking over her. "People thought it was extinct. Hadn't erupted in six hundred years, and then boom!"

The bus swerved again.

"Oooh, I'm not feeling very good," Nate heard Stephanie whisper to her brother.

"Yeah. Me neither."

Harold prattled on.

"That's where we'll be soon," he said, leaning forward to point a finger between Mateo and Nate. "In one of those voids... after we've gained a little altitude... that is on it."

Nate gritted his teeth. *How about giving it a rest, Harold?* he wanted to say. Instead, as if of one mind, he and Mateo responded to the monotonous geologist in like manner, by ignoring him and staying silently focused on the road.

And still the man kept talking.

"These long sharp spines you see traversing the tops of those mountains are volcanic ridges. Hogbacks, we call them back home. Smaller spurs jut out from them. If you've ever looked down a valley and seen hills that appear almost braided, those are interlocking spurs."

"Very impressive," Wilma commented softly from the rear seat.

"Yes," said Harold. "And very complex."

God. Is he ever going to shut up? Nate turned his head just enough to aim a flinty glance at his wife. They exchanged looks of annoyance, but then Sarah shook her head ever so slightly. She smiled indulgently at the man who loved his rocks, and turned away to gaze out the window.

"As we go farther," Harold continued, "we'll start seeing canyons and canyons within canyons, called sub-canyons...."

Nate's mind began to numb. He had no desire to be in a caldera. He had no desire to be in a cordillera or a canyon. He had no desire to be in this country, on this winding two-lane blacktop road labeled a national highway on the map in his lap. If this was a national highway, he could only imagine what the road would be like tomorrow, when they headed from Tuxtla into the Lacandon Jungle. The one it looked like they'd be taking was depicted with a broken line. And to make matters worse, the village of Mirador was not even on the map. *La Selva Lacandona* was, but it was just a blank spot, a vacant expanse of green.

After studying the map for a while, Nate held it up so Mateo could see it and pointed to the blank green spot.

"So, this is where we're going?"

Mateo glanced at the map, nodded.

"This must be an old map," Nate said. "There's nothing there."

"The Lacandon Jungle is..." Mateo scratched his head, struggling for the properly descriptive word. "It is... *despoblado,*" he finally said. "Not *un*populated, but... *under*populated. Few inhabitants. To most of the country, the people there are insignificant... perhaps even... invisible."

"I don't see any roads," Nate said. "They must be invisible, too."

"There are few roads, it is true. But they are there. No problem, my friend. I know them well."

"Ahh," Nate said, nodding, as if reassured, but in reality, dismayed.

Farther inland, the road descended—to the travelers' temporary relief—out of the higher elevations of the Sierra Madre into a long, straight run northeast across a high plain patchworked with more farms. Wilma marveled at the dramatic changes in the landscape. Midge groused that a cup of coffee from one of the plantations would be a comfort.

"But, of course, there are no rest stops or restaurants out here," she added. "You would think there would be with all these farms around. Back home there would be some place to get a cup of coffee and something to eat every few miles."

Unable to resist shooting her a disgusted look, Nate turned to see Harold put a comforting hand on his wife's knee and see Midge pick it up and fling it away. Turning back around, he saw a look of disgust flicker across Mateo's face and watched him take in breath as if to speak, then press his lips together, seeming to think better of it.

"Things are not as they appear," he said finally, keeping his eyes fixed on the road. "In Chiapas things are often not as they appear. What you are seeing is not prosperity—at least not for *los campesinos*. Far more wealth goes out of Chiapas than comes in."

He paused, as if considering whether to continue.

"This is the poorest state in all of Mexico," he said evenly. "The very poorest. Do not be fooled by what you see. Do not be fooled."

He swept a meaty hand gracefully through the air.

"These people have so little. And yet there are those who would take even that away from them. He shook his head. *Qué lástima. Qué lástima.* The farther we go, the worse it will get. Soon you will see. You will understand."

"But the land looks so rich," Sarah said, speaking for the first time since the border crossing. "And the people work so hard. It isn't fair that they should have so little."

Mateo glanced in the rearview mirror again—this time, Nate knew, seeking Sarah's eyes. "No, *Señora* Hunter, it is not fair, as you say. *Los indígenas* struggle just to have enough to eat while the natural treasures of Chiapas flow out through ranches and plantations. It is the tribute *los indígenas* are forced to pay to the overlords, the ones who exploit them and plunder their land."

"But that's not right," Sarah said.

Mateo shrugged. "They have no choice. They have no power... no education, no money...."

"I don't understand it. How can people treat other people that way? To stand by and watch while others suffer... to *contribute* to their suffering—"

"—when we are all God's children," the pastor said softly from behind her.

"Exactly!" Sarah said earnestly. "I don't understand it," she said, shaking her head. "I just don't understand it."

Sarah, Nate thought. That was Sarah.

Mateo shrugged again.

"Some say the people should take up arms... rise up..." Mateo said, making a graceful upward-sweeping gesture with a hand. "Their grandfathers did it almost one hundred years ago. Perhaps it is time for another revolution."

"Is that what *you* think?" Sarah asked, leaning toward Mateo. "Do *you* want to see a revolution?"

Mateo didn't answer immediately.

"No," he finally said. "No, as a servant of the church, I could not encourage bloodshed." He paused. "But I would understand if others did."

"Hunh," Sarah said, sounding surprised. She sat back in her seat and turned her gaze out the window again, absorbed in thought.

She wasn't prepared for that, Nate thought. He didn't blame her.

Mateo's hostility toward the landed aristocracy surprised him, too — unsettled everyone in the bus a bit, judging from the silence that descended. It seemed out of place for a man of Mateo's calling, though Nate was not entirely certain what that calling was. He reached back to pat Sarah's knee, and managed a ragged smile of reassurance. Sarah turned from the window just long enough to smile weakly back.

"Well, that's quite enough of that, thank you very much," Midge huffed in a tone that suggested she was practiced at making pronouncements and accustomed to getting her way. "I don't want to hear another word about bloodshed and revolution, do you hear me? Not one word. I'm sorry, but this is not what I was expecting. Burning up one minute, freezing the next. Soldiers. Guns. And now talk of revolution?"

Harold put a hand on her knee. She pushed it off and nodded in agreement with herself.

"We came here to work on a church, not fight a war," Midge continued. "Harold and I are not cut out for this. I've made up my mind. First thing tomorrow morning we're leaving."

"Now, Dear," Harold said soothingly.

"Don't 'Now Dear' me, Harold. I've made up my mind. We are leaving."

Harold sighed deeply, but didn't argue. Mateo studied the woman in the rearview mirror. Nate could tell he was bristling. For a moment, he thought Mateo might rebuke her outright, but he said nothing. Nate didn't like her any more than Mateo did, but he did take her point. Getting out of Chiapas first thing the next morning might, indeed, be the better part of valor, whether Sarah thought so or not.

Emboldened by Midge's outburst, Nate turned to Mateo. "I have some questions myself," he said. "First, who is this El Pitón? My Spanish isn't that great, but I think that soldier at the border was asking if you're afraid of him. He asked Sarah in English—"

"Ach," Mateo said, grimacing and waving a hand.

"You said you didn't know him."

"*Es verdad.* I do not know him."

"Meaning you've never met him."

Mateo frowned, nodded. "*Sí.*"

"But you know who he is."

A silence. And then, "*Sí.*"

"So who is he?"

Mateo shrugged. "No one of importance. *El jefe* of one of the local paramilitaries. He—"

"*One* of the paramilitaries?" Nate said. "There are paramilitaries here? More than one?"

"Uh...yes...a few...around the entire state. No cause for worry."

"No cause for worry," Nate repeated, dumbfounded.

"*Sí,*" Mateo said testily. "And I do not think this *El Pitón* is in Mirador very often, anyway."

"Not very often. Are you serious?"

"*Sí.* Most of the time, he is off in the mountains somewhere."

"Doing what, exactly?"

Mateo sucked air between his teeth. "*No sé, no sé.* Some people say he is the savior of Mirador. They say he and his men help keep law and order. That is what they call themselves. *La Ley y Orden.* The government says they are, how do you say—*vigilantes.*"

Nate chewed on that for a moment.

"*El Pitón.* What does that mean?"

"Oh... it is a name *los pobres* gave him. But they are timid and superstitious. No problem. No problem."

"But what does it mean?"

Mateo still did not answer. Nate turned to Wilma.

"What does it mean?"

"It means 'the python,'" Mateo answered before Wilma could respond.

Nate felt the hairs on the back of his neck stand up.

"Why do they call him that?"

"Ahh... who can say? I told you, the people are superstitious."

Nate backed off and asked the other question that had been eating at him.

"That man at the border... the one who was shot—"

"Excuse me, *Señor,* but we do not know the man was shot. We heard something, it is true. But that does not mean he was shot."

Nate studied Mateo's stony expression. He wanted to ask why Mateo was lying, and he would, in time. But not now.

"Who was he?"

"Who?"

"The man with his hands tied."

Mateo shrugged. "Just some poor *campesino.*"

"Why were his hands tied?"

"Who can say? Maybe...maybe...he was a thief. Maybe he stole a chicken."

Again, Nate studied Mateo intently.

Uncomfortable being scrutinized, Mateo lifted a hand from the steering wheel, and turned it palm-up in a gesture of helplessness. He widened his eyes, raised his shoulders, shook his head.

"I do not know, *Señor.* I simply do not know."

"Is there a war going on here, Mateo? Does this have to do with NAFTA?"

Mateo looked at him sharply, but he did not answer.

"I'm not completely ignorant, Mateo. I've read about NAFTA. I know about the reforms your president has enacted to attract American business. I know he's making it easier for foreigners to buy your lands. I don't blame you for wanting to *rise up,* as you put it."

Mateo flashed him an angry look. "Excuse me, *Señor.* Do not twist my words. I did not say I wanted to rise up."

"Okay. Okay. But is that why the army was at the border? Is something going on in Chiapas that we don't know about?"

Mateo smiled.

"No, no. Nothing is going on. Some say there are Zapatistas in the jungle, but—"

"There are what?" Sarah asked from behind Nate. He should have known she'd be listening. "Did you say *Zapatistas*?"

Mateo nodded. "Yes."

"You mean like Zapata?" Jeffrey called from the back seat.

Mateo registered surprise. "Yes. Very good, *Señor* Oliver. So you have heard of Emiliano Zapata, our famous peasant revolutionary. In that revolution—we have had many, you know—the rebels called themselves Zapatistas. But that was a long time ago."

"Enough!" Midge bellowed. "I said no more talk of revolution! I forbid it!"

"Okay, okay, you don't have to freak out," Jeffrey said, making his sister giggle. Then, to Mateo: "But no Zapatistas now, right?"

"*Sí.* Not now. No Zapatistas now. I do not think so."

Mateo glanced in the rearview mirror, waited for his passengers to settle back down, then looked at Nate.

"Did I say there are no Zapatistas?"

"Yes. You said it twice."

They drove on for a while in silence. And then Nate addressed Mateo again.

"You're not from here, you say?"

"No."

"So... why are you here?"

Mateo frowned. "I told you. I work with Father Javier."

"Yes, but what brought you to Mirador in the first place?"

Mateo made a graceful, dismissive motion with his hand. "Life," he said.

"You're not one of them?"

"What? One of..."

"One of the rebels. The Zapatistas."

Mateo frowned, then chuckled—a forced chuckle, it seemed to Nate.

"No. No. No. I am... I am no... Zapatista."

"How did you end up here?"

Mateo sighed. "We came for a short trip, my wife and I...from Mexico City." He glanced in his rearview mirror. "Like all of you, we came to help. That was seven years ago." Mateo shrugged. "I am still here."

"So, you're married?" Sarah asked brightly.

Mateo's face clouded.

"Was. My wife died. She is buried in Mirador."

"Oh, I'm so sorry," Sarah said softly. Then, after a respectful silence, "Is that why you stayed?"

Mateo nodded slightly, forced a small smile. "There is a saying. 'Once the dust of Chiapas settles on your shoulders, you can never truly go home again.'" He shrugged. "Perhaps it is true."

"What did you do before you came here?" Sarah asked.

"Do?" Mateo said, slightly confused.

"Your work. What was your line of work?"

"Oh. I was in the construction trade—homes, small office buildings, I was the project supervisor, *el aguacil.*"

"Valuable skills here, I'd think," Nate said.

Mateo nodded. "*Sí.*" He glanced at Nate. "And you work with computers."

"Yes, that's right."

"I remember. You are also an *aguacil.*"

"A supervisor? Yes, I'm a project supervisor."

"Your company. I am sorry. I have forgotten the name. But I remember I liked it."

"Stalwart Engineering."

Mateo pressed his lips together, raised a clenched fist.

"Stalwart. *Sí, me gusta. Un nombre muy fuerte, muy hombre.* You design how to put information on the Internet, no?"

"I design websites, yes, that's right. We talked about that." Nate remembered that Mateo had seemed very interested in his work when they had met at the gala. "It's a pretty new thing. Most people aren't that familiar with it yet."

"I do not know much, but I find it very interesting," Mateo said, straightening in his seat. "It is a new way of sharing information very quickly with many people in many places."

"Yes, that's right. It's really a revolutionary new means of communication."

Mateo waved a finger. "Ah, careful, my friend," he said. "*Señora* Bottomley has forbidden us to speak that word."

"You know I didn't mean that, Mateo," Midge said huffily.

Mateo suppressed a smile.

"So, tell me," he said to Nate, "what do you do with websites?"

"Design them, launch them, maintain them, set up networks. Pretty much everything."

"Nate is extremely good at what he does," Sarah interjected. "He's very respected in his field."

"Well..." Nate said, shrugging.

"It's true, Nate. You know it is."

It was true. Nate did know it and he was proud of it. But he didn't like braggarts and wasn't going to be one himself. He loved that Sarah was so proud of him, though. That was all he really cared about—making her proud.

Mateo nodded. "I am honored to be traveling with such an important person."

"Okay, okay."

"No, I am sincere, *Señor* Hunter. The power of words. The power of ideas. To be able to share them with the world, *toda la gente, inmediatamente.* That is a powerful tool. And you help people do that, no?"

Nate nodded.

"*Muy importante. Muy importante.* The Information Age is upon us, no?"

Nate was surprised. "You know that term? Not many people do."

Mateo shrugged. "As I said, I am interested in this new Internet. Very interested."

Mateo frowned. "But I am being rude." He looked into the rearview mirror again. "You are coming to Mirador at the perfect time, my friends," he said, drawing his other passengers into the conversation. "*Carnaval* begins soon."

"Awesome!" Jeffrey blurted out from the back. "What's *Carnaval?*"

"Ahh. . . it is magnificent. Days of feasting and celebrating. You will love it. All of you."

Mateo shifted his weight, pulling himself up and forward with the steering wheel. His manner became animated.

"It is a combination of the *Carnaval* before Lent and the celebration of the Mayan New Year. There are five lost days in the Maya calendar. *Carnaval* is the celebration of days that do not exist. It is a time when spirits walk upon the earth and everything is turned upside down."

"Wonderful," Midge said curtly. "Too bad we'll have to miss it, since we'll be leaving first thing in the morning."

In his enthusiasm about Carnaval, Mateo had sped up and he took another bend with a hard swerve.

"Ooooh," Stephanie moaned.

"Mateo, please," Wilma said meekly. "Can you slow down just a little?"

Looking slightly embarrassed, Mateo held up a hand and slowed the bus. "*Sí, sí. Lo siento.* No problem. No problem."

Mateo's catchphrase was starting to grate on Nate's nerves. He took no comfort from it. He had not a shred of doubt left that this trip was a mistake. He was cautious and deliberate by nature, heedful of consequences, not the sort of man to fling himself into the waters of uncertainty. But, here he was, having done just that.

Before heading south, Nate had, indeed, done his homework. He knew that President George Bush, Mexican President Carlos Salinas de Gortari, and Canadian Prime Minister Brian Mulroney had all signed the North American Free Trade Agreement, or NAFTA, as everyone called it, in December. It still needed to be ratified by all three countries, but Nate expected that would be perfunctory. He'd been all for it at first. Free trade had to be good, right? But then he had started hearing the dire warnings that American jobs would drain south to take advantage of Mexico's cheap labor and Mexico's cheap products would flood north to out-compete with American-made goods. He hadn't thought about that. He hadn't thought about what NAFTA might do to Mexico's small farmers, either, until he read that they were even more afraid of cheap U.S. agri-business crops flooding their markets. And that wasn't even the worst of it.

Delving deeper, thanks to his access to the new Internet information-gathering site called NexisLexis, Nate had learned that the Mexican government was canceling land reforms instituted after the Mexican Revolution to redistribute some of the land owned by domestic and foreign overlords to the peasant farmers who lived on it and farmed it. Now, that program was dead, and, for the first time, the land that had already been issued could be bought and sold.

Mateo was right, Nate thought. Even the little the campesinos had, more powerful interests were ready to take away, and what was to stop them? While doing his research, Nate had stumbled on a couple of human rights reports that documented the historic and ongoing persecution of the Indian populations of Chiapas and the brutal treatment inflicted upon them—arrest, imprisonment, and worse—if they tried to march or protest or press for basic services and the right to earn a living on their land.

Nate had shared his readings with Sarah and had quizzed Pastor Tom about the situation in Chiapas when the pastor had come for tea. But Sarah would not be dissuaded. The more she learned about how unjust things were for the people of Chiapas, the more determined she became to go on this trip. The minister had been more conciliatory. Yes, he had said, the political situation was unfortunate: the powerful exploiting the powerless yet again. But that was why the mission had to go forward—to show the people of Chiapas that they were not forgotten. Passing a plate of cookies to the minister, Sarah had nodded vigorously. "He's right, Nate. That's important." And there was nothing to fear, the minister had continued. He had traveled to Chiapas many times without incident. As members of an American church group, they'd be quite safe.

Nate had let himself be persuaded, had let *Sarah* persuade him, and had put all thought of a peasant revolt out of his mind. It was not as easy as hitting a key on a computer keyboard and watching a screen go blank, but he had been able to do it. The pastor was right, he had told himself. What did any of this have to do with a handful of American do-gooders on a church mission trip? *Nada.* And even if some of the peasants did try to rise up, as Mateo put it, how could a few gun-toting farmers expect to prevail against the interests of the United States and the forces of capitalism and free trade—especially now, with a truly revolutionary new communications technology at their disposal?

A new millennium was dawning. And Nate Hunter, rising star at Stalwart Engineering, Dallas, Texas, stood poised to play a major part in shaping and defining the new era through his work in computer technology and, more specifically, the growth of the World Wide Web. He knew that more than fifty websites were already operational and that by midyear, according to even the most conservative estimate, more than a hundred websites would be operating around the globe. A boom was taking shape — one that Nate knew would change the world. Sharing information, finding it and distributing it. Everyone would have instant access to documents, books, photographs, newspapers — the possibilities were limitless. People would be able to find anything, read anything, learn anything, just by turning on a computer. A librarian in New York, who was already a big fan of the new technology, had written an article about it in a library bulletin and had come up with a name for it: *surfing the Internet.* Nate liked it. And he was just where he needed to be to catch the wave. He was ambitious, smart, one of the best in his field, Sarah was right about that. God willing, in a few years he could see himself really making his mark. People could be writing about him and recognizing him as the leading computer expert in the country... maybe the world.

And, Sarah would be right there at his side. His lady fair, the golden-haired girl who had stolen his heart a little more than five years earlier, Sarah meant everything to him. Without her, none of it would matter a damn.

Nate first laid eyes on the love of his life in the fall of his second year of grad school at Southern Methodist University in Dallas. They were both on track to graduate that spring — Nate with a master's degree in computer engineering, Sarah with a bachelor's of nursing from nearby Baylor. They met at a party they both would have skipped if friends hadn't insisted they come. It became part of their courtship and marriage story later — how they almost didn't meet.

Nate was leaning against a wall, sipping a beer and talking to another computer geek, when Sarah came in with a girlfriend. Nate didn't notice the girlfriend, only Sarah. Her friend knew his friend, waved and walked over. Nate couldn't believe his luck.

It was not exactly love at first sight, or even second, but by the third or fourth the die was cast. It was, perhaps, the attraction of opposites.

Not polar opposites, but opposites nonetheless.

Nate was the cautious one, Sarah the plunger. He wanted to conquer the world, step by deliberate step. She wanted to save it, and do it in one fell swoop. Nate admired Sarah's gentle and passionate heart, loved her for it. Sarah admired Nate's dogged determination, his meticulous methodology. She liked to sneak over to the SMU Student Union late in the afternoon, she confessed to him later, to stand at an upstairs window and watch her new love leave the engineering building every day at precisely the same hour, an armload of books carried in precisely the same manner, and make his way down the sidewalk with exactly the same gait. She loved his reliability and his predictability.

That spring, as Sarah neared completion of her obstetrics rotation at the University Medical Center, she invited Nate to meet her at the newborn nursery one afternoon to see the babies in her care. One by one, she lifted them from their bassinets and held them to the window. She raised a tiny, pink hand and waved. That day, he took the head-over-heels tumble. They married that summer, after graduation.

Earlier in that school year, Sarah had joined a group of students on a one-week medical mission to *Río Bravo* in northeast Mexico. Nate had tried to talk her out of it, fearing for her safety. But Sarah wouldn't budge. She had felt the Samaritan call and would not be deterred.

In Río Bravo, she had helped deliver babies, tended the ill, treated injuries, dressed wounds, helped save lives. It was there that she had first confronted the more extreme consequences of poverty and desperation, when a twelve-year-old boy named *Fito* had come under her care. He and his mother, along with dozens of other refugees from the Guatemalan Civil War, had made their way across the border into Mexico and climbed atop a slow-moving freight bound for *El Norte,* the promised land. In the middle of the night, Fito and his mother had fallen or been pushed from the roof of the moving railroad car onto the tracks. Fito had lost a leg. His mother had died. Sarah had returned home, heartbroken and angry, with the gift Fito had insisted she accept: a small figurine of a jaguar that he had stuffed into his pocket before fleeing his home—a totem animal in the Mayan culture, she learned later, a symbol of power and strength.

"And the worst part is, the clinic director said that when he gets stronger, they have to send him back," Sarah had told Nate. He would never forget the way Sarah's eyes had glittered when she'd told him that. "Can you believe it, Nate? They're going to send him back!" And she had burst into tears. "It's so unfair. And there was nothing I could do."

That was Sarah. When someone suffered, she felt it. Whatever happened to others, happened to her. When she saw injustice, she felt compelled not just to lament it, but to confront and oppose it. She couldn't help herself. She seemed to see herself not as a citizen of the United States but as a citizen of the world, a member of an interconnected and interdependent human race. She cared for humanity, felt she had a stake in its welfare and a full measure of responsibility to help care for her fellow human beings. She saw easing suffering as her duty.

After her trip to Río Bravo, Sarah had talked often about going on another medical mission after graduation, perhaps back to Río Bravo, perhaps somewhere else in Mexico or Central America. "What I'd really like to do is start a clinic somewhere that doesn't have one," she told Nate one night as they snuggled in bed. "I could go down for a month or two to help set it up and then travel back and forth, depending on my work schedule here. What do you think?" She looked at him eagerly. Nate smiled and nodded. He didn't want to discourage her, but he had other ideas.

Instead, after graduation, they married, honeymooned briefly in Big Sur, returned to Dallas and got caught up in their demanding new jobs—Nate's at Stalwart, Sarah's in the cardiac unit at Children's Health—and, next thing they knew, four years had passed. Now, Nate was well on his way to professional distinction. He had only to stay on course. In another year, if he didn't stumble, if he didn't offend the wrong person or make a bad call on a project, he would break into upper management at his firm. Ahead of schedule, at only thirty-two. He felt like a man on the cusp of fullness.

Soon, he and Sarah would be able to sell their two-bedroom brick starter house on Lyndon Road near the SMU campus, the one that Sarah's parents had helped them buy, and purchase a somewhat larger and more expensive but still affordable place on the edge of Highland Park or University Park. They'd have a baby. It was time. Sarah's biological clock was ticking. A girl would have her golden hair and green eyes. A boy would have Nate's dark hair, light brown eyes, cleft chin. Their child would be beautiful and gifted. Sarah would be a fulltime mom if she wanted until their son or daughter started school. Maybe they'd have a second child by then.

A bright future lay ahead for Nate and Sarah Hunter. They both knew it. Now, though, all Nate wanted was to get himself and his wife back to Dallas as soon as possible and never sign up for a mission trip again.

CHAPTER 4

Masks of Mexico

The truth, Nate knew, was that he was the one who'd started this whole Chiapas thing by taking his wife to that gala at the Dallas Museum of Art back in November. Colleen Murray, the wife of Frank Murray, the senior partner at his firm, had organized the affair as a fundraiser for the American Cancer Society, and Nate had seen it as a chance to wine and dine and show off his beautiful wife. More than that, he had also seen it as an opportunity to mingle with rich and powerful people, to see and be seen. Everybody who was anybody would be there. For an up-and-coming young professional, a man poised on the brink of high achievement, status, and acclaim, attendance was *de rigueur.*

Eager to support her husband, Sarah had looked forward to attending the event. She knew her parents would also be there, and she always looked forward to seeing them. They were above pressing Sarah and Nate to see them more than the young couple's busy schedule allowed. But they were getting older and, as their only child, Sarah was beginning to feel a greater sense of responsibility toward them and more desire to spend time with them.

That was fine with Nate. He and Sarah's parents got along well now. They hadn't been thrilled about the marriage at first; he'd had to work to win them over. But he didn't blame them for that. Trevor and Katherine Blake, both descended from Irish immigrants, were moneyed people, well known and well regarded in Dallas society. Trevor, a distinguished silver-haired gentleman on the shady side of seventy, came from old money on the East Coast. With his third-generation wealth, he had built a greater fortune as a founding partner and investment banker with a firm headquartered in Dallas. Katherine's family had money, too—black gold, the largesse of the Permian Basin. Though it didn't show, except perhaps in her strong will and fearlessness, Sarah had been born to the purple, double-bred for claiming the center cut as her own.

Nate came from different stock. He had grown up north of the Red River, in a mid-size Oklahoma town. His parents, both dead by the time he met Sarah, had been ordinary folks. His father, John, had been the parts manager for a Chevy dealership. His mother, Dot, had been a housewife. He'd had a brother once, but didn't anymore. Nate had been the first in his family to go to college. A scholarship had opened the door for him. Student loans and a series of part-time and summer jobs had carried him through.

In the beginning, Nate had felt insecure about the difference between his background and Sarah's. But he had turned his insecurity to the good, letting it energize him, sharpen his focus. He was playing catch-up, and he knew it. He dreamed of success—not just modest success, but big-time success—and was determined to achieve it. And he would do it on his own. Of that he had no doubt.

That November night at the museum had brimmed with elegance. Linen-cloaked tables set with sparkling crystal and silver and extravagant floral arrangements filled the airy main lobby. Fine wine flowed freely. Chamber music played. Counterpoint to the strains of violin and cello were the low murmur of conversation, the tinkle of ice cubes in cocktail glasses, an occasional swell of laughter. Men in their penguin finery and women with bejeweled necks, manicured nails, delicate ears adorned with diamonds, strolled across white marble floors.

Dressed to impress, the Hunters, in Nate's assessment, made the handsomest couple at the event. Nate in black tie, Sarah in a strapless ivory gown by Carolina Herrera—a gift from her parents—they were outshone by no one. During the extended cocktail hour, wine glasses in hand, they wandered with the crowd of socialite art lovers from gallery to gallery and floor to floor, admiring paintings by Gaugin, Degas, Monet, Cézanne; sculptures by Rodin; *objet d'art* from Africa and Asia.

In time, they found themselves in the museum's Ancient American Art galleries, where an exhibit of masks captured Sarah's attention more than anything had so far that night. *Masks of Mexico*, the sign next to the entrance announced. The pieces on display, the text explained, were ancient ceremonial masks that had been used by pagan mummers of Mesoamerica in all manner of ceremonies and rituals, some involving human sacrifice. Arm in arm, Nate and Sarah strolled the gallery, regarding the work of craftsmen dead for a thousand years or more, their own handsome young faces reflected back at them in the display cases. Large stone carvings of Mayan gods stood posted like sentries at the corners.

"They remind me of some of the masks I saw in Río Bravo," Sarah said as they began to browse the display. She withdrew her arm to study the craftsmanship, and Nate took it back.

"Stay close," he said, seeing more people enter the gallery.

He was possessive and protective of his wife. He made no bones about it. Sarah was beautiful. With brilliant eyes, finely sculpted features, hair that had the quality of spun gold, she could not help turning heads. She was strong-willed and tough under her warm and friendly manner, perfectly capable of taking care of herself, as she reminded him often. But he had promised her parents, and himself, that he would always take care of her. Succeeding in his profession, rising to the top, making Sarah proud of him and providing her with a secure and comfortable life was all part of that pledge. It was his sworn duty and one he was determined to fulfill.

Earlier that evening, as they were dressing for the party, Nate had laid out his vision of the future to Sarah.

"In another two years, I'll make partner, move to a corner office, and have a staff of designers reporting to me," he said, standing at their full-length bedroom mirror to tie his bow tie. "I've already as good as gotten the nod from Frank. He likes me a lot, you know. Just the other day, he said, 'You be loyal to me, and I'll be loyal to you.'" He turned to Sarah. "How about that?"

"That's wonderful, sweetie," Sarah had murmured, smiling as she fastened her gold-link bracelet, letting him talk.

Nate turned back to the mirror. "It'll take a lot of hard work and long hours for the next couple of years. I'll have to show Frank I've got what it takes. But I don't mind that. You know I don't. I'd be a fool not to do it. Talk about right time, right place. This is it, Sarah. I can feel it. This Internet explosion is going to change the world."

Nate frowned then, turned and began pacing.

"I'll have to be careful, though," he said, wagging an index finger.

"Not make any stupid mistakes. Make sure the clients and the partners all trust and respect me. So far, so good. I'm on the right track there. I can tell you that for sure."

He paused, smiled at his wife again. "And just think. If everything works out—and it will, I'll make sure it does—my income will probably double. And who knows where things could go from there. I might start my own company like your dad did. I'd have to time it carefully, of course, have all my ducks in a row, not take any unnecessary risks. I mean, you have to be willing to take risks, but not foolish ones. I've seen what that can lead to. I've seen guys go down in flames. Not me." Nate scowled. "No, that I will not do. You just have to be careful... and determined."

Sarah sighed and gave Nate an indulgent look. "Sweetie, there's more to life than making money, you know."

Nate snorted. "Easy to say when you've always had plenty of it."

Sarah nodded. "I know. I know. But it's true. You know it is."

She looked up at her husband with tenderness in her eyes, and it was Nate's turn to concede.

"I know."

No amount of money or fame would be worth anything without Sarah at his side, he was thinking now as he threaded her arm safely through his again and walked with her along the museum display case. And he knew that no matter how close he tried to keep her, how much he tried to protect her, he could never keep her completely safe and could never relax his guard. Because things happened, no matter how careful you were. Sudden things. Horrible things. Like what happened to Jack.

Nate's older brother, Jack, had been the fair-haired boy of the family, their parents' favorite. Captain of this, president of that, straight-A student, good at everything he did, adored by all. Nate had idolized him.

One night, on their way home from a high school football game, Jack and his adoring kid brother saw a pack of hoodlums raising a ruckus in a parking lot across the street. They were loud and worked up over something, probably drunk or high on drugs. They were walking toward a woman standing with her back to them next to a parked car, digging in her purse for her keys. The leader came up behind her and the pack closed in around her. Nate was thirteen; Jack was eighteen.

"Hey, they can't do that!" Nate said, looking at his older brother.

"Ignore it," Jack said, walking on, looking at the sidewalk. "It's none of our business."

Nate couldn't believe it. "Jack, we can't—"

The punks started laughing and cheering. The woman cried out. Nate grabbed his brother's arm.

"Jack, we have to do something! We can't just—"

"Shit!" Jack snarled, eyes darting from his kid brother to the parking lot and back again. Nate had never heard Jack swear.

"Stay here," he said, starting across the street.

Nate began to follow.

"Stay here, I said!"

Nate backed away. He'd never seen his brother so angry.

He watched Jack run across the street and throw himself at the gang of thugs. They shouted at him—"Hey! What the..."—broke ranks and closed again around him. Nate heard scuffling, punches, grunts. He started running. And then he heard the woman scream, heard one of the thugs shout, "Oh, man! What did you do?" Watched them scatter, saw the woman standing over someone on the ground, hands over her mouth, sobbing, "Oh God, Oh God, Oh God."

Jack was lying on his left side on the pavement with a knife in his gut, blood pooling under him. He was dead before the ambulance got there. The woman couldn't identify her assailants. Jack's murderer was never caught.

The newspapers called Jack a hero. At the funeral, friends and neighbors did, too.

"Your son was a hero."

"Your brother was a hero."

And he was. But he was also dead. And it was his own fault—his and Nate's. Nate would blame himself for the rest of his life for reacting emotionally and urging his brother to get involved instead of analyzing the situation and realizing the smart thing to do would have been to go for help. But Jack was also to blame for acting impulsively and thinking he could handle more than he could—for trying to protect Nate and save a woman from a gang of thugs at the same time. Nate was tall for his age, looked older than he was. If the gang had seen both brothers coming at them, maybe they would have run. Jack had failed to assess his risk and the possible consequences of his acts, and his boldness and impetuousness had cost him his life.

Never again, Nate swore. These were mistakes he would never make again. From now on, he vowed, he would proceed with caution, keep his wits about him and his emotions in check. He would not be faint-hearted, but he wouldn't be foolhardy, either. He'd be careful, look before he leaped. No acting on impulse. No unnecessary risks.

Jack's death wrecked the family. John Hunter took to drink. When he had a load on, he got mean. Nate and his mom learned to stay out of his way until he passed out. It didn't help that Dot blamed her husband for their elder son's death. It was his fault, she told him, for teaching both of his boys, his firstborn especially, that a real man was tough, courageous, never admitted fear, never backed down from a challenge, never turned tail and ran away from a fight.

"Congratulations," she'd spit at him the morning after a bender, tossing scrambled eggs from the frying pan onto his plate as he sat at the kitchen table, hungover and holding his head. "Oh, you taught him to be a man, all right. 'Never run from a fight,' you said. Happy now?"

"Shut up," Nate's Dad would moan. "Just shut up."

And then he'd go on another bender, and it would start all over again.

Nate felt bad for his father, wanted to tell his parents, "But he didn't want to fight. I made him." But he couldn't do it. The only comfort they had was believing their cherished older son had acted bravely. Foolishly, perhaps, but bravely. Nate couldn't take that away.

Wandering through the mask exhibit arm in arm with his wife as waiters passed among the guests with trays of wine, Nate let Sarah set their pace, pausing whenever she did to examine another mask, studying every detail and reading aloud from the information card next to each piece. *"Un tigre." "Un iguana."* Grotesque faces—red, blue, green—grimaced at Nate and Sarah as if they had poked through the paper-thin boundary between past and present.

"Look at these, Nate," Sarah said in wonder. "They're amazing. Some date back to the time of Christ."

Nate's eyes fell upon a tenth century wooden carving of *El Diablo*, the devil himself, that Sarah seemed to find especially mesmerizing. The face burned brimstone red. At the sides of the helmetlike creation, oversized ears protruded and rose to sharp points. From the top, long bladelike horns extended and curved inward.

A few steps away, another display case held masks made of fur, leather, plant fibers: likenesses of bulls, crows, horses, dogs; masks symbolizing life and death and the inscrutable world beyond. Some of the faces sported mustaches and beards. One resembled a skull— empty eyes, ashen cheeks, rotten teeth. Some wore serene expressions, some seemed meant to evoke fear.

"Incredible," Sarah said, drifting to another case. Nate followed, keeping a tight hold on her arm and an eye on the crowd.

Sarah stopped suddenly and pointed to an oversize, elaborately feathered and painted wooden carving on the wall.

"Look, Nate. I think that's the feathered serpent."

The carving featured the large, long-snouted head of a snarling green creature with red eyes, pointy ears, a mouth full of curving white fangs, and a long, forked, red tongue. The creature wore a head-dress with tall feathers the length of a man's arm sticking up out of a high brim covered in crimson fabric and adorned with rectangular mirrors about the size of playing cards all around the creature's head.

"It's from Chiapas, the Lacandon Jungle," Sarah said, reading from the information card on the wall below the mask. "'*Quetzalcoatl*, the Plumed Serpent, supreme creator, god of the four elements, resurrection, reincarnation.'"

Nate nodded, only half-listening, sipping his wine, a good Merlot, and surveyed the room, searching for important faces. Suddenly, he went rigid, like a dog on point.

"Look," he said, squeezing Sarah's arm. She turned and he gestured discreetly with his chin, smiled ever so faintly. "See that guy? Sarah, see that short, bald, heavyset fellow over there with Frank? You know who that is? That's Henry Teague. He's the CEO of StarFire Communications, one of the biggest satellite communications companies in the world. I've mentioned him. He's one of our clients, a friend of Frank's. The guy's worth millions."

"Fantastic," Sarah murmured.

"You got that right."

"Look at those eyes. They seem to follow you wherever you go."
"What?"

Nate turned to find his wife transfixed by the serpent mask.

"Sarah, you didn't hear a word I said."

"Sure I did. He's worth millions." She read aloud again from the information card. "'Worn strapped on a dancer's back as part of *La Danza del Calalá,* the dance of the deer.' Well, that explains the size. Wow."

Nate glanced at the mask again, then took Sarah's hand. The crowd in the gallery was thinning.

"Come on. Let's go down and work the room."

"No. Wait. Don't you love it?"

"Sure. But we're not here to look at art. We can do that later."

Nate downed the last of his Merlot and when the waiter passed, silver tray in hand, traded the empty glass for a full one. On a mission now, he led his wife back down to the main floor and into the sea of milling, laughing, chattering people, privately pleased by how often they were stopped for hugs and handshakes, greetings and introductions. *And why not?* Nate thought. They were a golden couple, he and his beautiful wife, and their future was filled with promise.

After scanning the room for a while, they finally spotted and made their way to Sarah's parents.

"Hi, Mom. Hi, Dad," Sarah said, smiling brightly, giving her mother a careful hug that didn't muss either woman's makeup or hair, and pecking her father on the cheek.

Trevor Blake took his daughter in his arms.

"How's my girl?"

When he released her, Nate shook his distinguished father-in-law's hand with a firm grip and lightly embraced his elegant mother-in-law.

"Wonderful to see you, Nate," Katherine Blake said warmly.

"Did you see the masks?" Sarah asked her parents. "They're incredible, don't you think?"

The old man nodded vigorously. "Very impressive," he agreed.

Nate and Katherine exchanged a look. Nate suspected his father-in-law hadn't even seen the exhibit, but of course he would agree with Sarah's opinion. The man was known for being constitutionally incapable of denying or disagreeing with his beloved only child about anything if he could help it.

"They reminded me of my trip to Río Bravo," Sarah said, turning wistful. "I've been wanting to do another medical mission..." She paused. "That mask of the feathered serpent, the one from Chiapas. That one was really amazing. There was something about it..." She looked at her husband. "Wouldn't it be great to go there, Nate? See the people and the culture up close? Help out at a clinic..." She smiled at her parents. "I'd love to do that."

Trevor Blake beamed at his daughter, as Nate knew he would. Sarah's father was notorious for encouraging her appetite for challenge and adventure—summer rock climbing lessons and equestrian camps as a kid, Outward Bound in Canada during high school, a bicycle trip through France the summer after her freshman year of college.

Sarah's father opened his mouth to say something, but her mother cut him off.

"Go to Chiapas?" Katherine Blake said coolly, lowering her chin and raising her eyebrows at her daughter. "Lord. I don't know about that, dear. Do you have any idea how far away that is? It's not just across the border."

Sarah smiled and patted her mother's hand.

"Yes, Mother, I know."

Sarah's father frowned. "Now, Kitty, it isn't as if Sarah hasn't traveled before. And you know she can take care of herself."

That's true, Nate thought. His wife was perhaps the most capable and self-reliant woman he had ever known. Obstinate, too. When she made up her mind she was going to do something, stand aside. Now, all of a sudden, she wanted to go to Chiapas.

"Oh, I know that," Katherine Blake said, smiling at her daughter. "But still, Chiapas..." She caught Nate's eye. "Maybe if Nate went with you...I guess that would be all right. As long he was there to take care of you...."

"We take care of each other, Mother."

"Of course you do, dear, I only meant—"

Sarah smiled. "And there's no need for worry. Nate will protect me." Sarah winked at her husband.

"That's right," he said, doing a slight parody of a chivalrous bow. "I am her sworn protector." Everyone laughed, but Nate wasn't joking. He would always do whatever he had to do to protect his wife. Restrain her when her Irish was up, comfort her when she was frightened. He would smite the wicked, slay the dragon, go toe-to-toe with the devil. He would die for her—without question, hesitation, or doubt.

"Sarah," Trevor Blake said, touching his daughter's arm. "It's interesting that you mention Chiapas. I was just—"

And then everyone flinched at the explosive report of glass shattering on the marble floor. Music and conversation stopped as all heads turned in the direction of the terrible sound.

From where Nate and Sarah stood, Nate saw at its epicenter a round-faced young waiter with bronze skin and raven-black hair kneeling among the shattered remains of perhaps a dozen wine glasses, wearing the stunned and frightened expression of a young man who knew a momentary loss of balance had just thrust him into a world of trouble. And then, suddenly, Sarah was there, kneeling beside him in her designer gown, recovering pieces of broken glass from the floor. The young waiter sat back on his knees, his eyes wide.

"No, Señora."

Sarah ignored him and continued collecting pieces of glass.

"Nate," Sarah's mother said under her breath, prodding him out of his own state of astonishment.

As Nate approached, he saw the young waiter try to shoo Sarah's hands away.

"Señora, no," he pleaded softly.

Sarah smiled and laid a hand on his arm.

"It's okay. I don't mind."

A platoon of other young waiters arrived on the scene just as Nate did. He touched Sarah's shoulder.

"Come on," Nate said gently, helping her to her feet. "They'll take care of it. It'll be okay."

Sarah rose. But then she lingered uncertainly until the young waiter who had dropped the tray looked up, smiled shyly and gave her a grateful nod. The slight gesture seemed to provide the release she needed. She smiled at Nate and they rejoined her parents, who, like Nate, knew better than to chastise their daughter for her impulsive behavior. That was Sarah, and Sarah would always be Sarah. Nate handed her a fresh glass of wine lifted from a passing tray, and the evening resumed.

Nate went back to scanning faces. Sarah's father put an arm around his daughter and drew her near.

"As I was saying," he said, "It's funny you should mention Chiapas. I was just talking to a minister...."

Nate saw Katherine Blake frown at her husband, as if to silence him. Trevor Blake saw the look, ignored it and searched the room with his eyes instead.

"There he is, over there." He lifted his wine glass and pointed with one finger. "The little blond guy in the dark suit. He's part of some organization that does a lot of work in Mexico. I think he said he was going down there soon."

"Trev," Katherine Blake said softly.

"Going where? To Chiapas?" Sarah asked, looking where her father was pointing. Her interest was piqued.

"I'm pretty sure," her father continued. "He said something about restoring some church down there. And see that big guy in the dark suit talking to the waiter you were trying to help? He's here with the minister. He's from there, I think."

"Really? I'd love to meet them."

Sarah's father touched her elbow. "Come on. I'll introduce you."

Katherine Blake sighed. "I think I'll go say hello to the Bowmans, dear," she said, moving off in a different direction.

Nate followed his wife.

After introductions and an exchange of greetings, Pastor Thomas Butler—"Please, call me Tom," he said—explained his plans.

"We'll be going to Mirador. It's a small village in Chiapas, in the Lacandon Jungle. Very humble. I've been many times. There's a beautiful old church there, a Dominican mission that dates back to the mid-sixteenth century. The villagers still use it, but it's crumbling. We're hoping to restore it, or at least get the restoration process started. Spread a little good news. Let the people know that God has not forgotten them. That's about it."

"And you're looking for volunteers?" Sarah asked.

"Yes, we are," the minister said, smiling. "Do you think you might be interested?"

"I might be," Sarah said, returning the minister's smile. "Very interested."

"Sarah..." Nate tried to interject.

"When are you going?" Sarah continued.

"I'm not sure yet. It depends on how long it takes to get a group together. "You should go with us." The minister smiled at Nate. "You and your husband."

Nate shook his head. "I'm sorry. My wife forgets that we both have extremely demanding jobs."

"With two weeks of vacation time, Nate," Sarah said. "We haven't taken any vacation."

"That would work nicely," the minister said. "Our mission trips are seldom more than two weeks."

As Nate opened his mouth to respond, the broad-chested man who'd been off talking to the waiter joined them. Tall and solid with dark hair and eyes and brown skin, he also wore a dark suit instead of formal attire. The minister put a hand on his back.

"This is my old friend Mateo De La Cruz. Mateo, this is Sarah Hunter. You've met her father, Mr. Blake."

The two men nodded. Sarah offered her hand.

"*Mucho gusto,*" she said.

"*Igualmente,*" Mateo responded, bowing slightly. "You speak Spanish, I see."

"Not really," Sarah said, smiling. "I learned a little in high school. I need to work on it."

Mateo nodded. "I want to thank you for your kindness."

Sarah looked puzzled.

"For your help," Mateo said, gesturing toward the aggrieved waiter, who was now passing among the guests with a fresh tray of wine glasses.

"Oh."

The minister gestured to Nate.

"And this is Nate Hunter, Sarah's husband."

Nate and Mateo shook hands, and Nate almost winced at the unconscious strength of the man's grip.

"You're visiting from Chiapas, Mateo?" Sarah asked.

"That's right."

"And what brings you here?"

"Visiting friends." He nodded at the minister. "Tomás and I are old friends . . . since before he was a pastor. We are here tonight as the guests of Dr. and Mrs. Alejandro. He is a professor at the university."

"Which one?" Sarah's father asked. "I don't think I know him."

"University of Dallas," the minister answered. "The Institute for Religious and Pastoral Studies."

Trevor Blake nodded as Mateo searched the crowd.

"Over there," he said, pointing to an elegant-looking older couple. "And, we are organizing a mission trip."

Sarah smiled, nodded. "Yes, Pastor Tom was telling us."

"And they may be interested in joining us," the minister told Mateo.

"Well, I don't—" Nate began.

"Yes," Sarah interjected. "I'm very interested."

Mateo smiled.

"You are not a stone mason, by any chance, are you?"

Sarah laughed. "Afraid not."

"But she's strong, and she knows how to work," Sarah's dad chimed in.

Laughing, the Mexican turned to Nate.

"What about you, *Señor*? Are you a stone mason?"

"Hardly. I work with computers."

"Computers," Mateo said, looking surprised and interested. "And what do you do with computers?"

"I'm a computer engineer," Nate said, noting Mateo's change in tone. "I build websites for the Internet."

"Ahh...the Internet," Mateo said, nodding and looking impressed. "It will change the world, they say."

"So, you know about the Internet?"

"Of course. With the stroke of a computer key, news will be carried around the world. A single voice can be heard in every corner of the globe. And that voice can come from anywhere. Even from Chiapas, yes?" Mateo lifted his bushy eyebrows at Nate.

"Uhh...well, yes," Nate said, a little surprised that Mateo knew as much as he did and a little embarrassed at having assumed otherwise. "That is, with the right technology, of course. It's still very new." He sipped his wine and regarded the man. "And what about you? What do you do?"

"I help restore crumbling churches," Mateo said affably. "And I try to get people to help us." He grinned. "Just as I am doing now." He turned serious again. "But I am interested in learning more about this new Internet. Perhaps you will teach me. You will come to Chiapas and help us start the first Internet in the Lacandon Jungle. You will help us build a website..." He smiled at Sarah. "And *Señora* Hunter will help us build the church."

"Thanks, but I don't think—"

"That's a wonderful idea!" Sarah said, excited. "Don't you think so, Dad?"

Trevor Blake smiled at his daughter, a satisfied look on his face. "I do indeed, honey." He gave Nate a sly look. "What do you say, Nate?"

"Sure, it sounds good, but—"

A chime rang softly. Time to sit down to dinner.

"This is exciting, Nate," Sarah said, in that tone of voice he recognized as a sign of a mind already almost completely made up. "I think we should look into this." She turned to the minister. "Do you think we could talk again?"

"Of course," the clergyman said. "It would be a pleasure." He handed Sarah his card. "Please. Call anytime."

"Perhaps you both can come for tea," she said, smiling at Mateo.

"Ah, I am sorry, *Señora*, but I must return to Mirador soon. But Tomás will be here in Dallas, organizing things."

"I'm sorry, too," Sarah said, offering Mateo her hand. "I hope to see you again."

"In Mirador, I hope," Mateo said, taking her hand and bowing. He turned to Nate, his expression serious, his handshake firm again. "I hope to see you both there very soon."

Nate was extremely pleased to find that he and Sarah were seated with Frank and Colleen Murray; Henry Teague and his wife, Sandra, were also at their table, along with the CEO of the American Cancer Society, John Seffrin, and his wife, Carole, who had flown in from Atlanta for the event. After dinner and speeches, there was wine, music, dancing, more meeting and greeting, seeing and being seen—all of which seemed to center around their table.

At evening's end, Nate and Sarah strolled out onto a terrace overlooking the museum garden for some fresh air before heading home. The night was mild. Wine glass in one hand, his other arm around his wife's creamy shoulders, Nate sighed with satisfaction and let a contented smile play across his lips. For him, the night had been an enormous success, cementing his status as a rising star. He let his head fall back and gazed up at the cloudless night sky shot through with millions of celestial embers.

"What a night," he sighed. "What a night."

He set the wine glass down on a ledge and took Sarah in his arms. He kissed her and felt her arms encircle his waist. She leaned back, smiling, eyes large and shining, lips parted. He kissed her again and again.

"Mmmmm," she murmured. "Maybe it's time for bed."

Nate laughed softly. Relaxing his hold on her, he looked up again, searching the blackness above with purposeful eyes.

"Where is it?" he said, tapping the cleft of his chin with the edge of a forefinger. "Where is it?"

"Where's what?"

"The North Star. The pole star. Ahh. There." He retrieved his glass and raised it in salute. He finished his wine and set the glass down again a little clumsily, one arm still around his wife.

"Careful there," Sarah said in a playful tone. "I think you may be a little drunk."

"Of course, I'm drunk. You have to be drunk to understand the importance of this."

Sarah laughed. "I have no idea what you're talking about, my darling."

Nate laughed, too. He pulled his wife close and rifled his free arm toward the heavenly body that had captured his gaze, sighting along its rigid line.

"See that star? The bright one?"

Putting her cheek to her husband's chest, Sarah matched her line of sight with his. "Mmm-hmm."

"That's the North Star," Nate said.

"Ahh," Sarah said in stylized amazement.

"No, really. It's the North Star. The North Star. You have to understand this."

Sarah giggled.

Nate furrowed his brow and put a hand to his forehead.

"How does it go? Let me see."

He squinted and sighed, stared up into the face of heaven. "Ah, yes, that's it." He raised a finger, cleared his throat and recited.

"'But I am constant as the northern star, of whose true-fixed and resting quality there is no fellow in the firmament.'"

"Bravo," Sarah said, stepping back and applauding softly. "Nicely done."

Nate smiled, gave a little bow.

"Not bad, huh?"

"Not bad at all."

Nate pulled Sarah close and kissed her again.

She stepped back and smiled. "And?"

"And... what?"

"What about the next line?"

"The next line... Hmmm... I don't think I know it."

"Sure you do," she said, eyes twinkling.

She took Nate by the shoulders and slowly turned him around until he was facing the other way. She cleared her throat.

"Turn ye exactly one hundred and eighty degrees away from the North Star, and thou will be looking south."

She pointed.

"Chiapas is that way."

Nate frowned. "I don't think Shakespeare said that."

"Of course, he did."

But Nate had no intention of being drawn unwillingly into Sarah's plan. He wrapped her in his arms again and kissed her on the forehead.

"I'll tell you what. I'll get you a book on Chiapas. A picture book."

When Sarah started to protest, he silenced her with more kisses.

"You are incredibly beautiful," he said, cupping her face in his hands. "Do you know that?"

She smiled up at him. "You may have said that once or twice."

"Yeah, I think I have."

Her eyes went soft. "Do you have any idea how much I love you?"

Nate felt his heart would burst from the sudden rush of feeling. He kissed Sarah once more. A long, rapturous kiss. The touch of her lips and tongue, her sweet scent, the feeling of her body against his ignited within him a storm of desire. With his loins pressed against her belly, there was no disguising the effect she was having on him.

"I think I'd better get you home," Sarah said. "This is a public place, you know."

"I'm not sure I can wait that long. Isn't there a hotel nearby?"

"You can wait. Come on."

Sarah reached for the empty wine glass, grazed it with her fingertips, and nudged it off the ledge. Husband and wife reached for it, missed, and watched it fall and shatter.

Nate shook his head. "What is wrong with the glassware tonight?"

Sarah laughed.

"We should clean up the mess," she said, starting to reach for the shards. "Someone might step on it."

"No, Sarah," Nate said, pulling her back. "You've done enough clean-up for one night. We'll tell the staff. I think they can handle it." Nate put an arm around his wife's slim waist and guided her away. "Come," he said, nuzzling her hair. "Time for bed."

CHAPTER 5

Persuasion

Nate hoped the notion of going to a remote Mexican village on a church mission trip had been put to bed. It hadn't. Sarah said nothing about it for the next few days, giving Nate a false sense of hope. But early the next week, she told him that Pastor Tom Butler had called to invite them to his church's semi-annual potluck dinner.

"But we're not members of his church, Sarah."

"He knows that, Nate. He said he always likes to invite a few outsiders to these events to make them more interesting, and he enjoyed meeting us and hoped we'd come."

"And you said yes."

Sarah nodded. "I said yes. I was going to call him anyway...."

Nate didn't respond.

He went grudgingly to the church social, feeling set up and expecting to have a miserable time. But, to his surprise, it wasn't bad at all. The people were friendly and interesting, many of them young professionals like Nate and Sarah. The food was flavorful and all homemade. And when Pastor Tom sat down next to Nate with his own plate, instead of immediately bringing up the subject of the mission trip, as Nate expected him to, like Mateo at the gala, he seemed more interested in Nate's work.

"Tell me more about the Internet," the clergyman said. "And websites. What are those exactly? Are they like electronic information archives? I've heard a little bit about them, but I'm not really sure what they do. Should the church get one? Maybe you could explain a little about how they work."

"Of course," Nate said. Sensing a potential client who could bring in a new stream of clients, he was happy to oblige. He explained the basics as the pastor listened intently, and closed with a version of his usual sales pitch.

"So, to answer your question, yes, a website can function as a kind of information archive. But that's only part of what it can do. It also allows you to share news and information about almost anything, almost instantly, with thousands of people, maybe millions, all around the world, with just the touch of a computer key."

Pastor Tom nodded thoughtfully.

"So, after a website *goes live*, as you say, anyone with a computer and access to the Internet system can read what you wrote. And see pictures, too?"

"Pictures, too. And video. That's next."

The minister nodded again. "So I wouldn't be getting all my news from newspapers and radio and TV anymore. I could get it on the Internet."

"That's right."

"And if I wanted to tell people about something that had happened or was going to happen, I wouldn't have to depend on a newspaper or TV or radio station to carry the story. I could spread the news myself."

"Exactly. Sitting at your desktop computer at home or in your office, you can dial up and see it or send it yourself. Anytime you want. As long as you can get a connection, that is. We call it getting online."

"It would save time and money, too. No more mass mailings."

"That's right."

"It's fascinating, isn't it?" Sarah said, talking across to the minister from Nate's other side.

"Amazing," the pastor agreed. "Truly amazing."

"And nobody knows more about it than my husband," Sarah said, smiling and laying a hand on Nate's arm. "He's really a genius."

"I wouldn't go that far," Nate said, chuckling.

"Well, I would," Sarah said, planting a kiss on his cheek.

Pastor Tom sat back in his chair and regarded them both. "You know what I'm thinking now, don't you?"

Nate tensed. *Here we go,* turning forward and staring down at his forgotten plate of food.

Pastor Tom smiled, patted Nate's arm, pushed his chair back and stood.

"I've taken too much of your time," he said. "Enjoy your meal. And, please, think about joining us on our trip to Chiapas. I know Mrs. Hunter—"

"Sarah," Nate's wife interjected.

"Sarah," the minister corrected himself. "I know Sarah is interested. I hope you will consider it, too."

Nate shook his head.

"Thanks, but I'm afraid not."

"You don't have to decide right now. We haven't even set the date yet. Just think about it. Try to keep an open mind. We would love to have Sarah join us, of course. But I would hate for you to miss the opportunity to share this experience with your wife. The work is so enriching, and you have so much to give. Both of you."

After the social, Sarah again said nothing about the trip for a day or so. Nate also kept silent. She would go if she was determined, with or without him, he knew, in which case he would have no choice but to go with her. But if he didn't say that, if he let her think he'd let her go alone, maybe she'd decide she didn't want to go without him.

It was his only hope, and on Day Three, he saw that it was a false one. Sarah had made up her mind. Now she set out to bring her husband around. She began to talk about the trip more often, reading about Chiapas, picking up travel brochures, listening to language tapes, practicing her not-very-good Spanish, checking when their passports expired.

Nate pretended not to notice.

"You know, if we need any inoculations, it's better to get them sooner rather than later," she said casually one evening.

"We?" Nate said.

Sarah just looked at him.

Nate retaliated by doing his own homework and telling Sarah what he was learning about what was going on in Mexico to prepare the way for NAFTA, how it was starting to look to him like it would only add up to more exploitation and abuse of the indigenous people and how the government was dealing with early signs of resistance. "I don't know, Sarah. I don't think now is a good time to travel to Chiapas. I don't think it's safe."

Sarah responded by inviting the minister to tea. "No reason to worry," Pastor Tom assured Nate. "I've traveled there often. It's perfectly safe. We're a church group. The people appreciate what we're doing. And we're Americans. No one's going to do us harm."

The issue came to a head one morning two weeks after the minister's visit. Nate was in the bathroom, shaving, getting ready for work. Sarah was just getting out of bed.

"I forgot to tell you, Pastor Tom called yesterday. They've picked the date now. They're going down in February."

Nate glanced up in the bathroom mirror. Sarah had struck a beguiling pose in the bathroom doorway behind him, leaning nonchalantly against the jamb, hair mussed, lilac colored robe hanging open, tie dangling, arms crossed under her breasts.

"Good for them," Nate said coolly, resisting the urge to turn and slip his wife's robe off her shoulders, continuing to carefully drag the blade across his face.

Sarah made a pouty face.

"Come on," she pleaded. "We have so much, Nate. It's a way to do something good, give something back to the world." She pouted again. "I want to do this. It's who I am. You know that. And I want you with me."

Nate's hand lay across his mouth, pulling the skin of his cheek taut.

"I'm not responsible for the world," he said, his words muffled but resolute. "I'm responsible for you and me. Mexico? And not just Mexico but Southern Mexico, almost to Guatemala? I don't think so, Sarah."

"But you heard Pastor Tom. He takes groups there all the time."

Nate kept his eyes focused on his own reflection. Sarah was fighting dirty, posing like that in the bathroom doorway, calling on methods of persuasion she knew he couldn't resist.

"It's dangerous," he said. "They rob people in places like that... at gunpoint. Kill them. If they don't like you, they just put a bullet in your... I don't—"

Sarah had moved closer, close enough for him to pick up her scent. He stopped shaving, watched her in the mirror. She folded her arms again and lowered her chin, raised her eyes alluringly, gave him a playful, enticing smile. A bewitching silence fell. He knew then she was going to win. Sarah would have her way, as she always did. But Nate was not ready to give in yet. He continued shaving.

"I don't know, Sarah. It doesn't sound like a very good idea to me."

Inwardly, he felt himself starting to cave. He did think the trip was risky. He was not so naïve as to expect creature comforts and emergency care in Chiapas to be anywhere near what it was in the good old U.S.A., but even he had no real reason to think killers actually roamed the countryside waiting to murder them.

"Please?" Sarah pleaded softly, moving another step closer. "I need you to protect me. You will protect me, won't you?"

She was pulling out all the stops.

"Of course, I'll protect you."

"And it's only two weeks. How much protection can I need?"

Nate lowered the razor and turned to Sarah, making one last stand.

"In a place like Chiapas two weeks is a long time. If you want to go to Mexico, why don't we go to Cancun or Acapulco? How about a nice beach resort?"

Sarah did not answer. She lowered her head again, casting him another fetching expression. In a show of false indifference and as a last act of vain protest, Nate turned back toward the mirror and lifted the razor to his face.

Sarah stepped up beside him and touched his arm. He froze, disoriented by clashing images and sensations—a cold steel blade against his cheek, and Sarah's soft, warm hand on his arm.

"Think about it," Sarah said huskily, trailing a finger slowly up and down his left bicep. "Tropical nights. Palm trees swaying." She paused, gave him another seductive look. "Picture it, Nate."

Nate sighed, lowered the razor, let his eyes close. When he opened them, Sarah was gone, her robe lying in a silky heap on the bathroom floor. He took in a deep breath, inflated his cheeks, then exhaled through pursed lips, and followed his wife back to bed.

Later, rushing to finish shaving and make up for lost time, he grabbed the razor, pulled it quickly across his left cheek, did it again, and winced as a thin line of blood appeared bright red against his skin where his cheek was flecked with remnants of shaving cream. He pressed a fingertip hard against the nick and leaned into the mirror. He lifted his finger and watched the blood trail down his cheek.

They were going to Chiapas. And first blood had already been drawn.

CHAPTER 6

Tuxtla

The travelers soldiered on. As afternoon shadows began to lengthen, and light began to dull, they passed the outskirts of a hamlet called *Jiquipilas* and continued east, flanking the northwestern reaches of *El Valle Central*, which Harold informed them ran almost two hundred miles northwest to southeast.

"The heart of Mayan country," Nate added.

Mateo glanced at him. "You have done your homework," he said, nodding once in approval.

"We're climbing again," Nate said as the road jogged northeast. "I can feel the altitude."

"*Sí.* We are nearing *Ocozocoautla.* Over one thousand meters. Maybe thirty-five hundred feet."

"How much farther to Tuxtla Gutierrez?"

"About forty kilometers. We will be there by dark."

In a short time, the road gradually began to descend. Within the hour, they made Tuxtla.

"Well, thank the good Lord," Midge muttered as the VW bus approached the outskirts of the largest urban area the travelers had seen since leaving Oaxaca.

"So, how far would you say we've driven today?" Nate asked Mateo when they entered the city.

Mateo shrugged. "Perhaps three hundred miles."

"And do you do this often?"

Mateo shrugged again, but did not answer.

A few minutes later, the bus pulled up to the porticoed entrance of the four-star Hotel *Real*. With hardly a word passing among them, the road-weary travelers straggled into the lobby as two uniformed attendants saw to their bags. Waiting his turn to check in, Nate watched Mateo and the minister tip the attendants. Then the minister signaled Mateo to wait and crossed the lobby toward Nate.

"I'm sure you're looking forward to getting to your room," he said. "I'll see you for dinner."

"You're not staying here?"

"No, no. We're staying with friends. But I'll be back for dinner."

Sarah and Nate's second-floor room overlooked a central garden and small swimming pool. They stood at their window for a few minutes, arms around each other, exhausted, enjoying the view.

"I need a shower," Sarah finally said, smiling at Nate. "Join me?"

But the shower was only big enough to hold one.

Sarah sighed. "I guess we're not in Dallas anymore." She smiled and gave Nate a squeeze. "You go first. You're quicker."

Sarah was still in the shower when Nate finished dressing. "Why don't you head down and have a drink?" she called. "I'll be down soon."

Nate was just settling in at the bar with a cold brew when Pastor Tom arrived.

"May I join you?" he said.

"Sure, but just so you know. I'm having a beer."

The pastor gave a faint smile.

"I'll turn a blind eye. After this day, I'm tempted to join you."

"Feel free. I'll buy."

"Thanks, but I'd better pass."

"What about Mateo? He probably needs one, or something a little stronger." Nate looked past the minister. "He isn't joining us?"

"I don't think so. He's pretty bushed. And he has to get up early tomorrow to see if he can get the air-conditioning fixed."

Nate nodded. "That's right. I hope he's successful."

"Harold and Midge aren't coming, either. I heard her asking about room service, when they checked in. She turned to me and said, 'I'm sorry, Pastor, but we have not taken a vow of poverty.'"

The minister and Nate both laughed.

"To Midge," Nate said, lifting his bottle in salute and taking a long pull. Pastor Tom settled himself in his chair.

"I think I should apologize," the clergyman said, "for the rough beginning today. The border crossing... I know it was something of a shock."

"You might say that," Nate said dryly, examining his beer. "Not exactly what we were expecting... not that I really know what we were expecting."

"But by this time tomorrow we'll be in Mirador," Pastor Tom said, smiling. "We can get on with the work we came to do... if everyone chooses to stay, that is... That is on it."

He and Nate chuckled.

The pastor turned serious again.

"Our mere presence does make a difference, Nate," the pastor said. "Don't underestimate that. It shows the people they have not been forgotten by the world. That's what they fear most, I think — simply being ignored and forgotten. Mateo says we are fighting 'a war against oblivion.'"

"Mateo," Nate said reflectively. "Now there's an interesting guy. How do you know him?"

Pastor Tom smiled.

"A long story."

"I have nothing but time."

"All right. I didn't always want to be a minister. When I was in college, I wanted to be a professor of Latin American studies. I don't know why. I just always felt a pull toward Latin American history and politics. I did my junior year at *La Universidad Ibero Americana,* a small Jesuit college in Mexico City. I was there in nineteen sixty-eight, the year of the student uprising... right before the Olympics. The *Tlatelolco* massacre, in *La Plaza de las Tres Culturas.* Maybe you heard about it."

Nate thought, shook his head. "Sorry. No. I don't think so."

Pastor Tom nodded. "It was a long time ago. Twenty-five years this year. I can hardly believe it. You would have been a kid."

"You used the word massacre."

The minister nodded again. "It was just before the Olympics, as I said. The Mexican government had spent a lot of money on the Games, and the president didn't want any problems... That would be a polite way to put it. But the government was having major problems with the people then. It was a really corrupt, repressive government, and there was serious dissent and resistance taking shape. Students, labor organizers, farmers, everybody was coming together to press for change. And they were doing it peacefully. That was the remarkable thing. But then there was some fight between high school gangs, and the president used it as an excuse to send riot police into the schools, and then he sent the army onto college campuses...."

"Really."

"Yes. So the students organized a huge protest in the plaza. Something like ten thousand people, mostly students, but not all. Again, all peaceful... until it wasn't."

Nate stared at his beer. "Sounds like Tiananmen Square."

Pastor Tom nodded. "No tanks and not as many people killed, but, yes. It was part of what they call Mexico's Dirty War back in the sixties and seventies when it was trying to crush the student movement and political opposition. Dirty business, for sure. The government spent billions on the Games—that's billions, with a B—while its own people were starving, didn't have jobs, needed schools and clinics."

"How many people died?"

"No one knows for sure. Some say as many as three hundred. Some say more. And that's not counting the thousands who were wounded or rounded up and beaten."

"Were you there?"

The pastor was silent a moment.

"I was there."

"Were you hurt?"

"No. When the shooting started, I ran like a scared rabbit. I was one of the lucky ones. I didn't get caught. But that night changed me. I can tell you that."

"So, where does Mateo fit in?"

"He was a professor at the *Ibero*. I was one of his students."

"Really? He told me he was a construction supervisor."

The minister nodded.

"He didn't lie. That was kind of his sideline. His wife's uncle had a company. Mateo was good at construction, good with his hands, good at organizing and getting things done. He helped out."

Nate laughed. "And, oh yeah, I forgot to mention I was a college professor." He shook his head.

"What did he teach?"

"Philosophy."

Nate couldn't help smiling. "Ahh... philosophy. Why does that not surprise me?" He glanced at the minister. "Was he there?"

Pastor Tom nodded. "Oh, yes. He was one of the organizers."

Nate sat, ruminating on that interesting piece of information for a few moments.

"Was he hurt?"

"He didn't run, the way I did. He was arrested. Roughed up pretty bad. Spent a few months in jail. He doesn't talk about it, so I don't know for sure what they did to him." He looked sheepishly at Nate. "Don't think I want to know."

Nate nodded. "I knew there was more to him than he let on. He was one of the organizers?"

"Yes."

"That doesn't surprise me, either. He has that quality about him — a kind of 'leader of men' quality."

"I know what you mean."

"There's a certain look he gives you sometimes... It makes me feel like I should salute him. *Sí, Capitán!*"

The minister laughed and nodded.

"He's quite a fellow. I'm glad you've had a chance to get better acquainted."

"So how did the two of you get from Mexico City to Chiapas?"

The minister smiled. "That came later. Mateo and I remained friends. I went into the ministry. I'd visit him every now and then in Mexico City. He and his wife had a lovely house there. Then she convinced him to go with her to Mirador and... Well, you know the rest."

"How did she die?"

Pastor Tom frowned. "I don't think that's for me to say. That's something to ask Mateo. But I know it's still a very painful subject for him, so I'd let him bring it up."

Nate nodded. "I understand." The thought of ever losing Sarah — he couldn't even contemplate it.

"After her death, I guess his life in Mexico City didn't have the same meaning for him. So he stayed in Mirador and started working with the church. I came to visit him. And the rest is history." The preacher looked at Nate. "He has a heart for *los indígenas*. Always did. He's the kind of person who can't stand idly by while other people suffer. He can't see a wrong without trying to right it. Some people are like that.

Your Sarah, for example. They have an innate goodness, a sense of justice that is very rare, very precious. And they are naturally bold."

"That's Sarah, all right."

"I admire people like that so much. I always wanted to be one of them. Sadly, I'm not. I'm afraid I don't have that kind of courage."

"So, *El Capitán* is..." Nate counted on the fingers of one hand. "Professor, philosopher, political organizer, church-builder...." He looked at the minister. "Anything else?"

The minister smiled. "Yes, there are many sides to the man."

"And his mood changes on a dime. One second he's affable. The next, it's like something comes over him."

Pastor Tom nodded. "He likes to tell the old story of the Indian and the two dogs."

A quizzical smile shaped Nate's lips.

"You haven't heard it?"

Nate shook his head. The pastor leaned in.

"It goes like this. An old Indian was kind one day, cruel the next, kind one day, cruel the next. Finally, someone asked him how that could be, how he could change back and forth like that. The Indian said, 'There are two dogs inside me. They are at war with each other.' The person said, 'One dog will ultimately win the war. Which dog will it be?' The old Indian said, 'The one I feed the most.'"

Nate sipped his beer.

"He seems to know a fair amount about computers, too. On the drive today, that's mostly what he wanted to talk about. He wanted to know about the Internet."

"Yes," Pastor Tom said. "In addition to everything else, he's very innovative, very curious and creative. Very smart. He is what you might call a man of a different stamp." Pastor Tom looked up. "Ah, there's Sarah."

Nate looked up to see his beautiful wife in clean khakis and white shirt, wet hair tied up in a knot, leading the rest of the small band of missioners toward them.

"Shall we move to a table?" the minister asked.

Everyone seemed to feel relaxed and refreshed after showering and changing. The minister and Wilma ordered bottled water. Sarah and Nate shared a beer. The siblings ordered soft drinks. "No ice!" they said in unison, then broke into laughter that relaxed the group even more.

Over a late meal of well-cooked chicken, beef and vegetable dishes, tamales and fried plantains, rice and beans, the six people gathered around the table talked and laughed, and avoided the question they knew they had to tackle until coffee and a modest desert of cookies and chocolates were set on the table before them.

"Well," the minister said finally. "As you know, we have a decision to make. Forward? Or back?"

As Nate expected, Sarah remained undaunted.

"We came here to do something for people who have nothing," she said earnestly. "What happened today was horrible." Everyone murmured in agreement. "But if we turn back, what does that say about our level of commitment? And where does that leave the people we've come to help?"

Seated to Sarah's right, Wilma spoke next. "I agree with Sarah. I would have voted to turn around and go home if we could have after that...after that incident. But I'm glad now that we couldn't, because it gave me time to think. What happened today was awful. It was a crime." Again, everyone murmured agreement. "But we weren't hurt. And, as Americans, I don't think we will be. So, I vote to continue to Mirador." She looked down, as if embarrassed. "I can't speak for anyone else, but I don't think I could live with myself if I backed out now."

Wilma stopped speaking, and Sarah gave her a hug.

Pastor Tom nodded to the siblings. "Jeff? Steph?"

"We've already talked it over," Stephanie said, sounding surprisingly calm and mature. "And we want to stay, too." She looked at her brother, who nodded in agreement.

"We like to goof around, sure," Jeffrey said. "But we're not the total airheads people seem to think we are—which is our own fault, no doubt." Jeffrey smiled a lopsided smile that made everyone laugh. "But really. Steph and I know how fortunate we are. We've been blessed, and we're not kids anymore. It's time to start giving back. That's why we're here. We didn't sign up for a vacation. We want to do something to help people." He shrugged. "So...."

The minister smiled at them. Then all eyes turned to Nate.

"What about the rocker and his better half?" Nate said to Pastor Tom, stalling for time.

"Oh, I know Harold and Midge pretty well. They can be difficult, especially Midge. But they're good people at heart. Midge flusters rather easily but—"

"I wouldn't call that 'easily,'" Nate interjected.

"No, of course not." The minister frowned. "I didn't mean that. What I meant was, when something frightens or upsets her, she reacts strongly. But ninety-nine percent of the time, she comes back later and apologizes and will actually say 'I was wrong.' I don't know many people who can do that, so I have to say she's earned my respect... and my affection." He looked at Nate. "She'll be okay. Harold, too. He talks a lot but he's a pretty sturdy soul, and he's her rock, no pun intended." Everyone laughed. "Besides, there are more spectacular geological features to see. *El Cañon del Sumidero*, for example. They call it The Drain. Very impressive. We'll be skirting the southern rim tomorrow. Harold wouldn't want to miss that."

"So we're going down the drain?" Jeffrey wisecracked.

Everyone laughed except Nate. Now, all eyes were again on him.

"Sweetie?" Sarah said softly.

Nate leaned forward in his chair, put his elbows on the table, clasped his hands and stared down at them, wrestling with himself. *No,* he wanted to say. *No, Sarah. It's too dangerous. We didn't sign up for this.* But Sarah was sitting there, watching and waiting, her expression a heart-melting mix of worry and hope. Sarah wasn't leaving. He knew that. She'd made that clear. He sighed, nodded slowly.

"Okay. Let's go to Mirador."

CHAPTER 7

The Final Push

By seven-thirty the next morning, the travelers were back on the road, back in a bus with no air-conditioning.

"I am sorry," Mateo said when he came to pick them up. "The mechanic did not have the parts."

"Well, did you go somewhere else?" Midge asked indignantly.

Nate saw a look of annoyance flit across Mateo's face and disappear.

"*Sí, Señora,*" Mateo said calmly. "Many places."

"Between last night and this morning, I think Mateo has probably visited every auto mechanic in town," the pastor added.

Midge harrumphed. "I'm sorry, Mateo," she said, climbing into the bus. "I didn't mean to insult you."

"*Está bien, Señora.* No problem, no problem."

Once all the travelers were again settled in their assigned seats, Mateo started the engine and smiled into the rearview mirror. "Today, I will show you something special before we begin our journey."

"*El Cañon,*" Harold said, a hint of excitement in his voice.

Mateo nodded. "*Sí, El Cañon.*"

In less than an hour, they arrived at a scenic turnout that offered a commanding view of a steep, green river canyon. The travelers clambered out of the bus near a low stone wall at the edge of an overlook.

"Take a gander at that, will you," Harold said, walking right up to the wall, resting his elbows on its top and gazing over the edge. "Now, that's what I call a canyon." Midge stood a step or two behind him to his left. He turned to the rest of his companions, who were hanging back a few paces. "Come look at this!" he said, motioning them forward. "You really must see this. Some of my colleagues say it's one of the geological wonders of the world."

Nate and Sarah led the group forward. Mateo stayed behind, relaxing against the front of the bus. From the stone wall, they gazed down into a deep cleft in the earth with a narrow ribbon of blue-green river coursing through it. Flat-faced canyon walls, sheer and entirely unscalable, rose up a thousand feet or more on either side of the water. From the river gorge a seemingly boundless rain forest, trackless and wild, spread out in every direction.

"I think this is the biggest canyon I've ever seen," Sarah said softly, stepping up next to Harold and leaning out over the edge of the wall.

"Sarah, don't," Nate said, taking her elbow to draw her back.

"You haven't seen the Grand Canyon?" Wilma asked, hugging herself and taking a few tentative steps closer.

"Not yet, but if it's anything like this …."

"They started at about the same time, actually about thirty-five, forty million years ago," Harold said. "This one started as a crack in the earth's crust." He pointed down at the sunken, blue-green ribbon. "That's the *Grijalva* River down there. As with the Grand Canyon, the river did the rest."

"Why is it called The Drain?" Jeffrey asked. All of the missioners were now lined up at the wall, taking in the view.

"Those are limestone cliffs," Harold said, pointing. "They're riddled with caves. During heavy rains the water drains out of the caves and down the sides of the canyon."

"Cool," Jeffrey said, nodding appreciatively.

Sarah continued gazing out at the view. Nate lifted his camera and snapped a picture of her.

"There's some sad history associated with this place, too," the minister said. He nodded toward Mateo, who was leaning up against the front of the minibus. "Mateo told me the first time he brought me here. The Chiapa people lived in this area before the Spanish arrived, and they fought the Spanish invaders to the death. The story is that when the Spanish finally took their last stronghold up here in the canyon, the survivors jumped to their deaths."

"Whoa," Jeffrey said softly.

"Yeah," his sister echoed.

Everyone fell silent for a few moments.

Sarah bowed her head.

"We should get going," the minister said finally.

Back on the road, traveling eastward, the bus followed the rise of the land, tooling along the narrow, winding upland road through steep, rugged terrain. The old VW grumbled and coughed, laboring up foggy ridges and slumping into deep valleys, trailing a scent of carbon monoxide mixed with burning rubber each time Mateo applied the brakes. When the wind was right, everyone in the bus got a good whiff.

Very quickly, they came to *Chiapa de Corzo*. From there, departing the canyon-riven country, they pushed deeper into the central highlands. Air thinned and cooled. A profusion of tropical foliage encroached on the roadsides—shrubs, wildflowers, palm trees, vibrant-colored hibiscus and bougainvillea. High palisades of gray volcanic rock loomed over them to the south. To the north, the land fell away and opened up into expansive vistas of distant mountains that drew "oohs" and "wows" from the travelers. From time to time, as the road climbed higher, they could look down on the cloud forest, white layers of dense, moist air hovering in deep troughs between rocky rooster-comb ridges.

"How high are we now?" Nate asked Mateo.

Mateo glanced at Nate and raised his eyebrows. "High," he said. "Almost eight thousand feet."

About an hour after the mission-workers had piled back into the bus at The Drain, the road descended slightly into San Cristóbal de las Casas, nestled in a small valley surrounded by hills forested with massive pine and oak trees.

"The city is almost five hundred years old," Mateo said, as he guided the bus from the ramshackle outskirts of town toward the heart of the old city along narrow cobblestone streets lined with low, tile-roofed stucco buildings painted in bright colors, with ornate iron gates covering windows and doorways.

"Oh my goodness, what's that?" Sarah asked when they came to what looked like a walled and gated garden fronted by an old church facing onto a plaza.

"It was a church and monastery," Mateo said. "Then the monastery became a military barracks and prison."

"A what?" Harold said. "Did you say prison?"

Mateo nodded. "*Sí*. But it is not a prison anymore." He waved at the deteriorating complex. "It is very old. Many of the buildings are very old. This was one of the first cities the Spanish built in all of North America. At one time, it was the capital of Chiapas. Now, the capital is Tuxtla. But San Cristóbal is considered the cultural capital."

"I can see why," Sarah said. "It's beautiful."

They drove around the heart of the old city.

"There is the cathedral," Mateo said, pointing to a large, ornate, mustard-colored church facing onto another broad plaza.

"Oh my gosh, look at that," Sarah gasped.

"Beautiful," Wilma said, a catch in her voice.

"And there," Mateo said, pointing to a long white building facing onto an adjacent plaza to his left, "that is *El Palacio de Gobierno.*"

"The government palace," Wilma translated, looking out her window.

"Another beautiful building," Sarah said.

"Limestone façade. Tuscan arches. Wrought iron balconies," Harold observed. "Very nice, very nice. Wouldn't you say, dear?"

"It is," Midge said. "It's quite a beautiful old city. Thank you for showing it to us, Mateo."

"Yes, thank you," Sarah added.

Nate turned toward his wife and they exchanged a surprised look. Maybe the pastor had been right about Midge.

Nate consulted the map.

"We're still pretty high up, here, right?"

"Yes," Mateo said. "Over seven thousand feet."

"So, to the east, we descend. Right?"

"A little. But then the road will take us toward the *Altiplano, La Meseta Central de Chiapas.* There, we climb again. Then we descend again. As I said, up and down, up and down."

About half an hour outside San Cristóbal, they relinquished the Pan American Highway and turned northeast onto Highway 199, where, as Mateo had promised, the road dipped down a bit, then climbed again. The VW bus crawled over the edge of the platform mountain and struck out across high tableland. An hour later, they passed the outskirts of an urban area called *Oxhuc.* A little later, the road curved east and they gradually began to descend.

By degrees, they abandoned the upcountry and began wending their way steadily downward toward the Lacandon Jungle. By the time they reached the town of *Ocosingo*, not quite three hours after leaving San Cristóbal, they had descended to less than three thousand feet, giving up more than four thousand feet of elevation.

"Please tell me we are done with the high country, Mateo," Midge said. Nate glanced back to see her sitting with her arms folded tight around her chest, under her bosom, and her husband's arm once again around her.

"*Sí. Sí.* No more high country, *Señora* Bottomley."

"Thank the Lord."

At the northern end of *Oco*, they left the federal highway, looped right more than ninety degrees, and plunged southeastward on their first unpaved road. Nate checked the map again.

"This road doesn't have a name or number."

"No. No name, no number. Here, we are in the Lacandon."

"So what road is this?"

"The road to Mirador."

Until then, the roads had been decent. Two-lane blacktops, mostly. Not always smooth, sometimes no center line, but not too bad. Now, the formerly smooth roadbed gave way to corduroy. Corduroy gave way to washboard. Washboard gave way to corrugated. The passengers in the minibus bounced and bumped, bracing themselves however they could. Progress slowed.

They were on the downhill now, descending toward the low country along a ridge flanked by parallel ridges in both directions as far as Nate could see. With the gradual loss of another thousand feet of elevation, lowland heat returned, fiercer than ever.

After about three hours that seemed like an eternity on the nameless road of dirt and gravel, they reached *La Sultana,* a settlement that was little more than an outland way station, where everyone got out to breathe, stretch, relieve themselves discreetly and drink warm bottled drinks purchased from a roadside stand.

"How much farther?" Sarah asked Mateo, twisting and stretching to loosen cramped muscles.

"About sixty miles. Perhaps another three hours."

The travelers groaned.

"*Sí*, I know," Mateo said. "The road will be rough the rest of the way. But we are almost there now."

The road descended toward a river. Mateo negotiated the bus across a rickety bridge, turned southeast, and the terrain began to change again. The low-gear road took many turns. They crossed skinny fault-line streams and swollen rivers on more rickety narrow bridges, passed a high, cascading waterfall that plunged in a wide, blanched ribbon of water into foamy turbulence in the pool below. Occasional signs warned, *Curva Peligrosa*.

The travelers fanned themselves, pulled sweat-soaked clothing away from their skin, sipped their warm beverages.

"Boy, what I wouldn't give for an ice-cold Coke right now," Jeffrey sighed from the back seat.

The other travelers laughed weakly.

Mateo nodded. "This is a rain forest," he said. "It will be hot and wet. Rains are heavy for seven or eight months of the year. Rough country. There is a reason it is poor people who live here. Land is hard to clear and cannot take much tilling."

Mateo waved an arm.

"Here, *campesinos* try to coax meager crops of corn from rocky soil. Little else will grow. And when it does grow, it leaves the land exhausted."

He shook his head.

"It is a poor stake in the world for anyone. But it is all these people have. A difficult life. A difficult life, indeed."

Nate nodded, listening more openly, he realized, than he had the day before. He gazed out the window, letting his thoughts drift. He was glad he and the pastor had had that talk at the hotel bar. Knowing a little more about Mateo's background helped Nate see him in a different light. He hadn't told Sarah what he'd learned. After dinner, they had fallen dead asleep, and they hadn't had time alone today. Nate was looking forward to finally reaching Mirador. Maybe he and Sarah would have their own room. Just being alone with her for the night would—

And then, the bus was passing something Nate was not expecting to see—an Army outpost of some kind, a military camp swarming with armed troops clad in green fatigues like the ones at the border crossing. Armored vehicles. A barracks with green-white-and-red striped flags flying at the entrance.

Nate straightened in his seat at the same moment the other travelers saw what he was seeing. He heard gasps, a stifled whimper, a soft "Oh, no." But the bus passed without incident and the outpost soon disappeared from view. No one said a word.

Nate looked at Mateo with disbelief.

"So the army is way out here, too? You didn't mention that."

Mateo said nothing.

"Why?" Nate asked.

"Why what?" Mateo responded calmly.

"Why is the army way out here?"

"We are nearing the border with Guatemala. Of course, there are soldiers here. There is even a small garrison in Mirador."

Nate stared at Mateo. "There are soldiers in Mirador? Something else you didn't mention. Why is that?"

"I do not know," Mateo said stone-faced. "You would have to ask the army."

"I'm asking you."

Mateo waved a hand dismissively. "Mexico has an army. They have to be somewhere. No problem. No problem."

Hearing those empty words of assurance again was too much for Nate. He turned to Mateo, ready to confront him when he felt Sarah's hand on his shoulder. He glared at Mateo instead, choked his anger back down, turned to face out his open window, and took a series of deep breaths.

"What the hell?" Nate muttered to himself. "What the fucking hell...."

But Sarah had been right to check him. They were in too deep now. They'd had their chance to turn back and, for Sarah's sake, only for her sake, Nate had agreed to go on. Anger and insults wouldn't help anything. Nate needed to stay calm and focused. He needed to get through these next two weeks and get his wife home.

And then, when he thought things couldn't get worse. Rain. A sudden downpour that soon slacked off into a persistent drizzle, as relentless as the torrid stillness that had preceded it. Mist shrouded the jungle. Nate felt enveloped in steam.

"How much farther now, Mateo?" Sarah asked softly. "Are we getting close?"

Mateo shifted his gaze to the rearview mirror. Nate watched his expression soften. He liked Sarah. Of course he did. How could he not?

"Not much farther, *Señora* Hunter. We will be there soon. Our journey is coming to an end."

After another twenty minutes or so, the fine drizzle abated. About another twenty long minutes after that, as the bus rocked and splashed along a muddy road riddled with rain-filled potholes, signs of civilization returned. The Americans saw campesinos in the distance, clearing small tracts of brush with axes and machetes. Children driving donkeys hitched to homemade wooden carts mounted on automobile tires. Women, in groups of a half-dozen or more, sitting cross-legged on the ground, cooking around open fires, under lean-to shelters. A young mother walked along the side of the road carrying an infant in the hollow of her arm, one of her breasts exposed and at the ready. Only the dregs of the day's light remained now. Dusk was coming on.

The road rose and fell in hypnotic undulations. Some of the travelers slept. Nate was about to drift off, too, when the road lifted again and from high ground, a village—tinted bluegray by twilight shadows—came into view. Mateo stopped and idled the bus.

The passengers stirred. "What—" "Why are we stopping?"

Mateo pointed. A smile creased his face.

"Mirador. We have made it."

"What? We're really here? Really? We made it?" Jeffrey asked. "All right!"

His sister giggled. "Hip, hip, hooray!"

The other travelers laughed in relief.

The village wasn't much to look at. It occupied a hollow scooped out of a ring of heavily forested, humpbacked hills. From their perch, the pilgrims gazed down upon a sprawl of low, squalid-looking structures set in a maze of narrow streets and alleyways, the village bounded on all sides by what looked like a two-lane, gravel road.

Mateo put the bus in gear. "We must go. *Tatic* is waiting."

The road insinuated into the valley from the northwest. Near the village, the VW clattered across a wooden beam bridge that spanned a shallow creek. On the other side of the bridge, the road branched. Mateo stopped and idled the bus again to give the new arrivals their bearings.

"We have come in on *el camino principal*, the main road," he said, pointing at the road behind them.

"Not much of a road," Nate muttered.

"*Sí*, that is true. Still, it is the busiest thoroughfare in Mirador."

Mateo pointed to the road ahead.

"Here, it continues south along the west side of the village. There..." He indicated where the road branched off to his left. "... it runs east, then south, then west again. The two roads join again at the southwest boundary of the village. Then the road goes on to the Guatemala border."

"So the road makes a loop," Nate said. Seemed simple enough.

"*Sí*, like a noose," Mateo said. "That is what people call it... *La Soga*. The noose."

"How cheering," Midge commented dryly.

"What's our elevation here, Mateo?" Harold asked.

"About one hundred twenty meters," Mateo said. "Maybe four hundred feet."

"And the population?" Sarah inquired.

"About one thousand souls, give or take."

Nate and Sarah exchanged a look, both struck by Mateo's choice of words. Nate would have expected it from the minister, but to hear Mateo refer to people as souls surprised him.

"The village seems to shrink a little every day now, though," Mateo added. "It... *marchitarse*... what is the English word?"

"Wither," Wilma responded. "It withers."

"Yes, it withers."

They drove on. In the village, Mateo guided the bus southeastward down gravel lanes lined with slat board houses and dirt-floor shacks. Tumbledown huts of wattle and daub. Tarpaper shacks and packing-crate shanties. Weathered structures of plank and batten, others cobbled up out of a hodgepodge of scavenged materials—corrugated sheets of metal, green plastic, large pieces of plywood, fragments of shutters, pieces of wooden shipping crates—many with slanted roofs constructed of nothing but blue tarpaulins stretched tight between poles. The yellow lights of candles and oil lamps flickered and seeped through chinks in the walls and the rifts left by the imperfect joinery of siding boards. They passed yards littered with junk—old tires, car parts, odds and ends of broken-down pieces of furniture and other cast-off wooden objects. At least the wood could be used for cookfires, Nate thought.

Mateo waved a finger toward a cluster of barefoot, half-naked children standing outside a shanty. Their bellies were swollen. Sarah came forward in her seat and peered out the window. She put a hand to her heart.

"My God. Those poor kids. They're starving. They can't live long like that."

Mateo nodded.

"Here, children suffer from malnutrition and tapeworms, dysentery. They die of diseases that are easily cured where you come from. It is what you Americans call a hardscrabble life. We had a doctor and a clinic once. But no more. Now we have nothing."

"No medical care at all?" Sarah asked, sounding dismayed.

"We have a midwife, but no western medicine, no. Not since the clinic closed."

Sarah sat back and shook her head.

Mateo glanced over his shoulder at her.

"My wife, Elba, was a nurse there."

Nate felt like he'd been punched in the stomach.

"Your wife was a nurse?" Sarah said, clearly surprised. "I didn't know that, Mateo. Why didn't you tell me? What did—"

Just then a bony black colt—very young—bounded suddenly into the road from the underbrush. Mateo slammed on the brakes, throwing his passengers forward in their seats, as the colt shied and jumped in circles in front of the bus.

Mateo spun around at the sound of their cries and shouts.

"Is everyone okay? Is anyone hurt?"

The travelers were rattled but uninjured.

"Next time you're going to hit the brakes like that, Mateo, try to give us a little warning, will you please?" Midge said archly, patting her hair.

"*Lo siento, lo siento,* I am sorry. But if I had hit him…."

Mateo eased the bus forward to herd the colt off the road. It jumped sideways to the edge of the trackway and cavorted along on Nate's side of the bus in a show of youthful bravado. And then it veered and disappeared back into the brush.

Mateo laughed.

"I envy him for his youth and innocence. He does not seem to know he is poor. *Verdad?*"

Nate nodded, saying nothing. He was still reeling from Mateo's revelation that his wife had been a nurse. He waited for Sarah to resume questioning Mateo, but she didn't. He turned to see her gazing out the window, lost in thought.

Nate reached back and squeezed Sarah's hand, caught her eye and gave her a smile. She smiled back. But inside, he felt a deep well of anger rising up. Mateo's wife had been a nurse. She had died in Mirador. Mateo and the minister had known that when they recruited Sarah and Nate. And no one had thought to mention it until now. Nate clamped the lid back down on his anger. He didn't want a scene. But he would discuss this with Mateo later—Mateo and the minister both.

He went back to looking out the window, observing life in Mirador. Barefoot men rode bareback on gaunt horses—malnourished animals, sides caved, ribs protruding like barrel hoops. Scrawny dogs wandered in twos and threes, hip bones jutting against sagging hides. Two mongrels fought over a food scrap at the road's edge, snarling, growling, lunging at flanks and throats. Others watched, some with hackles raised, some with tails tucked, mouths open, tongues lolling.

They passed a man sharpening a machete on a stone, women in colorful cotton dresses—red and blue, yellow and green—carrying loads of firewood, nursing their babies, cooking tortillas on grills set over open flames. The aroma permeated the dense air.

The road widened a bit and the huts and shanties gave way to homes of somewhat better quality. *The better part of town,* Nate was thinking when, approaching an intersection, Mateo suddenly shouted "Hold on!" and slammed on the brakes again. The bus skidded to a stop in the mud just as a pickup truck full of drunken hooligans—laughing, shouting, waving bottles—barreled through the intersection, narrowly missing them. A few of the young toughs brandished rifles. One looked directly at the bus, raised a hand and gave the travelers the finger as he sped past.

Again, Mateo spun around to make sure his passengers were unhurt. They were flustered, but unharmed, having had a split-second to brace.

Assured that no one was injured, he turned forward again, clenched his sizable fist, and shook it in the air.

"*Cabrónes chingados!*" he snarled, his face reddening. "*Cabrónes chingados!*"

Nate heard Wilma gasp.

Breathing heavily, Mateo clutched the wheel and tried to calm himself. He turned again to the seven Americans behind him, their faces wiped clean of all expression, drained of all color.

"*Lo siento. Lo siento.* Forgive me. Please, forgive me. From time to time, I am known for using... *palabrotas*... bad words. It is a character flaw. But when I see these... these... young men... riding around drunk on that poison, waving guns. And laughing!" He pounded the steering wheel. "*Madre de Dios!*"

"What were they drunk on?" Nate asked, keeping his voice level.

Mateo grimaced. "*Posh,*" he muttered.

"What's *posh*?" Nate asked calmly.

"Homemade corn liquor. Very strong." He looked at Nate. "Stay away from it unless you want to end up dead or blind."

Nate nodded slightly.

"Shouldn't be a problem."

They drove on, past other intersecting streets and alleys—some gravel, some dirt, some little more than muddy pig trails. A few streets farther along, they passed a small wood-frame building with a wide covered porch and shattered windows. It looked abandoned.

"What's that?" Nate said.

Mateo was silent a moment. "It was once the clinic. But it is closed now."

Nate studied it as they passed, turned to Mateo. "What did—"

"Ah, at last, my friends," Mateo said, smiling and pointing ahead.

The road had dead-ended into a tree-filled square. Mateo swung the bus left along the northern side, then right along its eastern boundary. Slightly ahead and to his left, Nate saw a church facing onto the square, the only white building in view. Mateo pulled up in front of it and cut the engine, turned and smiled at his passengers.

"We are here," he said, gesturing toward the church. "*La Iglesia de la Ventana de Luz.* The Church of the Window of Light. Built by Dominicans in fifteen sixty."

It was a humble village church set back from the road by some thirty feet of stone forecourt, not all that different from other rural mission churches Nate had seen in guidebooks. Whitewashed stucco walls, flaking in places. Tiled roof with narrow eaves. A large central entrance. Massive double doors made of some kind of weathered hardwood hung on great iron hinges set within an archway outlined in blue-green tile. Fluted Doric half-columns flanked the doorway. A bull's-eye window was centered over the door, above a plain molded cornice that stretched the width of the building. Above the cornice, a flat façade tapered upward from the sides to a curved pediment that soared above the roofline, giving the church an illusion of height. The crowning parapet featured a diminutive arcaded belfry framing three bronze bells suspended from heavy timber yokes. A weathered wooden cross surmounted the belfry. The cross leaned slightly to the north.

Nate took it in. *So this is what we've come all this way for,* he thought. *This is our holy grail.* He turned to see what his fellow travelers thought. All were silent, gazing and craning with slightly worried or puzzled expressions on their faces. The siblings exchanged a look. Midge pursed her lips and frowned. Nate looked over his shoulder at Sarah. He caught her gaze, raised an eyebrow and shook his head.

This is it? his look said. *This is why we're here? For two whole weeks? I don't believe it.*

Sarah frowned slightly and turned her attention back to the church, but Nate knew she had received his message.

He gave the church another appraising look, shook his head again.

Mateo was still smiling. "We are here," he repeated. "Welcome to Mirador." ▲

CHAPTER 8

End of the Road

Beneath a rapidly dimming sky, Mateo hoisted himself from the driver's seat and stepped heavy-footed around the front of the vehicle to the opposite side. There, he threw open the doors and welcomed his passengers again with outstretched arms.

"*Bienvenidos a Mirador,*" he said, smiling. "At long last. *Sí,* at long last. We are here. Welcome. Welcome, my friends."

Nate offered a gracious expression, flimsily constructed, and a slight nod, but said nothing. Muscles taut with caution and cramped from sitting, he swiveled to his right, eased himself to ground and stood for the first time in too many hours. He shuffled forward a few half-paces, stuffed his hands into his pockets, arched his back, gingerly took his neck through its full range of motion and looked around.

Encroaching darkness allowed him to discern mostly vague images, black figures, gray shapes. Through a blue veil of dying light, he made out a motley of impoverished dwellings clustered near the church, curtained windows yellowed by the muted glow of interior lights. In the square across from the church, partially hidden in a copse of tall shade trees, he saw an octagonal kiosk-type bandstand capped with a louvered cupola, a couple of wrought iron benches. A few shop fronts dotted the perimeter of the square. Beyond the square to the west, in the direction of daylight's hurrying retreat, the slope of a distant hill was darkly etched in irregular patches that he speculated were vegetable gardens.

Sarah appeared at Nate's side. She looked up at him, eyes questioning. He put an arm around her shoulders, pulled her close, kissed her at the temple. He drew in a deep breath, puckered his lips, and let it out slowly, gazing out over the far hillside in dwindling light.

"Are you okay?" he asked in a near whisper.

"Sure. You?"

Nate nodded.

"Peachy," he said. "Just peachy."

Their other traveling companions had begun shuffling in their seats, collecting their belongings. Nate watched Mateo help them clamber stiffly out of the bus, one by one—first Midge, then Harold, then the minister and the kids, and finally Wilma. Rubbing their necks and backs, grimacing, stretching, each stood on unfamiliar ground and looked around without speaking. Last, came Pastor Tom. When all had exited, the minister went to Mateo, smiled and patted his old friend on the shoulder as if to congratulate him on a feat of derring-do.

Nate observed the two men. *Old friends, all right,* he thought. Anger rising again, he took a step in their direction and felt Sarah hold him back. Gripping his bicep firmly with both hands, she gave him a solicitous look... and put a finger to her lips. Nate hesitated, rolled his eyes slightly, took a few slow, deep breaths, then—with his lips sealed—stared into the gathering darkness, taking in the local sounds and smells. Mournful strains of a guitar somewhere in the distance. Cry of baby, bark of dog, low hum of gasoline generator. The still, humid air bore a faint odor of woodsmoke, a hint of engine exhaust. *Where are we?* Nate thought. *Where the hell are we?*

"Thank *God!*" Midge proclaimed dramatically, fanning her sweaty cheeks with one open hand and setting the other, fisted, on the crest of a hip. "I thought we'd never get here."

"Yes. Yes," Mateo said, smiling and crossing himself. "*Gracias a Dios.* Always. Always. But we are here. We are in Mirador. Home."

He turned and pointed again to the little church.

"*La Iglesia de la Ventana de Luz,*" he said. "A place of hope and salvation."

The travelers regarded the church again. For at least a full, measured minute, no one spoke.

"Well... " Wilma finally said with obvious effort, "really... in its own way... it is... beautiful... don't you think?" She turned to her companions.

"Awesome," Jeffrey said, smiling. "For sure. I bet people come from miles around to see it."

Stephanie giggled, poked her brother and forced the smile off her own face. "It is... like... really... cool," she said, trying to sound sincere.

"It is an interesting structure," Harold observed. "They make stucco from native limestone, you know. The Mayans have done it for centuries. It's a complicated process. It deteriorates rather quickly in this climate, though. That is on it."

He looked at his wife with a satisfied smile. She glowered.

"Thank you for that little lesson, Harold," she said. "I'm sure everyone appreciates it."

The pastor cleared his throat. "Actually, Jeffrey, people do come to this church from miles around," he said gently. "But they aren't tourists. They are *campesinos*."

"*Los indígenas, sí*," Mateo said, gazing up at the church again. "For those who have nothing, *esta iglesia es muy importante*. Here is where they speak to God, where they feel God hears their prayers."

"I'm sorry," Jeffrey said, looking at his feet. "I didn't mean—"

"No, no, of course not," Pastor Tom said, smiling and patting his arm. "No harm done."

He would never admit it, but now Nate felt a little ashamed of his own initial reaction. Even in the gathering darkness, he could see that the modest building was in poor repair—scabrous walls dappled with water stains and veined with cracks, broken and missing steps. He saw no ventana, no heavenly luz. But if the church's interior was in the same or worse condition, now at least he had some idea of what their work would be once it actually got underway. He still couldn't envision how the well-intentioned coterie of gringos could provide assistance that would be of any real value, but maybe with Mateo as their foreman, they could at least get the restoration process started. Why were the pastor and Mateo so focused on restoring a church, though, when the village didn't even have a clinic? Clearly, it seemed to Nate, Mirador needed that more. Nate didn't understand it and intended to say something about it. But never mind that for now. Never mind anything. They were here. It was late. All Nate wanted was a good meal and a good rest, with Sarah in his arms. *Go with the flow,* he told himself. *Go with the flow.*

Nate studied his fellow Americans. All appeared deflated, exhausted and equally doubtful—all save one. He could tell by looking at

Sarah's face that she saw everything—the window, the light, the good they might do. She had a purer vision than he did, saw things with different eyes.

"Come," Mateo said, pointing with one arm and beckoning everyone forward with the other. "We will leave the luggage for now. It will be perfectly safe. Come, everyone. I will take you to the rectory. We will eat and drink and you can freshen up, make yourselves comfortable. Come. Come. Follow me."

Moving in a tight cluster, like a covey of watchful birds, the party of Americans followed Mateo along a well-trodden path of cinder paving that wound around behind the church. Sarah walked at Mateo's side, questioning him intently about something. Nate couldn't hear what. Lingering a moment for a last look around at the darkening world, he found himself bringing up the rear. Up ahead, Nate saw a modest brick house nestled in a secluded bower of tall trees. The group stopped to admire one tree that towered above the others. Nate had never seen anything like it. It had a tall smooth trunk, high spreading branches and deeply incised furrows of buttress roots as tall as Mateo surrounding the base of the trunk like the stiff folds of a giant skirt.

"Oh, my," Nate heard Sarah say as he came up to her. "Now, that's impressive."

"Yes," Mateo answered. "A Ceiba tree. The ancient Mayans believed the trunk connected the underworld, the terrestrial realm and the skies. They called it the Sacred World Tree, or the First Tree of the World."

"I can see why," Wilma said softly. "It's beautiful."

"Even today, the Maya believe it is sacred," Mateo added. "They do not cut it down."

"The roots and trunk look like a volcanic plug, don't you think, dear," Harold said to his wife. "They remind me of Devil's Tower in Wyoming."

"Mmm," Midge said half-heartedly. "Mateo, if you don't mind. I'm very tired."

"Oh, sí, sí. Please. This way."

Squinting through the semidarkness, Nate studied the house they were approaching. It was painted gray and had a peaked roof with some kind of plaster frieze decorating the triangular gable. Beneath the gable, a horizontal beam supported by four tall, square columns formed a shallow porch that ran the length of the building. A low flight of concrete steps led up the middle of the porch to a heavy double door flanked by casement windows that seeped stalks of light from between drawn drapes. Coming closer, Nate saw that the frieze was of winged angels and that the door was the same material and design as the church door—made of heavy hardwood and hung on iron hinges. Except this one was painted blood-red.

At the base of the steps, Mateo stopped the group.

"Be careful," he said, pointing and extending a helping hand. "The steps are old and uneven. Please, be careful. I will introduce you to—"

Just then one of the double doors flew open and light spilled out, illuminating the silhouette of a man standing in the doorway.

"Mateo! Tomás! You are here!"

"Tatic!" Mateo called back heartily. He turned to the group. "Come, come, carefully now, carefully. You will meet Tatic."

One by one, the travelers slowly ascended the steps onto the porch, where a barrel-built man, little more than five feet tall, stood with hands clasped over his chest. He had an exquisitely hairless pate rimmed by a narrow band of white fuzz at the level of the temples, bushy white brows and mustache, eyes the color of strong coffee magnified through the lenses of wire-rimmed spectacles perched awry on the bridge of his ruddy nose, pink cheeks, and a smile that even Nate found warm and welcoming. He wore a short-sleeved white shirt with a small stain near the top button, khaki slacks, and a pair of severely worn *huaraches* with heavy white socks. He looked...older, but Nate couldn't tell how old—he seemed so vigorous and alive.

After all the travelers were safely ushered onto the porch, Mateo and the man embraced, the diminutive priest all but disappearing in Mateo's bear hug. Then Mateo stepped back, smiling, and Pastor Tom came into the priest's open arms.

"Everyone," Mateo said, turning to the group with a grin on his face. "This is Father Javier Carrillo. He is called Tatic. It means father, or grandfather." He turned back to the priest. "Tatic, this is...this is...everyone," Mateo said, laughing.

The old man stepped forward to greet the new arrivals. With perfect manners, he broadened his smile, shook hands with the men with a firm two-handed grip and offered the women the lighter touch of a single hand, and a half-bow.

"Hello. Hello," he repeated. "*Bienvenidos. Bienvenidos.* Welcome. Welcome. God bless you for coming to our little village. God bless you."

The old cleric waved them into the rectory.

"Come. Come in," he said. "You are tired. You have come a long way. You must eat and drink. We will talk, and then you will rest. Mateo, come. We must make our guests comfortable."

Tatic led the way inside. Tired, hungry, the travelers followed like children.

Nate and Mateo hung back. Mateo turned to Nate. "My friend . . . do you think they will stay?"

Nate had assumed Mateo knew about the vote the group had taken at dinner the night before. Apparently not, or not yet. Nate looked down, thinking about all that he knew now, that he hadn't known then. If he had, he and Sarah might not be here now. Then he glanced up and saw Sarah standing with Tatic inside the doorway, talking, smiling, touching his arm. Nate sighed.

"Yeah. . . yeah. . . I expect they'll stay."

"And you?" Mateo said. "Will you stay?"

Nate looked Mateo coldly in the eye. "If Sarah wants to stay, we'll stay."

Mateo smiled, joggled his head.

"And, she will want to stay," Nate said. She would. He knew she would. "So. . . yeah. I guess we'll stay. Only for two weeks, though. That's all."

"*Sí.* Two weeks. Two weeks. *Gracias. Gracias.* Now come. It is time to eat and drink. . . and rest."

Mateo marshaled Nate ahead of him through the doorway as, outside, an avalanche of dark swept over the village. Once they were both inside, Mateo closed the door and threw the heavy iron locking bolt home with a loud clang that jerked heads around. Eyeing the solid lock and bolt, Nate was impressed and perturbed. He liked the idea of the security a locked door might provide. But the notion that such heavy security might be needed troubled him. And, if it was needed, he knew in reality the lock would be little more than an inconvenience to a determined intruder. There were the windows, after all. He caught himself. Scanning for danger, always scanning for danger and assessing risk. It was automatic, almost unconscious. He ordered himself to stop, to think of something else. *Let it go,* he told himself. *Let it go.*

Now that everyone was inside, Mateo introduced the travelers by name. Tatic went around the group again, clasping hands, repeating names. Then he stepped back, turned and beckoned an old woman forward.

"This is Lourdes," he said, placing a gentle hand on the bony shoulder of a stooped, brown-skinned woman with a leathery face, lively dark eyes, and a great mane of iron-gray hair. "She does us the kindness of cooking and cleaning for us." The woman nodded but said nothing. "She is also the midwife here in our village," Tatic continued. "I think I can safely say that all of the fine citizens of Mirador who were born in the last fifty years or so were brought into the world by Lourdes."

Tatic spoke to Lourdes in rapid Spanish, apparently telling her what he had just said, and she laughed heartily, flashing a wide and almost toothless smile.

"*Es verdad,*" Mateo said to Nate and Sarah, standing with them just inside the door. "See her hands? Her skin is like leather. Her fingers are stiff and gnarled from years of labor. But those hands are strong, even now. And gentle. For most of the people in Mirador, her touch was the first they knew. For some, it was also the last."

"I can't wait to get to know her," Sarah said softly.

Mateo smiled and nodded.

"She will love you. And you will love her. In addition to being a midwife, she is also a *curandera*, a healer. Like you."

"Is she the only source of medical care in Mirador now?"

"Yes," Mateo said, nodding. "We have no doctor, no nurses, no clinic."

"I wish I'd known. I could have—"

"Ah, there he is," Mateo said, smiling and jutting his chin toward a boy leaning against a wall across the room. Either he hadn't heard Sarah or had chosen to ignore her. Nate suspected the latter.

"And this is Rafael," Tatic said, walking over to the boy and placing both hands affectionately on his shoulders. He was a dark-hued wraith of a boy, who looked to Nate to be maybe twelve years old. Reaching for a pair of crutches, Nate hadn't noticed until then, the boy stood and gave a slight bow. He was missing his left leg.

"Rafael is *Tzotzil*," Tatic said. "We are teaching him Spanish and English. He came to us about a year ago from a nearby village. He lives here in the clergy house. He is a part of our family now." Tatic patted the boy's shoulders. "Isn't that right, Rafael." The boy nodded shyly.

Sarah was standing with her hand over her mouth, her eyes glistening, and Nate suddenly remembered the boy she had met in Río Bravo.

"What happened to him?" Sarah asked Mateo softly. "How did he lose his leg?"

"He is... *un huerfano*... an orphan. He lost his leg to a grenade. Someone in a passing truck hurled it into a crowd of *campesinos* waiting to board a bus to Oaxaca. His mother and father were killed."

Sarah gasped. "Oh, my God. Who would do such a thing?"

"The paramilitary," Mateo answered matter-of-factly. He shrugged. "That is what everyone suspected, anyway. It was never proven, of course."

Nate felt a chill run down his spine.

"I don't understand it," Sarah said. "I'll never understand it. Why would anyone want to hurt innocent people?"

"I am afraid they do not care," Mateo answered. "They care about power. That is all. They say they maintain law and order. That is what they call themselves—*La Ley y Orden*."

"Yes, you told us," Nate said coldly.

Mateo nodded. "*Sí, sí.* But they do not keep law and order. They make their own laws. They use brutality to punish and silence people for demanding a voice in their own affairs. They ride around drunk, terrorizing *la gente*—"

"Wait a minute, wait a minute," Nate interrupted. "Are you talking about those drunks in the pickup who almost hit us? They're paramilitary? The same people who threw the grenade? They're right here in Mirador?"

Mateo sighed, nodded once.

"But you said—"

"*Sí, sí,* I know what I said," Mateo said, frowning. He turned to Nate. "I am sorry, *Señor* Hunter. They go where they want, when they want."

"It's so unfair," Sarah said, still focused on Rafael. "A child doesn't know anything about politics. He doesn't care."

"Of course not," Mateo said. "But now he knows the pain of a lost limb, and the fear of being alone. He knows despair. He knows too much for a child his age."

Nate turned toward Mateo, crossed his arms, straightened his back.

"Look—"

"Ah, time to eat," Mateo said.

Tatic was beckoning the travelers to a long, plank table that had been set with platters of tamales, beans, and tortillas. Jugs of water.

"Please, please... everyone... sit... sit... eat. We have prepared a feast. A modest one, of course, but we hope you will enjoy it. The water has been boiled and is safe to drink, I assure you. Please, eat and drink."

Mateo crossed the puncheon floor and pulled out a chair for Sarah. He sat down on her left. Nate sat on her right, his mood dark. There was a paramilitary in this town. Drunken hoodlums armed with rifles. That changed everything. Forget their agreement to stay in Mirador for two weeks. If he could pull it off, he and Sarah would be heading north in the morning. He'd explain the situation to her later tonight, and she would understand. If she didn't, he would force the issue. He had never forced her to do anything. But he would now.

At his side, Sarah was quizzing Mateo about the one-legged boy, who had resumed his post against the wall with downcast eyes.

"He looks afraid," she said to Mateo, "even though he must know he's safe here. That poor child. With the horrors he's seen, it's no wonder."

"Yes," Mateo said. "He has hardly spoken since the day his parents died. He communicates with Tatic and Lourdes, sometimes with me, but no one else. Except Quina." Mateo nodded toward a slender, dark-haired young woman who had appeared in a doorway that seemed to lead to the kitchen. "That is Quina. Her name is Joaquina. But no one calls her that."

Nate found himself gazing at a young woman in a simple, loose dress, belted at the waist, who appeared to be in her late twenties. She was slender but well proportioned, with satin, sepia-toned skin, dark eyes, bold cheekbones and a mass of raven hair that fell with a high sheen to her shoulders.

Hearing her name spoken even softly, the woman glanced up, and for a fraction of a second, Nate's gaze met hers. Nate smiled politely, but the woman immediately looked down.

"Oh, my, she's lovely," Nate heard Sarah say. "Who is she? Tatic didn't introduce her before."

"No, she was in the kitchen," Mateo said. "She's... shy with strangers. She prefers to keep to herself."

Sweet Sarah. It didn't surprise Nate that she was so quick to ac-knowledge another woman's loveliness. His beautiful wife didn't have a jealous bone in her body. Truth be told, Nate had to admit that he agreed with his wife's assessment. Quina was lovely in every respect. But it was her eyes that Nate found most captivating in the brief mo-ment he had gazed into them. Large and round, deep umber in color, they told of a woman possessed of wisdom and experience beyond her years. A woman who knew sorrow and determination.

When all were seated and platters began passing, Tatic went from guest to guest again, practicing names, smiling, laughing, nodding.

"Welcome, welcome, all of you," he said when he finally took a seat at the head of the table to Nate's right. "Thank you all again for coming. You cannot know how much your presence here means to the people of Mirador." The Americans would be working side by side with the villagers for the next two weeks, helping to do much-needed repairs on the church, Tatic explained. "And that is a blessing. We need the help." But of far greater importance, he said, was their mere presence here—the friends they would make and the bonds they would form, the bridges of understanding they would build during their stay. That was the true purpose of their visit—making friends, building bridges between people and cultures.

"No one wants to feel forgotten," Tatic said, looking around the table. "No one. Your presence here tells the people of Mirador that they are not forgotten, that the world sees them and cares about them, even though they have nothing. You bring with you that gift, and it is a gift the people here desperately need. You are God's own messengers. You are bearers of good news. More than that, you *are* the good news. God bless you for that. Bless you."

Mateo turned toward Sarah and Nate and discreetly lifted a forefin-ger in the direction of the old priest.

"He is impressive, no? He has boundless energy, despite his years."

"How old is he?" Sarah said.

"Who can say? He says Methuselah was a boyhood friend. Actually, not so old as that, I think. But close, perhaps."

"He hasn't stopped smiling since we arrived," Sarah said. "He's hardly taken a breath. Does he ever slow down?"

"No... no. Never. And as you see, there is no plate in front of him. He doesn't eat much, either. He is what you might call a force of nature... or a force of God. Despite all his hard experience, all the suffering he has seen, he never loses his hope, never becomes bitter or angry. His faith never falters, not even for a fraction of a second. Always, he sees brighter days ahead and believes that one day the injustices of the world will be redressed, wrongs will be righted, the people will escape their miseries. He truly believes that, one day, good will win out." Mateo shook his head. "I envy him."

"You're not that kind of man, I take it," Nate said, somewhat severely.

"No, I am not."

The Americans settled in to eating. Though simple, the food was surprisingly good, obviously homegrown and homemade. Around him, Nate heard sighs of satisfaction. Lourdes and Quina stood together against a wall, ready to refill platters.

Sarah smiled at them. "Thank you, Lourdes, Quina," she said, nodding to each woman in turn. "*Gracias.*" She turned to Mateo. "Mateo, how do I say, 'The food is delicious'?"

"*La comida está deliciosa.*"

"*La comida está deliciosa,*" Sarah repeated haltingly. Lourdes laughed in delight, eyes twinkling. Quina returned Sarah's nod.

"After dinner," Tatic said, "Mateo will show you to your quarters and we will bring your luggage. Compliments of Colonel Delgado, the *comandante* of the garrison, you will be staying in the old barracks which is very near here. In the corners on both floors are the rooms of *los sargentos*... very nice. Enough for all of you."

"Yes," Mateo said quietly. "All compliments of the good colonel."

He cast a hard glance at Nate.

"Colonel Delgado regards himself as a very generous and kindhearted man. He likes to think that, one day, his kindness will be rewarded."

Mateo nodded slowly.

"I also believe that one day he will get what he deserves."

Nate let the remark pass.

"So, if we're staying in the barracks, where is the army staying?" Nate said.

"There is a new barracks about one mile west of the village."

"Oh, well, that's different. That makes me feel better. The garrison is actually one mile away."

"Nate," Sarah said softly. Nate ignored her.

"Why, Mateo?" he said, giving the man a hard look. "Why is the army here at all?"

"I told you before," Mateo said irritably. "Because the border with Guatemala is near. The Mexican government wants soldiers in uniform to be the first thing visitors from the south see when they arrive in Chiapas. It is the same everywhere, I am afraid. The southern border of the United States, for example. *Es verdad, no?* There is always someone in uniform. Governments like their borders. And they like men in uniforms."

Nate narrowed his eyes at Mateo and started counting on the fingers of one hand.

"So, there's the army. And we know about the state police. *Gangsters,* I think you called them. Quite a few people in uniform, it seems. And then, of course, there's the *para*military. Can't forget them. Any other people with guns we should know about?"

Mateo scowled. "No," he answered curtly.

"Okay, back to the paramilitary. As I started to say before, you told us they weren't here. But they *are* here."

Mateo shrugged, looked down at his hands.

"It is hard to know sometimes. As you saw, they do not wear uniforms. And... they are not often in Mirador. They are usually traveling around the countryside somewhere, or off in the mountains." He shot Nate an irritated look. "And there are no state police in Mirador. No problem. No problem. They have more bark than bite, anyway."

"More bark than bite?" Midge piped up from Mateo's left. "What about that poor man at the border? Somebody did more than bark at him, wouldn't you say?"

Midge had everyone's attention now. She nodded toward the place Rafael had been standing before disappearing into the kitchen with Quina and Lourdes. "And what about that poor child? That grenade didn't just bark at him, either."

"That was the paramilitary, not the state police, dear," Harold chimed in from the end of the table to Midge's left. "And, we really don't know what happened to the man at the border. He may still be alive... that is on it."

"Oh, thank you for clarifying that, Harold," Midge said sarcastically. "That's very helpful."

"I'm just saying—"

Looking around and realizing everyone was listening, Midge softened her tone. "I know what you're saying, dear."

At the mention of the man at the border, Wilma began tearing up.

"I'm sorry," she said, dabbing at her eyes with her handkerchief. "I agree with Harold, though. The man still could be alive... couldn't he?" She looked around the table. No one answered.

Sensing that the group's decision to honor their two-week commitment was going off the rails again, Pastor Tom tried to lighten the mood by changing the subject.

"Tomorrow is Sunday," he said, smiling. "Market Day. And the first day of *Carnaval*. It's a wonderful feast day here in Mirador." He looked at Mateo. "Mateo, tell them about it."

Mateo nodded. "You will enjoy it, I am sure," he said, looking around the table. "Here in Mirador, our life is a blend of the old ways and the new, ancient Mayan traditions and modern Christian beliefs. You will see that in the music and the dancing. Even on a regular Sunday, Market Day in the main square is very lively, many people and children coming into town from the countryside, many stalls, much food. But the first day of *Carnaval* is very special. You will find it fascinating."

Mateo glanced around the room again. *Checking to see if he's winning us over,* Nate thought. When Mateo turned to him, he remained impassive, saw Mateo look down and frown slightly.

"Tomorrow, we can also visit *la iglesia,*" Mateo continued. "You can see it in the daylight and from the inside. You will see how much work there is to do, and how much your help is needed."

"I will celebrate the Mass very early," Tatic said, smiling at his guests. "You are all welcome to attend... "

The travelers shifted uncomfortably and murmured softly among themselves.

"But please do not feel obligated," Tatic continued. "You are tired from your travels, and may want to sleep."

From around the table came sighs of relief.

"And some of you may not be churchgoers," Tatic said, smiling even more warmly. "That is fine, too. You are here. That is what matters. If you do choose to come to services, though, our parishioners will make you feel welcome, you can be sure of that. And then you can enjoy *Carnaval*."

Tatic motioned for Mateo to continue.

"And then later," Mateo said, "perhaps you would like to visit a Mayan temple."

Sarah sat up straight. "Really, Mateo?" she said eagerly, touching his arm. "Could we do that?"

Nate fumed in silence beside her.

"*Sí, sí, Señora* Hunter," Mateo said. "There is a site not very far from here. It is very impressive."

"Really," Harold said, intrigued. "And you've been there, Mateo?"

"Oh, yes, many times. I would be happy to take you."

Sarah turned to Nate. "Nate, wouldn't that be wonderful?"

Nate looked around the table, saw Harold murmur something to Midge, saw Wilma and the kids confer.

Mateo glanced at Nate, shrugged.

"Of course, if you want to go home, I will take you. No problem. No problem. But perhaps you will want to stay for one day at least. Tomorrow is Sunday, the day of rest. You can sleep, see the village, enjoy *Carnaval*. And then if you still want to go home...." Mateo shrugged again, turned up his hands.

The travelers consulted. "That sounds reasonable." "I think it's a good idea. I could use a day of not traveling." "We've come all this way. We could at least see the sights a little before—"

Bam! Bam! Bam! Everyone startled at the sound of fists pounding on the heavy wooden doors followed by a woman's half-muted cries.

Bam! Bam! Bam! "Tatic! Tatic! Lourdes! *Abra la puerta! Abra la puerta!*"

The travelers sat frozen, wide-eyed. Nate saw Tatic and Mateo exchange a look as they rose and moved briskly to the door.

Bam! Bam! Bam! "Tatic! Lourdes!"

The old priest reached for the latch. Mateo put a hand on his arm and said something in Spanish. Tatic listened, nodded, peered up at Mateo over his wire-rimmed glasses, smiled and patted his friend's hand. Then he turned, threw back the bolt, and opened the door.

In stumbled a thin woman half-carrying a young girl who was leaning heavily against her—*mother and daughter*, Nate surmised. The woman had cowled one end of a long, dark shawl she was wearing over the girl's head and around her shoulders as if to shelter her. The girl, who appeared to be in her early teens, seemed only semi-aware of her surroundings. She stood hunched over, barefoot, in a worn, knee-length dress, trembling and moaning, hugging herself with one arm, clinging to her mother with the other. The shawl slipped off her shoulders as Tatic closed the door behind them, and Nate saw that the girl's belly was slightly swollen. He felt Sarah grip his arm.

"Nate, I think she's pregnant," Sarah whispered. "And look at her. She's just a child. She can't be more than fourteen or fifteen."

Sarah pushed her chair away from the table to go to the girl. Nate gripped her arm to hold her back just as Lourdes came into the room, wiping her hands on her skirt.

"*Quién me llama? Qué pasa?*"

"*Lourdes, Lourdes, por favor,*" the woman pleaded, clutching her daughter more tightly as the girl moaned in pain.

"*Itzel está enferma. Está...* " She paused, suddenly realizing there were other people in the room. "*Está... embarazada,*" she said, looking down. She looked up again, tears welling in her eyes. "*Ella tiene un aborto espontáneo.*"

Sarah took in a breath. "Nate, I think she may be about to miscarry."

The girl named Itzel gave a sharp little cry and bent over, clutching herself harder. Lourdes went to her at the same moment that Sarah bolted from her chair.

Nate reached for her.

"Sarah—"

But she was already across the room, helping Lourdes slowly walk the girl and her mother toward a back room as Tatic followed, speaking softly to Lourdes, giving her some kind of instructions.

Mateo returned to the table, shaking his head. Following him with his eyes, Nate noticed that the door was ajar. He was about to say something about it when a violent *Bang!* sounded, drawing cries and shouts from the travelers. Frozen in his seat, Nate saw Sarah and Lourdes turn and tuck Itzel and her mother more tightly between them just as the door flew open with the force of being kicked by a heavy boot or blasted with a battering ram. No one moved. No one breathed.

CHAPTER 9

First Night

A lean, bronze-skinned man dressed in a starched white shirt and neatly pressed black trousers strode in. With quick, determined steps, the heels of his polished black boots clomping against the floor, he moved to the center of the room and stopped, posture erect, feet apart, knuckles on hips, a slender cigar cupped in the palm of his right hand.

Nate saw Lourdes look down and cross herself. The man turned his head, and Nate saw the scar—a jagged white scar slithered like a snake from the bridge of his nose across his right cheekbone to the lobe of his right ear. The others at the table saw it, too. *El Pitón*, Nate thought. *It has to be.*

Nate tensed in place. He felt Mateo stiffen beside him. Silence descended, broken only by Itzel's soft whimpers.

Easy, Nate told himself, the thoughts coming automatically. *Careful, now. Stay calm. No stupid moves.* He studied the man standing before him. He had struck a military stance, but there was nothing really military about him except his bearing, his air of cool arrogance. And, the fact that he was armed. He carried a pistol wedged in the front waistband of his trousers. The ivory grip peeked over the shiny black leather of his belt.

The man clearly took pride in his appearance. Carefully slicked-back hair, the color of darkness, neatly trimmed and parted on the left, tapering to dagger-point sideburns. A narrow face, high cheekbones, sharp features, proud chin, dusky eyes set close together, beneath pencil-thin brows that looked shaven or plucked. Lean and sinewy, the man had an epicene quality about him. He struck Nate as vain, a strutter and a poser.

A second man—beefier, shorter, dressed in scruffy jeans and a sleeveless black t-shirt—now appeared in the doorway, holding an assault rifle across his chest. Nate jolted upright. He heard gasps behind him, felt Mateo laying a calming hand on his arm. Walking somewhat hunched over and bandy-legged with a rolling, almost simian gait, the second man positioned himself one step behind and a little to the right of El Pitón. He was younger, round-faced, shaven-headed, with massive muscles and nervy eyes that skittered around the room from face to face to face and then fixed on his master. Sweating profusely, he stood coiled, ready. *His henchman,* Nate thought. The man adjusted his grip on the rifle, flexing his massive arm and chest muscles and flashing the tattoo on his bulging right upper arm—a snake slithering up from his elbow, forked tongue flicking at his sharp-cornered shoulder.

Having held stockstill at El Pitón's entrance, Tatic now came back to himself. He whispered something to Lourdes, and, with a gentle touch turned her and Sarah around to continue walking Itzel and her mother into the next room. He then moved toward the intruders.

"*Señores,*" he said. "*Por favor—*"

"*No!*" El Pitón thundered, cutting the priest off and striding past him in a few quick steps to stand in front of the women. He blocked their way.

"*No, ella no va con ustedes,*" he commanded, seizing the girl's wrist. "*Va conmigo.*"

"*No!*" the girl cried, wresting free and collapsing against her mother. "*No. Por favor, no.*" The women held her tightly, pulling her back and away. Nate and Mateo started out of their seats. El Pitón snapped his fingers and his henchman took a step toward them. They sat back down.

Nate felt powerless. *What should I do? What should I do?*

El Pitón stepped forward and reached for the girl again. But Sarah was faster. Acting on instinct, she moved in front of Itzel, pushed El Pitón's hand away and shielded the girl with her own body.

"No! Stop it!" she said angrily, putting a hand in his face like a traffic cop. "Stop it!"

El Pitón momentarily startled. Then his face reddened.

Horrified at his wife's impetuousness, Nate jumped to his feet again to go to her. The henchman took another step.

"No Nate!" Sarah said, stopping him with the same traffic cop gesture.

He froze in a standing position, heart pounding. Mateo rose slowly from his seat and stood next to him. "Easy," he said under his breath.

Sarah turned back to El Pitón.

"Please, *por favor*, this girl is sick," she said, speaking more calmly but still forcefully. "*Está... está...* " Lourdes whispered the word to her. "*Enferma.*" Sarah repeated. "*Está enferma,*" she said to El Pitón. "She is sick. You can see that." She moved slightly aside, still shielding the girl but allowing El Pitón a glimpse. "Look at her," she said, passion rising again. "She is pregnant and she is about to lose her baby. She needs help. *Necesita ayuda.* I'm a nurse. I can help. Now, please. Move out of the way."

Nate felt sick. *No, Sarah. No.* Beside him, he heard Mateo suck air between his teeth.

Tatic tried to intervene.

"*Señor, por favor,*" he said, taking a step toward the women.

El Pitón halted the old priest with the same gesture Sarah had used on him and stood unmoving, glaring at her, his face reddening to the hairline, lips curling to a sneer. Nate watched him raise his cigar to his lips with long, almost elegant fingers, take a puff and slowly exhale a thin stream of smoke into Sarah's face. She closed her eyes and coughed once, but didn't move. He took a step back and slid the tip of his tone along his lips—*Like an adder's tongue,* Nate thought—as he looked Sarah up and down, studying her. Nate heard a soft rustle and saw Quina and the boy standing half in shadows in a doorway, watching.

El Pitón took a step toward Sarah, pointed a finger in her face. "*Ella es mía!*" he said angrily. "*Es mía! Entiendes? Sin mí, es nada. Se hace puta. Sin mí, está muerta.*"

He pointed his cigar at the girl's mother. "*Quién se encarga de ustedes?*" he said accusingly. And then in heavily accented English, "Who protects you? Who feeds you? *Cuando ustedes privan de comida, quién traiga comida? Quién?*"

The mother turned her head away, avoiding his eyes.

"*Yo. Yo cuido de ustedes,*" he said, tapping his fist against his chest. "*Yo traigo comida. Ustedes saben. Las dos. Es verdad.*"

Itzel cried out again, doubling over.

"Enough," Sarah said, stepping immediately to her side. "She's a child. She's sick. She needs help, and we're taking her."

She pulled Itzel closer to help support her and nodded to Lourdes and the girl's terrified mother.

"*Vamos*," she said. "Come."

Keeping herself between El Pitón and the other women, Sarah led them slowly past him and out of the room. El Pitón sneered at Sarah as they passed, his eyes hard. But he let them go. Nate couldn't believe it. El Pitón let them pass.

After they were gone, El Pitón turned his attention to the Americans sitting at the table, erect and precarious as bowling pins. Resuming his quasi-military stance and demeanor, he contemplated every face in the room. "You," he said, pointing to Mateo. "You will translate." Then he addressed the norteamericanos.

"*Este no es su país. Ustedes son extranjeros aquí, y este lugar es muy peligroso. No me desafíe. No tengo pacencia. Pero tengo una memoria larga. Y no perdono a nadie.*"

El Pitón rambled on a bit more in what sounded to Nate like a mixture of Spanish and an indigenous tongue. Then he waved a finger at Mateo to translate. Mateo stared at the floor a moment, as if weighing how much to repeat.

"The man says the world is cruel," he said finally, his face and voice expressionless. "He did not make it that way. But that is the way it is. To survive and keep order, he must sometimes be cruel. 'When I see a fly,' he says, 'I do not kill it with a fly swatter. I kill it with a sledgehammer.' The man who is weak dies. He is not a weak man."

El Pitón nodded curtly. "I am a reasonable man," he said. "But I warn you. *Cuidado.* We must have law and order. That is my job. It is my... responsibility. *La Ley y Orden. Entienden?*"

El Pitón ran his tongue over his lips again and traced a thumb over the ropy keloid on his cheek as he gave each of the norteamericanos a long, withering stare. Then he snickered and shook his head in disgust.

"*Chingaderas!*" he said. "*Qué chingaderas!*"

Then, he spat... right on the floor. He turned to Tatic.

"You are a foolish old man, priest. One day you will go too far."

El Pitón regarded Mateo again, the faintest ghost of a smile on his face. He drew on his cigar and exhaled a long, thin stiletto of smoke in his direction.

"And you..." he said almost softly. "You are nothing. A weak old woman."

Mateo didn't respond in any way. He simply remained standing next to Nate, silent and still, returning El Pitón's gaze, until El Pitón looked away.

Last, El Pitón turned to Nate, and gave him a scorching stare, but said nothing. He turned and walked over to his henchman, turned back and flashed a tight-lipped grin.

"Buenas noches, damas y caballeros. Y buena suerte."

He clicked his heels, bent slightly at the waist and crooked a finger. "Chuy."

He turned toward the door, and his henchman followed him out.

Silence returned—deafening silence. Stunned amazement and disbelief sifted down like fine dust. No one moved. The travelers hardly dared breathe. What if he came back?

Finally, Tatic crossed the room and closed and latched the door. He turned to the others. "If you will excuse me, please," he said quietly. "I will go check on Itzel and *Señora* Hunter."

At the mention of his wife's name, rage and fear overwhelmed Nate and he turned on Mateo, grabbing him by the arm and shoving his face in Mateo's face.

"What the hell have you gotten us into?" he said, seething. "You're a liar. You said El Pitón was nowhere around here."

Slowly, without breaking eye contact, Mateo peeled Nate's fingers off his sleeve with one hand and pushed him back with the other.

"Do not do that again, *Señor* Hunter," Mateo said slowly, releasing Nate's hand. "And do not ever call me a liar."

"You said this guy El Pitón was not in Mirador."

"I said I did not think he was. I am very sorry, *Señor*. Very sorry. But he is gone now. He will not be back."

Nate was stunned. "Really," he said, sarcastically. "And you actually expect us to believe that?" He shook his head. "How can we believe anything you say?"

Around the table, the other travelers began emerging from their collective state of shock. "Uhh... yes," Harold said. "I don't know, Mateo. Perhaps we should forget about visiting the ruins. I think Midge and I would prefer to leave first thing tomorrow, after all. This paramilitary business is very troubling. Very upsetting... that is on it."

"I think I agree," Wilma said, her voice quivering. "It's frightening." She looked from Nate to Mateo with tear-filled eyes. "*Tengo mucho miedo.*"

"Me, too," Stephanie said softly.

"Yeah," said Jeffrey. "Me, too."

"No. No. *Es verdad. Es verdad,*" Mateo said, patting the air, trying to calm everyone. "He is gone. No problem. No problem."

Nate snorted in disgust and started to go after Tatic, then turned back, hands clenched into fists, knuckles pressed into his hips.

"And who was that other idiot? That juvenile delinquent with the rifle, what was his name?"

"Chuy."

"That's right, Chuy. Who's he?"

"No one," Mateo said. "He is from another village. Do not worry. He is no one of importance."

Nate shook his head in disgust. "No one of importance," he repeated. "Right. No one of importance, just a guy with an assault rifle."

Mateo began to reply, then stopped, and Nate saw his expression brighten. Turning, he found Sarah approaching them, drying her hands with a clean rag, looking tired and lost in thought. She gave Mateo a distracted smile as she let Nate wrap her in his arms.

"How's my girl?" he said, holding her close and kissing the top of her head.

"She's resting," Sarah said. "Lourdes and Quina are with her."

"No, I meant you," Nate said. "How are you?"

"Oh, I'm fine. A little tired, but I'll be okay." Sarah gave him a squeeze and patted his chest. "Listen, I'm going to be here for a while. Why don't you get some rest?"

Nate frowned. "What are you talking about?"

Sarah stepped out of his embrace and wiped a stray lock of hair from her forehead with her arm.

"Everyone's exhausted," she said, nodding toward the travelers still sitting around the table. "Look at them."

Midge and Harold had pulled their chairs closer together so Midge could rest her head on her husband's shoulder. The kids had their heads down on the table, resting on their crossed arms. Pastor Tom and Wilma were sitting with hands clasped, talking softly, looking down.

Sarah fixed Nate with a no-nonsense look. "You're exhausted, too, sweetie. I can tell."

Nate didn't argue.

"So why don't you let Mateo take you all over to the barracks where you can get some sleep. It's been a long day."

Mateo nodded. "*Sí*. It has been a long day."

Nate stared at Mateo in disbelief, then turned to his wife.

"Leave you here?" Nate said. "No, Sarah. Not a chance. Are you crazy? No. If you're staying, I'm staying. We need to stay together."

But Sarah had made up her mind and she became impatient. "Nate, please. I'm too tired to argue, and I have to get back. I'm a nurse, remember? There's a girl in there who could lose her baby. I'm staying and you're leaving, and that's the end of it. I don't need to be worrying about you, too. Please. Go get some rest and let me do my work. I'll be okay, really. Mateo will walk me over later, won't you Mateo?"

Mateo bowed slightly. "Of course, *Señora* Hunter."

"Sarah, you can't—"

"Good, that's settled." Sarah kissed Nate on the cheek. "I love you. Now go." And she turned and walked away, allowing no time for protest.

Nate started to go after her, stopped, turned back and glared at Mateo, who looked away. He felt powerless and humiliated. He had lost all control of events. *That does it,* he thought. *That absolutely tears it. Tomorrow, we are out of here. We're leaving if we have to walk all the way home.*

Tatic reappeared and beckoned Mateo over. They conferred quietly. Then Tatic addressed his guests.

"Friends," he said. "My dear American friends." The travelers roused themselves.

"The girl," Wilma said, eyes wide with worry. "How is she?"

"Resting," Tatic said. "The pain has subsided a bit."

"Oh, that's good, that's good," Wilma said. "The pastor and I have been praying."

Stephanie gave Wilma a shy smile. "Us, too," she said.

Midge looked at Harold, who nodded. "Us, too," Midge said gruffly.

"Thank you, my friends. Thank you, all of you. And please accept my apologies. You have had a very long and difficult day, and an even more difficult evening."

The travelers murmured in exhausted agreement.

"Those men," Wilma said in a low, trembling voice, rubbing her arms as if she felt a chill.

"Yes, I know," Tatic said. "I am sorry. We were not... expecting them. But they are gone now."

"*Sí, sí,*" Mateo said, nodding. "They are gone."

"But what if they come back?" Stephanie asked in a small voice.

"They will not come back," Mateo said.

"But how can you be sure?" Midge asked.

Mateo frowned. "They will not come back."

The Americans exchanged worried glances, but said no more.

"So you see, you are safe now," Tatic said. "And now you must rest." He gestured toward Mateo. "Mateo will help you collect what you need from the bus and take you to the barracks. You will have a good night's sleep. Come now. Mateo and Tomás will show you the way."

The travelers pushed back their chairs, too tired to argue, stood and gathered in the entrance hall to go back out the way they had come in.

"Today has been a trial," Tatic said, handing flashlights to Mateo and Pastor Tom. "But with the Lord's help, we have survived the day's challenges. The trouble has passed, and we must put it behind us. You will have a quiet night, and the world will look better in the morning. *Siempre el mundo parece mejor en la mañana. No es verdad?*"

Nate, was the last out the door. He wasn't buying it. But he didn't say a word.

B eneath a waning moon, accompanied by the droning of insect choristers, Mateo and the pastor led the missioners back to the bus to fetch toiletries and a change of clothes.

"You can leave the rest," the pastor said. "Your things will be safe in the bus. We will bring everything later."

"You forget that some of us are planning to leave in the morning," Midge said coldly. Others murmured agreement.

"*Sí, sí.* No problem, no problem," Mateo said. "But sleep first. Tomorrow is Sunday. You will visit the market, have breakfast in the square. Then you can decide."

Satisfied with that offer, the travelers let Mateo and the pastor lead them down a footpath that paralleled a wide, unpaved avenue leading south from the square. Mateo lighted the way with his flashlight. The Americans followed in silence.

After they had been walking for about ten minutes, Mateo doused the light and pointed to a long, narrow, two-story wood-frame building standing on a cinderblock foundation. The crawlspace beneath was thick with weeds.

"Your accommodations," Mateo said. "Compliments of Colonel Delgado."

Nate made out two rows of double-hung windows running along the north wall—covered by screens but no curtains. Concrete steps and a steel pipe handrail led up to a small latticework wood porch at the west end of the building facing the road. A single yellow lightbulb housed in a green metal fixture hung from the porch ceiling, illuminating the door with a jaundiced glow. A cloud of gnats seethed around it. As the group got closer, Nate could see that the building was painted a pale bone color and that almost every square inch of paint was peeling.

Mateo led the travelers up the steps, then quickly opened the front door, reached in, turned off the porch light and ushered everyone inside. *"Bichos.* I mean bugs," he explained, closing the door behind them. "It is better to have the light off when you open the door." He switched on the interior lights. "It is not a four-star hotel," he said, "but it is better than the homes of most people in Mirador."

The long room was lined with two rows of rusting metal cot frames, one on either side of a center aisle. Nate saw two private quarters on either side at the far end of the room and a third to the left of the entrance. To the right was a latrine. Inside, a row of seven lidless toilets lined a wall. No toilet stalls. The toilets faced the showers. Four showerheads protruding from the far wall. No dividers, no curtains, all open to the room.

"Running water," Mateo said. "In Mirador, that is a luxury. No air conditioning, of course. Not much privacy, either, I am afraid."

"But it will be fine," the pastor assured them. "The men and women just have to take turns. You'll see."

No one spoke. Mateo continued the orientation.

"In the other corners, there are private rooms. Enough for all of you."

"Oh?" Nate said. "I count three."

"There are also rooms on the second floor," Mateo said. He smiled mock-subserviently. "Warmer, but a better view."

They peeked into the room to their left. It was small and square with windows facing north and west onto the road. It was furnished with two army cots separated by a small wooden desk with a straight-back chair in front of it and a chest of drawers against the opposite wall. The cots were dressed with thin tick mattresses, olive drab military blankets and clean white sheets. A flashlight and two bottles of water sat on the desktop. Two worn but clean towels and washcloths lay atop the bureau. A naked bulb dangled from a cord at the center of the room.

Stephanie dropped her backpack on one of the cots, plopped down and ran a hand over the sheets. "Not too bad," she said, smiling up at her fellow travelers. "Who made up the rooms, Mateo?"

"Lourdes," Mateo said. "And Quina."

"That was nice of them," Stephanie said. "We'll have to thank them."

Jeffrey dropped his pack on the second bunk. "So, I guess this'll be our room." He looked around at the rest of the group. "I mean, unless someone else wants it."

"I'm sure that's fine," the pastor said. "Midge, Harold and Wilma, why don't you take the other two downstairs rooms. The stairs can be tricky at night. Nate, if it's all right with you, I thought you and Sarah would take an upstairs room."

"What about you and Mateo?"

"You forget that I live here, Señor," Mateo said. "Mirador is my home. And when Tomás is in Mirador, my home is his home."

"Of course," Nate said numbly. "Sorry. I'm tired."

Mateo nodded. "And I am also sorry that today was so... difficult," he said to the group. "I apologize again for the rocky beginning to your visit. But, as Tatic says, the world will look brighter tomorrow. Sleep well, my friends, and do not worry about setting any alarm clocks. You are on Chiapas time now. I encourage you to take a look around the village in the morning. I think you will enjoy it. Then you can decide what you want to do. If some of you still want to leave, I will take you back to Oaxaca."

"Or maybe just to Tuxtla?" Wilma said tentatively. "That would be a shorter drive, wouldn't it? Maybe we could wait for a flight from there?"

"Yes, that is on it," Harold seconded.

"As you prefer," Mateo said. "No problem. No problem."

The pastor handed Nate his flashlight. "For the stairs," he said. "And now Mateo and I will bring your luggage and leave it inside the front door. Then, we will say goodnight."

Mateo addressed Nate. "And, please, do not worry about your wife, *Señor* Hunter. "I will see that she returns safely. You have my word."

It struck Nate that he had never heard Mateo say that before—"You have my word"—and he immediately understood that these were not words the man spoke lightly.

Nate nodded. "Thank you."

Nate didn't know how long he had been lying on his cot in the warm, dark room, staring at the ceiling, listening to night bugs buzz and thump against the window screen, when he heard the sound of the front door to the barracks open and close, followed a few moments later by the shuffle and creak of footsteps on the stairs. The dim beam of a flashlight played on the ceiling through the open door to his room.

"Thank you, Mateo," he heard Sarah whisper. "Goodnight. See you in the morning."

Nate was on his feet and in the doorway as Sarah came slowly up the last few stairs. She looked exhausted, wrung out. He took her in his arms and kissed her on the forehead, then the lips.

"Are you okay?" he said, walking her into the room and sitting her down on a cot. "I've been going nuts in here worrying about you."

"Itzel lost the baby," Sarah said softly.

Nate drew her close. "I'm sorry, sweetie."

Sarah started to cry.

"Oh, honey. That bad, huh?"

Sarah shook her head. "No. I mean yes. Every miscarriage is awful. But I've seen miscarriages before, and hers was early, which, if it has to happen...." She took a crumpled handkerchief out of her shirt pocket, wiped her eyes. "She'll be okay. She lost some blood but she's young and strong. She'll recover."

"What about the old woman?"

"Lourdes? She was amazing, Nate. So capable and knowledgeable just from all her years of experience, and with such a gentle, healing way. She really has a gift. I understand why people call her a *curandera*. I could learn a lot from her."

Sarah ran her hands over her face. "But that animal. That *animal*." She turned to Nate. "He raped her, Nate," Sarah said, voice trembling, eyes wet and blazing. "He raped her and then he beat her. Raped her and beat her. Over and over again. Maria told us."

"Who's—"

"Itzel's mother. He saw her working in the garden one day, and he just took her. And when she tried to run away, he beat her. Then he threw her out, and then he came back for her. That's how that monster gets his kicks. He rapes her, beats her, then throws her out. But he always comes back. Maria says he thinks he owns her because he sometimes gives them food, as if he could buy her for a few crumbs of bread. He tells Maria that he loves Itzel, but she needs discipline." Sarah pounded the cot with a fist. "He's a monster, Nate. And there's nothing they can do about it. When I suggested they go to the police, Lourdes and Maria and Quina just looked at one another and shook their heads. Quina said, '*La policía no hace nada.*'"

Nate nodded. "Because El Pitón helps them keep *la ley y orden.*"

"Yes. That's what Maria kept saying. '*La ley y orden, Señora. La ley y orden.*'"

Nate held Sarah close. She was shaking.

"She's only a child, Nate. Fifteen years old. And now she's already been pregnant and had a miscarriage. Who is going to want her when he's through with her? What kind of future does that poor girl have? And the worst part is that Maria says Itzel blames herself for what's happened to her. She said that when El Pitón throws Itzel out and she comes home, she hides herself. She won't even go to the market because she feels so ashamed. She doesn't want anyone to see her. She tells Maria, 'It's my fault, Mama, it's my fault. I'm sorry. I'm sorry.' Maria worries that... that... Oh, Nate, why does there have to be so much suffering in the world? Why do people have to be so cruel?"

Sarah laid her head on Nate's chest and closed her eyes. Nate gently took the band out of her pony tail, let her hair fall free.

"You need to get some sleep," he said, standing and laying her down.

"Mmmm."

"Then, we need to get out of here," Nate said, covering Sarah with the thin sheet and leaning close to kiss her.

Sarah opened her eyes and smiled. She rested the edge of a forefinger against the cleft of his chin.

"Shh. Shh. We'll talk in the morning." 🔺

CHAPTER 10

In Dreams Foretold

Day had not yet broken over Mirador when Nate rose from his cot. Standing at the screened window, arms folded, he stared into predawn darkness. Like a sentry on a wall, he watched, he listened, he chewed his lip. He mopped sweat from his eyes with a sleeve. The first light of day was just beginning to dilute the blackness of night, and the morning air was already burning.

Sleep had come easily to Sarah. Not to Nate. He had tossed and turned for hours, too tired for sleep, too uneasy. Finally, his body had surrendered, but only for a while. He had risen in darkness and taken his post at the window facing north toward the church and square, waiting for night to end.

Nate turned and studied his wife in the grainy luster of false dawn. She lay sleeping on her back, utterly still, golden hair framing her head on the thin pillow, white sheet pulled to her chin, arms folded atop it across her breast. Her face looked almost waxen in the half-light. Nate could not detect so much as the flutter of an eyelid, the slightest rise or fall of her chest. Suddenly afraid, he reached for her just as the church bells started tolling, calling the faithful to Sunday morning Mass. Sarah stirred. She shifted, gave a bit of a sigh. Nate leaned back against the window, watching her, weak with relief. She massaged her eyes with thumb and forefinger. Finally, opened them. Outside, the sky paled. A rooster heralded sunrise. Sarah stretched and wriggled, turned on her side, saw her husband at the window watching her, smiled a sleepy smile.

"Good morning," Nate said.

"Good morning. Are you the captain of the watch?"

Nate shrugged.

Sarah propped herself on an elbow. She sniffed, then wrinkled her nose.

"Did it rain?"

"A little. About an hour ago."

"I can smell it."

"Sleep well?" Nate said.

"Oh, yes. I had a wonderful dream. I dreamed I was flying."

Sarah raised herself to a sitting position, shoved her pillow to the wall and put her back against it. She drew up her knees, girding her legs with her arms, and smiled expectantly at her husband. Nate gave up his vigil at the window, sat down beside her and put his arms around her.

"Flying, huh? Where?"

It was one of their morning rituals, when time allowed—snuggling and sharing their dreams.

"I was floating above you," Sarah said dreamily. "I wasn't sure where we were, but I remember all the light was golden. I kept floating higher and higher. You kept calling to me to come back...."

Nate stroked his wife's hair. "And did you?"

She yawned. "I'm not sure. I was looking down at you, feeling such love for you. I wanted to call back to you, tell you not to worry. And then bells started ringing, and I started floating up toward the sound of the bells...." She shrugged. "And then I woke up."

Sarah smiled at her husband. "It was beautiful, Nate. So beautiful."

Nate felt a strange chill. He kissed his wife at the temple, withdrew his arms, and sat down on the cot across from her. He leaned forward, forearms on thighs, hands together, palm-to-palm. The room was now steeped in the light of early sun streaming in through the window.

"Sarah, I think we should leave. Head back to Tuxtla."

Sarah rubbed her eyes with the heels of her hands. "Oh, Nate, do we have to discuss this right now?"

"It isn't safe here, Sarah. This isn't what we signed up for, and you know it."

Sarah sighed. "Can we give it one day, Nate? Just one day?"

"I don't know, Sarah."

"Nate, I know last night was rough."

"I'd call it more than rough."

"Okay, you're right. But that man is gone now...."

"But he could come back."

Sarah nodded. "Yes, he could. But Mateo doesn't think he will. Not soon, anyway. And I don't want to leave until I know Itzel's okay."

"The old woman can take care of Itzel. You said so yourself."

"But we haven't seen Mirador yet. We haven't even really seen the church."

"I don't care about Mirador... or the church. I care about you."

Sarah sighed heavily, got off her cot and sat down next to her husband. "One day, Nate. That's all I'm asking. Today is Sunday, Market Day, and the first day of *Carnaval*. How many chances are we going to get to see that?"

"Sara—"

"Hear me out. We just got here. I'd like to have at least one day of not traveling in that awful bus, and I want to make sure Itzel is okay. Mateo said he'd take us back anytime we want to go. So, please. Let's just try to enjoy this one day. And then, tomorrow, if you still want to leave...."

Nate considered Sarah's proposal. He had expected her to put up more of a fight, was surprised and relieved that she didn't. *One day,* he thought. *I can give her that.*

He nodded. "Okay."

Sarah smiled and kissed him on the cheek.

Nate rubbed his hands together.

"Are you hungry?" he asked.

"Famished," Sarah said brightly. "And I could use a cup of coffee."

"That shouldn't be hard to find around here."

Sarah stood and picked up her toiletry kit.

"What do you say we get cleaned up and take a look around this little berg?" she said, giving him an impish grin. "See if we can find a tortilla and a cup of Joe."

"Mmm... tortillas and coffee. My favorite."

Nate hesitated.

"Shouldn't we check with the others? See what they want to do? If everyone else is set on getting out of here today—"

"They can find us and tell us," Sarah said. "It's not that a big a place."

"True," Nate said. "You can probably throw a rock from one end to the other."

Sarah took his hand, pulling him to his feet.

"Come on. *Carpe diem.* Let's take a quick shower and get out of here before the others wake up."

A short time later, while their companions still slept, Nate and Sarah descended the concrete steps of the barracks and stepped boldly into the bright morning. Wearing sandals, a white linen blouse tucked into lightweight jeans well suited to her figure, her wet hair in a ponytail, Sarah glowed. She turned her face to the rain-washed sky, smiled, took Nate by the hand and headed back north in the direction of the church, homing in on the sounds of people and activity coming from the square. Nate, clad in a blue chambray shirt, sleeves turned up to the elbows, khaki chinos and tan boat shoes with no socks, let himself be pulled along, his mood cautious. The road was wet. In places, it was a stew of horse manure and mud. Sarah charged ahead, paying the minefield of puddles and droppings little mind. Nate tried to keep pace while navigating around them.

The church bells rang again. From a distance, Nate and Sarah saw parishioners in colorful indigenous dress streaming out of the church and heading into the square, which was beginning to stir with mercantile activity. Turning west along the perimeter, they saw peddlers setting up shop, arranging neat piles of fruits, baskets of vegetables and buckets of flowers on rows upon rows of sawhorse display tables. Many of the displays were set up under tarpaulin canopies or large, multicolored umbrellas for protection from the blistering sun and inevitable rain. Craft vendors were arranging displays of handwoven fabrics and embroidered tunics, beaded jewelry and cloth dolls, wooden masks and clay pottery and figurines on low tables and blankets spread out on the ground. Traders and hucksters were hawking tools and wares, cookpots and utensils, trinkets and toys. Musicians were uncasing instruments—horns and pipes, keyboards and accordions, drums and guitars—and tuning up for the day's musicale. Nate was sorry he didn't have his camera, but after the incident at the border he and Sarah had agreed it might be better to leave it behind.

Walking hand in hand up a row of stalls toward the center of the square, Nate and Sarah were surrounded by laughter and conversation, the clatter of pots and pans, the smells of woodsmoke and cooking oil, toasted tortillas and roasted corn, pastries and sweets. Everywhere they strolled, the square had a bustling, inviting look. It shimmered with a celebratory air. Nate could see that the alacrity and energy of a feast day had roused Sarah's eager curiosity and appetite for adventure and had caused her to relax her guard. Walking close at her side, Nate remained on high alert.

Reaching the east side of the square, Nate and Sarah got a good view of the church for the first time in the full light of day. The doors were open and villagers were wandering in and out. Some were traversing the forecourt that fronted the church on their knees, carrying clutches of flowers. Others paused at the stone font near the front doors to anoint their foreheads with holy water and made the sign of the cross over themselves as they entered the church.

"Oh, look, Nate," Sarah said. "The doors are open. Let's go inside."

Sarah stopped at the font, dipped a finger in the water and touched her forehead. Nate did the same.

The church was like no church Nate and Sarah had ever seen before. The nave was simple and boxlike with a coffered ceiling surfaced with jigsaw pieces in varying shapes and sizes, painted red and green. In the main room, there were rows of simple wooden benches. The stone floor was carpeted with pine needles, and dozens of knee-high clay pots holding bouquets of flowers occupied the corners of the room, scenting the air with a mix of pine and perfume. Candles burned everywhere—in ornate sconces and racks, on shelves and long narrow tables located around the room, standing in rows lining the walls like heraldic torchbearers standing at attention. Indigenous music played at low volume from a radio or cassette player somewhere near the front of the church—a discordant blend of guitar, accordion, drum, and an almost caterwauling violin that struck Nate as shrill and singsongy and yet tinged with melancholy.

Nate and Sarah sat down on the rearmost bench on the left and gazed up at vaulted ceiling beams. The multitude of flickering candle flames bathed everyone and everything within the church in an amber glow.

"I can feel the warmth," Sarah said in a hushed tone.

Inside a low chancel gate at the front stood an altar, clothed with a white lace runner and set with an open Bible and an ornate golden cross. On the back wall above the altar hung a naïve wooden likeness of the crucified Christ, in three-quarter size, painted streaks of blood lining his face and torso, twining his arms and legs. Fading, cracked and peeling frescoes of angels adorned the side walls, interspersed with gilt-framed, painted-tin *retablos* of the Holy Virgin and decorated niches housing doll-size painted-wood carvings of saints draped in royal blue robes.

For several minutes, Nate and Sarah sat silently together, taking it all in as the parishioners went about their business, lighting candles, arranging flowers. Some knelt or sat in prayer. Some prostrated themselves at the altar. Others wandered the church, stopping and crossing themselves before each portrait of the Virgin Mary, humming along with the indigenous music as they made their rounds, neither ignoring the Americans nor staring at them, but seeming simply to accept their presence with the understanding that all are welcome in God's house.

Nate assessed the interior of the church more critically. The walls were veined with cracks, blemished by patches of fallen plaster, greened with mold and blackened by smoke. The frescoes were faded and water-stained. The paving stones were cracked and uneven, some of the rafters were badly splintered. There was clearly work to do here—work worth doing, Nate had to admit. But Mateo and Pastor Tom and the old priest would have to find someone else to do it. He would try to enjoy their one day in Mirador, and then, tomorrow, he would take Sarah home.

Nate drank in his wife's profile as she sat, smiling, eyes glistening, taking in her surroundings. She was so happy, so young, so beautiful and full of life. She lowered her head and closed her eyes, seemed to murmur a prayer. Her serenity and contentment brought him ineffable joy. Now, for the first time, in spite of himself, he was glad he had brought her to this place. *God, I love you, Sarah. There aren't words to tell you. You are beautiful. You are good. And you are mine.*

Perhaps sensing her husband's thoughts, Sarah looked up at Nate and smiled. But then, her eyes misted, as if, at the margins of her happiness, a trace of sorrow lurked.

Sarah reached for Nate's hand and held it tightly, and he had the strange sense for some inexplicable reason that she was not just holding his hand, as she so often did, but that she was holding on to him.

"Is something wrong?" he said quietly.

"No, nothing," Sarah said, smiling, eyes shining and wet. "Nothing at all."

Nate smiled back, squeezed her hand and didn't probe, happy to sit in silence until she was ready to go. After a few minutes more, they rose. Glancing back once at the image of Christ on the cross, they took their leave.

Outside, Sarah clutched Nate's arm, lifted her face to the sun, took a deep breath.

"That was amazing," she said.

"It was," he agreed. "It truly was. And so are you. Did you know that?"

"You've mentioned it," she said, giving him a playful smile.

"Are you okay, Sarah? For a moment, you looked sad in there."

She shook her head. "No, I'm fine. Never better."

Nate held her close, kissed her on the temple. She leaned into his kiss. And then, arm in arm, they headed across the road and back into the plaza, now teeming with vendors, shoppers, and strollers. It was charged with energy, a collage of color.

"These people may not have much," Nate said, "but nobody's robbed them of their sense of style. That's for sure."

"I know," Sarah agreed. "What a fashion show."

Like performers in a pageant, shoppers and vendors of all ages, male and female alike, were dressed in shirts and blouses, dresses and shawls, vests, scarves, and aprons in a dazzling array of hues and tints, from bold primary colors to soft pastels. Everywhere Nate and Sarah looked, their eyes were caught by splashes of blue and red, daubs of pink, patches of green, streaks of yellow. Unshod, bronze-skinned women had decked themselves out in colorful blouses and long, black woolen skirts sashed at the waist with a wide band of red cloth. Others wore rectangular shaped blouses of unbleached muslin, yoked with red brocades and embroidered bibs in intricate geometric and floral designs. Women wore their long raven hair in braids that fell almost to the waist, plaited with pink ribbons and tied together at the ends to form a loop. Some wore loose turbans of lemon-colored fabric, the tail dangling to their shoulders like a havelock. Mothers swathed themselves and their babies in deep-purple shawls or tied their shawls into slings to carry their young ones on their backs. Other women turned their shawls into a kind of headdress worn folded into a flat square atop the head.

The men were equally turned out in their finest sleeveless, knee-length woolen tunics—some white, some black—worn over long-sleeved white shirts with pointed collars peeking out at the tunic's V-neck. Like the women, the men cinched their tunics with bands of brightly colored fabric. Some of the men were barelegged and barefooted beneath their tunics. Some wore simple sandals. Others wore blue jeans and cowboy boots and either the local style of low-crowned, broad-brimmed straw hats or the type of high-crowned felt hats favored by cattlemen of the American West.

Nate and Sarah wandered along the aisles and rows of slant-roofed trading stalls, past displays of colorful fruits and vegetables: tables stacked with bananas, oranges, mangoes; baskets filled with onions, cauliflowers, avocados, radishes, and other oddly shaped tubers Nate could not identify. Burlap bags brimmed with coffee beans, potatoes and shucked kernels of corn in a variety of autumn colors. Others held coffee beans, potatoes, and other comestibles.

At one stall, a gray-haired avuncular-looking pitchman held glass jars containing what looked like various nostrums, herbs, and native medicinals up to the light one by one and wiped smudges away with a cloth like a barman polishing glasses. Other vendors stood or sat behind wooden crates filled with round cakes of what looked like mineral salt or soap, bundles of pinewood kindling standing on end and trussed up with jute twine, waist-high stacks of straw hats that looked like they were about to topple over, trays of crucifixes and rosaries, bunches of wildflowers for church offerings.

In the meat and poultry section of the market, Nate and Sarah passed crates of plump, white rabbits peering out of their stick-made prisons with little pink eyes, caged and free-roaming chickens. One vendor had arranged paillards of what appeared to be raw veal or chicken on a hand-carved wooden tray set atop a card table. Another had hung pigs' heads, pink and bristly, on a steel stanchion that resembled a hat rack and had draped long links of sausages between the heads. No ice, no refrigeration, no netting to protect against the flies the vendors kept waving away. Smell of raw meat and blood. Nate and Sarah kept walking. Music seemed to be coming from everywhere. Pine incense tinged the air.

In another section of the market, two men tended a trio of fatbellied earthenware jugs filled with a clear liquid. Nate leaned in to sniff and quickly pulled back, nose and eyes burning. *Posh,* he thought. *Has to be.*

One of the vendors stepped forward, smiling, lifted a gourd cup that was hanging from a lanyard looped around the wide neck of a jug, and offered it to Nate. *"Quieres probarlo?"*

"No, gracias," Nate said, smiling, waving his hands and stepping back. The vendor shrugged amiably and went back to talking to his friend.

Nate and Sarah exchanged friendly smiles with marketers, said, *"Buenos días."* Sarah especially tried to strike up conversations. But most of the merchants were *indios* who didn't speak Spanish, and Nate and Sarah could make no sense of the indigenous languages being spoken around them with their guttural sounds and complex cadences that resembled no tongue or dialect they had ever heard. People were invariably friendly. Some tried to communicate in a mix of English and Spanish and their indigenous tongue. But most of Nate's and Sarah's efforts prompted pleasant looks, but few verbal replies.

Nate finally gave up and contented himself with an exchange of nods and smiles. But Sarah was not so easily discouraged and finally encountered one kind-faced old woman sitting cross-legged on the ground behind a blanket stacked with handwoven fabrics who knew a little more Spanish and attempted to teach Sarah the words for some of the things she was seeing.

"Qué es eso?" Sarah said, pointing to the woman's intricately embroidered blouse.

"Este?" the woman said, patting her blouse. *"Este es un huipil."*

"Huipil," Sarah repeated. *"Y eso?"* she asked, pointing to one of the long, multicolored handwoven shawls displayed on the blanket.

"Este es un rebozo," the woman answered.

"Rebozo, Sarah repeated. "It's very pretty," she said, smiling at the woman. She searched her memory for the Spanish words, found them. *"Es muy bonito."*

The woman nodded, clearly proud of her work.

"Gracias," Sarah said. *"Gracias."* The woman smiled and nodded again.

Walking on, they saw a young woman wandering through the press of people carrying an aluminum tray piled high with what looked to Nate like some kind of small, toasted snack, stopping every now and then to let people buy a handful or pop a couple into their mouths. As she came closer, she extended the tray toward Nate and Sarah, who found themselves gazing down at a platter of narrow, leggy, brown-toasted bugs.

Nate recoiled involuntarily. Sarah held steady and tried to smooth over the awkward moment by practicing her Spanish.

"*Qué es eso?*" she said, smiling.

The young woman smiled back. "*Chapulines,*" she answered.

"What did she say?" Nate asked.

"I'm not sure." She addressed the young woman again. "*Qué?*" she asked.

"*Chapulines,*" the young woman repeated.

"Ah," Sarah said, nodding. "*Gracias.*"

The woman returned her smile and moved on.

"So, what were they?" Nate asked after the woman disappeared in the crowd.

"I'm not sure," Sarah said. "But I think they were fried grasshoppers."

"Oof!" Nate said. He shook his head, gave Sarah a wry smile. "I guess we're not in Dallas anymore, are we?"

Sarah laughed, took his arm. "No, sweetie, we definitely are not."

Ambling on, they encountered a cluster of middle-aged-looking women spinning wool into yarn, old women with gnarled fingers and crooked backs shelling corn by rubbing cobs together, young girls laboring on their knees over low stone platforms, grinding kernels of corn into meal with an unvarying rhythm. They passed women sitting in circles on the ground, making tortillas on large, flat, standing griddles set up over open cookfires. Sarah and Nate watched as the women took fistfuls of dough from a bowl, flattened them with wooden presses, then laid them to sizzle and brown on the heated, greased griddle. Other women made tamales, thrusting their hands into great aluminum vats, kneading moist meal, molding it, stuffing it into cornhusks. The aroma restored Nate's appetite.

And finally, the strong aroma of coffee wafting from pots set over the flames of small propane camp stoves.

"Nate, look!" Sarah exclaimed. "Coffee!" She smiled at her husband. "Your turn!"

Nate smiled at the woman sitting on the ground behind the camp stove. "*Dos, por favor,*" he said, pointing to one of the pots and then to himself and Sarah. The woman nodded and poured steaming brew into two clay mugs. She handed them to Nate, who handed them to Sarah.

"Mmmm," Sarah said, closing her eyes and inhaling. "That smells divine."

Nate pulled some Mexican bills and coins out of his pocket, arranged them in the palm of his hand, shrugged at the woman in a gesture of helplessness and held the money out to her. She reached over, pulled his hand lower to see what was in it, plucked a few coins from his palm and pushed his hand away.

Sarah handed Nate his mug. He took a careful sip.

"That'll put hair on your chest," Nate said. "Strong as granny's breath."

"Good, isn't it?"

"I'll say. How about we get ourselves a tortilla or a tamale to go with it?"

"But we have to return the mugs, don't we?"

Sarah turned to the woman who had sold them the coffee. "*Por favor*," she said. She pantomimed walking away with her coffee, lowered her chin, lifted her eyebrows in question.

"*Sí, sí*," the woman answered, gesturing them away with the backs of her hands.

"*Gracias*," Sarah said. She turned to Nate. "I guess she trusts us."

They worked their way back through the crowd to where the women were making tamales and tortillas and were trying to decide which to get when Mateo appeared at Sarah's side.

"*Buenos días*," he said, beaming. "You are up early. You slept well, I hope."

"Yes," Sarah said, returning Mateo's smile.

"No," Nate said, ignoring it. Seeing Mateo brought back the events of the night before, which Nate had been managing to not think about for a while.

Mateo frowned. "I am sorry to hear that, *Señor* Hunter." He waved an arm to indicate their surroundings. "But today is a beautiful day, and Tatic is right, no? The world always looks better in the morning."

He turned to Sarah. "I have been to the rectory, and Tatic asked me to tell you that Itzel is doing well."

"Oh, thank you, Mateo," Sarah said, laying a hand on Mateo's arm. "I should go to her."

"No, that is not necessary," Mateo said. "Maria is taking her home. Lourdes is going with them. She will be back soon." He patted Sarah's hand. "Do not worry, *Señora* Hunter. Lourdes would not let them go if Itzel was not well enough."

"Yes, I'm sure that's true," Sarah said thoughtfully. "She is a very special person, isn't she, Mateo?"

Mateo nodded. "Yes, she is."

"But, is Itzel safe there?" Sarah asked, looking suddenly worried. "That monster knows where they live. What if he comes back? Maria said he always comes back."

"Sarah, come on," Nate said. "Try not to think about that right now."

"But Nate—"

"*Señor* Hunter is right," Mateo said. "She is going home to rest. That is all that matters now. Tomorrow will bring what tomorrow will bring. But for now, let us try to enjoy this beautiful day."

"Mateo's right, Sarah," Nate said. "Remember what we talked about."

Sarah started to protest, but thought better of it. She sighed. "You're right. Okay."

"*Bueno*," Mateo said, smiling at both of them. "So, tell me, what do you think of our little village?"

"We haven't seen much of it yet," Sarah answered. "Just the church and—"

Mateo's eyes lit up. "Ah, you have been inside *la iglesia*. And how did you like it?"

"Oh, I love it. It's very charming."

"And very much in need of repair, as I am sure you saw. What do you think, *Señor* Hunter?"

Nate nodded, but said nothing. He didn't want to give Mateo an opening to try to persuade them to stay longer than one day.

Mateo studied him, then changed the subject. "And how have you been enjoying the market?"

"Oh, it's fascinating, Mateo," Sarah said. "There's so much to see. I just wish we spoke better Spanish. And that other language everyone seems to speak, what is that?"

"*Tzotzil*," Mateo said. "Many of the people here are *Tzotzil*."

"Do you speak it?"

"A little. If you have lived in Mirador as long as I have, you would learn it, too."

Sarah laughed. "Oh, I doubt it. Language isn't exactly my strong suit. I try but...."

"You know more Spanish than I do," Nate said, automatically defending his wife even from her own self-criticism.

Sarah laughed again, turned to Mateo. "You should see us, Mateo. It's all we can do to buy a cup of coffee."

Mateo smiled, gave a little bow. "Please, then. Allow me to be your guide."

They returned their empty mugs to the coffee vendor and, with Mateo leading the way, continued touring the market, eventually meandering out into the northeast corner of the square, where a two-person *marimba* band was playing catchy, happy, fast-paced music in the kiosk—one person on a wooden xylophone, the other on drums, as people clapped and called, swinging their hips and tapping their toes.

"It's like a big party," Sarah said, eyes shining.

"*Cómo no,*" Mateo said, smiling. "It is *Carnaval.*"

Next thing Nate knew, a colorfully dressed troupe of male minstrels filed past, playing more cacophonous indigenous music on a strange mix of instruments. An old man with a drooping mustache led the way, beating out a crude rhythm on a rustic version of a colonial military drum that Mateo called a *tambor.* Following behind, oldest to youngest, another older man used what looked like a deer antler to pound a large tortoise shell figured with Mayan glyphs; a middle-aged man played a short reed flute; a younger man of perhaps twenty piped on a small clay whistle shaped and painted like a bird; a teenager played an accordion; and a younger-looking teen played a horn.

A crowd of people followed close behind the minstrels like a wave surging northeast out of the square.

"Come," Mateo said. "It is starting." 🔺

CHAPTER 11

Blood-Red Banners

Mateo and Nate and Sarah followed the parade out of the square and east along a gravel road north of the church. Ahead of them, they saw crowds of people gathered in the street under rows of colorful banners strung from rooftop to rooftop across the road. Jewel-colored streamers and tissue paper cut-outs that resembled oversized lace doilies fluttered and snapped in the breeze.

The street was now so jammed that Sarah, Nate, and Mateo could hardly move. Nate didn't like it. He put a protective arm around Sarah and shot Mateo an angry look. Mateo nodded. "Follow me," he said. "We will go where we can see better." Letting one massive arm hover protectively behind Sarah and Nate and using the other to clear a way through the crowd, Mateo led them to the side of the road and onto the elevated porch of a boarded up cantina. From their new coign of vantage, they watched the pulsating crowd part at the center and press back to the sides of the road as a team of men tied two large, black, crimson-headed turkeys to a cable that had been lowered to the street. At their signal, other men on the rooftops hoisted the cable back into the air. The turkeys hung by their feet from the rope over the middle of the road, jerking, squawking, and flapping their wings, as the crowd pressed back farther and all heads turned to the east.

Sarah leaned out over the low porch rail and looked up the street to see what the crowd was seeing. Nate gripped her upper arm and tried to pull her back, but she resisted and strained for a better view.

"Nate, look! Look!"

Farther up the street, four young men dressed in white smocks and white headbands sat bareback astride four powerful horses, controlling their mounts with taut reins and muscled legs calipered against their sides as the excited animals danced in circles, throwing their heads, stamping their feet. "What's going on?" Nate asked Mateo.

"Watch," Mateo answered.

A man costumed in a black woolen cape and a low-crowned straw hat, festooned with multicolored ribbons cascading over the wide brim, walked to the center of the street carrying a firebrand as long as his forearm. He held it aloft, turned in a slow circle, then made his way to a skyrocket held upright by a length of steel pipe planted at the side of the road. He lit the fuse. The ignition sent the missile soaring, hissing and arcing, etching a thin white contrail across blue sky. At the peak of its ascent, the rocket exploded with a loud boom and a shower of sparks. The crowd roared, and the young riders took off at a hard gallop, charging down the graveled lane toward the flapping gobblers, jostling and battling for position near the center of the road. Passing at a full gallop beneath the birds, the riders reached up, plucking a handful of feathers on the fly. Hooves thundering, the young men flailed their horses to the west end of the street, reined them about sharply and charged the turkeys again. The spectators roared.

"That's cruel!" Sarah protested to Mateo. But Mateo had joined in the cheering and didn't hear her, or chose not to.

"Nate," Sarah said, turning to her husband. The pleading look in her eyes triggered a flash of white-hot anger Nate had to struggle to control. *What am I supposed to do, Sarah? Look around you. What the hell do you expect me to do? Why are we even here? We wouldn't even be here if it weren't for you.*

Nate pressed his lips together, breathed deeply, forced the anger back down. But Sarah had seen it. She turned away.

The riders made a third pass at the birds and the crowd roared again. Then the riders reined in their horses, and two men dressed all in black—black blousy shirts, baggy black trousers, faces blacked with wood char—strode into the center of the street accompanied by musicians and took down the partially plucked, flapping and squawking birds.

"Thank goodness," Sarah sighed just as, in almost perfect unison, each man secured a turkey under his left arm and wrung its neck, ripping off its head with his bare hands.

Sarah's hands flew to her mouth as the men tossed aside the still-flapping bodies, smoothed the feathers on the detached turkey napes, and popped the bleeding heads into their mouths, beaks out, eyes still blinking.

"Oh, my God," Sarah said softly, covering her eyes.

Nate and Mateo exchanged a look, but did nothing.

In the street, the two men in black were now hopping around to the music, gobbling and flailing their arms in some kind of strange turkey dance.

"What in the world are they doing, Mateo?" Sarah asked, watching the performance.

"The men in black are The Dead," Mateo explained. "The turkeys are sacrificed for the forgiveness of sins."

"Whose sins?" Nate said.

"All sins. Yours, mine. Sins of the past. Sins of the future."

After hopping and flailing for a while, each man grabbed a turkey carcass and, holding it by the feet, slung it over his shoulder. Side by side, the men started marching east along the street with the musicians following along. Removing the turkey heads from their mouths, the men started whooping as they walked—"Whoop! Whoop! Whoop!" A spectator raced forward holding a bottle and a lit cigarette, poured a drink into one decapitated turkey beak, and stuck the cigarette in the other. The crowd erupted in laughter. Mateo threw back his head and guffawed.

As the turkey men continued up the road, the crowds of spectators began moving with them. After the street had cleared a little, Mateo led Nate and Sarah down from the cantina porch, and the three of them fell in with the procession. With no more men biting off turkey heads in front of her, Sarah got back into the spirit of the celebration. The costumes, the music, the dancing and jostling crowds, the strangeness of it all. Watching his wife grinning and taking it all in, Nate could tell that she found it thrilling. Nate, on the other hand, felt nervous and out of control. He didn't like being in a crowd, never had. Didn't like that he and Sarah sometimes got separated and he had to move fast to regain hold of her arm. When he turned to ask Mateo where the procession was leading and discovered that Mateo was gone, Nate became truly apprehensive.

"What happened to Mateo?" he called to Sarah, shouting to make himself heard.

She looked around. "I don't know. He was just here."

Okay. We're getting out of here. Nate grabbed Sarah's hand and led her sideways out of the procession, along the street and into the open doorway of a nearby grocery shop, where an old woman with a head of shaggy white hair stood at a stove in the back of the room, stirring what smelled like a cauldron of beans. She glanced at them, but said nothing.

"Amazing," Nate said, watching the rest of the procession pass from the safety of the open doorway.

Sarah smiled broadly. "Can you believe we're here, seeing this?"

Enjoy it while you can, Nate wanted to say. *We're still getting out of here tomorrow.* But Sarah was happy and enjoying herself again, so he kept quiet.

As the procession and music moved off to the east, Nate became aware of an amplified voice shouting something he couldn't understand, staticky words scratching out from a bullhorn coming from the west end of the street, back toward the square.

Peering out the doorway toward the sound, which seemed to be getting louder, Nate saw a crowd of indígenas advancing toward them. First came a row of musicians playing guitars and accordions, then the man with the bullhorn, who kept shouting as the musicians played. Behind them came a crowd of people waving signs, chanting unintelligible slogans, shaking their fists in the air.

Those people aren't revelers, Nate thought. *They're angry.* His senses went on high alert.

Some of the marchers carried poster-size photographs of two Mexican men—one a dignified-looking gentleman with slicked down hair, wearing a dark jacket, high-collared white shirt and black tie; the other darker-skinned with a bushy mustache, wearing a wide-brimmed sombrero and *bandoleros* crisscrossing his chest.

"The one in the suit," Sarah said. "That's Benito Juarez, isn't it?"

"I think so," Nate said. "And the other one has to be Emiliano Zapata."

Sarah's breath caught. "Nate," she whispered. "You don't think...."

He moved her back a step deeper into the shop. "We'll just stay here until they pass."

As the marchers approached, Nate saw that some were waving

blood-red banners emblazoned with the words *Tierra y libertad!* in white letters. Others carried black flags with a five-pointed red star at the center. Some of the women carried enlarged photographs of men and boys of different ages, each bearing a name and inscribed with the word *DESAPARECIDO* in bold black letters.

Sarah put her hand on Nate's arm. "Disappeared, Nate. It means disappeared, I think."

The crowd of approaching protesters swelled. Nate estimated its size at more than two hundred people—men, women and children of all ages. He turned to the old woman still working at the stove. "Who are they?" he said, waving an arm toward the doorway. "What are they doing?"

The woman looked past him, and Nate turned to see Mateo in the doorway.

"What the hell happened to *you?*" Nate demanded.

"The crowd. We got separated. I am sorry."

"Is this what I think it is?"

Mateo frowned. "*Sí. Zapatistas.*"

Nate stared at Mateo, suddenly drenched in sweat.

"But you said—"

Mateo held up a hand, angry now. "I know what I said. I did not know this was going to happen. I would not have brought you here if I did."

Nate threw up his hands. "Oh, that helps a lot."

"Come," Mateo said. "We should not stay here. We should go to the rectory."

Nate and Sarah looked at each other in stunned silence.

"Come!" Mateo insisted. "We do not want to get caught in this." He peered out the door to the west, then the east. "Come quickly!" he said, motioning impatiently for them to follow.

Mateo led them swiftly east, away from the marchers, "We will go around this way," he said, motioning toward a corner not far ahead, where they could turn south off the road and head for the rectory. But, as they neared the intersection, an army truck roared through and screeched to a stop, blocking their escape and disgorging a small platoon of men in olive drab fatigues and helmets carrying M-16s at hip-level.

Mateo turned Nate and Sarah around. "We will go back," he said, then saw that they would have to pass through the approaching throng to return to the shop where they had taken shelter before. He looked around. "This way," he said, leading them to another shop doorway. But the door was locked. He tried another and another. Every door he tried was now shut and locked.

We should have stayed where we were, Nate thought angrily. *Damn it! We should have stayed where we were!*

The soldiers fell in behind their commander, an authoritarian-looking figure, who also carried a bullhorn.

"*Alto!*" the commander shouted at the approaching marchers. "*Alto! Regresen a sus casas! Regresen!*"

But the protesters ignored the command and continued to advance. The soldiers widened their stances, gripped their weapons. Mateo tried another door in a sheltered entrance. Finding it also locked, he motioned for Nate and Sarah to crouch in the doorway beside him, Nate on his left, Sarah on his right.

To their right, the soldiers began to advance toward the marchers, rifles now chest high. The protesters kept coming.

"*Alto!*" the commander ordered again through his bullhorn. "*Regresen a sus casas!*"

"*Adelante!*" the leader of the march shouted through his bullhorn.

"*Adelante!*" the protesters called, cheering, raising fists and waving signs.

From their hiding place in the doorway, Nate and Sarah heard a great tramping and shuffling of feet getting louder and closer on each side as the two armies closed in on each other. Around them, they saw other people huddling in doorways, hunkering down against building walls. Women crossed themselves, then clasped their hands at their breasts. Mothers drew their children close.

The army officer with the bullhorn again demanded that the protesters disperse. Again, they answered with shouts, arms held high, fists clenched. They continued marching. The army continued advancing.

And then, it happened. Gunfire. Pandemonium erupted and swept down the street. People were screaming. Bodies were falling. The stench of gunsmoke and terror filled the air. Sarah screamed and covered her head with her hands. Mateo flung out his arms, pinning Nate and Sarah in place and shielding their chests.

As suddenly as the shooting started, it stopped. Now, there was only crying, wailing, weeping, people running and shouting, people on their knees, people on the ground. Anyone who fell was trampled.

Mateo held Nate and Sarah down with a firm hand on a right and left shoulder until they heard the army truck roar off.

"No," he said, pressing Sarah down again when she struggled to stand. He waited a while longer, then hauled them to their feet.

"Now," he said.

Sarah made a quick move toward the nearest group of kneeling, weeping people, but Mateo was quicker and, keeping a firm grip on her arm, led them west back toward the square, away from the heart of the carnage, tugging Sarah along firmly when she tried to stop, to kneel, to help.

"But, Mateo, I have to—"

"No," Mateo said firmly.

Nate didn't argue.

Heading south at the square, they saw that the market had been abandoned in panic, tables and chairs overturned, umbrellas knocked over, displays of produce and wares toppled and scattered on the ground.

As they passed the church and turned onto the cinder path to the rectory, Sarah tripped on a paving stone and almost went to her knees. Mateo caught her by the shoulders, steadied her, and kept moving. Even in the confusion, Nate was struck again by how quick and light-footed Mateo was for a man of his bulk.

Lourdes had been watching for them. Tatic and Pastor Tom pulled open the door to the rectory as they mounted the steps. Inside, they found the other members of their mission group already assembled around the table, sitting silent and pale-faced, a replay of the night before.

Nate sat Sarah down next to Wilma, and she immediately began sobbing.

"Oh, sweetheart," Wilma crooned, taking Sarah in her arms.

Nate turned on Mateo, vibrating with rage.

"*No Zapatistas!* No problem! No problem! You son of a—"

"*Basta!*" Mateo bellowed, eyes burning.

"Please. Mateo, *Señor* Hunter," Tatic said, stepping between them. "This is not the time for anger. You are all unhurt. We must be thankful."

Mateo and Nate glared at each other but said nothing.

Pastor Tom crossed from the door and put a calming hand on Mateo's shoulder. "Tatic is right, everyone. The question now is, do we stay or do we go?"

"Stay? I should say not!" Midge erupted. "We are leaving!"

"That is on it," Harold seconded.

"No, no, you misunderstand," the minister said. "I'm sorry. No, of course, we cannot stay now." He glanced at Mateo.

"No," Mateo agreed. "There will be reprisals."

"But why would anyone want to hurt us?" Stephanie asked in a small, shaky voice. "We just came to help build a church."

"And we're American," Jeffrey added. "Doesn't that protect us?"

"Not from a bullet," Nate said angrily. "It didn't protect us from almost getting shot five minutes ago."

"*Señor* Hunter is right," Mateo said. "It is too dangerous now."

Tatic sighed. "I am so sorry, my friends. We have been a peaceful village until now."

"The question," Pastor Tom said, "is, do we wait a day, let things quiet down, or do we leave today?"

"I think we should wait," Harold said. "Hole up here, let the trouble pass, then go tomorrow... that is on it."

"Not me," said Midge imperiously. "I'm ready to get the hell out of here right now."

"You want to be out there with all those crazies?" Jeffrey said. "I don't know about that."

"I want to stay," Sarah said softly. She had collected herself and was sitting calm and erect now, head bowed, hands folded in her lap. Nate marveled again at his wife's courage and strength.

"I agree," Wilma said in a trembling voice, eyes filled with fear. "I think we should leave tomorrow."

"I don't mean that," Sarah said calmly. She looked at Nate. "I mean I want to stay."

"Sarah—"

"People have been shot, Nate. They're lying out there, bleeding and dying. I'm a nurse."

"No, Sarah," Nate said calmly. "We're leaving. We made a deal, remember?"

"Nate, please," Sarah begged, eyes filling with tears. "People are hurt."

But Nate would not be moved.

"No, Sarah. No. We're leaving. Don't make this harder than it has to be."

Sarah closed her eyes, lowered her head. "God forgive us," she said softly.

Nate turned back to Mateo and the minister. "All right. So, the question is do we leave today or tomorrow? I think what Harold says makes sense. We hole up here for the night, wait for things to calm down and leave first thing tomorrow."

"Yes, I agree," Wilma said. "Why get out in the streets now? It's safer here, isn't?"

Mateo shook his head. "No," he said, his tone final. "We cannot wait for things to calm down, as you say. Things will not calm down. There will be reprisals. It is simply a matter of when. We must go now, before they come back."

"Before who comes back?" Nate said.

Mateo looked him in the eye. "The Army. *La Guardia. La Ley y Orden.* Any of them. All of them. There has been an uprising. Things will not simply calm down."

"I'm afraid Mateo is right," Pastor Tom said. "We should go now, while we can."

"But how do we know—" Jeffrey began.

Mateo held up a hand. "No more talk. The bus is parked at the barracks. You will have a few minutes to gather your essentials—money, passports. But you must be quick. Come now. We must go."

Mateo and the pastor embraced Tatic quickly and led the Americans out the back door of the rectory. Looking back once, Nate saw Tatic make the sign of the cross over them and saw Lourdes, Quina and the boy in the doorway, watching them go.

In less than fifteen minutes, they were back in the bus, in the same seats they had pried themselves out of less than twenty-four hours before. Mateo guided the bus south along the muddy street, then west, then south, then west again, down rutted alleyways lined with squalid shacks.

Nate was confused. "Why the back alleys?"

"Too narrow for army trucks. Too confusing for *los paramilitaristas.* We will come out on the far side of town and get on the main road there. We will be okay then. No problem. No problem."

Nate clenched his fists. *If he says that one more time.* But it didn't matter now. *Just get us out of here. Just get us out.*

All was silence in the bus as Mateo wrestled the VW down the narrow, rutted alleys, jostling and bouncing the passengers, who braced as best they could. No one complained. No one said a word. Nate turned to check on Sarah. She sat staring out the window with large, sad eyes. He put a hand on her knee. She lay a hand atop his, then took it back, bracing again, keeping her face turned away. Beside and behind her, the other passengers had also withdrawn into themselves. The pastor sat with eyes downcast, lips moving silently in prayer.

The alley they were negotiating finally opened onto a gravel road, wide and empty.

"*Bueno,*" Mateo muttered.

"Where are we now?" Nate asked.

"Southwest of the village. On the loop road."

He turned right, heading north.

"We should be okay now," he said, shifting gears and picking up speed. "No problem. No problem."

Nate took slow, deep breaths. *Soon,* he thought. *Soon this will be behind us.*

And then, rounding a bend, Nate saw a barricade ahead, and his blood turned to ice. Two pickup trucks sat facing each other, blocking a muddy stretch of road. A knot of men, none of them in uniform, several armed, loitered around the trucks as if they had every right to be there and nowhere else to go. They saw the bus approaching, but made no move to clear the road. There was no way around. It was too late to turn back. Mateo clutched the steering wheel, set his face in stone and slowed the bus.

Nate heard Sarah gasp, felt her grip the back of his seat. He reached up and squeezed her hand. "It's okay. We'll be okay."

"Fuck!" Jeffrey swore from the back seat. "Fuck! Fuck! Fuck!"

"Please, everyone, let's stay calm," Pastor Tom said. "Calm and quiet. Mateo will speak for us."

Mateo stopped the bus about thirty feet from the trucks. No one moved or spoke. A young tough leaning against the back of the west-facing truck stood suddenly as two men came around from the far side with M-16s slung across their chests. The one leading the way was lean and neatly dressed with slicked-back hair and walked with a strut, puffing on a long thin cheroot. The one following was short and muscular, dressed in a t-shirt and jeans and walked with a hunched-over roll. Even from a distance, there was no mistaking who they were.

"Oh, my Lord," Midge gasped.

"Shhhhh," Harold hushed her, putting a finger to his lips and slipping his other arm around her shoulders. "Shhhhh."

Midge let herself be hushed and held still.

Through the mud-slaked windshield, Nate watched El Pitón saunter casually toward them, down the middle of the road, followed by his henchman. He stopped, cocked a hip, took a long puff on his cheroot, and exhaled slowly, keeping his right hand on his M-16. He leaned forward slightly and squinted in through the windshield. Nate couldn't tell if he recognized them or not. Then he stuck the cigar between his teeth, put both hands on his rifle, sauntered around to Nate's side of the bus, and peered inside. His black eyes slid coldly past Nate and Mateo. When they settled on Sarah, his eyes crinkled and his lips thinned to a smile. He removed the cigar from his mouth, leaned and spat. He took another step forward.

"*Afuera*," El Pitón commanded, motioning with his rifle for everyone to get out of the vehicle. "*Todos afuera.*"

Mateo sat like a stone, gripping the steering wheel and staring straight ahead. No one else moved.

"*Afuera!*" El Pitón commanded again, swinging the muzzle of his rifle upward and firing an ear-shattering burst of bullets into the air over the bus. The firing triggered terrified reactions inside the bus— flinching, screaming and crying, people ducking their heads, covering their ears. Mateo grimaced but did not move. Frozen in panic, Nate watched a skein of brass shell casings spew from El Pitón's rifle and tumble through the air as if in slow motion.

"*Afuera!*" El Pitón shouted, angry now.

Chuy stepped up beside him. "*Él dijo que se fuera!*" He lifted and pointed his rifle. "*Vámonos! Ahorita!*"

Mateo muttered something under his breath as he shut off the engine, opened his door, and slowly stepped out. He came around the front to Nate's side of the bus and stopped, meaty paws in the air.

"*Por favor. Son Americanos. Vinieron aquí para ayudar—*"

"*Cállate! Yo sé quiénes son. No me insulte! No me haga enojado!*"

Mateo nodded. "*Lo siento. No quiero ofender.*"

"He's trying to reason with him," Wilma whispered in a trembling voice.

El Pitón waved his rifle toward the bus, keeping his cold gaze fixed on Mateo.

"*Todos afuera.*"

Mateo sighed. "*Por favor, Señor.*"

"*Ahorita!*" Chuy barked.

Mateo nodded again. "*Jefe. Los Americanos* have done you no harm. They are showing you respect. You yourself said they do not belong here, that this is not their country, *recuerda usted?* So, they are leaving. They are going home."

Nate felt a small stirring of hope. Mateo's argument was nimble. It might work.

El Pitón stepped back, drew on his cigar, narrowed his eyes at Mateo, and looked him up and down. Then he stepped forward and spat at Mateo's feet.

"*Basta. Afuera. Todos afuera.*"

Mateo sighed heavily, walked over and slapped a hand twice on Nate's door. "Out," he said. He moved to the back door, pulled it open, motioned everyone out. "Come. Everyone out. Right now. He says right now."

Blank-faced, ears still ringing, the passengers clambered out. El Pitón motioned with his rifle for them to stand against the bus. Silently, they lined up in the muddy road. First Mateo, then Sarah and Nate, Midge and Harold, Stephanie and Jeffrey, Wilma and Pastor Tom. Nate put an arm around Sarah's shoulder, pulled her close.

Clamping his cigar between his teeth, El Pitón approached Nate and Sarah. "You," he said, pointing and wagging his rifle for them to step apart. Nate squeezed his trembling wife, kissed her hard on the temple, dropped his arm and took a half-step to his right.

Mateo stepped forward, tried again to reason with the gunmen.

"*Señor. Jefe. Por favor....*"

"*Cállate!*" El Pitón barked, raising a hand to silence him.

"*Pero—*"

Before Mateo could utter another word, El Pitón snarled and caught the stout Mexican full across the jaw with a ferocious backhand, drawing startled cries from the women. Mateo's head wrenched sideways, snapped back, and Nate saw a flare of anger in his eyes, deadly intent. Startled, El Pitón took a step back. That quickly, Chuy shouldered his rifle, and, just as quickly, the old Mateo returned, slump-shouldered, subservient. The men loitering by the trucks hooted and laughed, bellowed insults. Chuy snickered and lowered his rifle. It all happened so fast Nate wasn't sure if he'd seen what he thought he'd seen in Mateo's eyes. He and Sarah exchanged a look. No, he hadn't imagined it. She'd seen it, too.

Stay calm, Nate thought, reaching for and squeezing Sarah's hand. *He wants to scare us a little, that's all. Humiliate Mateo. Show off for his men. Then he'll let us go. We're Americans. He's not going to hurt us. He can't be that stupid.*

El Pitón lifted the strap of his rifle over his head and handed it to his sideman. Hands forked on the crests of his hips, he swaggered down the row of Americans and back up again, like a drill sergeant inspecting his new recruits, and Nate noticed that, in addition to the pistol El Pitón kept in the waistband of his trousers, he carried a knife with a long blade and silver-mounted handle in a tooled leather scabbard attached to his belt at his left hip. Cold steel. One of the most ancient instruments of war.

Maybe El Pitón would just let them go. Maybe he'd take their money and credit cards and then let them go. That would complicate things, but Nate could live with that. But he didn't like the way El Pitón had smiled when he had seen Sarah in the bus, and he didn't like the way he had licked his lips and flicked his tongue at her as he sauntered past. If he made a move toward Sarah, then what?

Think, Nate told himself. Chuy was holding El Pitón's M-16 now, leaving him a little more vulnerable. Nate could go for the gun tucked in El Pitón's waistband, but that would mean going at him directly. The knife, though, hung on his hip. If he moved fast, he could have it out of the scabbard and into the man's heart or back or neck before he knew what hit him. Nate would probably end up dead, too, but that didn't matter. Sarah was the only thing that mattered.

Nate tried to work out a plan as El Pitón did another slow stroll down the row of Americans, turned and started back, puffing on his cigar.

If he makes a move now, I can grab it. But where do I put it? Can you get to the heart through the sternum? The ribs? Maybe I should go for the belly? Or the throat? How do you cut a man's throat? Do you stab? Do you slice? Would he still be able to fight? How fast would he die?

El Pitón strolled back toward them, stopped in front of Nate. He stared into his eyes. Nate swallowed hard, felt the blood drain from his face, his right eye twitch. His mind went blank.

El Pitón studied him, chuckled, put the smoldering pastille back in his mouth, puffed, took it out. Gracefully he inspected the glowing tip, returned the cigar to his mouth and turned away.

But then he turned back and squared himself to Sarah. Head inclined, eyes icy, El Pitón studied the fair-haired American woman, the one Nate had sworn before God to protect. He looked her up and down, took the cigar out of his mouth.

"*Ah, sí.* I remember you," he said softly with a scornful curl of lip. He drew on his cigar, brought his face close to hers, causing her to shrink back. He sneered, exhaled a slow stream of smoke in her face. Sarah closed her eyes and coughed once but didn't' move.

"I tell you, eh?" El Pitón said softly. He took a step back. "*Les dije a todos!*" he bellowed, waving his cigar. "I say, '*No me desafie! El Pitón no olvida! Y no perdona!*'" He stepped closer to Sarah again. "But you," he said in a low voice. "You defy me."

"You're an animal," Sarah said calmly to his face.

"Oh God, Sarah. No!" Nate gasped.

El Pitón cocked his head sideways. "*Cómo?*" He leaned in close again. "*Cómo me llamaste?*"

"Sarah," Nate pleaded.

"You're a monster. You raped that girl."

"Sarah!"

El Pitón stepped back, traced a thumb along the scar on his cheek, a sinister smile forming on his face. He raised a hand and crooked a finger, indicating for Sarah to follow him, turned and began walking back toward the trucks blocking the road.

Nate seized Sarah's hand, holding her in place, scrambled for what to say. *Wait. Stop. Don't.* But he said nothing.

When El Pitón realized Sarah was not following, was defying him again, he whirled and strode back, his face red with rage. Planting himself in front of Sarah again, he pointed a rigid finger like a gun at her chest.

"You! I say come!"

He turned away again, took a few steps and stopped, his back to the Americans, hands on hips, as if waiting for Sarah to fall in behind him.

Now! Nate commanded himself. *The knife! Go for the knife!* He caught Mateo's eye, saw him frown and shake his head, as if he knew what Nate was thinking. But Nate had to act. He had to do something. This was his moment. *I could get to the knife before Chuy killed me,* he thought. *I could hurt the bastard. I could at least hurt him.* But then Nate had another thought. *But what if I don't kill him. Then what? What would he do to Sarah then?*

He stood without moving, clutching his wife's hand. His feet had taken root. His arms had turned to slabs of stone.

El Pitón raised his face to the sky, sighed, turned and approached Sarah again, his expression inscrutable. He put the back of his hand to her left cheek. She shrank from his touch and turned her face into Nate's shoulder.

Do something! Nate commanded himself. *Do something!*

"Please... sir... " he heard himself say in a neutral tone, voice trembling. "Please... leave her alone."

A plea, not a command. Measured. Careful.

El Pitón examined him with amusement.

"Please," Nate repeated, this time in a stronger voice. "Leave her alone." He took a small step forward and to the left, wedging himself between Sarah and El Pitón. "We don't want any trouble. We just want to go home." Nate took another step, pulling Sarah behind him as he did so, until the two men stood with chests almost touching, Nate standing a good head taller than the man with the pistol and the knife.

El Pitón sneered, took a step back, as if to reduce Nate's height advantage, looked him up and down again, turned his head away and spat. He glanced at Chuy and put out a hand for his rifle. Then, in one fluid motion so quick Nate had no time to defend against it, he slammed the butt against Nate's left jaw. The force of the blow spun him around and threw him against the side of the bus. When he turned around, a second slam of the rifle butt across his left ribcage sent him collapsing to the ground in an explosion of pain.

He heard shouts and screams, heard Sarah cry, "No! No!" Felt her fall to her knees next to him.

"You monster! You monster!" she shrieked.

No, Sarah, no. Lying on his right side, unable to move or speak, Nate saw El Pitón hand the rifle back to Chuy, step forward, reach down and seize Sarah by her golden ponytail and yank her to her feet. He heard Sarah shouting "Let me go! Let me go!" Saw Mateo turn into a snarling animal and rush for El Pitón. Saw Chuy leap between them and catch Mateo under the chin with the butt of El Pitón's rifle, knocking him flat. He heard screams, cries, whimpers as Chuy turned the gun on the Americans, daring anyone else to move.

"Oh, God, we're going to die," he heard Wilma whisper. "We're all going to die."

Sarah! He had to get to Sarah. He tried to get to all fours, collapsed back in blinding pain. El Pitón watched, a satisfied look on his face, still gripping Sarah by the hair. He yanked her head back, forcing her face to his, flicked his tongue, ran it over his lips.

Repulsed, enraged, Sarah fought, tried to push him away, free herself, but El Pitón was powerful. He held her hair fast, grabbed her wrist and bent her back as if to kiss her.

"No! No!" Unable to escape or turn her head, Sarah Hunter curled her lip back and spat in El Pitón's face.

"Ach!" El Pitón released her hair to wipe his face, and then flung her down hard in the mud.

Nate tried to get up again but crushing pain on the left side of his head and body staked him to the ground. He tried to call to Sarah, but he had no voice. *Stay down!* he wanted to shout when she began struggling to her feet. *Stay down!*

But she didn't stay down, and as she came to her hands and knees, El Pitón grabbed her by the hair again, pulled her into a kneeling position, reached down with his other hand, grabbed the front of her linen blouse and, in one fierce movement, ripped away the front and tore open her bra, exposing her pale perfect breasts. Sarah lost her balance and went down again on her back.

Chuy grinned. *"Chiches,"* he snickered, craning his neck to gape. The thugs loitering by the trucks hooted and called. The American men averted their eyes. The women turned away, whimpering and clutching the fronts of their blouses, covering their breasts with their forearms. But El Pitón did not want them.

Sarah rose to her knees, steadying herself with one hand in the mud, covering her chest with the other.

Sarah! Sarah!

Sarah looked up suddenly, as if she had heard Nate call her. She turned, searching for him, found him, fell into his eyes.

Sarah, I'm sorry. I'm so sorry. I'm sorry, Sarah. I love you. I love you.

Sarah sat back on her knees in the mud then and gazed at her husband with such serene tenderness that Nate could hardly bear it. And then she smiled, green eyes shining.

I love you, too, baby. Don't worry. I'm fine. Everything is okay.

It was too much. Nate closed his eyes. When he opened them, El Pitón had Sarah by the hair again and was fumbling with the front of his trousers. "No!" Mateo roared, conscious again and struggling to his feet. "No!"

Faster than Nate thought him capable of moving, Chuy was on top of Mateo, kicking him hard in the back, sending him sprawling on his stomach and pinning him down with a heavy foot between his shoulders and the muzzle of a rifle to the base of his skull.

Pushing through blinding pain, Nate struggled to rise, managed only to claw and push at the mud.

El Pitón opened his pants, pulled out an erect penis, moved in front of Sarah and waved it in her face.

"Kiss it," he ordered. "You are going to kiss it."

Sarah yanked her face away.

"Kiss it!" he hissed, yanking her head back.

"Never!"

El Pitón brought his face close to Sarah's.

"Kiss it," he hissed again. "Or I will kill you."

Sarah didn't answer, didn't move.

"Stupid American *cabrona*. You think I will not do it?"

As Nate watched, helpless, El Pitón took a tighter grip on Sarah's hair and pulled his revolver from his belt.

The women shrieked, the men shouted.

"No!" the pastor cried, falling to his knees and raising his clasped hands toward the heavens. "Please! No! *Señor Jefe!* I beg you. In the name of God and Jesus Christ his only son, I beg you, let her go."

Nate clawed and pushed with everything in him, dragged himself forward a few inches, another few inches, tried to yell, produced only a half-suffocated grunt. El Pitón looked from Nate to the preacher, smirked, looked down at Sarah.

El Pitón had lost his erection. He stuck his pistol in a back pocket, and stuffed his penis back in his pants. Then he retrieved the pistol.

"Jesus Christ," he scoffed. He spat in disgust. Then his face darkened. He thumbed back the hammer of the revolver, put the muzzle to Sarah's left temple. Sarah closed her eyes.

"You," El Pitón said softly, pulling her hair down to turn her face up to his. "You believe in *Jesucristo*?"

Sarah did not respond.

El Pitón pulled her head back farther, pressed the muzzle of the gun harder against her skin.

"*Contestame!*" he demanded, loud and angry. "*Crees in Jesucristo?*"

Sarah took a breath. She sighed as if from the depths of her soul.

"Yes. Yes, I do."

And then, El Pitón pulled the trigger. The shot rang out amidst more screams and cries, and Sarah crumbled to the ground, her life's blood pulsing from a small hole in her skull.

No! No! No! No! No! Sarah! Sarah! SARAH!

El Pitón stuck his revolver back in his waistband, adjusted his belt, smoothed his hair with both palms, and walked away. Like a well-trained dog, Chuy immediately took his foot off Mateo's back and fell in behind his master. Together, they sauntered back toward the trucks as the other Americans stood or slumped motionless against the bus or down to the ground, frozen and silent in a fog of confusion, terror, and disbelief.

The moment Chuy's foot came off his back and the cold muzzle of the rifle lifted from his neck, Mateo flipped over and sprang to his feet. Seeing Sarah, an animal cry escaped him. He rushed to her, fell to his knees, weeping, and tried to staunch the bleeding with his hands.

"*No! No! No! Madre de Dios, no, no, no!*"

Summoning strength from somewhere beyond his own power, Nate half-crawled, half-dragged himself to where his wife lay and rested the unshattered right side of his face over her heart.

Nothing.

Weakly, he pushed Mateo's hands away and clumsily, painfully, stretched out on the ground beside her, cradled his wife in his arms.

Holding her, kissing her blood-soaked face, ordering the chaos of her hair with his fingers, he wept. And wept. And wept.

It started to rain. ▲

Part Two

QUINA

CHAPTER 12

Going Home

Mateo struggled to his feet, hands and clothes stained with Sarah's blood, face smeared with mud and tears. He stood fierce vigil over Nate until the sound of El Pitón's truck driving off faded into falling rain. "We must return to the rectory," Mateo said then.

In shock and all-encompassing pain, passing in and out of consciousness, Nate was vaguely aware of being turned and lifted. Then he was lying on his back in the bus with Sarah in his arms, and the bus was moving. He heard tires crunching on gravel, soft weeping.

By the time the travelers reached the rectory, Nate had come around enough to follow behind Mateo, supported by Harold and Jeffrey, as Mateo carried Sarah up the steps and through the door. The women had gone ahead, and Tatic stood ready to anoint Sarah as Mateo cradled her in his arms, tears coursing down his face.

But we're not Catholic," Nate thought vaguely.

Then Lourdes took charge. She led Mateo to a small back room with whitewashed walls. With the sweep of an arm, she directed Mateo to lay Sarah on a cot and Harold and Jeffrey to lower Nate into a straight-back chair she pulled up beside it. She covered Sarah's body with a sheet, then waved everyone out.

The moment the others were gone, Nate fell to his knees beside the cot, his every breath and movement an explosion of pain. He pulled back the sheet.

"Sarah . . . Sarah . . . . "

He stroked his wife's hair, kissed her forehead, eyes, lips, then put his arms around her, lay his head on her breast and closed his eyes.

Let me die. Let me die. Please let me die.

After a while, Nate didn't know how long, he felt a strong, tender hand on his shoulder and let Lourdes help him back up into the chair. Standing silent against a wall, Quina came forward now and gently placed the sheet back over Sarah's head as the old curandera pulled up a stool and sat and commenced doctoring Nate's wounds.

With soap and water, Lourdes cleaned Nate's face of dirt and blood, and examined his left cheekbone and jaw with the tips of her fingers. Despite her light touch, the pain was massive.

She sat back, looked at Nate and spoke in a mix of Spanish and another language while miming a slash across her cheek, then sewing with needle and thread. Nate nodded. *Bad cut. Needs stitches. Got it.*

Lourdes daubed the laceration with a cloth soaked in an astringent that smelled like turpentine and burned like fire. Nate grimaced.

"No," Lourdes said sternly. She held up a needle and thread soaked in the same astringent and said something to Quina, who was again standing quietly in a corner.

"She says you must be still now," Quina said to Nate in surprisingly good English. "No..." She waved her fingers next to her cheek and scrunched up her face.

Nate nodded, closed his eyes, stilled his facial muscles and grasped the sides of his chair.

"*Bueno,*" Lourdes said and went to work, swiftly suturing the wound with ordinary sewing thread. Almost before the pain could register, she was done.

Next, she removed Nate's shirt and examined his chest. Every touch hurt. Every breath. Lourdes sat back and mimed breaking sticks, one by one, putting the insides of her fists together and then turning them up: *crack, crack, crack.*

Nate nodded, held up three fingers.

"*Sí,*" Lourdes said. Three broken ribs.

She spoke to Quina, who left the room and returned with a basket filled with strips of cloth torn from bed sheets and a clean button-front man's shirt folded atop them. The two women helped Nate to his feet, and Lourdes bound his upper torso. Then she and Quina helped him into the clean shirt. It was too big around and too short in the sleeves. *Tatic's shirt.*

When Lourdes had done all she could for Nate, she shifted her attention to Sarah. The old woman knelt at the side of Sarah's cot, crossed herself, put her gnarled hands together and bent her head in prayer. She reached out a hand for Quina to help her to her feet, and when she turned, Nate saw that her wrinkled face was wet with tears.

Quina left again and returned with Mateo. Lourdes beckoned him over and spoke quietly to him. He nodded and turned to Nate.

"She says you must go now and leave Sarah in her care."

"No, I'm not leaving."

"She says this work is for old women. There is no place for men here. Even Quina must leave."

Lourdes took Nate's hands in hers and spoke softly again.

"She asks that you please let her prepare her in the right way," Mateo translated. "She says she loved *Señora* Hunter very much and will take good care of her."

Nate looked into the old woman's eyes. They were clear and kind. He nodded and let Mateo and Quina escort him out of the room.

"Now, I am sorry," Mateo said to him, "but we have another difficult task."

Mateo led Nate back out to the bus, gave him a folded blanket to hold against his chest to protect against bumps and jostles, and drove slowly to the new garrison house to report the murder to Colonel Delgado.

"He will impress you," Mateo told Nate on the way. "His English is very good, and he will be very solicitous. But do not be fooled. Colonel Vicente Delgado cares only about himself. He is a pragmatist, dedicated to advancing his own career. Everything he does, he does for that reason."

Twenty minutes later, Mateo and Nate sat in two gray metal chairs across a gray metal desk from the comandante. A narrow-shouldered man with a slight frame, dressed in crisp green camouflage fatigues, hair freshly barbered, mustache and sideburns neatly trimmed, Delgado sat with back erect, hands clasped on the desk, a look of concern and commitment to duty on his face, smelling faintly of aftershave and hair tonic.

Nate sat silent, lost in a miasma of pain, grief, and self-loathing as Mateo recounted the details of the murder and named the murderers. The colonel listened, frowning, nodding, shaking his head, and sat silent for a few moments, after Mateo had finished speaking, as if considering how to respond.

"This is a great tragedy. A great tragedy, indeed," he said slowly, carefully shaping each word to polish off any heavy traces of accent. "You have my deepest sympathies, *Señor* Hunter. And the sympathies of the Mexican government." He looked down, studying his clasped hands. "Now, your safety and the safety of your friends must be our first concern," he said. He thought for a moment, looked up. "I believe you should leave Mirador as soon as possible. I think that would be best for everyone. We have entered a time of unrest here. This terrible business in the street today. I cannot be responsible for what might happen if you stay. I am sure you understand."

"But *Comandante*—" Mateo interjected.

"We have a telephone here," the colonel continued, holding up one hand to silence Mateo and gesturing with the other toward the black push-button console sitting on his desk. "You are welcome to use it to call *Los Estados Unidos* and make all necessary arrangements. Anything we can do to help, anything, will be done. But your safety must come first, as I said. You should leave Mirador as soon as possible."

Nate stared at the colonel.

"My safety?" he said, slurring his words slightly because of the stitches and the pain. He snickered, sending another bolt of pain through him. "Do you honestly think I care about my safety? My wife is dead. She was murdered."

"And we take your wife's death very seriously, I assure you. A thorough investigation will be conducted. Very thorough. We will do all that we possibly can to identify those responsible for this terrible crime and bring them to justice. Have no concern about that. Have no concern."

"You already know who did it" Mateo said. "I told you. It was El Pitón. He and his men. *La Ley y Orden.*"

The colonel frowned and shook his head, lifted himself from his chair by the armrests and repositioned himself at the front edge of the seat. He smoothed his mustache with the edge of his index finger, first one side then the other, rubbed his palms together, sighed, laced his fingers, rested his hands on the desk. He leaned forward.

"As I said," he said slowly in a perfectly modulated voice, looking directly at Mateo, "we will do an investigation. There are no local police here, as you know. No state police. The army is the only civil authority. So, it is my... our... responsibility to investigate thoroughly."

He gave Mateo a stony look, then turned a more solicitous expression on Nate.

"These are challenging times in our country, *Señor* Hunter," the colonel said. "People are on edge because of this NAFTA. You have heard of it, perhaps. The government is taking great pains to prepare. It cannot afford..." He raised a hand, fluttered his fingers, and gazed down at his desktop, searching for a word. "Distractions," he finally said. "Yes, it cannot afford distractions."

The colonel smiled, but then canceled the expression quickly. Mateo sat back in disgust. If Nate had had a gun, he would have shot the man dead right there.

"A distraction," he said levelly. "That's what you call my wife's murder. A distraction."

"No, no no," the colonel said, waving his hands. "Please do not misunderstand me, *Señor* Hunter. I was speaking of the trouble today in Mirador. The government cannot afford such distractions. But it will want to take great care with a matter such as yours. The investigation must be very deliberate."

"*Basta!*" Mateo almost spat. "You know who killed *Señora* Hunter. We told you. It was El Pitón."

"Ahh... yes... so you said. But are you certain of this?"

"We have eight witnesses."

Colonel Delgado knitted his brow, pressed his lips together and thought a moment. He swiveled his chair to the right, leaned back, folded his arms on his chest, looked up at the ceiling, then lowered his gaze and spoke as if talking to the wall.

"There are *bandidos* in this district, you know. From time to time, they commit crimes of violence. Sad but true. Perhaps it was *bandidos*, who shot the American woman."

He glanced sideways at Mateo at the same moment that Mateo leaned forward and put both hands on the colonel's desk.

"The American woman has a name," Mateo said. "Her name is Sarah Hunter. *Señora* Sarah Hunter. Perhaps you should write it down. And her killer also has a name. Would you like me to spell that for you? E... L... P... I... T... O... N."

The colonel swiveled his chair toward Mateo and fixed him with a threatening look. Nate had seen that look before. Where had it been? And then he remembered.

The colonel softened his manner. "You are no doubt certain of what you *think* you saw, *Señor*. But, forgive me if I find that difficult to believe. This *El Pitón*, as the *campesinos* call him... he is a hard man, it is true. But his job is a difficult one. Maintaining law and order in this remote region is not easy. Still, the man knows his limits. This... killing... this murder...I..."

"You intend to let him get away with it," Nate said calmly. He turned to Mateo. "We're wasting our time. This is a joke."

"*Señor* Hunter, please," the colonel said with an offended air. "I assure you, this is no joke. If, as you claim, an officer of the paramilitary has been involved in a serious crime...well...well...that is a complex matter...very complex."

"No," Mateo said, stone-faced. "It is a simple matter. El Pitón murdered *Señora* Sarah Hunter, an American citizen, on *el camino principal* in Mirador this morning. Many witnesses saw it. They will swear to it. The man must be arrested and punished."

The comandante shook his head. "I am sorry, but it is not that simple," he said, irritated. "As I said, there must be an official investigation. It would be bad enough if *bandidos* committed this crime. But if it was committed by a member of the paramilitary, as you claim. Well...that would be a horse of a different...a horse..." He struggled to come up with the metaphor, but failed. "Well, that would be a different thing," he said finally. "That would reflect poorly on my... on our ability to keep peace in our community, and it would show disrespect for my...our authority. So, we must investigate very thoroughly, go through the proper channels. I must report the incident to my superiors. They must report to their superiors, and so on...."

The colonel turned his attention back to Nate. "Such an investigation will take time, of course."

"How much time?" Mateo asked.

The colonel gave a half-shrug.

"*Quién sabe?* Perhaps a great deal of time."

"How much time?"

"Weeks, perhaps months. Who can say? And the body...forgive me, I mean *Señora* Hunter...will have to remain in Mirador until the investigation is completed."

The colonel shook his head, a concerned look on his face. He sighed. He flattened his palms on the desktop, slid them back and forth as if smoothing out wrinkles in a tablecloth.

"But, of course, we have no proper facilities here...no mortuary. We will have to move the body... *Señora* Hunter... to San Cristóbal, and we will have to do that quickly. Tomorrow at the latest, I would think. And she will have to stay there until the investigation is completed." He aimed his eyes at Nate. "An unpleasant business, I admit, but unavoidable, I am afraid."

He raised a finger and canted his head, eyes still on Nate.

"If, on the other hand, you told me that the killers were *bandidos*, and you were unable to identify them because they were wearing masks..." The colonel shrugged. "Then, there would be no need for an investigation. What would be the point?" The colonel looked squarely at Nate. "In that case, *Señora* Hunter could go home immediately, which I am sure would be a great comfort to you and your family."

Nate understood exactly what the comandante was doing. A glance at Mateo's scowling face told him Mateo understood, too. The man was trying to strong-arm them into changing their story and making any difficulties or embarrassments for him go away. And he was using his power to hold or release Sarah's body as a bargaining chip.

But what did it matter? There would be no justice for Sarah here. El Pitón would never be punished. *We're not in Dallas anymore, Sarah.* All Nate wanted now was to take Sarah home.

As if reading his thoughts, the colonel opened his desk drawer, took out a piece of paper, and laid it on the desk before him. In a lithe movement, he removed a fountain pen from his breast pocket, uncapped it, and began to write. He wrote in silence for a few minutes, picked up the paper, turned it one hundred and eighty degrees with his fingertips, and pushed it toward Nate. He set the pen beside it.

"I have taken the liberty of preparing a statement to the effect that the murderers were *bandidos. Bandidos desconocidos.*"

He coughed into his fist, looked at Nate.

"Unknown outlaws. Unknown...and unknowable. *Hombres malos de la selva.*"

Nate cocked his head slightly, studying the man with the impeccable uniform and perfect posture. The colonel sat with hands folded, calmly returning Nate's gaze.

"You have my word that your wife's murder will be investigated whether you sign this paper or not, *Señor* Hunter. Officials with powers greater than mine will want to know what happened here, I assure you. And, of course, officials in your government will be notified, as well. But if you sign this paper, we will not have to keep your wife here until we complete an official investigation. You can avoid all the red tape, as you Americans say. You and your wife will be free to go."

Mateo was right, Nate thought. The man was impressive—unctuous, heartless, and slick.

"Do not do it," Mateo said under his breath to Nate, narrowing his eyes at the comandante. "You cannot trust him."

The colonel kept his gaze fixed on Nate.

Nate stared at the paper. Even in his brain-fogged state, he understood there would be no investigation whether he signed the paper or not. But, if he signed, he could take Sarah home.

He reached for the paper and pulled it closer. Mateo put a hand on his forearm, but Nate ignored it. He took the pen in his blood-stained fingers, scrawled his signature on the line marked with an X, put the pen down and pushed the paper back toward the colonel. The colonel picked it up, examined Nate's signature, blew it dry, and deposited the now official document in his desk drawer.

Mateo slumped back in his chair and shook his head sadly.

The bargaining completed, the colonel rose. He tugged at the tail of his camouflage blouse, adjusted the pistol belt at his waist. Mateo stood, grasped Nate's arm and helped him to his feet.

The colonel cleared his throat.

"You have my deepest sympathies, *Señor* Hunter. We will keep you informed of the progress of our investigation. *Vaya con Dios.*"

The colonel extended his hand. Nate looked at it, looked the colonel in the eye, and turned to leave.

Then he turned back.

"You said you have a phone."

The comandante gave them his office, closing the door behind him and leaving it slightly ajar. Mateo sighed heavily, picked up the receiver and pressed a button. He spoke in rapid Spanish, waited, spoke again, waited, repeated the numbers Nate recited to him, waited, then handed the receiver to Nate.

Nate heard a telephone ring in a different universe, heard someone pick up.

"Helloo."

He took a slow, painful breath. "Trevor... It's Nate."

"Nate! Good to hear from you, son. Let me get Kate on the line. How's the trip going? How's my girl?"

By the time Nate and Mateo returned from the garrison house, Lourdes had finished preparing the body of Sarah Hunter for her journey home. Grave and deliberate at her task, she had cut off Sarah's clothes and bathed her in warm water boiled with laurel leaves. She had scrubbed off the dried blood crazed on Sarah's face and brushed and picked out the gouts of blood matted in her golden hair. She had dressed Sarah in a stark white burial shift and anointed her with fragrant oils. She had tied Sarah's feet together with a length of twine, to keep them from splaying, closed her mouth with a pink ribbon wrapped around her head and tied in a bow under her chin to hold the lower jaw closed, sealed her closed eyes with silver coins.

In accordance with Mayan custom, Sarah's body was then laid out with her head pointing west, feet pointing east, on a reed mat turned upside down on the floor of the small white-walled room. Lourdes had then placed Sarah's head on a deep, soft pillow that framed her face and concealed the bullet wounds at her temples and covered her up to her neck with a fine linen sheet. She had sent Quina to retrieve the ornate golden cross from the church altar and had laid it on Sarah's breast, then arranged Sarah's arms and hands atop the linen sheet so that her fingers were wrapped around the base of the cross. She had arranged votive candles flickering in glass cups in a luminous circle around Sarah. She had sprinkled wildflowers within the circle and set a cake of pine incense smoking in a ceremonial censer. Then the old *curandera* had seated herself in a wooden chair placed against a far wall, folded her hands in her lap, and bowed her head. Because the newly dead could not be left alone.

This was the vision that greeted Nate when Tatic guided him back to the small room where he had left his wife.

Sarah. Look at you. Look how beautiful you are, even in your sleep. I won't wake you. Not yet. I'll just stand here a while and watch you, like I did this morning.

Tatic quietly left the room and returned with a small bottle of holy water. The other travelers filed in silently behind him and spread out around the room. Softly, Tatic led them in the Lord's Prayer. As they stood with heads bowed, he sprinkled Sarah's body with holy water and made the sign of the cross over her. Then he crossed himself and quietly led the other mourners out of the room. Mateo hesitated, then followed. Lourdes stood slowly, walked over to Nate, placed the palm of her right hand gently over his heart and said some soft words Nate didn't understand but that felt like a prayer. Then she followed Mateo, leaving Nate alone with his wife.

Nate stood outside the moat of flickering candlelight, and studied his wife's pale face. *Time to wake up now, sweetie.*

He whispered her name. "Sarah." But she did not stir. He whispered it again. And again. "Sarah. Sarah." He sank to his knees, reached to touch her cheek, drew back and clasped his hands between his knees. He lowered his head. He wanted to pray, but he could not.

He covered his face with his hands. "Oh, God," was all he said. "Oh, God."

Nate felt a warm hand on his shoulder.

"It is time, *Señor* Hunter," Tatic said in a gentle voice.

Nate nodded numbly, and Tatic and Mateo helped him to his feet and led him out of the room.

A man of means and action, Trevor Blake had wasted no time hiring a private jet to fly him and his wife into the small regional airport outside San Cristóbal the next morning to bring Sarah, and the other members of the mission group, home. Before leaving the colonel's office, Mateo had arranged for a funeral parlor in San Cristóbal to receive Sarah's body that night, and, no doubt to insure their swift departure, the comandante had insisted on providing two Humvees to transport the Americans so Nate and Mateo could convert the bus into Sarah's hearse.

A simple pine coffin now sat outside the room where Sarah lay. Nate and Mateo walked past it into the main room, where the other travelers were assembled. Lourdes, Quina, and the boy stood against a wall, heads bowed. Four young men from the village stood at the rectory's entrance with hair neatly combed and hands clasped in front of them. Tatic spoke softly with one of the men, then beckoned to

Lourdes, who escorted them to the back room.

Tatic turned to Mateo and Nate.

"Cholo says the bus is ready. They have removed the back seats."

He turned to the other travelers. "And the colonel's vehicles are here. They are waiting at the church."

The travelers pushed their chairs back from the table and began gathering their things. No one spoke. Lourdes reappeared and nodded to Tatic, who moved to the door of the rectory and opened it wide. He stood Nate and Mateo on one side of the entrance and directed the rest of the travelers to stand on the other side.

The four young men from the village approached the entrance carrying Sarah's coffin. Tatic invited Nate and Mateo to follow behind it and the other travelers to follow behind them. Then he moved to the front of Sarah's coffin and led the procession out the door, down the steps and along the cinder path back toward the church. Two other young men from the village stood waiting at the rear of the VW bus. They opened the back hatch and helped slide the raw wood coffin inside.

Before the door closed, Tatic offered a prayer. "May the Lord bless and keep you. May the sun never smite you by day. Nor the moon by night." He turned to the travelers and prayed that their travel would be safe. Then, as they divided into two groups and headed to their respective military vehicles—Harold, Midge, and Wilma to the Humvee parked in front of the bus; Pastor Tom, Jeffrey, and Stephanie to the one behind—Lourdes stepped forward and put her wrinkled hand flat on the VW's cracked rear window glass. Nate hadn't even known she was there. She bowed her head, closed her eyes, and spoke a few words in her native tongue, her voice throaty, cadence irregular, words inscrutable. But the loving-kindness and sorrow in her heart were unmistakable. Nate turned to Tatic for a translation.

"May your heart suffer no more."

The old woman whispered again. Standing beside Nate, Mateo crossed himself and wiped his eyes. Nate turned to Tatic again.

"She said, 'May God watch over this dead one.'"

Lourdes turned to Nate now, took his hands in hers and gazed deep into his eyes. *Thank you,* Nate wanted to say. *Thank you for loving Sarah.* He couldn't form the words, but the old *curandera* seemed to understand his thoughts. She nodded, patted his hands, then turned and walked away.

Mateo directed Nate to his usual shotgun seat. Gingerly, Nate eased himself into the bus, accepted the folded blanket Mateo handed him to cushion his broken ribs, fixed his gaze straight ahead. Head drumming with pain, every breath a knife stab to his chest, he held the blanket over his chest with his left hand, clutched the door handle with his right, braced himself the best he could against the bumps, jostles, and swerves he knew lay ahead, and nodded.

"Okay. Let's go."

Nate and Mateo rode in silence as Nate replayed in an endless loop the questions and accusations Trevor Blake had hurled at him over the phone. *How the hell did this happen? How could you let this happen? You were supposed to protect her! We trusted you! That's the only reason Kate let her go! My God, she was your wife! You swore to protect her! And now you're alive and she's dead? Why didn't you do something? Why didn't you stop it?*

From time to time, Mateo broke the silence with a question or a comment. "How is your head?" "How are your ribs?" "Only a couple of hours more." Nate didn't respond.

It was well past dark when the missioners arrived in San Cristóbal. Mateo drove directly to the *funeraria* while the army vehicles took the other travelers to the Casa Na-Bolom, where Mateo had arranged for them to spend the night. At the funeral home, Nate and Mateo sat silently in the entrance lobby until the morticians had finished their work and transferred Sarah into a casket of higher quality than the simple pine box in which she had arrived. The casket was closed and placed in a small viewing room. When all was completed, Nate was led in and eased into a chair.

"Go," he said hoarsely to Mateo.

Mateo hesitated, then nodded. "I will return in the morning."

The next day, with the sun high in the sky, Nate sat again next to Mateo in the shotgun seat of the dilapidated bus, following behind a black Cadillac hearse, decades old, as it made its way slowly to the old regional airport. Both vehicles parked at the edge of the tarmac, among patches of weeds rising from cracks in the concrete, to await the arrival of the chartered plane. The other travelers had already arrived and were waiting with their belongings in the small office building. Mateo got out of the bus and leaned against the driver's door, arms folded. Nate remained in his seat.

At the expected hour, the plane appeared in the sky, gleaming white against wild blue. Nate watched it circle and land and taxi closer to the airfield's small hangar. A tanker truck drove up for refueling. After it drove off, at a signal from a man in brown coveralls, Mateo climbed back in the bus and followed the hearse closer to the plane.

The hearse stopped a short distance away. Mateo turned off the engine, got out of the bus again and came around to help Nate to his feet. Nate walked with Mateo to the driver's side of the bus facing the plane but would go no farther. Sighing, nodding, Mateo left him standing there and made his way to the jet.

The passenger door opened and the steps came down. Sarah's parents appeared in the doorway and slowly descended the steps. Mateo reached to shake hands with Trevor Blake, but Sarah's father did not respond. Dressed in black, their faces carved in grief, Trevor and Katherine Blake stood still as stone statues. Mateo lowered his head and seemed to offer words of sympathy. He gestured toward the hearse and stepped aside, out of the way.

The Blakes went to their daughter, Katherine leaning heavily on her husband. Her eyes flicked to Nate, then flicked away. Trevor ignored Nate entirely. Sarah's mother cupped her hands on the glass of the hearse's rear window and peered in. The sight of the casket broke her. Her legs gave way. Weeping bitterly, she started to crumble to the pavement. Her husband held her upright and led her back to the plane and up the steps. Nate did nothing.

The driver of the hearse got out of the car, walked around to the back and waved over four young men in brown coveralls standing a short distance away. Under his supervision, they removed the casket from the hearse and carried it to the plane and carefully maneuvered it through the rear cargo door.

Watching them, Nate imagined Sarah inside the casket, sleeping. *Careful. Gently. You'll wake her.*

After the cargo door was closed, the hearse drove off and the other travelers were led out to the plane and up the steps. The young men in coveralls carried their luggage up after them. Then, Sarah's father came down the steps again and walked over to Nate. Standing before him, no more than an arm's length away, Trevor Blake fixed Nate with a hard black gaze. His lips quivered and parted as if he might speak. But he did not speak. And Nate did not speak. He didn't try to explain, made no plea for forgiveness, no show of outrage, no angry vow of blood vengeance. He just stood there mute and unmoving in suffocating, shame-laden silence.

Trevor Blake shook his head and walked away. Nate watched him board the plane. He felt a hand on his shoulder.

"Time to go, my friend."

Nate didn't move. *Go where?*

And then he heard her voice.

Nate! Nate!

He whirled. *Sarah was calling him. Sarah!* She was standing at the edge of the tarmac, waving, smiling, her golden hair catching the sun. *Sarah! Oh, thank God!*

He moved toward her, felt a gentle but firm hand on his shoulder again.

"My friend, they are waiting."

"But… Sarah…" Nate pointed, turned back toward Sarah. But she was gone.

"She is on the plane," Mateo said gently. "They are all on the plane."

Mateo guided Nate forward with an arm around Nate's back.

"They are ready," Mateo said. "You must go now. It is time to go home."

Nate was confused. *Go home?* But home was with Sarah. And Sarah was here. He had just seen her. They had always said that if they ever got separated, they would go back to the place where they had last been together and wait for each other there.

Sarah was here. She would be waiting. How could he leave?

The Blakes remained sequestered with their daughter's casket in the plane's private aft cabin during the flight. Nate resumed his vigil in a rear-facing seat just forward of the bulkhead. The other travelers sat in the front of the plane. The flight was smooth, endless.

"Nate? Can I join you for a moment?"

Nate looked up and saw Pastor Tom standing over him. He sat down in the seat facing Nate. Nate turned his gaze toward the window.

The pastor waited a moment, then cleared his throat. "Nate, we haven't had a chance to tell you how sorry we are about Sarah. All of us. I've been asked to express our condolences. We are heartbroken.

Sarah was... She was such a beautiful human being."

Nate glanced coldly at the preacher. He was sitting hunched forward, wringing his hands. His eyes were red. Nate went back to gazing out the window. The two men sat in silence.

"Forgive the intrusion," the minister said finally. "I will leave you to your contemplations." He stood, put a hand on Nate's shoulder. "If there is anything I can do, Nate, anything at all...." Nate stared out the window. The minister patted his shoulder. "I'm sorry, Nate. We're all sorry. Please know that I'm here for you should you ever need me. That's all I wanted to say."

Nate didn't respond. The pastor returned to the front of the plane and Nate was not bothered again.

The airplane made its final approach to DFW at dusk, vermillion afterglow of day smeared low across the western sky. *Like blood,* Nate thought. Sarah's blood. His head throbbed. Face and ribs ached. He touched his cheek with his fingertips.

The other members of the mission trip exited the plane first. When the way was clear, an attendant informed Nate that Mr. and Mrs. Blake had requested that he exit next. A shiny black hearse, one of the current model year, waited on the tarmac, undertakers in black suits attending. Two limousines waited behind. The driver standing near the second one held a sign with his name on it. He walked toward it, then stopped and turned at the sound of the plane's cargo doors opening. *Sarah.* After the casket had been transferred to the hearse, Sarah's parents came down the steps of the plane, got into the first limousine and drove off.

"This way, please, Mr. Hunter." The limousine driver opened the passenger door for Nate. One of the other travelers had left his camera and knapsack on the back seat.

Nate got in the car. He was going home. Alone. ▲

CHAPTER 13

The House on Lyndon Road

B ent under the weight of darkness, Nate dragged his broken form onto the porch of the house on Lyndon Road that had been his home with Sarah. His legs were rubbery. He crossed the porch slowly, testing each step, sensing that one careless step with his full weight could cause the porch, the ground, the earth to collapse beneath him. A mere four days had passed since he last had stood at this threshold. He recalled the precise time he and Sarah had left for the airport, consulted his watch, calculated. One hundred eight hours, ten minutes. That long ago, that recently, he had stood right here on this spot with his beloved wife. That recently, they had brimmed with hope and plans. A long, full life had stretched out ahead of them.

The key slid into the lock as it always had. Nate had unlocked this door how many times? Perhaps he should attempt to tally that, too. Perhaps it would have some meaning, some purpose, might inject some order into chaos. Okay. He and Sarah had moved into this house the first Saturday in May of 1990. The day of the Kentucky Derby, The Run for the Roses. They had watched it on television. He had bought her a dozen red roses to mark the occasion. *Red. Red. Like Sarah's blood.*

So we moved in almost three years ago. Two years, nine months, one week and three days, to be exact, so let's say one thousand sixteen days. He would have entered this door at least once every day—except when he and Sarah were out of town, of course. Like when they went on that ski trip with her parents to Vail. Those days would have to be deducted. If he applied himself to the task, he could probably come up with something close to the exact number of times he had put the key in the door and walked in. Surely, there had to be some purpose in that, some benefit to be derived from such precision, some... comfort.

Nate turned the key. Feeling the bolt slide back, he nudged the door open. It swung freely on its hinges, groaning, arcing along its course until it bumped the wall, shuddered, and fell still. For a long time, Nate stood and stared into the silent emptiness within. When he finally entered the house, he felt like an archaeologist excavating an ancient, abandoned dwelling. Treading carefully, touching nothing, he noted objects of everyday life left behind by the people who had once inhabited this place. In the living room, a newspaper lay neatly folded on the coffee table. He picked it up and read the date. Thursday, February 11, the day before he and Sarah left for Chiapas. On the dining room table, a stack of bills lay in an orderly row. Sarah had sat at that table, on that chair, only five days prior, organizing those bills. *"Okay. I've paid the ones that have to be paid before we leave. These can wait until after the trip." Was that it? Was that what she said? Were those her exact words? No. No. "I'll pay them when we get back." Yes. That was it.* He had to get it right.

On the kitchen counter, a single white ceramic coffee cup stood in the dish drainer. Sarah's cup. Sarah's lips had touched the rim of this cup. Sarah's sweet, inviting mouth.

In the bedroom, the unmade bed looked as if someone had just climbed out of it. Sarah had been so worried about missing the flight, she had left it unmade. *So unlike her to do that. She's such a neat freak.* Nate used to tease her about always wanting things in perfect order before they left the house. To him, it made no sense to expend so much energy cleaning the place just to leave it. "I like to come home to a clean house," Sarah would say. But that morning she had left the bed unmade. He had noticed but said nothing, thinking he'd tease her about it when they got home. But she was not coming home. Did she know? Was the messy bed her little joke? Did she want him to laugh about it when he came home alone? *Did she know? No, of course, not. Of course, she didn't. We were running late that morning. That's all. And it was my fault. I made us late. But did she know?*

The soft pillow on Sarah's side of the bed lay bunched up and compressed where her head had rested on it. *Her head made this impression. When she was sleeping beside me. For two years, nine months, one week and three days we slept together in this bed. Four nights ago, we slept together in this bed.* Nate walked over to the bed, put a hand on the sheets, feeling for her warmth. Nothing. Of course, nothing. *I'll never touch her pillow. I'll never sleep in this bed again.* He noticed a long strand of her golden hair on the pillow. Beautiful. Fine. Not matted with blood. Sarah's blood. He heard a sound in the hall. *Sarah?* He hurried out to look. He checked the living room, the kitchen. *Sarah, is that you?* No. Of course not. No.

The life, the love that had permeated this house still lingered here. Nate had been a part of it. He and Sarah had created it. The two of them, together. Now, he felt like an intruder, a trespasser. These were not his possessions. This was not his home. He would stay until he figured out where to go. But he did not belong here. He belonged with Sarah, and Sarah wasn't here. Home, now, if he had one, was in Chiapas. On the edge of the tarmac in San Cristóbal, where Sarah had waved and called to him. Or on that bend in the loop road on the outskirts of Mirador, where she had drawn her last breath. On that patch of muddy ground, hallowed by her blood. He had to go back. He had to find her. He had to bring her home.

The Blakes asked to be allowed to handle the funeral arrangements. "Kate thinks that would be best," Trevor Blake said stiffly when he called Nate the next morning.

The funeral. That's right, there has to be a funeral.

"She's right. Yes, that would be best."

"We'd like to have the service at our church," Trevor Blake continued matter-of-factly.

"That's fine."

"And we'd like to bury Sarah in the family plot."

Nate and Sarah didn't have plots. Until two days ago, they had thought they had forever to get around to that. Until two days ago, they had seen their lives as just beginning.

"That's fine."

"We thought we'd have people here afterward, if that's acceptable."

"Of course."

"Thank you. I think that's everything. My secretary will get back to you with details. Your presence is expected, of course."

"Of course."

Two days later, the mortal remains of Sarah Hunter were returned to the earth.

After a simple memorial service at the church, the mourners drove in a doleful rain to the cemetery. For appearances' sake, Nate shared a limousine with the Blakes. He rode up front. They rode in back. No one spoke.

At the graveside, Nate sat numb in his folding chair next to Trevor Blake as the minister from the Blakes' church offered prayers, a man Nate and Sarah hardly knew and whose remarks during the church service Nate had already forgotten. Nate gazed around at the other mourners. Sarah's aunts, uncles, and cousins. Her parents' friends. Lots of those. They had filled the church. Sarah and Nate's friends, whose presence registered vaguely. His boss, Frank Murray, and Frank's wife, Colleen, who'd chaired the gala where Sarah had seen the masks. *We should never have gone. I should never have taken her. If I hadn't taken her, she'd still be alive.* Other colleagues from work. Sarah's friends and coworkers from the hospital. The other members of the mission trip. They were all there: Harold and Midge, Wilma, the kids standing with a distinguished-looking older couple Nate guessed were their parents. And Pastor Tom. Oddly, Nate realized he was sort of glad to see the pastor. For some reason, right now, Nate felt closer to him than to anyone else there. He remembered that the pastor had come to him on the plane, encouraged him to call anytime. But that wasn't it. Maybe it had been his honest admission at the bar in Tuxtla that he lacked boldness, that he was not the man Mateo was, that when the protest in Mexico City had turned violent, he had run away in fear. *Like a scared rabbit.* Of all the people here, the preacher was probably the least likely to condemn him for Sarah's death. The way Sarah's parents condemned him. The way he condemned himself.

Nate scanned the rest of the faces. He knew how it would go for most of these people. He had been through it with Jack. They would talk about how wonderful Sarah was, how beautiful and good. They would shed tears, pay their respects to the grieving parents and young husband. They would express shock and sadness over the loss of such a wonderful person. They would hug and kiss, say how sorry they were. And then they would move on, taking comfort in the fact that fate had not centered the crosshairs of misfortune on them, that Death had taken someone else. They would experience a new thrill, a new joy at simply being alive. They would feel more consciously grateful for every day. Even so, the untimely end of a good life would remind them of their own impermanence. For a while, they would feel vulnerable. They would take no unnecessary chances. They would tread lightly on the earth for fear of upsetting the delicate balance of life and drawing Death's attention to them. But, little by little, they would forget and begin taking life for granted again. The illusion of invincibility and immortality would return. They would walk through the world confident and assured, shooing away like a pesky mosquito any annoying reminders that we are all mortal, that the number of times each of us will hear our loved ones speak our name is finite, that every day, every hour, every minute could be our last. Nate could read their thoughts, tell their futures. And he resented them.

When all the prayers had been recited and the hymns sung, the *amens* repeated, mourners began to take their leave, some to gather again at the Blake residence, others to head home. Operating on automatic pilot, Nate returned the handshakes and hugs of those who approached him at graveside. He thanked people for coming, thanked them for their condolences. But he sensed coolness in their words and touch, censure in their eyes. When they turned away, whispering among themselves, he knew what they were saying. The women: "Poor Sarah. Can you imagine? Your own husband lets someone pull out a gun and shoot you to death? What kind of man does that?" The men: "I'm surprised he's able to show his face. You'd think he'd be too ashamed. Standing by while your wife is murdered? I wouldn't have let it happen, I can tell you that."

He rode back to the Blake residence with Sarah's parents to put in a short appearance at the gathering. It was the last time he would ever enter their home, he was sure. He ate nothing, drank nothing, took a chair in a corner of the great room and concentrated on not saying what he was dying to say in response to the thoughtless and insincere things people said to him.

"I can't even begin to imagine how you must feel." *No, you can't. You didn't see your husband shot down in front of you, did you?*

"It must have been terrible." *Of course, it was terrible. Do you want to hear the gory details?*

"No one blames you, dear. I'm sure there was nothing you could do." *Oh, but you do blame me. And you should. I alone am responsible for my wife's death. And there is something I could have done. If nothing else, I could have died with her.*

"I've never heard of such a thing happening on a church mission trip. Our church does them all the time, and the worst thing that has ever happened is someone getting dystentery." *Is that supposed to comfort me? Am I supposed to find solace in the fact this never happened before?*

And then these words: "You're young. You still have your life ahead of you. You'll marry again." *You don't understand. My life isn't worth living without Sarah. I don't want to marry again. I want Sarah. I want my wife.*

When he could take no more, Nate stood and headed blindly for the door.

"Nate." Pastor Tom was suddenly at his side. "You're leaving? I won't keep you." He put a hand on Nate's arm. "I just want to say again, if there's ever anything I can do...."

Nate looked at him. "Do you have a car?"

"Yes."

"Take me back to Sarah."

The pastor hesitated, thought, then nodded. "Of course."

The rain had let up but the sky was still leaden. They drove in silence. Nate gazed out the window, as he had on the plane. At the cemetery, the pastor found his way back to Sarah's gravesite.

"I'll wait here," he told Nate. "Take your time."

Nate got out of the car and walked through the wet, cold grass to his wife's grave. It was closed now. He stood, staring at the freshly turned ground, saw Sarah in her closed casket, sleeping.

Sarah. Oh, God. Sarah.

Turning away, he closed his eyes and raised his face to the troubled sky. Rain dotted, then streaked his forehead and cheeks.

"Forgive me, Sarah. Please forgive me."

Walking back to the pastor's car, Nate saw that his shoes and pant legs were covered with mud. Mud and blood. Sarah's blood.

Weeks passed. Months. March, April, May. All a blur. People telephoned—friends, coworkers, the missioners, Pastor Tom. Nate let the calls go to the answering machine and didn't return them. People sent cards, notes, fruit baskets. He didn't respond. Neighbors came to the door with casseroles. The minister rang the doorbell twice. Nate didn't come to the door. He went to work and came home. That's what Nate did. For some feeble reason he didn't try to understand, he felt compelled to make a show at his office of handling his loss and his grief well. It was his standard operating procedure—maintain control, stick to the routine, keep on top of things, stay organized.

It had always worked before. But not this time. Nate could not purge from his memory the image of Sarah lying on the ground, green eyes open and vacant, blood matting her golden hair, the leaden limpness of her body when he cradled her in his arms, the stunning lack of responsiveness, the undeniable and overpowering absence of life.

Guilt—relentless, ever-increasing—haunted him. The passage of time did nothing to assuage or diminish it. Time merely meant more opportunity to relive every millisecond of that last day in Mirador. The roadblock. The burst of machine gun fire in the air. The harsh order to exit the van. Stench of gunpowder. Smell of cigar. The knife in its scabbard. The pistol in El Pitón's waistband. The slam of the rifle butt. The smell and feel of the muddy earth. Sarah on her knees. Sarah on the ground. Trying to reach Sarah. Trying to call to Sarah. The pistol shot that shattered the world. He remembered it all. Relived it all. Over and over. Every image. Every moment. Every word.

Again and again, Nate saw Sarah, felt Sarah. She came to him. Not in dreams, for he seldom slept. He glimpsed her getting in and out of elevators in his office building, walking down a crowded sidewalk, crossing a busy street. He sensed her presence in the home they had shared. Tasted her lips in the morning before he opened his eyes, picked up the scent of her hair, held her hand, talked to her.

"Sarah, where have you been? How did this happen?"

She wouldn't answer, but he knew she was there.

"I've missed you so. Never do this again. Promise me. Please, don't ever leave me again."

And then his alarm would go off. A door would slam. A car horn would honk. Nate would open his eyes. And Sarah would be gone.

Nate felt himself slipping. His boss, Frank, had insisted he see a doctor before returning to work, and his physical injuries were mostly healed now. He still had twinges in his side and tenderness in his jaw, and he still didn't quite recognize himself in the mirror, the man who looked just like him except for the scar on his left cheek. But he was young and his body was strong and getting stronger, even as he felt his other faculties failing.

It became harder and harder for Nate to think, to concentrate, to focus. He couldn't read a newspaper anymore. He could make it through a headline, but that was all. He'd read it slowly out loud to himself, repeating it over and over until he could make sense of it. But if he tried to read the story, the words would swim.

He was off his game at work. He would sit in his office, staring at a black computer screen, sometimes simply staring at his own reflection, sometimes gazing into the past, watching his entire time in Mirador play out over and over like a black-and-white movie. Sometimes, he imagined he could rewrite the script, change the ending. He'd see himself jump to his feet after being knocked to the mud, grab El Pitón's gun, bash his head in, shoot Chuy square in the chest, toss the gun aside, lift Sarah to her feet and take her in his arms. Why hadn't he done that? He could have done that. *Why didn't I? Why?*

Nate never talked about Sarah's death. He allowed no one to talk about it to him. Speaking about it would validate the truth of it, make it unchangeable. When anyone offered a word of sympathy, Nate grunted or thanked them curtly to discourage any further conversation.

The physical healing that came with the passage of time angered him. He didn't want to feel better. He wanted to suffer. He deserved to suffer. He should have died with Sarah. He should have died instead of Sarah. Surely, if there was a God, He had not meant to take her. *Did God make a mistake? Did he take Sarah when he meant to take me? Did she somehow get in the way?*

And then Sarah began to leave him. He didn't see her as often in a crowd, heard her call to him less and less. When he woke in the morning, he didn't taste her lips, smell her hair, feel her beside him. He didn't see her face as clearly. His memory of her smile, her laugh, her quirks and mannerisms began to fade. *No, Sarah! Don't leave me.* But, little by little, she did. No matter how he begged, how he fought to keep her with him, the love of his life continued slipping farther and farther away. And Nate felt his hold on reality slipping away with her.

Nate began tumbling over the edge at work one Friday morning, trying to pour fresh-brewed coffee into his cup. Hands shaking, he half-missed the cup and sloshed the scalding liquid onto his fingers. He didn't feel a thing.

"Whoa! Watch it there, bud! You better run some cold water on that." Nate looked up to see Vic Perry, a member of his development team, standing beside him. He recognized the look Vic gave him. Disbelief. Concern. Worry. He'd been getting it a lot lately.

Vic cleared his throat. Poured himself some coffee, added sugar, stirred for a while. "Say, a few of us are going out for a couple of beers later. Me, Steven, Mike, that new guy Kurt. The usual band of outlaws. Why don't you come?"

Nate felt himself closing down. He didn't want to go for a couple of beers with anyone. Not today, not ever. He didn't want to laugh and he didn't want to hear anyone else laugh. But Vic was a guy Nate had always liked. Good-humored, easygoing, he had a natural kindness about him; and when Nate saw Vic give another worried glance at Nate's shaking hands and then shoot him a more penetrating look, Nate decided he had to do something to convince Vic he was doing okay, nothing to worry about, no problem, no problem. So he said yes.

The pub was crowded and noisy by the time they arrived, filled with laughter, shouting, plates clattering, bottles clinking, music blaring—Aerosmith, Madonna, Janet Jackson, Billy Ray Cyrus, Brooks and Dunn. The sounds of TGIF revelry. Kurt had gotten there early and grabbed a table in the back. Nate took a seat, ordered a beer, let the noise and conversation wash over him. He looked around at all the grinning faces. He felt like an alien. He had nothing to say to these people.

Then the talk among the beer-drinking young Turks at his table turned to politics, and then to NAFTA.

"Anybody know anything about it?" Vic said. "You hear more and more about it all the time."

"Supposed to be a great thing," Kurt said. "They say it'll create jobs. That's good for everybody. And free trade, right? What's wrong with that?"

"Plenty," Steven shot back. "A disaster in the making."

Vic rolled his eyes at Nate. Steven Becker was known around the office as Conan the Contrarian, the guy with the affected courtly manner who was always eager to hear someone else's opinion on a topic so he could explain why it was wrong.

"It'll cost us billions of dollars," Steven continued, "run up the deficit... all of which we do not need. It's a crock, if you ask me."

"Conan speaks," said Mike in a deep-throated, theatrical voice. "Doom and gloom, doom and gloom." Mike Haggerty was the nonconformist of the group, if it had one. He wore his dark hair on the longish side and sported a goatee, and nobody said "boo" to him about it because he was so smart. Nate was pretty sure the guy was a genius.

"I don't buy it," Mike said to Steven. "That's not what I hear. I hear it'll be good for the little guy. Bring down the price of goods, create new markets for small businesses and farms, drive competition." He grinned at Steven. "Help make the world a better place."

"Who are you hearing that from?" Steven countered. "Giant corporations, that's who. Globalization, my friends. That's the plan. Big guys gobbling up the little guys and smashing any little guys that get in their way. Yeah, NAFTA's a great deal... for them. But it ain't good for the little guy. That's for damn sure."

Nate listened impassively, sipping his beer. Talk. Empty talk. Young hotshots showing off, matching wits, trying to one-up each other. It was a game to them. An intellectual exercise. Should he tell them about the marchers? The shootings? Should he tell them about Sarah? No. He would never talk about any of it. Never.

"So you're taking up the cause of the little guy now?" Vic said to Steven. "Standing up for the guy whose working for the man every night and day. Big wheel keep on turnin'? Proud Mary keep on burnin'? That kind of thing? Well, here's a news flash for you—the big guys are our clients. They hire us to do what we do. Their money pays our bills. It bought these beers. So, let's don't get too self-righteous."

Nate sipped his beer, tried to look like he was listening. The truth was he didn't care what they thought about NAFTA, didn't care if it was good or bad for the little guy or the big guy. He didn't care about anything. Nothing mattered. Nothing was real. He wasn't really sitting at this table with these people. He didn't know where he was... Somewhere far away....

The debate droned on.

"If you ask me," Steven said, "even the name is a damn lie. Pure artifice, my friends. Free Trade? Come on. Nothing free about it."

Steven finished his beer, belched loudly.

"These sonsabitches just want to make it easier for *the man* to make money. Then *the man* gives some of it to them and lets them keep their little government jobs, wear their fancy suits, eat their fancy meals, live in their fancy houses. It's like everything else. In the end, it's about money. Money and greed."

Mike snorted.

"Yeah, well, I don't see you giving up your little slice of the man's pie. Nice tie you're wearing, by the way. How much did that set you back?"

Steven looked down at his shirt front, stroked the high sheen of his blue silk paisley neckwear, grinned at Mike.

"Like it? It's Ralph Lauren. I have it in maroon, too."

Vic shook his head.

"Don't mind him," he said to Nate. "He can't help it. He's what Spiro Agnew would call a 'nattering nabob of negativism.'"

"Well," Steven said, "it's better than being a pusillanimous pussy-footer or a hopeless, hysterical, hypochondriac of history." He laughed. "Spiro Agnew. You gotta love him. He may have been a crook, but he could sure turn a phrase."

"Him and his speechwriters," Kurt said.

They all laughed.

Encouraged by the positive response to his first contribution to the conversation, the new guy loosened up a little.

"I gotta tell you, all this NAFTA talk...." Kurt said. He whistled and zipped the flat of his hand over his head. "You know?"

The others laughed again. Emboldened, Kurt turned to Nate.

"What about you, Nate? Didn't I hear something about you being in Mexico recently? Were they talking about it down there?"

Dead silence. Winces. Pained looks.

Kurt looked around the table. "What?" He turned his hands up. "What...."

Nate felt his expression harden. He put his beer down, narrowed his eyes at Kurt.

"Let me tell you something," he said, seething. "I don't give a damn about NAFTA. It doesn't mean jackshit to me. And I don't care one little bit about Mexico. As far as I'm concerned, the whole country can go fuck itself. And so can you."

"Hey, man, take it easy," Vic jumped in. "He doesn't know. He was just trying to make conversation."

Kurt looked around the table again, more confused than before. "Doesn't know what?" he said. "What don't I know?"

"You want to talk about Mexico?" Nate said before anyone else could speak. "Let's talk about Mexico. Yeah, I've been there. Swell place. That's where my wife was murdered. You want to hear the story? You want to know how it happened? Want to hear what I did to try to stop it?"

Nate looked from face to face to face to face with burning eyes. Nobody responded. Nobody returned his gaze.

"Nothing!" he shouted, hammering the table with his fist. "That's what I did to stop it! I didn't do one damn thing!" He fell back in his chair, smirking. "Should have. Could have. But I didn't. I just laid there in the mud and let it happen." He looked around the table again. "Okay? Happy?" He smiled and flipped up his hands. "So, there you go. Now you know about Mexico. Great place." He lasered in on Kurt. "You should visit. Take your wife. I know a little village I bet she'd love."

"Hey! Look, I'm sorry—"

Nate shot to his feet, knocking his chair over backwards.

"Whoa! Hey! Nate! Come on! Sit down, man—"

Heart banging in his chest, he took a wad of bills and a handful of change from his pocket and threw them on the table. He wheeled about and began pushing his way through the crowded pub toward the front door. Vic came after him, reached him as he burst into unforgiving dark.

"Hey, Nate. Nate," Vic said, stepping in front of him with palms up to block his way. "Nate, come on. Kurt didn't mean anything, you know that. He just didn't know. It's my fault for not telling him. But we all know you never want to talk about it, so I figured you wouldn't want us talking about it either. I'm sorry, man."

Nate was still breathing rapidly, his heart still pounding. He put his hands on his hips, looked down, tried to slow his breath.

Vic put a tentative hand on his shoulder.

"Wanna come back inside? Have another beer?"

Nate shook his head. "No, I don't think so."

"Or we could go somewhere else, just you and me. Have a drink. Maybe talk."

Nate shook his head again. He looked up at his kind-hearted colleague, saw the concern on his face. "No. Thanks, Vic. I'll see you Monday."

"You okay to drive?"

"Yeah, sure."

Vic gave him an assessing once-over. "Okay." He nodded. "See you Monday, then."

Nate drove home, parked the car in the driveway. But he couldn't go inside. He got out of the car and started walking. For hours, he wandered, dazed, lost in a raging darkness blacker than night, swirling with noise and confusion, rent by spasms of boundless grief, gut-wrenching sobs, torrents of tears. He hurled curses at the heavens. Cursed his wife's killer. Cursed God. Cursed himself. He had promised to protect Sarah, die for her if necessary. He had failed her. He had broken his vow. And now, he wanted to die, too. Die the same way she died.

I'll get a gun. That's it. I'll get a gun.

If he died exactly the way Sarah had died, maybe it would be easier to find her in the afterworld. It hadn't been that long. Maybe he could catch up.

Without intending it, not knowing how he got there, Nate found himself standing later that night on Pastor Tom Butler's front porch.

If I can do anything at all, Nate.

Nate reached a hand toward the doorbell, drew it back. Reached again and pressed the small, round, lighted button. He heard the doorbell ring softly inside.

Nothing. Nate stood in the dark on the doorstep. And then the porch light came on. The door opened. Pastor Tom appeared in the doorway, tying his robe.

"Nate!" the pastor greeted him, looking surprised.

Nate said nothing.

The minister glanced away, then back at Nate. He forced a weak smile.

"I've tried to reach you, you know. Several times."

Nate nodded.

"Well... come in." The pastor stepped back into the foyer, opening the door wide. "Please... come in."

Nate's feet wouldn't move. Pastor Tom took him by the arm and led him inside, closing the door behind him, and ushered him into what looked like a library or den.

"Here. Sit here," the minister said, guiding Nate to one of a pair of armchairs flanking a cold fireplace.

Nate sat. The minister lowered himself into the other chair and pulled it closer.

"May I offer you... Would you like... "

Nate raised a hand in a peremptory gesture. He shook his head.

"No. No. Nothing. Thank you. I...."

Nate fell silent. The pastor sat and waited.

"So, how are you doing?" Pastor Tom asked finally. "What have you been doing?"

"Oh... working... just carrying on... you know."

"Have you heard anything about... the investigation?"

"No... not really. Sarah's father is working on it. He hired some investigator in Mexico to try to track El Pitón. Paid a lot of money for no results. 'Disappeared in the mountains.' Those were his results. He's trying to pressure the State Department, calls his congressman and his senator twice a day." Nate shrugged. "Nothing. No surprise there, I guess, with this NAFTA thing ramping up."

Pastor Tom nodded. "So you're still in touch with Sarah's parents."

Nate shook his head. "No, not really. I talk to the old man's secretary. She keeps me updated."

Another silence.

"Well, I should be going," Nate said, starting to rise.

"No, Nate. Stay. Please. I'm glad you came. I've been hoping to see you."

Nate sat back down.

"You're sure I can't get you anything? Water? Juice?"

Nate shook his head. Another silence fell. From another part of the house, Nate heard the soft ticking of a clock. He leaned forward, put his elbows on his knees and massaged his forehead with his fingers.

"I think I may be going crazy," he said slowly and deliberately, aware of feeling a weight lift off his shoulders as he faced the truth. "It's like the pieces are all there, but they're all mixed up. They're not put together right. Nothing makes any sense." He dropped his hands, looked at the minister with red, watery eyes. "I think I'm coming apart. I... I don't think I'm going to make it."

Pastor Tom started to argue, checked himself. "I'm listening," he said softly.

Nate stood and started to pace.

"I keep track of time," he said, his breath catching. I can tell you exactly how many days, how many hours and minutes it's been since I last saw Sarah, since I last touched her. I've figured out what we did during the last month of her life. I mean everything, minute by minute. I've written it down. I can tell you exactly what she said to me and what I said to her. I can tell you where she was standing when she said it, how she moved, what she was wearing, what she did with her hands, the look on her face."

Nate rubbed his face with his hands. He took a deep breath, blew it out. He suddenly felt exhausted, frightened.

"But then other times, it's like she's fading... disappearing. I used to see her. She'd visit me. She'd come in the morning when I was in bed, and we'd talk. I'd talk. But that doesn't happen anymore. Sometimes I close my eyes and think of her and I can't remember what she looked like. Can you believe that? I can't remember what she looked like. I have to look at her picture."

The minister sat silent, hands folded, head bowed. Nate returned to his chair, stared blankly at the fireplace.

"I don't know. I feel... I feel like I need to go back... to Mirador."

Pastor Tom looked up. "Why?"

"I'm not sure. I... I... just feel like I need to go back to that place... that place where she died. I need to stand there and look at it. It all happened so suddenly. She was alive. And then she wasn't."

He snapped his fingers.

"That quick. Gone. Everything ended. All gone. That's too fast. I can't... It's too fast. I can't make sense of it. It's like it didn't happen. It's not real to me. I have to make it real somehow, and the only way I can think to do that is to go and stand where she drew her last breath, say something, put a flower on the ground...."

Nate glanced at the minister.

"We didn't even get to say goodbye. No last kiss. Nothing."

Nate rubbed his face with his hands.

"I can't shake the feeling she's still there, some part of her... a shadow, some... residue... waiting for me."

Nate gave a half-laugh. "I know it sounds crazy. But I have to do it. I have to go. I have to—"

Raw grief seized him. He struggled to breathe, struggled for control.

"I have to say I'm sorry. I have to... apologize. I have to tell her that I know I let her down. I have to ask her forgiveness. And I have to do it there."

Nate dropped his head in his hands. "Maybe I can stop this... stop this... make amends. Do something to turn things around."

He drew his hands down over his mouth.

"Or maybe I can die there myself. I don't know. I don't know."

The minister eased forward in his chair.

"Nate, it wasn't your fault."

"Don't *tell* me that!" Nate yelled, exploding out of his chair in fury. "Do not tell me that! I'm tired of people telling me it wasn't my fault! It *was* my fault! It was! I should have protected her! I should have died for her! I shouldn't be here. It's not right. And the worse thing is, that thug who killed her is still down there, and nobody's gonna do a damned thing about it. *He* goes on living. *I* go on living. *You* go on living. But Sarah's dead!"

Pastor Tom nodded, sighed softly.

"Nate, you can't go down there. Sarah wouldn't want that."

"How do *you* know what she'd want? She was *my* wife. We loved each other. You'll never know how much we loved each other. She'd want me to do what I feel I have to do."

The pastor sat silently for a moment, looked up at Nate with compassion in his eyes.

"Even if it means getting killed?" he said softly. "Would Sarah want that?" He shook his head. "I don't think so, Nate."

Nate batted away the minister's words. "I might get killed? Is that supposed to frighten me? Sorry. No. I was thinking of doing it myself, if you want to know the truth. It seemed like a pretty good idea until I thought of going back to Mirador."

Nate stood in front of the minister, turned his hands up, lifted and lowered them back and forth like an uneven scale.

"One or the other. What do you think?"

Pastor Tom looked away.

"I can think of a lot of things I should say. I should tell you that Sarah's in a better place, that she's not suffering, that you'll feel better in time, that you'll be with her again someday." He shook his head. "It's all true, but I can't say that. I can't."

The minister looked up at Nate, his eyes moist.

"And I can't try to stop you from going back. Who am I to know... what ought to be done? After all, I'm the one who set the whole thing up. I'm the one who took you to Mirador. I'm the one who convinced you to go. If anyone's responsible, I am."

The minister looked down at his clasped hands. "I'm the one who should ask forgiveness, Nate," he said softly. "I was trying to do something good. And look what happened." He looked up at Nate again. "I didn't know, Nate. Please believe me. I've been to Mirador... I can't count how many times. And nothing like this has ever happened. How was I supposed to know things would get so crazy?"

Nate didn't answer. He sat down heavily again. Both men fell silent.

"I don't know what to do," Nate said finally, his voice cracking. "I know I can't go on living here, like this. Not anymore. Everything I loved, everything I wanted in life, I lost on that road. There's nothing here for me anymore. Nothing...."

The preacher turned his gaze out the darkened window, sighed, examined his thoughts in silence, then turned back to Nate.

"Maybe you should go," he said. "Maybe you do have unfinished business there." He looked down at his hands. "Maybe we all do."

Pastor Tom stood, walked over to Nate and put a hand on each shoulder.

"Go if you have to go, then. Do what you have to do. And may God go with you."

On Monday morning, Nate headed south. 🛕

CHAPTER 14

The Killing Ground

Nate spent his first night back in Mexico at a hotel near the bus terminal in Oaxaca. Early the next morning, muscling his way through crowds of passengers outside and inside the station, he made his way to a window and bought a ticket to San Cristóbal de las Casas. Although the sign over the ticket window said *Primera Clase*, the quality of the rolling stock was a far cry from that. No air-conditioning, no legroom, an engine that belched black exhaust, a slight list to the right. And it was packed with people: indígenas in Indian attire, mestizos and campesinos in work clothes, city folk in pressed slacks and shirts. All locals, no tourists. Wedged in, the passengers sat sometimes more than one person to a seat. Young and old. Husbands and wives. Babies in their mothers' laps. Mostly, the other travelers kept to themselves, said very little. When they did talk, it was in low voices. From time to time, they applauded when the driver did something worthy of praise, like avoiding a tumble over a sheer cliff.

The travel was tedious. The bus stopped at every town and village, every place in the road that was wide enough to pull over and let passengers off, every time someone waved it down from the side of the road in the middle of nowhere. It stopped twice to fill up with gas. After every stop, for whatever reason, when the bus lurched forward and got underway again, the passengers all crossed themselves. Everyone. Every time.

Crossing into Chiapas at the same checkpoint he and Sarah and the other missioners had passed through in the church bus almost exactly four months before, Nate found himself strangely reassured that nothing had changed in this place. Everything was familiar. The line of vehicles, the barrier, the soldiers. The women and children at the side of the road. And beyond: the green stillness, dense humid air of the lowlands, the low-lying clouds of the Altiplano. The notion of changelessness comforted him. He wanted to believe that here, in a place like this, the past might dwell close to the present, that things that had happened, or seemed to have happened, weeks, months, or years ago might not be sealed in the past, but might linger in some sort of extended present, some purgatory of time—that, here, past events might be irresolute, malleable, perhaps even reversible.

It was past dark when the bus arrived in San Cristóbal. Nate spent the night at a decent hotel a short walk from the main square and, the next day, with the help of the clerk at the front desk, hired a driver to take him to Mirador.

The driver, Enrique, made clear immediately that he would not take Nate all the way.

"No one will go there anymore," he said. "Not since the killings. Perhaps you have not heard, *Señor*. There was a march. *Los soldados* killed many people. It was during *Carnaval*. They say an American woman was killed, too. She was visiting *la iglesia*." Enrique crossed himself and shook his head. "Mirador is no place for visitors now. No place for you either, *Señor*."

Nate considered telling him then, but thought better of it. If he did, the man might refuse to drive him anywhere at all.

"Thank you, Enrique. But I am going, and I need a driver. Can you get me close?"

Enrique waggled his head. "Close? *Quizás*. We shall see."

"Good. Let's go."

Enrique's courage ran out about three hours later, just north of Ocosingo, where the route turned southeast off the federal highway onto the unpaved, unnamed road to Mirador.

Enrique steered the car to the side of the road and stopped. He rested a forearm atop the steering wheel and tapped the nail of his index finger on the windshield, pointing to the road ahead.

"This is the road," he said. "I am sorry, *Señor*. But I must turn back now. *Por allá....*" He grimaced. "Too much killing. It is not safe." He gave Nate a sidelong glance. "Perhaps you also want to go back?"

Nate shook his head. "No, *gracias*."

Enrique shrugged.

Nate pulled out his wallet, paid Enrique generously, grabbed his backpack from the rear seat, and got out of the car. *"Gracias,"* he said. *"Muchas gracias."*

"Vaya con Dios, Señor." Then Enrique turned the car around and drove away.

Nate threw his backpack over a shoulder and started walking. He followed the road southeast, striding stolidly along, not seeing another person or vehicle for what seemed like hours. A few cars passed finally, but he made no attempt to flag them down and the drivers paid him no mind. He continued walking, keeping to the edge of the road, head down, mind and body numb.

A few miles into his trek, on a steep, winding incline, a rattletrap flatbed truck rounded a bend behind him and lumbered past, carrying some twenty or more *campesinos* packed in with their belongings between the high, wood-plank siderails in the back. The truck halted about fifty yards in front of Nate, the driver leaned out his window and shouted, and all the passengers, male and female—every one clad in indigenous attire—clambered out. The driver shifted to a low gear and began coaxing the laboring vehicle up the grade, engine coughing and sputtering. The passengers followed close behind. Without a word, Nate fell in with them and saw why the driver was having so much difficulty getting the truck up the hill. The tires were almost bald. When the truck began to falter again, the passengers took up positions on each side and in back, bent forward and pushed. Finding himself behind the truck, Nate pushed with them.

When the truck crested the hill, the driver stopped, and, one by one, the travelers climbed back aboard. Nate was about to veer back to the side of the road when a man who had just boarded the truck leaned down and extended a hand. *Why not?* Nate tossed up his pack and accepted the offered hand, hoisting himself up to join the others. Finding a sliver of space between two campesinos sitting at the front of the truck with their backs to the cab, he lowered his haunches to the truck's steel bed and put his pack on his lap. To his right, a woman held a russet-colored chicken with a twine leash around its neck. To his left, a man was holding and stroking a pale gray rabbit.

When everyone was settled, a few passengers waved their arms and shouted, and the truck ground into gear and jerked forward, sending

all the passengers swaying back and forth in unison, like water sloshing in a bowl. Sitting shoulder to shoulder with his new companions,
Nate pulled his knees up closer to his chest and hooped them with his
arms. A cool breeze rustled his hair as the truck gathered speed. He
felt a chill and rubbed his shoulders, hugged himself. He'd dressed for
heat in chinos and a thin shirt, comfortable for walking. But he'd forgotten how cool it was at elevation and noticed now that the campesinos were wearing a lot of wool.

Seeing Nate's discomfort, the woman sitting next to him holding
the chicken reached into her bindle and fished out a crumpled brown
fedora. She belled out the crown, creased it, straightened the brim,
and handed it to Nate. He nodded his thanks and put it on. All of his
fellow travelers were watching. Blank faced, they considered his new
appearance. Then they laughed. Nate smiled.

"You are American?" the man holding the rabbit asked in a thick
accent. He was short and powerfully built with dark hair and eyes and
skin like cracked leather, from age or a lifetime of hard work in the
sun, or both. Nate couldn't tell.

Nate nodded. "*Sí.*" Was it that obvious?

"I am *Tzotzil*," the man said, putting a hand to his chest. "I am
from *La Realidad. Por allá.*" He waved a hand back over his head up
the road.

Reality, Nate thought. A harsh name for a town in any country.

"You are a farmer?" the man asked.

Nate shook his head no.

The man nodded.

"We are farmers," he said, stroking his rabbit and pinning down its
ears with rough brown hands. "We work the land, *la tierra*. My father
and his father and his father. My uncles and their uncles. *Toda la com-
munidad.* We work our land. *Our* land," he repeated, thumping a fist
against his chest. "*Nuestra tierra. Entiendes?*"

Nate nodded.

His companion frowned.

"The government says it is our land and we can get the *certificado* so
everyone knows. *Es nuestro ejido.*" He looked at Nate again. "You know
that word? *Ejido?*"

It sounded familiar, but Nate couldn't place it. He shook his head.

The man shrugged. "*Pues,* we fill out the papers and we wait. We have hope. *Esperanza, sí?* We wait and we wait. *Mi familia...*" He waved his arm. *"Toda la comunidad."* His face darkened. He stroked the rabbit. "But then, *el gobierno dice no más ejidos.*"

Listening, the other campesinsos grumbled, nodded and frowned, and Nate remembered why the word sounded familiar. He had come across it in his reading while preparing for the mission trip. NAFTA again. Ejijdos were communally farmed parcels of land campesinos could claim title to under land reforms introduced after the Mexican Revolution—reforms the current government had canceled to pave the way for NAFTA.

The man shook his head. "So we lost our hope. And then, *los paramilitaristas*, they came." He fell silent. "We lost more."

The man turned to Nate.

"I am Rominko," he said, putting a hand on his chest

"I'm Nate."

"Con mucho gusto."

"Con mucho gusto."

"A donde vas, Nate?" Rominko asked. "Where do you go?"

"Mirador."

Rominko's eyebrows shot up. He pursed his mouth and nodded. Yes, he knew it. It was not far from La Realidad.

"Los paramilitaristas," he said. "They came to my village. And now they have come to Mirador."

When the paramilitaristas came to La Realidad, Rominko told Nate, they took many people away. The young ones, mostly. The bold ones, who were trying to organize the community. *"Los Desaparecidos,"* he said softly, stroking his rabbit. "You know *Los Desaparecidos?*"

Nate nodded. He did. He remembered the photographs some of the women marchers had carried during the uprising in Mirador.

"The disappeared ones," Rominko translated. His family had not been spared. They had taken his oldest son, Takil, he said. "Good boy. Smart. *Muy fuerte.*" Rominko lifted an arm, clenched his fist and flexed his muscles like a bodybuilder.

Like Jack, Nate thought, and it struck him that he hadn't thought about Jack in a long time.

Takil had simply vanished. Los paramilitaristas came and he disappeared. One day he was there. The next he was gone. "It broke his mother's heart," Rominko said softly. "And mine." He shook his head and sighed. He looked up at Nate. *"Tiene hijos?* Children? You have children?"

"No," Nate said.

"Ah, lo siento. I have four sons. Two are gone now. My first and my second. Takil and Pakal."

Rominko shook his head again. "Also a good boy. Not as smart." He tapped a finger to his temple. "But also very strong. *Más fuerte* than his *hermano.* He went to find Takil. 'I will bring him back,' he said. "And now he is one of the devils." Rominko wiped his eyes with one hand. "Chuy, we called him. He has broken our hearts."

Nate stiffened. *No,* he told himself. *There must be dozens of men with that nickname in La Realidad alone.*

"His *jefe,"* Rominko continued. "They call him El Pitón. It is *un serpiente.* You know it?"

"The Python," Nate responded woodenly. "Yes. I know it."

"He has a scar." Rominko drew a slash across his right cheek with his thumb.

Nate nodded.

"You have heard of him," Rominko said.

"Yes."

"They say he was in Mirador. Now they say he is in the mountains. Chuy came to see us when they passed near our village. His mother cried and begged him to stay." Rominko scowled. "But no. He is proud to follow his *jefe.* He thinks he is a big man now. *Muy macho."* He shook his head. "He has a tattoo. Right here." Rominko pointed to his right upper arm. *"Un serpiente. Muy feo.* But he is proud."

Rominko sighed again, put his head back against the rail, closed his eyes and stopped talking. Recounting the facts of his life had tired him. Nate said nothing. What could he say? *I'm sorry for your loss? Your son helped kill my wife?* He leaned his head back and closed his eyes, too, letting the groan of the engine, sigh of wind, drone of indecipherable conversations around him dull the edge of what would otherwise have been a terrible silence.

The rocking of the truck became rhythmic and soothing. Nate drifted between wakefulness and sleep, his thoughts turning, as they always did, to Sarah. Questions he couldn't answer or stop asking assaulted him. *When did Sarah die? When exactly? At what hour? At what minute past the hour? When did her life actually end? The instant the bullet struck her skull? Or a millisecond later when it entered her brain? Did she feel the bullet hit her temple? Did she know what was happening? Did she experience fear? Pain? Does life end in an instant? Or does it fade like the light of day? When does the soul leave the body? Do you just close your eyes, then open them to a new world? Or is that all there is? After death, nothing?* Nate did not try to fend away these questions. It seemed necessary to consider them. But they exhausted him.

For the rest of the afternoon, Nate rode in the back of the truck with the campesinos, thinking of Sarah, drifting, dozing, being jolted awake each time the truck stopped to let people jump off or climb on. The cantankerous old vehicle followed corkscrew roads that, at times, became almost impassable. It crooked around rockfalls and mudslides, negotiated hairpin curves, flirted with sheer drop-offs and unguarded edges. Months before, when he had traveled these roads the first time in the front seat of the VW bus, these high, narrow stretches had made him nervous and he had often reached over the seatback for Sarah's hand. Now, rattling and bumping along close to the edge, he felt nothing.

Gradually, the road descended, the temperature and humidity rose, and the vegetation thickened. Nate removed his fedora and returned it to the woman with the chicken.

"*Gracias,*" he said.

She nodded and stuffed the hat back in her bindle.

A little later, the truck stopped at a river and everyone got out to lighten the truck's load across a rickety bridge. Nate remembered the bridge. Once the truck had safely reached the other side, the passengers crossed on foot and climbed back aboard. The driver followed the road southeast along the river for a while, then turned off into the rain forest on a road that was little more than a mud path. Nate didn't remember this turnoff. He remembered turning onto a better road that passed by an army barracks. *Ah, smart,* Nate thought. *He's detouring around.*

The oppressive heat silenced conversations. Nate dozed again as the truck slowly rocked and bumped along. Then the driver made another turn and the road widened and smoothed.

Nate was drowsing again when Rominko put a hand on his shoulder. He pointed to a village in a green valley toward the southeast. "Mirador," he said. He pounded a fist on the truck cab. When the vehicle came to a jostling halt, the two men wrestled themselves to their feet. Rominko tucked his rabbit under one arm and cleared a path through the tightly packed jumble of people. Nate followed him, stepped over the low tailgate and jumped to the ground.

Rominko handed down his pack.

"*Gracias.*"

"*Vaya con Dios.*" Rominko raised a hand and signed a cross in the moist air. Nate nodded, but said nothing. Rominko nodded back, stroked his rabbit, and turned to make his way back to his seat.

When the passengers were all settled again, the truck, now lighter by a man, pulled away. Nate stood alone on the muddy road and took his bearings. Mirador lay before him. In the distance, he could just make out the white bell tower of the church. He was back. For better or worse, he had made it.

If he remembered correctly, this road would take him southeast, then south to the northwest corner of the village. If he kept to the right where the road branched after crossing a small bridge, he'd be on the loop road that ran along the western edge of Mirador—the road Mateo had taken north from the southwestern corner of the village after negotiating a maze of back alleys in an attempt to get the missioners swiftly out of town after the riot broke out. *And we thought we were safe when he made it to that road. We thought we were home free. And then we came around that bend....*

Nate shouldered his pack and set off, keeping to a resolute pace as he headed down the hill. He would know it, he would recognize it— the exact spot where Sarah had fallen. And in that place, that killing ground, he would find...

What? What would he find? Nate felt a sickening dread rise up within him. He had come here out of obsession. He had come on a mission, as a duty, an act of contrition. But now that he was actually here, he felt a draining away of intensity of purpose, a waning of his strength. His anxiety mounted. His pace slowed.

Voices from above seemed to whisper a haunting requiem. Nate lifted his gaze, but saw nothing. *Wind. Wind in the trees.* Was someone following him? He glanced over first one shoulder, then the other. Nothing. He came to the bridge, the fork in the road, kept to his right, continued walking. *It was here, near here, somewhere around here.* He shortened his stride, scanned the ground in front of him with each step, became cautious, nervous. *What am I doing? Why am I doing this?*

He halted. From a small remove, he saw what he had come to see. *There.* Just a few yards ahead. The bend in the road, the clump of trees off to the side, the heavy branch arching high over the roadway. *This is where it happened.* He moved to the shoulder of the road and walked the perimeter, remembering, studying the ground. *The bus was here. No, it was over there. The trucks were down there. No, they were closer. We all lined up facing this way, toward that hill. No, wait. That's not the hill.* He turned in circles, studying the road, the trees, the hills, the sky. *Is this the place?* It had happened so fast. He'd been knocked out, down on the ground. *Maybe this isn't the place.*

Nate started to panic. He had come all this way. He had done what his driver Enrique had lacked the courage to do. He had come to Mirador. To stand here. In this sacred place. And now, he could not be sure this was the place at all. There was no blood, no chalk outline of a body, no memorial cairn. Not even a roadside cross with plastic flowers.

Just as his courage had, he thought, his memory was deserting him when he needed it most. His panic flared. *Maybe over there?* He raced some twenty feet down the road and stopped. He studied the ground, the vegetation. *No.* He jerked around and rushed back up the road. *Here. No. Yes. Yes!*

Yes, he was sure now. This was the stretch of road where it had happened, but that wasn't enough. Nate had not come just to visit this bend in the road. He had come to stand exactly where Sarah had fallen, to drop to his knees on that very ground, the few square feet of dirt hallowed by her blood. But he wasn't sure exactly where that was, and the more he searched, the more he tried to remember, the more uncertain he became.

"I can't remember," he said aloud in a thready voice. "I can't remember." Nate collapsed to his knees where he stood. "Sarah, forgive me. I can't remember."

Nate felt a great sinking of the heart, a great weight of despair. An intense wave of sadness and guilt washed over him. He fell prostrate to the ground, weeping bitterly. Sarah was dead. She was not coming back. And this was the day of her death. Not the day of the shooting, but today. Right now. There was no more denying it. No more trying to keep her alive. No more hoping to find her, see her again. Sarah was dead. She was gone.

Nate wept. "Sarah, I'm sorry. I'm sorry. I'm so sorry. I should have protected you. I should have done something. Forgive me. Please forgive me. Please. Please."

Dusk was gathering when Nate finally built himself to his feet. He began walking. He had no thought of where he was going. It didn't matter. Nothing mattered.

By dark, Nate had drifted into Mirador. In a fugue state, he ambled with languid steps along littered streets, down a muddy alley, hands pocketed, head low, mud caked on his shoes, feet leaden. A light rain fell and matted his hair to his forehead. Old women roasting ears of corn beneath lean-to shelters looked up when he passed. "*Elote,*" one woman said, reaching up to hand him an ear of corn. Nate gave no response. In the distance, he heard guitars, melancholy music.

A woman walking toward him, cowled in a dark shawl, glanced up at Nate as they crossed paths, halted and stepped back, as if she recognized him. Nate kept walking. A little farther down the street, Nate heard the muffled sound of *mariachi* music and then a man calling to him.

"*Amigo.* Hey, *amigo,*" the man crooned, his tone inviting, calculating.

Nate stopped and turned. He saw a man sitting in a chair under a leaky awning next to an entryway of some kind, a flap of canvas for a door. His face was bronze leather, deeply furrowed. He wore glasses with one lens blacked-over.

"Hey, *amigo,* you like posh? We have posh. Best in Chiapas." He took a drag on his cigarette, eyed Nate. "Girls, too. Best girls."

When Nate did not respond, the barker rose, flicked his cigarette into the mud. He threw back the coarse cloth that hung over the entrance and waved Nate in.

"Come, my friend."

Nate stepped through the doorway.

The first thing to hit him was the smell—a rank mix of unwashed bodies, cat urine, thick tobacco smoke, and exhaust fumes. A single fluorescent ceiling light cast everything in a dim, sickly green glow. As Nate's eyes adjusted, he saw that he was in a large room with a hard-packed dirt floor and raw-plank walls. About a dozen men stood hunched over a makeshift bar to his right. Others sat at wooden tables and benches scattered around the room. Three girls in tight, low-cut dresses, all heavily made-up, sat together at a center table, smoking and sipping their drinks, eyes downcast, expressions bland. A handful of scurvey-looking felines lay about. A quartet of mariachis played in the far corner. The exhaust fumes were wafting in from a gasoline-powered generator running outside an open back door.

Nate found a table in the back and plopped down on a wooden chair. Three hardcase hombres with sweaty faces and dirty shirts studied him from a nearby table. Another man snoozed on a bench against the wall.

A man appeared with a bottle and a glass and set them on the table in front of Nate.

"*Cincuenta pesos,*" he said. "*Muy barato.*"

Nate pulled a handful of coins from his pants pocket and put them on the table. The barman took what he wanted and left. Nate stuffed the rest back in his pocket, then pulled the cork from the bottle and poured the colorless liquid into the glass. He took a drink. The first gulp went down hard. The second, not so much. By the third, he couldn't taste it anymore and he was well on his way to becoming numb and witless.

Over the top of his glass, Nate studied the young women at the center table. They were eyeing him back boldly. One wore a thin, skintight white dress with the vague shadow of a black bra showing through. Her almond-shaped eyes were heavily outlined in thick mascara, her lips painted red. She could not have been more than sixteen years old, not much older than Itzel. Nate guessed she was probably pretty under all that makeup, but she already had the worn look and manner of a woman with long years of experience making her living on her back. Slouching along the road she was traveling, Nate thought, she'd probably be dead from disease or violence before she turned twenty-one. *Good for you,* Nate thought. *Wise choice. Why delay the inevitable?*

Nate drained and refilled his glass. His lips were getting numb, his tongue thick and unwieldy. His eyelids grew heavy. He slid down in his chair, dropped his chin to his chest, and closed his eyes.

He felt a hand on his shoulder, shaking him. He looked up, his vision blurry. The sloe-eyed girl in the white dress stood over him, her scarlet lips thinned into a smile. She smelled of sweat and cheap perfume, a combination that reminded Nate of pickle juice.

"*Hola,*" she said in a high, thin voice. "*Quieres ir a cama?*"

Nate didn't understand. The girl tried again.

"You want me? We go to bed. *Cincuenta pesos.*"

Nate considered the proposition. *What the hell.* Mustering what remained of his coordination, he finished the whiskey in his glass, set the glass down on the table, stood on wobbly legs, grabbed the back of his chair for balance, dredged a handful of coins from his pocket and tried to examine them. He couldn't focus.

When he looked up again, a burly, dark-haired man was standing in front of him. He seemed angry.

"*Vete!*" the man snapped at the girl, waving her away like a sniffing dog. "Go!"

The man put a heavy hand on Nate's shoulder and pushed him down onto his chair.

"Hey!" Nate protested drunkenly. "What the—"

"I heard you were here," the man said, dragging a chair over from another table and sitting down heavily.

What? Who...?

Through a drunken haze, Nate studied the man's face.

"Oh... Mateo." Nate slapped the table. "My old *amigo* Mateo. No problem, no problem Mateo. The man with all the answers." He fell back in his chair, waved toward the bottle. "How about joining me for a drink?"

Mateo glowered at him.

"So this is what you are now? A drunk? A man who goes with little girl whores?"

Nate poured more posh into his glass, spilling some on the table, and threw it back. He slammed the glass down and tried to focus on the face swimming around across from him.

"What of it? What business of it... what business of it... It's none of your business."

"Why do you do this thing?" Mateo challenged him, crossing his meaty arms on the table and putting his face in Nate's face. "To feel alive? To remember your wife? This is how you honor her? By keeping company with whores?"

It vaguely registered with Nate that he was being insulted. He didn't care.

Mateo sat back in his chair, studied Nate. "Ahh," he said, jerking his head back and nodding. "You do this to forget. *Sí. Sí.* Not to remember. To forget. To feel nothing, make yourself nothing. To feel dead, eh? Maybe you even want to die?"

"Bingo!" Nate raised his glass in a drunken salute.

Mateo snorted in disgust. "Okay, *bueno*. You want to die, that is your business." He leaned in again. "But why here, my friend? You could drink and whore back home, no? Why come here?" He stared hard into Nate's eyes. Even in his drunken state, Nate felt the intensity of his gaze.

"Ah," Mateo said finally. He sat back in his chair and fixed Nate with a cold stare and a cold smile. "Ahh, yes. Yes... to have *justicia, sí?* Justice. What we all want, but so few get."

Nate poured himself more posh. Mateo was boring him.

"And revenge, too, *sí? Sí,* revenge. To die a hero." Mateo waved his arm in a grand flourish. He shook his head. He leaned forward, put an elbow on the table, stole a look at the darkly brooding men sitting nearby, turned back to Nate and spoke in a low voice.

"*Escúcheme,* my friend. Listen. If you want to be dead by morning, all you have to do is stay right here. Those men"—he cocked his head—"will slit your throat and take your money and leave you dead in the street."

Nate looked over at the other table, squinted at the men. They were all staring.

"Okay. Good. Sounds like a plan." He threw back his drink, grimaced, and belched up a low laugh. That's what he and Sarah always said when they made up their minds about something. *Sounds like a plan.*

Mateo sat and watched Nate drink, a disgusted look on his face. "You think I am joking," he said. "You are a fool, Nate Hunter. You do not know what can happen here."

Nate had heard enough. "Hey. Why... don't... you... just... shut... the... fuck... up?" Nate said in a half-strangled voice, his whiskied lips and tongue leaden, slurring his words.

Mateo stared at him, said nothing.

"Hear... me? Why... don't... you... shut... the... fuck... up?"

Mateo sat watching him, still said nothing. Nate leaned forward, face low to the table.

"What's the matter? You can't hear? Cat got your tongue? What's the word? What's the Mexican word?"

Nate leaned back in his chair, looked up at the ceiling. "Cat, cat... " To his surprise, the word came to him. "*Gato!*" he crowed, snapping his fingers ineptly in the air. "That's it! *Gato.*"

He leaned forward again, hands and chest on the table.

"Fucking *gato* got your *el tongue-o?*"

Nate burst into loud, blubbering laughter, put his forehead on the table, smacked the table with his hand. *Gato. Tongue-o. God that was funny. Fucking hilarious.* He laughed and laughed, lifted his head, reached for the bottle of posh. But it wasn't there. He looked around for it. The men at the other table watched him search. While he'd been laughing, Mateo had taken the bottle off the table.

"Oh, no. No. No. No." Nate waved a pointed finger in the air.

"Oh, yes," Mateo said. "*Si˝. Si˝. Si˝.*"

Mateo lifted the bottle from under the table and set it on the table behind him. When Nate got up to reach for it, Mateo seized his arm and rose, blocking his way.

"No more, *amigo.* Time to go home."

"Time for *you* to go home," Nate said, trying to pull free. He couldn't. The man's grip was like a vice. Mateo let him go, but remained standing before him.

"*Sí.* Time for me to go home, and time for you to go home, too."

"Well, you see, that's a problem. Because I don't have a home anymore." He stumbled. Mateo righted him. He waved his hands. "No. No. No. That's not right. No, I have a home. I have a *new* home." He waved his arms around unsteadily. "This is my home."

Nate, staggering forward, a step, put both hands on Mateo's huge chest and pushed.

"Now get out of my way."

Mateo did not budge. Nate put a hand on the table, steadied himself, staggered forward and tried again.

"I said get—"

But Mateo did not allow Nate to finish the sentence. He moved so fast that Nate didn't even see him lift his hand, felt only the stunning impact of being smacked hard across the right side of his face with the back of a meaty paw. Nate stumbled back, tried to regain his balance, made a fist, cocked an arm. And then everything began to spin, and he crumbled. Mateo caught him, stood him upright, lifted him in his arms like a sleeping child and carried him out the door. ▲

CHAPTER 15

The Jaguar God

The night that followed stretched long and arduous for Nate. Unconsciousness wrought by hard drinking and Mateo's backhanded blow lacked the power to deaden his disgust with himself and only flung open the doors to the phantom demons that came to call. Ghouls and ogres advanced in waves, brandishing bloody knives, grinning, blood dripping from their mouths. Shrieking harpies swooped down, claws extended, and tore at his chest, clawed at his head. They had no pity. There was no escape. Nate writhed in pain.

And there were dreams, nightmares, grotesque visions of death and destruction. A giant black-and-yellow orb-weaver spider with the head of a dog chased half-naked children with bloated bellies, caught a one-legged boy and wrapped him like a mummy as soldiers and state policemen pointed and laughed.

Then Nate was in a bullfighting arena, watching a massive beast thunder angrily around the ring, huffing, pawing, throwing his head, brandishing deadly horns. The raucous crowd of spectators, overflowing the climbing rows of amphitheater seats, cheered and called for blood. But it wasn't the beast's blood they wanted. It was Sarah's. She stood alone, in a simple white shift, her back against the far wall of the ring, no champion to defend her, no matador to slay the bull.

The beast lowered his head, snorted and blew, eyes locked on Sarah, burning brimstone red. He pawed the crushed rock beneath his hooves, nostrils flaring, slobber streaming from the corners of his mouth. He charged. *Sarah!*

And then, Nate was in the ring, too, desperately searching for Sarah, trying to reach her, save her, but he couldn't see her, couldn't see any-thing. He was lost in a dense fog. He heard Sarah cry out to him. *Nate! Nate! Help! Please, help me!* But he couldn't tell where her cries were coming from. They were coming from everywhere. *Nate! Help me!* And then he saw her standing against the wall, but he couldn't move. His feet were blocks of concrete, his arms were bars of lead.

Now, Nate saw that the beast had spied Sarah, too. The bull lowered his head, pointed his horns, pawed, snorted, charged. *Sarah!* The bull tore into her, mauled her, gored her. Flayed her with razorous hooves as the crowd cheered. Frozen, unable to move, Nate watched it hap-pen. He couldn't close his eyes. Couldn't look away. *Sarah! Sarah! I'm sorry! I'm so sorry. Sarah! Forgive me! Forgive me!*

Nate's eyes flew open to an explosion of light. He sat bolt up-right. Pain shot through his body like a flash of branched lightning. He felt hammer blows to both temples. He was drenched in sour sweat, a dark choker of moisture staining his shirt at the throat, half-moons at the armpits, a wet splotch between his shoulder blades. He sucked in air and tried to reckon out where he was. With bloodshot eyes and fogged vision, he looked around. He was sitting on a cot in a small white room. The room seemed familiar, like he'd been there before. And then it came to him. The rectory. The room where Sarah had lain, first on a cot... This cot? Then on a mat, surrounded by flickering candles.

Was he really here? Or was he dreaming?

Nate swung his legs off the cot, kicking his knapsack to the floor. He put bare feet on the cool stone. The light pouring in through an open window hurt his eyes. His temporal arteries throbbed. His mouth tasted foul as carrion. His ears were ringing. His belly roiled, a turbu-lent ocean of bile and posh. His hair was plastered to his forehead. A growth of beard stubbled his cheeks. The air around him fumed with the odor of his own filthy body.

Nate rubbed his face, looked around the room again and saw Ma-teo sitting on a straight-back chair in a darkened corner. The two men stared at each other with eyes that expressed no emotion.

"So... you are alive," Mateo said, breaking the silence.

Nate put his hands to his temples. He closed his eyes and swallowed. His throat felt swollen and raw. He tried to talk, but his encrusted tongue did not cooperate. It was like learning to speak all over again.

"I'm not so sure I am alive," he finally managed, his voice so low and raspy he didn't recognize it. "I'm—"

Everything suddenly lurched sideways. Nate grabbed the cot rail with both hands to steady himself.

"Is this room moving?"

Mateo shook his head.

"I do not think so."

Mateo rose. He approached Nate slowly. Looming over him, Mateo looked down stone-faced.

"Get up," he said gruffly. "Clean yourself up. The lavatory is out back. Lourdes left you some washing water." Mateo gestured with a thumb to a pitcher and a basin sitting on a low wooden table along with a cloth and a sliver of soap. "Then come to the kitchen. Take coffee. We will talk." He turned and left the room.

Nate lifted his pack and carried the pitcher, basin, cloth and soap out back. He relieved himself, took off his clothes, washed as best he could, rinsed his mouth, combed his hair with his fingers and changed into his one spare set of underwear, shirt, and pants. He stuffed his dirty clothes into his pack and made his way to the kitchen. His head still throbbed, his mouth still tasted awful and his stomach still roiled, but he could walk a little more steadily. The earth continued to lurch unpredictably but it didn't spin under his feet.

Nate hadn't been in the rectory kitchen before. It was a warm, light-filled room rife with cooking smells: roasted corn, eggs, tortillas, coffee. Potted flowers lined the window ledge. Inside, Mateo sat sideways in a wooden chair at the far end of a small, rectangular oak table, sipping coffee from an earthen mug, gazing out a window, frowning, lost in thought. Nate paused in the doorway. Hands deep in his pockets, he put a shoulder to the jamb and studied the man. He was powerful, smart, wily, serious. Very serious under his mask of affability. But who was he? And why was he really here in Mirador? Mateo was a mystery to Nate. It was almost as if the more Nate learned about him, the less he understood.

Sensing Nate's presence, Mateo turned.

"Come in," he said. He pointed to a cane-bottom chair across from him. "Sit."

Nate shuffled in, fighting off a sudden wave of nausea, leaned against the table and collapsed into the chair. Mateo rose, took an aluminum coffee pot with blackened sides from the wood-burning stove, filled another earthen mug with the steaming brew and put it on the table in front of Nate. Nate raised it to his lips and drank. He closed his eyes and with the fingertips of his free hand skimmed the right side of his face, massaged it. He opened his mouth and worked his jaw.

"Did somebody hit me?"

Mateo did not answer. He refilled his cup and sat down across from Nate. Both men drank. Nate rubbed his jaw again. The strong coffee was helping to clear his head. He looked up.

"Now I remember. Yeah... you hit me."

Mateo did not respond. He gave no sign of agreement or protest.

"You pack a pretty good wallop for a... for a... for an altar boy... or whatever you are."

"I am no altar boy, my friend."

Mateo sipped his coffee. Nate caught and held his gaze.

"Then what are you? Some kind of preacher's assistant?"

Mateo remained silent. He drank more coffee, closed his eyes as if savoring it.

Nate shrugged. "Oh, well. It doesn't matter."

Another long silence.

Again, Nate was the first to speak.

"Whatever you are, what are you really doing in this armpit of the world?"

Mateo looked at Nate with cold eyes. "I told you. I came here to help. Same as you."

Nate nodded. "Yes, I know. But why did you stay?"

Mateo's face flushed with irritation. "I told you that, too, my friend. Perhaps you did not listen. My wife is here."

Nate held up a hand. "No, I know that. I didn't mean that. I meant, you could have taken her home. Why stay here?" He wanted to ask Mateo how his wife had died but decided to wait.

Mateo gave Nate an assessing look. He reached into his hip pocket and took out a battered wallet, opened it, pulled out a small, worn, black-and-white photograph. He wiped a white smear of flour off the table with his hand and set the photograph down in front of Nate.

"Elba," Mateo said. "My Elba. The finest person I have ever known."

Nate picked up the picture carefully and studied the image. Long, lustrous, raven hair. Dark skin, smooth complexion. Bright, intelligent eyes. High cheekbones. Dazzling smile.

"Very pretty," Nate said sincerely. He handed the photo back.

"Yes," Mateo said returning it carefully to his wallet. "And kind. She wanted to come to Chiapas... to help *los indígenas*. That was my wife... always wanting to help, to do something good, to make a difference." He nodded to Nate. "Like your Sarah." Mateo put his wallet back in his pants pocket, sighed a weary sigh. "But people like your Sarah, like my Elba. Such people are at great risk in the world. They are sparrows...." Mateo fluttered his hands in the air with the gracefulness that always surprised Nate. "Sparrows in a sky filled with hawks."

Mateo shook his head, heaved himself up from his chair, took his mug to the stove and stood with his back to Nate. Then he turned, holding his mug in both hands, and gestured in the direction of the kitchen doorway with a slight inclination of his head.

"She is buried out there in the little graveyard behind the church."

A silence fell.

"How did she die?" Nate asked finally.

Mateo sighed deeply, his gaze still turned toward the graveyard.

"She was killed."

He looked at Nate.

"She was murdered. She and another woman, Xoc, her assistant at the clinic."

Mateo carried his cup back to the table and sat down heavily. "They were taken away. Raped and shot. It was three days before we found them."

Nate felt his stomach turn. "But who would—"

"No one knows," Mateo said calmly. "But I know."

"But why would—"

"They gave medicine and care to everyone, anyone who came to them. *Soldados, paramilitaristas, campesinos.* Everyone. The military did not like that. They said, 'No *alborotadores*... troublemakers.' But Elba and Xoc said, '*Sí, todos.*'" Mateo shook his head and smiled slightly, glanced up at Nate. "And she was teaching the children to read. Adults, too, who wanted to learn, but mostly the children. The military did not like that, either. Oh, no, my friend. They told her to stop. But my Elba would not stop." Mateo sat back in his chair, straightened his arms, put his palms flat on the table. "So...."

Nate suddenly felt ashamed. "I'm sorry," he said, knowing even as he said it how empty the words sounded.

Mateo nodded.

Nate studied the dregs of coffee in his cup through another long silence.

"So it was the military. Delgado?"

Mateo shook his head. "No. Yes and no. *El comandante* did not do it. But he did not stop it."

Nate studied the dregs in his cup again.

"El Pitón?" he finally said.

Mateo nodded with cold deliberation. "*Sí.* Him and his men."

More silence, and then Nate felt a chill. "Wait a minute. So, you were lying when you said you'd never met El Pitón. And when he was lecturing us and told you to translate, you acted like you'd never seen each other before."

Mateo slid a hand across the table, grasped Nate's left wrist and squeezed. Hard.

"I told you once, my friend," he said, his tone calm and steely. "Do not ever call me a liar."

He released Nate's wrist and sat back.

"No, I had never met him. We had never stood face to face until that moment. He did not know me. But I knew him. *Todos los campesinos conocen a El Pitón.*"

Nate massaged his wrist, looked Mateo dead in the eye. "Don't ever," he said slowly, enunciating carefully, "grab me like that again."

Mateo lifted his palms in a gesture of appeasement.

"Okay, while we're on the subject," Nate said, the cold inside him spreading. "Here's what I want you to explain. Your wife was a nurse. She was murdered by El Pitón. I'm sorry about that. I really am."

Mateo nodded.

"And yet," Nate said. "You brought us here anyway. You brought Sarah here, anyway. And now Sarah is dead." He fixed Mateo with an icy gaze. "Why? Just tell me that. Why?"

Mateo looked down, shook his head sadly, looked up again directly into Nate's eyes.

"I am sorry your wife is dead," he said calmly, his gaze steady. "But I did not bring her here. She came because she wanted to come. I did not persuade her. I spoke with her once at *el museo.* You were there."

"But you knew she was a nurse."

Mateo nodded again. *"Sí."* He looked sadly at Nate. "We saw no reason she should not come. Remember, you were coming to restore a church, not to work in a clinic. The fact that your wife was a nurse... that was..." Mateo looked down, shook his head. "That was coincidence..." He looked up at Nate, turned his hands palms up. "That is all."

"Coincidence," Nate repeated, his tone dripping with venom. "A coincidence that ended up getting her killed."

Mateo looked down again, frowning hard, his face reddening, struggling to contain strong emotions. He took a deep breath, let it out, took another.

"If I had known El Pitón was in Mirador," Mateo said in a hoarse whisper. "If I had had any reason to suspect... I never..." He broke off, pinched his brow, put his hands flat on the table and sat silent with his head lowered for a long time. He looked up at Nate with deep, sad eyes.

Nate returned his gaze, remembering all Mateo had done to try to save Sarah—charging at El Pitón, getting knocked to the ground, struggling to his feet, getting knocked down again. *He did more than I did,* Nate thought. He tipped his head back, closed his eyes. *Oh God, oh God. Sarah....*

The two men sat in silence.

"Xoc wanted to be a nurse, too," Mateo said after a while. He shook his head. "Another sparrow," he said, fluttering his hands. He shifted, put his forearms on the table and held his cup between both hands. "You remember the girl, Itzel? Her mother brought her here the night you arrived."

Nate nodded. "Sarah helped take care of her."

Mateo nodded. *"Sí.* Xoc was her aunt. Itzel's mother, Maria, and Xoc were sisters." Mateo grunted. "He came back for her, you know. Before they went to the mountains. Lourdes told me. He came to her home, like a suitor with flowers in his hand. The girl was still weak. Maria tried to send him away, but he refused to leave. When he told her to bring the girl, she almost lost her mind. She called him names. *"Monstruo! Asesino!"* She told him her daughter's blood and the blood of her baby were on his hands. *La sangre de mi hija y su bebé está en sus manos!"* Mateo held up his hands and shook them as if to show blood on them, acting out the scene. "But El Pitón did not care. When he went to take Itzel, Maria attacked him with her fists. He threw her to the floor, threw the flowers at her, took the girl and left." Mateo shook his head. "She has not been seen since. May God protect her."

Nate couldn't believe what he was hearing. "May God protect her," he repeated sarcastically. "Yeah. Sure. Just like God protected Sarah... and your wife."

Mateo absorbed this. "You are angry, my friend."

Nate snorted. "You're kidding, right?" He leaned across the table toward Mateo. "My wife is dead," he said slowly. "She was murdered." He glared at Mateo. "Yes, I'm angry. Damned right I'm angry." He sat back in his chair. "You're not?"

Mateo nodded. "Yes. I am angry." He looked up at Nate. "But not at God."

Nate laughed out loud. "Not at God. That's a good one." He looked at Mateo. "So you *are* an altar boy."

Again, Mateo was silent for a while. "I swore I would kill El Pitón," he said slowly. "I took an oath on my wife's blood." He looked Nate dead in the eye. "That is why I am here, my friend. The same reason you are here." He shook his head. "No, I am no altar boy, Nate Hunter. And I am no preacher's assistant."

Nate had no idea what Mateo meant or what he would say next, and it struck him that it didn't matter. He'd gotten what he could from the man. He didn't need anything more.

"Nate Hunter," Nate said slowly as if testing out the sound of his own name. He looked at the man across from him. "I call you Mateo. You call me Nate Hunter or *Señor* Hunter."

Mateo said nothing.

"Do me a favor. Don't call me that anymore. Call me Nate."

Mateo grunted, nodded, sat quietly for a moment as if considering something. He downed the last of his coffee. Set the cup on the table and stood.

"Come with me... Nate."

The VW bus was parked near the church. They climbed in, and Mateo drove north, then east until he hit the gravel loop road at the outskirts of the village. He turned south and drove in what Nate judged to be a southeasterly direction through cultivated lands that gave way to rough country, dense jungle encroaching on either side, layered tree canopy overhead. Nate sensed they were descending. After about an hour, the road changed from gravel to dirt, then from dirt to little more than a trail.

"Where are we going?" Nate asked. Mateo didn't answer. Nate asked again. "Where are we going?"

Mateo glanced at him. "Does it matter?"

Nate thought, shook his head. "Not really."

Mateo said no more.

The trail they were on became increasingly narrow and overgrown, hardly more than a mule track. They stopped when it played out altogether near a river of sluggish, blue-green water.

Mateo swung the bus around and backed it into a choke of trees and thick, tall vines until it was nestled so deep in the shore bracken that only the front windshield was clear. He grabbed his rucksack off the back seat, then scrounged under the driver's seat and came out with a machete with a long, rusty blade.

"What's that for?" Nate said.

Again, Mateo did not answer. With no word of explanation, he climbed out of the bus and signaled Nate to follow. Nate stayed put. Ignoring him, Mateo moved behind the bus and began whacking at branches and vines. *Whomp!* A stack of cuttings landed on the roof of the bus. *Whomp!* Another stack slid down the windshield. Mateo worked methodically until the bus was so covered in branches and vines that Nate could no longer see out any of the windows. A small gap opened on his side of the windshield, and Mateo peered in, looking irritated. The gap closed. Nate picked up his rucksack, pushed the door open against vines and branches and squeezed through. Mateo grunted, motioned for him to step back, and returned to his task.

It was late morning now. The throbbing sun was pounding Nate like a pile driver. Thick jungle air was so humid he could hardly breathe. Humming clouds of mosquitoes descended upon him, targeting every bit of bare skin—his face, neck, arms, ankles. Nate rolled down his sleeves and buttoned the cuffs, buttoned and turned up his collar and scrunched his neck down, batted hectoring mosquitoes away from his face, slapped them off his head, neck, hands, and ankles. It did no good. They kept swarming and biting. He wanted to run, but where? Mateo kept working, seeming unbothered. Why weren't they attacking him?

A sudden, high-pitched barking and rustling of leaves and branches overhead snapped his head skyward, throwing him off balance and almost landing him in the brush. Mateo glanced up. "Spider monkeys," he said. "Watch out they do not piss on you." Recovering his balance, Nate saw a tribe of monkeys, at least a dozen, staring down, hanging from vines by their long arms and tails, barking and shaking branches at the humans below. They moved on through the canopy, small primate voices crackling, leaping and swinging from branch to branch with the grace of trapeze artists. Watching them, Nate spotted a medium-sized bird with a green head and wings, bright red breast, short yellow beak, and long green tail feathers perched on a high branch, twitching its head from side to side. A *quetzal*. It had to be. He and Sarah had talked about how exciting it would be to see one. *Sarah, look!* And then he remembered, and the searing reality of her death almost brought him to his knees.

"*Bueno*," Mateo said, appearing at Nate's side and putting down the machete to brush leaves and twigs off his arms and chest. Nate turned to check the bus, but it was no longer there. Mateo had concealed it so well that the jungle appeared to have consumed it. Mateo picked up the machete, moved to the river's edge and stood, scanning the dense bank in both directions, downstream and up. *What's he doing now?* Watching him, slapping madly at mosquitoes, Nate was startled again by a sudden shrieking and flapping of wings off to his right. Spinning around, he saw two large raptor birds, hawks of some kind, fighting over something in the marshgrass. A coral snake. Deadly. Nate made out its black and red bands as the raptors fought for it, grasping and lifting the writhing viper, then dropping it as they battled for possession.

One hawk finally gained control of the prize and both birds flapped off. The jungle was suddenly quiet. Mateo was out of sight on the riverbank. Nate was alone. And then he heard another animal sound from somewhere behind him. It sounded like a cough. It sounded close. He turned and looked hard into the brush, listened. He heard it again, like rough breathing. It sounded closer. Scrutinizing the bush, he caught a slight movement low in the foliage, a ripple of black and tan, glints of golden-green. Like eyes. Watching. Nate had a sudden chilling feeling that he was being stalked, that he was staring into the amber eyes of a jaguar, and that he could hear the big cat breathing, creeping closer. A blade of icy fear slashed through him. Every muscle in his body locked in a paralytic spasm of fear.

"*Señor* Hunter! Nate!" Mateo called from the river's edge behind him. "Come!"

Nate flinched. Heart pounding, he backed up toward the river, step by careful step, eyes fixed on the spot where he was sure he'd seen a pair of smoldering feline eyes, braced for a sudden charge of muscle and claws and teeth. Glancing quickly over his shoulder, he saw that he'd made it halfway to the marshy bank. He stopped, tensed. Nothing.

"Nate! *Ven!* Come! We must go!"

He waited a while longer, watching, listening. He didn't see the golden-green glints anymore, heard no coughing or raspy breathing, saw no rustling in the bush. Jungle sounds returned. The hum of mosquitoes and din of cicadas. The cries of monkeys, calling of birds. He took a deep breath, let it out slowly and turned toward the river.

He'd never seen water this color. More blue than brown, more green than blue. A dusky jade except where the sun struck it just right, creating bright pools of emerald green. *The green of Sarah's eyes.*

A short distance downriver to his right, the banks rose up and funneled the water through a narrow corridor between high, rocky cliffs. Upriver to his left, Mateo was searching for something in the undergrowth.

"Ah, there it is."

He stooped and then straightened and leaned backward, dragging the bow of a small dugout canoe halfway out of a brushy cache toward the water. It looked just like the ones Nate had seen in archival photos at the mask exhibit, the ones los indios of the Lacandon Jungle and their Mayan ancestors had used for centuries. Hewn from a single tree trunk, it was long and narrow, smooth on the outside and gracefully tapered at both ends. From what Nate could see of the inside, it had either been hollowed out in the old way with a stone or shell adz or burned out and shaped with hot coals. It was slightly wider across the beam than the ones he'd seen in photos and had a deeper belly and higher sides. It had one long, slender paddle inside. No seats.

Mateo lowered the canoe, tossed the machete and rucksack inside, moved around to the back end and shoved the wobbly craft across the loam, halfway into the water. He lowered it again and stood upright. Sweat beading on his forehead, he squinted and looked around as if checking to see if anyone was watching. Satisfied that they weren't being observed, he turned to Nate and gestured toward the bow with his right hand.

"Get in."

Nate hesitated.

"Where are we going?"

Mateo gave him an icy look. *"Otra vez.* Does it matter?"

No, it really didn't. Nate tossed his knapsack into the canoe, climbed in and sat down clumsily at the bow, facing forward. Mateo nosed the canoe away from the shore and climbed over the lip at the stern, rocking and nearly overturning the vessel in the process. He did not smile ingratiatingly or chuckle at his awkwardness or apologize as Nate might have expected... before. His expression serious, he simply knelt, took up the paddle with his rugged hands, sculled the slender craft out of the backwater, coaxed and yawed her about. With its shallow draft, the canoe was quickly seized by the sluggish current and carried steadily downstream. Glancing back over his shoulder as Mateo steered the canoe—cutting the surface with the paddle first on the right, then the left, using the blade as a rudder, leaning one way, then the other—Nate knew he'd done this before.

Watching the riverbank glide by, Nate experienced a faint stirring of exhilaration. He was going somewhere. He knew their direction— they were on a southeasterly course. But that was all he knew. He didn't know where they were going, and he didn't know why. And it didn't matter a damn.

Sheer canyon walls, dusty brown in color, flanked the river, rising a good three hundred feet above the water. Coursing through what felt like a great cleft in the earth, Nate craned his neck and studied the rockface on either side. Fractured everywhere by faults and joints, it was an intricate hodgepodge of angles, rifts, bulges, slabs, cracks, chinks, fissures, and crevices. Entirely unscalable by mortal man, he judged.

High up near the rim, a grand wide-winged bird with slate black feathers and white underside leaped from its cliffside aerie and patrolled the sky above. Riding updrafts, it circled and glided, swooped down low over the water, rose up again. *A Harpy Eagle,* Nate thought. He knew from his reading they were known to inhabit this region. To Nate's right, near the water's edge, the shadowy hollow of a tree blackened by fire seethed with the membranous wings of a colony of bats, fanning a hint of guano.

Farther ahead, Nate sensed movement on the opposite bank. A crocodile, at least the length of the boat, slid into the river. A deliberate beast, silent and slow but also capable, Nate knew, of great bursts of speed and strength, the creature lurked in the river's shallows. Nate tensed, watching the reptile closely as they passed. Mateo paid it no mind.

"What—" Nate faked a cough to cover the shakiness of his voice. "What river is this?"

Behind him, reading the water, guiding the craft, Mateo did not answer.

Maybe he didn't hear me. Nate turned to Mateo, asked again. "What river is this? Does it have a name?"

He waited, watching Mateo watch the river, still not sure Mateo had heard him.

Finally, Mateo answered.

"It is called *El Río Lacanjá.*"

Lacanjá. Lacandon. That makes sense.

"I call it *El Río de la Revancha.*"

"*Revancha.* What does it mean?"

No answer. Nate asked again.

"What does *revancha* mean?"

Mateo answered without looking at him.

"It means *revenge.*"

Like a rock tossed into a river, Mateo's answer sank to the core of Nate's being and settled there, solid and heavy.

Revenge.

The two men floated on.

"Caves," Mateo said, pointing up the craggy battlement on his right.

Shading his eyes from the sun, Nate looked where Mateo was pointing and saw dark openings in the rockwork.

"Sacred caves," Mateo said, turning his attention back to the river. "The ancient ones believed they are where the jaguar god enters the underworld."

Nate vaguely remembered reading something about a jaguar god.

"What kind of god was he?" he asked Mateo. "About like ours? Absent? Blind? Cruel?"

"He was a bloodthirsty god."

"Ahh... human sacrifices, right?"

"*Sí.* The people believed that each morning the jaguar god transformed himself into the sun and traveled across the sky, and each night he returned to the underworld and had to battle the forces of evil to emerge again the next day." Mateo cocked his head toward the caves. "Portals to the underworld."

Nate gazed up at the caves again.

"What's the underworld supposed to be like?"

"A terrible place. The world of death. The ancient ones called it *Xibalba*, The Place of Fright."

"What about the sacrifices?"

"To prevail against evil, the jaguar god needed the nourishment of human blood. So, sacrifices were made. Men. Women. Even children. Then, in the morning, the jaguar was reborn as the sun."

"Do people still believe that?"

"Some. Perhaps."

"Do you?"

Silence. Nate turned to see a look of disgust on Mateo's face.

"Do I believe it?" Mateo said, his tone sarcastic. "Do you?"

Conversation ended. Mateo steered and paddled. Looking back from time to time, Nate caught Mateo also glancing back as if to make sure they weren't being followed. *Who would follow us?* he thought. *We are lost to the world here.* And that was precisely where Nate wanted to be. He could fall out of the boat or step off into the jungle and never be found. No one would ever know. His only link to the world was a wobbly, wooden canoe with one paddle... and a companion whose destination and purpose were a mystery.

Day crawled on. Tediously, they were making time downriver. Twice, Nate thought he glimpsed a jaguar padding along the crestline of the high canyon wall. But it might have been the shimmer of heat. Murderous sun had cleared the edge of the canyon now and was bearing down on Nate's head, his hands, and the back of his neck with a ferocity he had never known. Sweat stung his eyes. He could feel runnels of it working down his spine and the backs of his calves. His shirt was soaked through. The boat's rough belly was killing his backside. The sun and heat, his drunken wilds the night before, and the sweat pouring off him left him with a parched throat and a desperate thirst. He'd heard about the dangers of heat exhaustion. Was he succumbing to it now? Did it matter? No, he told himself, it did not. Nothing mattered. Not anymore.

The distant sound of falling water roused Nate from his lethargy. Ahead, he saw water spilling from a gash high up in the jagged rock-face on his right. Transfixed, he watched it cascade in a long, pale green ribbon down to a churning and frothing blue-green pool in the river below. Approaching the base of the falls, Nate felt cooling spray on his face. He let his head fall back and rolled it from side to side, saw Mateo watching him.

The river! Jesus, what a city slicker he was, sitting there dying of heat and thirst with fresh water all around. He ladled up a palmful and splashed it on his forehead, splashed more on the back of his neck. It cooled and revived him.

Overcome with thirst now, Nate leaned carefully over the starboard bulwark and lowered his face, dipped his hand and saw something strange pass beneath them on the river bottom just as Mateo roared, "No!"

Nate jerked up, recoiling instinctively, jostling the boat.

"But I'm thirsty," he said, his voice a mere squeak.

"Not that water." Mateo nodded toward his rucksack. "In there."

Nate let the river water drain though his fingers, wiped his hand on his shirt, and rummaged through Mateo's rucksack for the flask of water. It was warm, almost hot. But it was water. He took a couple of thirst-quenching gulps, then turned and offered the flask to Mateo.

Mateo shook his head. "Later," he said.

Nate stowed the flask, faced forward again and fell silent. He found a semi-comfortable position—knees up, arms around them—and gazed out at the river, thinking about what he'd seen in the water. A submerged object of some kind. *A canoe? A scuttled boat perhaps. Was that what it was? And there was something in it? Something big and bulky wrapped in cloth. It looked like....*

"Mateo," Nate called. No response. "Mateo, back by the waterfall. I thought I saw something." He turned, caught Mateo's eye. Mateo frowned, looked away. The new Mateo, silent, stern—the real Mateo, Nate couldn't help think—did not answer. *He knows, but he won't tell me.* Nate faced forward, didn't ask again.

They floated on. The sounds of the jungle echoed on the water, rolled away down the canyon. Cries of birds. Shrieks of monkeys. Rasp of insects. Rocking and creaking of the boat. Dip and splash of the paddle. Rhythm of the river's flow. Nate's mind dulled. He crossed his ankles and let his knees fall open, rested a hand on each gunwale and let his head fall forward, chin to chest. His body, demanding rest, went slack and still.

The little skiff carried its passengers deeper into the canyon of *El Río de la Revancha*, deeper into the jungle. Nate slept. ▲

CHAPTER 16

Baptism

The river had no end. When Nate roused again, the rockscape, the water, everything looked much the same. It seemed that the river would go on forever, circling the globe, winding itself around it again and again like an endless spool of thread.

"*El río infinito,*" Mateo murmured, paddling through a long stretch of flat water. "*El río infinito.*"

Listless and dull-eyed, Nate stretched out on his back in the bottom of the boat, his head against his knapsack, arms folded on his chest, legs splayed across the tapered gunwales of the bow. Dozing, waking, dozing and waking again, he saw that the canyon had now widened, the river broadened. Skyscraper cliffs receded, yielding to a stairway of lower bluffs covered by tall grasses. The vegetation along the river banks grew thicker.

And then, the river changed again. The current quickened and carried the canoe swiftly through monotonous, thick jungle that grew right down to the water's edge. Nate sat up, letting the dense green landscape pass before him in a blur, until, for the second time, he was startled by the sight of something gruesome: what appeared to be a human corpse on the tangled right bank—rigid, kneeling, arms upraised, as if pleading or in prayer. He straightened and stared hard. But then he realized, to his relief, that what he was seeing was only the burned-out trunk of a tree, its two darkened branches lifted like arthritic arms, the stump transformed by fire and heat into a distorted wax cast of a human body, head, and face. Mateo saw it, too. "He prays for salvation, no? Or, perhaps, revenge. Or, maybe it is a warning from the jaguar god that we are entering a place we should not go."

There had been a time, not so long before, when the combination of such a bizarre sight and Mateo's sinister remarks would have provoked in Nate Hunter a dark sense of foreboding. They would have aroused in him an irresistible urge to be cautious, to proceed slowly, or even turn around, to insist at the very least that Mateo tell him where they were going. And why. But that had been a different Nate Hunter. This Nate Hunter was strangely unperturbed. He simply slumped back in the canoe, eyes half-closed, not moving or speaking, letting Mateo and the river determine his course. All cautiousness had left him, replaced not by courage, not by boldness, but by indifference.

Nate dozed again. When he woke, the canyon walls had steepened once more and the sun no longer beat down on his head. Now it was hammering away at his back. In his groggy, semi-hallucinatory state, the play of light and shadow in the canyon deceived him. It turned fallen trees into recumbent men. Rocks became jaguars and crocodiles. A gnarl of branches transformed into a baroque indigenous Pietà. Nothing was what it seemed.

From time to time, now, Nate noticed small standing waves on the surface of the water and wondered absently what might be causing them. An awakening of the current? A decline in elevation? A whisper of wind? They passed another waterfall, but this one was different—darker and stronger. Sheets of brown-green water poured over the canyon rim, as if issuing from overflowing pockets of rainfall, and plunged in a spiraling band into the turbid basin below.

They passed another pour-over, then another and another. The canyon walls began closing in. The river narrowed, and the current swiftened in earnest. Water began sheering more rapidly against the canoe. Ahead, rocks jutting out from both banks funneled riffled water into a strangled channel. And then, in the distance, a new sound rose up, a sound unlike all others Nate had heard on the river. It was a dull roar, like a speeding train.

"What's that?" Nate called to Mateo.

Mateo did not answer. Nate looked back and saw Mateo, his face fraught with uncertainty and concern, studying the water ahead, working the paddle to control the canoe in the rushing current.

The freight train rumble grew louder and closer.

"Mateo!" Nate called. "What—"

"*Agua grande,*" Mateo finally answered. "*Muy grande.* You better hold on, my friend. I have never seen it like this."

Nate felt his insides knot up. Sarah had tried to get him to go white-water rafting once. He had adamantly refused. The idea of being at the mercy of raging water held no appeal to him whatsoever. Not then. Not now.

Nate just had time to grab the gunwales before the rushing water was on them. Now, he watched over his shoulder as Mateo put muscle and mind into navigating the wild river. He trued up the bow, feathered the dugout onto his chosen course with short rapid strokes of the paddle, then held the blade broadside in the water in a two-fisted grip to try to slow their forward surge. Facing the front again, Nate saw that Mateo was tacking toward a tongue of dark water that looked like a clear passage. He made it through a stretch of choppy waves licking at the hull, and put his back into skirting the boil line of a developing rapid.

Looking good, Nate thought. *Looking good. Keep it up! Keep it up!* And then, just when Nate thought they might sneak past the turbulence, the current seized the boat, rocking and tossing it as if it were weightless and empty. Nate felt the awesome power of the river god now. There would be no more guiding or steering. The river would have its way.

The canoe rocketed toward the narrows. Glancing one last time over his shoulder, Nate saw Mateo sitting ramrod straight, staring downstream, still paddling hard, surrendering nothing. Nate turned forward again to confront the rushing river. He gripped the splintery sides of the dugout's prow and dug deep within himself to summon some semblance of the fierce determination he had seen on Mateo's face.

And then they were in the rapids. Rooster tails, side curlers, backrollers, water bludgeoning them on all sides, cresting and collapsing in tunnels and gyres. And dead ahead, a garden of car-size boulders rose up, shredding the rushing river into mounds of frothy water and spray.

"I don't like this!" Nate shouted into the roar of the river.

"Neither do I, my friend!" Mateo shouted back. "But we are in it now! Hold on!"

The canoe pitched and bucked. Nate tightened his grip on the vessel's forward gunwales until his fingernails cut into the wood. Heart pounding, he scouted the hydraulic maelstrom ahead. *Which way? Which way, dammit? How do we get through? Where do we go?*

Mateo shouted. "There! There!" Nate glanced back to see him pointing downriver. He shouted again, neck veins bulging, but his words were lost in the roar of the angry river. Nate faced forward again and cried out as the explosive whitewater engulfed them.

Miraculously, Mateo managed to keep the boat upright and pointed downstream. Paddling for all he was worth, he aimed for a cramped chute in the chain of iron-colored river rocks stretching from bank to bank and narrowly threaded through.

Nate felt a jolt of animal joy. *He did it! We made it! We made it!*

But then, the river bent. The roaring water hurled them around a bulge of land and they found themselves racing toward a precipice, a drop-off where the river simply fell away.

Good God Almighty. No. No.

The canoe shot over the edge. It descended a good ten feet down a near-vertical falls into a frothing whirlpool that sucked in the snout, heaved up the stern and spun the boat around, catapulting its occupants through the air and into the icy waters. Nate caught a glimpse of Mateo falling backward, his paddle cartwheeling over his head, before the river swallowed Nate whole, tumbled him and jerked him, tossed and yanked him in a frigid black world of swirling bubbles and muffled bellow of rapids with no up or down, no gravity or direction, no beginning or end. There was no struggling against it. Lungs straining, Nate fought simply to hold on, to keep from gasping, until the river let him go. *Air! Air! Air!* And then he felt his panic and will to fight subside and peace envelope him. Silent. Calm. Dark.

Sarah was there, garbed in a cloak of light, smiling, golden hair ruffling. *Sarah.* The sight of her calmed him. She reached out her hand. *Sarah. Oh, Sarah.* And then the rumble of big water returned, the darkness paled, the bubbles thinned, and in a spasm of rejection, the river coughed Nate up and spat him out.

He broke the surface, gagging and gasping for breath, slapping the water, kicking his legs wildly. Aware that the river was sweeping him downstream, he curled up, protecting his head with his arms, parrying with his feet and shoulders blows delivered by rocks lurking just below the water's surface. Above the water's roar, Nate thought he heard a shout. *Mateo!* He yelled back, heard the shout again, or thought he did. But the roaring water was too loud, too cold, too brutal. It rolled and tossed him, took him wherever it wanted, and he could do nothing but try to fend off impacts and seize gulps of breath when his face broke the surface. *Now! And... now! Now!*

And then the iron grip of the current slackened, the river slowed, widened. Nate uncoiled his body, turned on his stomach and began breaststroking against the current toward the right bank. Exhausted, weighed down by wet clothing, he had taken only a few weak strokes when he saw Mateo floating toward him, face up, arms splayed, gasping, head rising and sinking, rising and sinking, a few feet away. Nate lunged for him, seized him by the back of his shirt and held on. Kicking hard, lungs burning, he struggled to keep both their heads above water as he sidestroked toward shore and into the quiet of a back eddy.

Able to stand now, Nate turned and grasped Mateo from behind, forearms under his armpits, fought back on his heels and hauled his thick-framed, weakly coughing companion across the silty shallows and through the marsh weeds onto a grassy bank. With a massive heave, he propped Mateo against a sun-heated slab of rock and collapsed beside him. Both men were shivering and coughing, gasping for air. Mateo bent forward and barked up lungfuls of water. He tried to speak, but could not, couldn't catch his breath. Nate put a hand on Mateo's arm. *It's okay. It's okay. You don't have to talk.* After a few failed attempts, Mateo found his voice, looked at Nate, his face pale beneath a scurf of river slime and leaves.

"*Gracias. Gracias, amigo. Gracias.*"

Nate nodded, coughing, spitting water and debris, sucking in air, picking off leaves plastered to his face. Mateo leaned his prodigious head back against the rock, raised it and let it fall again. Nate did the same, felt the warmth of the feverish granite against the back of his head.

Chests heaving, bodies trembling, the two half-drowned river rats looked at each other, Mateo's stunned expression mirroring Nate's state of mind. He was having trouble believing what had just happened. They had come close to dying. And now they were here. On dry land. Alive.

The two men stared into each other's eyes for a few moments longer, grim, silent. And then, Nate wasn't sure how it happened, their lips began to quiver and smiles crept onto their faces. Each man gave up a sort of moan, and then, somehow, Nate didn't know how, little by little, their heaving and gasping turned to laughter. First, tentative and restrained, tempered by disbelief. Then stronger and heartier. And soon full-bellied and loud.

We made it! We did it! We're alive! Good God, we're alive!

Unable to speak now because they were laughing so hard, Mateo put a heavy hand on Nate's shoulder, and Nate patted the weighty paw with the affection of a genuine friend, the two forever bonded by their shared brush with death. Nate suddenly noticed his feet, looked at Mateo's feet, pointed. Nate had climbed into the boat earlier that day wearing canvas sneakers. Mateo had worn sandals. They both still had their shoes on. After all they'd been through. The two men stared at their feet, stared at each other and began laughing again. They laughed and laughed and laughed until it hurt to laugh anymore, and then they leaned their heads against the rock and rested. The sun was warm on Nate's face. The shore quiet. Nate closed his eyes, still smiling. His breath slowed. He began to drift off.

And then a shadow blotted out the sun. Nate opened his eyes, blinked to clear them and looked up. Above them, stood two men with rifles pointed at their chests. ▲

CHAPTER 17

Fresh Water

A ll around them, the world stilled. The river went silent. Birds didn't sing. Monkeys didn't chatter in the trees. Insects didn't trill.

Trying to avoid even the slightest movement, Nate studied the armed men standing over them through damp lashes caked with mud. The one standing over Mateo looked older and tougher. The one nearest Nate looked younger and slightly nervous. They had dark hair and eyes and brown skin and wore mismatched fatigues—the older one, olive drab pants and a black t-shirt; the younger, black pants and a hand-stitched brown shirt. Each wore a soft-billed military fatigue cap and a red bandana around his neck. Both had their pant legs tucked into the high tops of rubber farmer boots. Web belts circled their waists. Full bandoliers crisscrossed their chests. Machetes in leather scabbards hung from baldrics at their sides.

The river god has a sense of humor, Nate thought. *He saves us from drowning so we can be shot dead by paramilitary thugs.* He almost wanted to laugh.

Out of the corner of his eye, Nate saw Mateo wriggle his stout frame higher against the rock, put a hand to his brow to shade his eyes, and squint up at the men standing over them.

Careful, Nate thought. *They have guns.*

But Mateo seemed strangely calm. Glancing sideways, Nate saw Mateo's lip start to curl into a smile. A faint smile, but a smile nonetheless. And it was widening.

Is he crazy? Does he want to get us shot?

Next instant, Mateo chuckled.

"Oscar?" he said, addressing the man standing over him.

The man scowled, aimed his rifle at Mateo's chest.

Mateo sat up and wiped mud from his cheeks. He swept his wet forelock from his eyes, leaned forward and squinted up again, straining against the afternoon sun to make out the face of the armed man looming over him.

"Oscar? *Eres tu?*"

The man took a step back, lowered his gun, bent and squinted.

"Mateo?"

Nate watched, confused, as the armed man slung the rifle over his shoulder and extended a hand, saw Mateo take it and let the man help him gain his feet. Mateo's face broke into a wide grin. He compassed the man with his arms, holding him in a mighty bear hug, lifting him briefly from the ground, rifle and all. The two men laughed.

Sitting up slowly, Nate watched the incongruous interplay, but remained on the ground, keeping an eye on the younger, more nervous-looking man standing over him. This man did not laugh or speak. He didn't lower his rifle.

Oscar turned to the man and waved a hand in a gesture of reassurance.

"*Está bien. Está bien. Él es mi amigo.*"

The other man kept his rifle pointed at Nate's chest until Oscar pushed the muzzle down and away.

"*Calmate, Sebastiano. Está bien. Dije que es mi amigo. Ese hombre debe ser su amigo.*"

The man called Oscar took a U.S. Army canteen from a pouch on his belt and handed it to Mateo, who passed it down to Nate.

"Drink," Mateo instructed him.

Nate was too confused to respond. *Who are these men? What's going on?*

"*Está bien,*" Mateo assured him. "It is all right. They are friends. Drink. Drink."

Nate raised the canteen and swilled down cool, fresh water. Head back, eyes closed, he swallowed again and again, stopped, lowered the canteen, and gasped for breath. He wiped his mouth with the back of a hand, glanced at the armed men, then at Mateo.

Mateo nodded. "It is okay. Drink."

Nate quaffed down more.

It was the sweetest water Nate had ever tasted. From some pure spring, he imagined, unsullied by civilization, unpolluted by men and their bloody schemes.

Nate passed the canteen back up to Mateo. Mateo took a long, slow pull, then squatted before Nate, easing his sizeable haunches down on his heels.

"Feel better?"

"Yes."

"Can you walk?"

"I . . . I think so."

"We must go then," Mateo said, standing up again. "They will take us to the camp."

Revived by the water and his second reprieve from death, Nate shook his head and tried to make sense of what was happening.

"Wait. What camp? Where?"

Mateo did not answer. "Come," he said, putting out his hand and hauling Nate to his feet. "We must go."

Mateo turned to follow the armed men, who had moved off a few paces and were waiting. Nate reached for Mateo's arm.

"Wait a minute. Where are we going?"

Mateo turned, smiled, lifted a bushy eyebrow. "Does it matter?"

It wouldn't have before, no. But things were different now. Something had happened to Nate on the river. He felt changed somehow. Almost reborn.

"It might," Nate said soberly, fixing Mateo with a level gaze.

Mateo returned his gaze, then smiled.

"Do not worry, my friend," Mateo said, patting Nate on the shoulder. *"No te preocupes."* He turned back toward the two armed men. *"Vámonos."*

Mateo nodded to the men, and in single file they climbed the riverbank and headed into the jungle. Nate hesitated. *But my alternative is what?* He staggered up the bank and followed. Before going very far, the four men struck a narrow trail through the brush and, reordering themselves, set their feet upon it. Oscar took the lead. Mateo followed Oscar. Nate followed Mateo. The younger man called Sebastiano brought up the rear, more relaxed in the way he looked at Nate now but still maintaining a cautious three hundred sixty-degree lookout, rifle at the ready.

On the narrow trail, under the thick rain forest canopy, sunlight turned to shadow. The slanting brightness filtering through the treetop confusion of vegetation diffused and dimmed. The sun was still shining somewhere in the sky, but Nate had no idea where. A sort of bluish haze settled over the rugged country as the men trekked in silence. Following Mateo as closely as possible, seldom lifting his eyes from the muddy, narrow, stump-and-vine-tangled trace, Nate's thoughts circled back to what Mateo had told him on the river about the jaguar god—that each night, he entered the underworld to do battle with the forces of evil and needed human sacrifices, the spilling of blood, to prevail. Nate thought about the eyes he'd seen, or thought he'd seen, staring at him from the brush as Mateo searched for the boat. Senses sharp, nerves taut, Nate had the prickly feeling that the bloodthirsty beast was tracking him again now, moving silently on padded paws through the foliage, head low, eyes glittering, biding his time. He felt like clumsy prey. And he was sure he was being stalked.

Stop it. Just stop it. There is no jaguar. There's nothing out there. He was imagining things, he told himself, letting fear get the best of him. Fear—the unavoidable consequence of his renewed desire to live. *Lust for life and a horror of losing it. The two go hand-in-hand.* Nate had stopped feeling fear when he stopped caring about living. Now, somewhere in this unnamed, unmapped, roadless wilderness, Nate felt a rising sense of terror. Fear of what lay ahead. Fear of facing another moment of truth. Fear of being tested again, as he had been on the road outside Mirador, and showing himself once more to be ineffectual, a coward, a man of no account. He had endured and survived that first confrontation. But just barely. If he were to be tested again and fail again, this time, he knew, there would be no redemption. Judgment—his own judgment—would be final.

Moving slowly and carefully, two men ahead of him, one behind, Nate picked his way along the increasingly soggy path, climbing and descending through ever thickening vegetation, straining with each step to break the suction of the mire on his feet. Sometimes he bogged down entirely, legs stogged to the ankles in mud, tracks oozing to invisibility ahead and behind him. The lethal jungle was trying to swallow him up.

Colossal trees roofed the trail. Mahogany? Rosewood? Nate remembered reading that they grew here, but he wasn't sure what they looked like. He did recognize Ceiba trees like the one near the rectory in Mirador. Looking up, when he paused for a breath, he marveled at the arboreal trestlework overhead—arches and trusses, beams and cantilevers, masts and crosspieces. In places, stately trunks and their offshoots resembled flying buttresses. Branches sprouted from branches, layer upon layer. Shoots laced through and around each other. Vines dangled in green loops and coils, draped the jungle foliage like giant cobwebs. Nate recognized climbing philodendron. He knew that plant from his office. His office. A past life. No longer real or relevant. He saw thickets of ferns, masses of thorny briars, leaves as big as elephant ears, some bigger. On the jungle floor, he slipslogged across blankets of velvety green moss. Stepped over shadowy patches of mushrooms. The immense, intricate array of flora appeared in every generation— runners, suckers, mighty timbers, fallen and decayed trunks, sprouts just beginning their rise to lofty heights from the jungle floor.

Nate saw beauty in the wildness, even delicacy. Pale purple orchids stood out against lush, green backdrops. He caught glimpses of other trees and bushes bearing different kinds of flowers—large-petaled and waxy, delicate and drooping, red, yellow, pink, white. The air was strong with a cloying sweetness. Combined with the earthy odor of humus, it almost overpowered him.

Nate heard rustling and scurrying in the trees and in the vines overhead. Birds called. Monkeys screeched and howled. A small lizard cut across the trail. A butterfly, the size of his own hand, blue as the clear sky, flitted past on dusty wings, rising, falling, gliding. Nate felt like an interloper in an alien terrain, a trespasser in a verdant world ruled by species other than man.

The going became increasingly difficult until the trail was almost impassable. It rose and fell steeply. It meandered through the jungle, along streams, disappeared in blind turns around large rocks, infiltrated vegetation that presented an almost impenetrable breastwork for two-legged creatures. Sometimes, Nate could not tell if his feet fell on a trail at all.

Despite the arduousness of the journey, in front of Nate and behind him, the two armed men kept their steady, obdurate pace. They could cipher the trail when he could not. They advanced into the wilderness without hesitation, seemingly without fear, bushwhacking through the overgrowth with machetes when necessary, scrabbling along, clinging to vines, reaching for low-hanging tree limbs, pulling themselves forward, grappling hand-over-hand. They always appeared to know where they were going. Mateo followed without hesitation, obliging Nate to keep up.

It was hard going. Nate trudged along splay-legged to keep his balance, grunting with exertion, huffing with every step, fighting the mud-slicked slope of the trail and his own mounting fatigue. His steps were uncertain, his handholds unsure. Purchase often eluded him altogether. When the trail jinked hard to the left or right, he fell, thrashing, crashing to all fours. But no one paid him any mind. The pacesetters were all ahead of him now, surefooted creatures of the jungle breed passing him by, penetrating the wildness as if they could continue walking forever with no expectation of rest. Oscar, the point man, glanced back at him periodically to make sure he was still there but never stopped to help, never slowed his pace.

No one spoke. When communication was required, spare hand signals sufficed. *Stop. Come. This way. That way.* Nate fell in with the silence, was fine with it, preferred it, until a squadron of flies and mosquitoes swarmed and attacked, zeroing in on his neck and face.

"Shit! Shit! Shit!" he swore loudly, slapping himself and waving his arms around his head. Mateo and the others immediately halted, whirled and glared at him with fire in their eyes. He got the message. Felt the sharper sting of looking and feeling like a fool, resolved not to make another sound.

Toiling along in silence, Nate considered his situation. He had not the remotest idea where he was or where he was going. For all he knew, one of the armed men would turn on him in a few paces and separate his head from his body with a swift blow from a machete. If he did, no word of it would reach the outside world unless Mateo relayed the news later, and why would he? There would be no search for him, or no serious one at least, no quest for justice or retribution. His life would end, and the world would wag on, indifferent to his passing. His name might come up in idle chatter at cocktail parties back home. "Whatever happened to Nate Hunter?" "Couldn't tell you. I heard he never came back from Mexico." But that would be it. He would be known simply as the man who never returned.

Notwithstanding, Nate accepted his situation. He did not know his new companions or where they were taking him, how many miles they had traveled or how many more they had to go. But that was okay. Being alive and on the move was enough right now. They slogged on.

Nate lost track of time. It seemed to him that he and his companions had been trekking nonstop for hours, but it wasn't dusk yet, so it couldn't have been that long. Finally, at Oscar's signal, the men took a breather. Footsore, dripping with sweat, Nate breathed heavily. His bones ached. He was thirsty again, but he dared not ask for more water. The other men squatted on their haunches. Oscar pulled out his canteen, drank some water, passed it to Mateo. Nate was about to lower his backside onto the hefty trunk of a fallen tree when Oscar lifted his machete and tapped him on the leg with the flat of the blade. Nate froze. Oscar pointed the machete at a shallow crotch in the tree trunk where Nate was about to sit. Coiled inside, still and silent, blending perfectly with its hiding place, lurked a snake.

Petrified, mesmerized, Nate studied the serpent. It could have been a vine, a shadow, barely visible in the dim light of the jungle. He hadn't seen it at all. He looked at Oscar. The man shook his head, frowned, and made a slicing motion across his throat with a thumb. Nate slowly straightened and took a step away. Mateo handed Nate the canteen, and he took a welcome drink. Again, he got the message. A big message. *Be alert. Be aware. Look and think before you speak or move. One mistake here and you're dead.* Nate had always prided himself on being cautious and careful. He realized now that he didn't know the first thing about what to watch out for in this alien environment. Not the slightest thing at all.

Break was over. The other men stood and arranged themselves— Oscar in the lead, Mateo behind him. Sebastiano patted Nate on the shoulder and winked at him as he took his position in the rear. Silently, they resumed their march.

Again, Nate lost track of time, of how long they kept moving through the fetid jungle along a path he could no longer discern. Exhaustion and exertion, climbing and descending, plunged him into an almost hypnotic state. Walking. He kept walking, to the beat of his own heart, the rhythm of his own breath, as the dim light faded to blue twilight and deepened.

As night approached and Nate felt he was about to founder, they stopped on the crest of a ridge. Across a narrow valley, through humid haze, near the top of the next ridge, Nate spotted the faint glow of yellow lights. Scenting the dank odor of the jungle, he detected a hint of woodsmoke. Oscar closed his eyes, lifted his chin and inhaled deeply. He pointed.

"Home," he said. He nodded, turned to Mateo. "Home."

Mateo patted him on the shoulder, then turned to Nate.

"We have arrived."

Nate squinted into the gathering darkness, unsure what he and the other men were looking at. Overwhelmed by trees and other jungle growth, the place Oscar called home was largely concealed.

"Hard to see," he said.

Mateo grunted. "That is why we like it."

"We? Who's we?"

Mateo ignored the question. "Come. It is getting dark."

"Where are we? Does this place have a name?"

"We call it *La Libertad.*"

We again.

Without another word, the men filed down the steep ridge and across the darkening valley floor, and started up the slope on the far side. As the night turned black, they arrived at their destination. Before them rose the imposing entrance to a high-walled compound with makeshift parapets at the corners where sentries were stationed. A mysterious jungle fastness hidden from the world in its remote isolation, the fortresslike structure resembled a medieval castle abandoned centuries before and left to crumble and decay. Overgrown with enormous trees, the ground around it returned to brush and rocks, it was well on its way to being reclaimed by the jungle. *Like the ruins I've seen in books,* Nate thought.

"It is an old colonial hacienda," Mateo explained as the men wearily approached the tall, arching entranceway and massive wooden doors. "More than two hundred years old. Here, they used slave labor to grow sisal. It was exported to make rope and twine. Before that, sugar cane. Now, lost and forgotten."

"Incredible," Nate said, taking in the massive structure. He looked at Mateo. "You've been here before."

Mateo shrugged.

"It was at one time a world of its own," Mateo continued. "Completely self-sufficient. There are natural underground springs and wells and a complex system of cisterns and aqueducts."

"Must have been prosperous."

"*Sí.* The blood of slaves greased the wheels of the great machine. Now, descendants of those slaves use it to fight descendants of their masters."

Nate stopped walking.

"Wait a minute," he said. "What do you mean, 'use it to fight'? Where are we? What is this place? Some kind of Zapatista stronghold?"

Mateo patted his shoulder. "Do not worry, my friend. You are safe here."

Nate tensed, waiting for Mateo to utter his usual "No problem, no problem." But Mateo didn't say it—hadn't said it once, Nate realized, since they had met again in the bar, *when was it*... Nate couldn't believe it had been only the night before.

Mateo gave Nate's shoulder a gentle nudge, and the two men continued walking, joining their escorts outside the tall, arching entrance. When all were assembled, as if at some signal, the massive wooden doors creaked open on their crude, iron hinges and a trio of armed men—one standing in the doorway, two handling the door—positioned themselves in sentry stance beneath the archway, each man silhouetted by dim light from within.

Oscar approached and exchanged a few words with the guards in a tongue that reminded Nate of the one the campesinos had spoken during the truck ride to Mirador—*Was that yesterday? The day before?* Then Oscar turned and waved the others forward.

"Come," Mateo said, and Nate passed with his companions through the entrance into another new world.

Inside the compound, the hacienda transformed into a walled village with a large rectangular central courtyard filled with people and alive with activities. An arcade ran the length of more than a city block along the right side of the courtyard. At the far end stood a large, two-story building with stucco walls. *La Casa Mayor*, Mateo said, walking Nate around the square. A crumbling collection of more modest outbuildings lined the other sides of the quadrangle.

"Two centuries ago," Mateo said, pointing, "they were workers' quarters, stables, granaries."

In the open area at the center of the compound, women carried babies on their backs wrapped in dark rebozos or knelt at cookfires, forming tortillas, patting them flat, tossing them onto sheet-metal griddles.

Children roamed and scampered unattended. Scrawny dogs ambled about. In one corner of the compound, in a rustic corral made of split, unpeeled saplings, a few mules and burros and a couple of horses grazed on stooks of hay. A little ways off, outside a small coop, a woman wrung the neck of a chicken. In another part of the square, young men played what looked like a game of stickball by the light of torches. Near one of the cookfires, two men sat cross-legged on the ground, playing guitars and singing. Against another wall, a skinny, grizzled-looking old man sat on a straight-backed wooden chair, puffing on a pipe.

Everywhere Nate and Mateo wandered, Mateo greeted people by name and they responded as friends, smiling, nodding, shaking his hand, patting him on the shoulder. And yet, beneath the friendliness and camaraderie, Nate sensed cautiousness, edginess, tension.

"Okay, Mateo. What is this place?"

Greeting another friend, Mateo did not answer.

"Mateo, I asked you a question. Where are we?"

Mateo walked on.

Nate caught up with him, rested a hand on Mateo's arm, looked him in the eye and spoke firmly, but with respect.

"Look. I'm not a tourist, Mateo. And I'm not exactly going to walk out of here and go spilling any secrets. So tell me. I want to know. Where are we? Is this some kind of rebel camp?"

Mateo returned Nate's gaze. He was silent for a moment. Then he nodded.

"*Sí. Un avanzado.* An outpost."

Nate stared at him. "A Zapatista outpost?"

"*Sí.*"

The two men stared at each other.

"I asked you if you were a Zapatista during our drive to Mirador," Nate said slowly. "Do you remember that?"

Mateo nodded.

The word *liar* formed on Nate's tongue. He swallowed it.

"You told me no. Now you're telling me yes."

Mateo frowned at the ground.

"Things happen," Mateo said. He looked up. "People change."

"All of a sudden, just like that?" Nate said, snapping his fingers in the air. "One minute, priest's helper? Next minute, Zapatista?"

Mateo scowled. "No."

"So what then?"

"It is a long story."

"So tell me."

Mateo shook his head. "Tomorrow. Now it is late."

Nate pressed his lips together, narrowed his eyes. "When we left the rectory, is this where you were taking me?"

Mateo was silent a moment. He nodded. "*Sí.*" He looked hard and deep into Nate's eyes. "You came to Mirador looking for something." He paused. "Yes, I was bringing you here."

Nate was confused. "But why? I don't understand."

Mateo smiled, put a hand on Nate's shoulder.

"We will talk later. It is late now and we are both tired and hungry. Come. Eat."

Mateo led Nate to one of the fires and greeted the old woman tending it. When she looked up, Nate saw that it was Lourdes. She smiled at Mateo, squinted up at Nate and gave him a slow nod, almost as if she'd known he was coming, had been expecting him.

Lourdes handed Mateo a plate of corn and beans, a tortilla, clay mug of water. He passed them to Nate.

"Here. We will eat and drink."

Lourdes handed Mateo another plate and mug, and the two men sat down on the ground near the fire.

"Lourdes, too?" Nate asked Mateo as they settled in to eat.

Mateo nodded. "The uprising. The killings. Many people were affected." He pointed to Nate's plate. "Eat."

The fare was simple but fresh and good. Nate ate heartily. Glancing around as he stuffed the last of his tortilla into his mouth, he saw another familiar face. Quina, the other woman from the rectory. She stood a short distance away, talking to Oscar. In the dusky glow of open fires and through a thin veil of smoke, she looked mysterious and even more beautiful than when he had first seen her in Mirador. As Nate watched, she frowned and waved a hand at something Oscar had said, turned her head and saw Nate. Their eyes met, held. Then, with no sign of acknowledgment, Quina looked away and strode off into the darkness, Oscar at her side.

"Eat," Mateo said again, putting another tortilla on both their plates.

The first taste of actual food in almost two days revealed to Nate the depth of his hunger. He wolfed down the second tortilla, accepted more rice and beans. For a while, both men were too busy eating to speak. When Nate had finished, he put down his plate and shifted slightly to look at his friend.

"Okay, Mateo, I'm asking you again. Why did you bring me here?"

Instead of answering, Mateo got heavily to his feet.

"*Gracias*, Lourdes," he said to the *curandera*, handing back his plate and mug and glancing sharply at Nate.

Nate felt embarrassed. "*Sí, gracias,* Lourdes," he said, returning his mug and plate. "Thank you."

The old woman nodded.

"Come," Mateo said, turning from the cookfire and gesturing for Nate to follow him.

Mateo led him across the courtyard to one of the decaying buildings tucked away within the compound and stopped outside the doorless entrance.

"You will sleep here tonight," Mateo said.

It was a small room, bare but for a wood-framed cot and a packing crate turned upside-down to serve as a makeshift table. The cot was furnished with a corn-husk mattress, small pillow and a wool blanket woven in an intricate diamond design. A candle guttered in the neck of a glass bottle atop the table. A simple wooden crucifix hung on the flaking stucco wall over the bed.

"How long are we going to be here?" Nate asked Mateo.

Mateo looked at him, cocked his head. "Does it matter?"

"Maybe. Maybe not. I don't know yet."

Mateo rubbed his chin.

"It is late. We are both tired. Tomorrow I will answer all your questions. Tomorrow will be soon enough."

"And the world will look better in the morning, eh?" Nate muttered.

"*Sí.* You are in Mexico now. Here, we always have tomorrow."

Nate looked at him coldly. "No, not always. Sarah didn't." He couldn't help saying it: "Elba didn't."

Mateo looked down, nodded. "*Sí,*" he said calmly. He looked back up at Nate. "And now we are here. Both of us. Remember the name of the river that brought us here."

"You mean the river that almost killed us."

Mateo shrugged. "Almost. But we are here." He patted Nate's shoulder. "Rest now. Tomorrow we will talk."

This corner of the compound was quiet and dark. After Mateo took his leave, Nate sat on the edge of the cot, peeled off his clothes and still-soggy shoes, and snuffed out the candle. The room went black. He lowered himself to the homemade tick, stretched out, pulled the blanket over him and plummeted into dreamless sleep. ▲

CHAPTER 18

La Libertad

Nate woke the next morning before first light. From his cot, beneath the prickly blanket, he watched the blackness of night pale until he was able to make out the entrance to his quarters. He rose, shook out his clothes, put on his shirt and pants and stepped out into the central square, barefoot.

Smoldering remains of nightfires dotted the quadrangle. Skeins of smoke ascended lazily from the embers, spiraled, flattened out, lingered low to the ground. Through the haze, Nate had his first good look at the rebel camp. It bore no resemblance to any military installation he had ever seen or ever could have imagined. He saw couples bedded down with their children on pallets beneath trees, under lean-to shelters, in small alcoves. Men of all ages slept on the ground in clusters of three and four, some in sleeping bags, some under coarsely woven *serapes*, some with their arms pulled inside their shirts. Others sat snoozing in niches, broad-brimmed straw hats raked forward on their heads. Nate counted upwards of two hundred people—as many women and children as men of fighting age. *Pretty sorry excuse for an army*, he thought to himself.

Nate heard a cock crow. The melodious calls of jungle birds heralded the new day. He saw the camp's residents begin to stir, rise drowsily from their pallets, stretch, yawn, and set about their morning chores. He saw a few women already tending cookfires, Lourdes among them. From a distance, rubbing his chin stubble, Nate watched her at one of the fire rings, legs folded beneath her, dark skirt heaped over them, stoking a bed of embers until she brought it to flame. She added coffee grounds and water to a soot-stained aluminum pot, set it on the grill to brew and charged a second pot as the first began to perk. Soon, the air began to smell like breakfast.

Glancing up from her work, Lourdes saw Nate watching her and, in a gesture of hospitality, raised a chipped enamel cup in his direction. Nate put a forefinger to his chest and arched his eyebrows. Lourdes nodded, raised the cup again. Nate walked toward her across the quadrangle.

"Good morning," he said. "I mean... *buenos días.*"

Lourdes nodded, but did not speak. She poured coffee into the cup, handed it to Nate and, with the downward sweep of an arm coaxed him to sit. He put down the cup and seated himself tailorwise on the ground, facing the compound's massive wooden doors. The light was coming up now. Out in the center of the square, Nate saw cur dogs lying back to back, some lying atop each other, some rising and stretching. Guinea fowl clucked and roamed. Looking up at the tops of the walls surrounding him, he saw armed sentries manning the parapets at each of the four corners of the compound. Above the walls, nacre mist shrouded the jungle like a sheer linen veil, lit by a muted glow emanating from Nate's left. *East. So that's east.* For the first time since landing half-drowned on the bank of *El Río de la Revancha*, Nate Hunter had a sense of direction.

Gripping the cup with both hands, he sipped the steaming brew.

"*Bueno,*" he said, sighing. "*Muy bueno.*"

Lourdes responded with a tilt of the head, a half-smile, then filled the cup again.

"*Gracias,* Lourdes." And then Nate remembered his manners. He knew her name, but he wasn't at all sure she knew his.

"*Me llamo* Nate," he said, touching his chest. "Nate Hunter."

The dark-eyed old woman leaned toward him.

"Hoon... tare?" she repeated, smiling, wrestling with English pronunciation.

She had a soothing voice, gentle manner. Nate understood why Sarah had taken to her so quickly. *Sarah. My beloved.*

"Yes. *Sí.* Hun-ter."

"Hoon-tare," Lourdes said again, her accent a blend of Spanish and some indigenous tongue, producing a rendering of his name that Nate had never heard before.

Lourdes's eyes lit up. "Ahh," she nodded. "*El cazador.*"

"What? I'm sorry. I don't understand."

Lourdes aimed a gnarled finger at Nate.

"*El cazador,*" she repeated, miming the act of lifting and drawing a bow and releasing an arrow.

"Ahh. Hunter." Nate chuckled. "*Sí. El cazador.*"

Lourdes fixed him with a tender, penetrating look.

"*Y qué busca usted?*"

Nate shrugged his shoulders and turned his palms up in a gesture of helplessness, shook his head.

"I'm sorry. I don't understand. *No entiendo.*"

"She wants to know what you are hunting," Nate heard Mateo say from over his shoulder.

The burly mestizo squatted beside him.

"*Qué busca?* What are you searching for? What do you seek?"

Nate weighed the question. He considered making an attempt at humor. Or taking a stab at a truthful response. But he had no jokes in him. And he couldn't answer the question honestly because he didn't know the answer. So, he said nothing. He just shook his head.

Mateo stood again, put his hands on his hips and rocked back on his heels, waiting. Nate finished his coffee in silence, then got to his feet.

"*Gracias, Señora,*" Nate said, handing his cup back to the old woman. "*Gracias por....*" Lourdes looked up at him, waiting. He knew the word for coffee, but not the word for kindness.

No matter.

"*De nada,*" Lourdes said warmly, returning to her cookery.

Mateo nodded to the old woman, then put a hand on Nate's shoulder.

"Walk with me," he said. "I will show you La Libertad."

Strolling through the compound with Mateo in the morning light, Nate saw rifles almost everywhere he looked. Some standing on the ground in teepee-like stacks. Some leaning in orderly rows against crumbling stucco walls. Others propped in clusters of two or three against trees. All looked to be of World War II vintage or older, obsolete by modern military standards: .30 caliber carbines, single shot bolt action rifles, pump action shotguns. Nate even spotted some carved wooden rifles, mere facsimiles of weapons—good for training, good for children's play, but useless in a real battle, it seemed to him. Weaponry befitting an army of peasants, Nate thought, people long on hope and courage but short on materiel.

The outpost began to stir as others in the compound rose and set about the day's business and the quadrangle filled with the sounds of an awakening community—clang of pots and pans, cries of babies, sneezes and coughs, talk and laughter, the din and rhythm of daily life.

Everyone appeared to have a job. Cook, firekeeper, water-drawer. Young girls cared for younger children. Young boys fetched kindling for the cookfires. Mothers nursed babies wrapped in swaddling cloth. In one corner of the compound, an old man labored on his knees in a small vegetable garden. In another, an old woman was making tallow candles, placing them in mason jars. In the distance a few young men and women stood gathered around a well, laughing and chatting as they took turns filling their buckets. Inside the corral, one man fed the livestock as another cleaned the horses' hooves with a pocket knife. As they walked, Mateo again greeted everyone by name.

They passed a young woman sitting on the ground with a book in her lap and three young children gathered around her.

"That is Mirasol," Mateo said. "She teaches *los niños*. Quina is her mentor. Because of them, children will learn to read and write."

Quina. The mention of her name aroused Nate's curiosity about the woman with the inscrutable eyes, who had looked right at him the night before, then abruptly turned away.

"Yes, I saw Quina here last night," Nate said. "Who is she? What do you know about her?"

"She is from San Cristóbal," Mateo said. "She came to Mirador with her husband. She is a teacher. He was a doctor. He is dead now."

Nate wanted to know more. *When did he die? How did he die?* But Mateo had moved ahead as if to avoid further questions.

"Come," he said, beckoning to Nate with a graceful wave of his hand. "There is more to see."

They came to a small, strange-looking structure in another recess of the compound. Flat-roofed, consisting of a pole framework lashed together with ropes and covered with a thick layer of mud plaster, it measured about ten feet square and less than six feet high, a little shorter than Nate. A jaguar skin hung over the small, low entrance-way, and a beehive-shaped kiln made of rock and mud protruded from a side wall. The entire structure sat nestled under a peaked thatch roof, about a foot overhead, that sheltered it from the elements.

"This is our sweat lodge," Mateo said. "Have you ever used one?"

Nate shook his head. "No. You?"

"*Sí*. Not this one, but yes. We call it *temazcal*. We use it when we are sick. People here have faith in its power."

"Did it work for you?"

Mateo shrugged, turned up his meaty paws. "I am here. I can still paddle a canoe..." He grinned. "And tame a *boracho.*"

"What's that? A horse?"

Mateo's grin widened. "No. An ass."

A little farther on, half-hidden among trees in another corner of the compound, they came to a small, freestanding *casita* with a heavy wooden door painted a blue-green color that reminded Nate of the color of the river that had almost taken his life. A gasoline generator sat outside. Mateo paused, moved toward the door, then stopped, gave Nate an assessing look, and turned instead toward the center of the square. "Come," he said. "Lourdes will have breakfast ready."

"*Desayuno,*" Nate said. "One of the few words I know."

Mateo nodded. "You will learn more. Come."

Turning away from the casita to follow Mateo, Nate caught a glimpse of Quina across the hazy quadrangle, standing beneath a tree, brushing her wealth of shoulder length black hair. Nate couldn't take his eyes off her. When her eyes accidentally met his, the brushing stopped. She turned away and resumed brushing.

Nate caught up with Mateo, who led him to a crude, slatboard table in a small pavilion in another part of the square.

"Sit," Mateo instructed Nate, pointing to a wooden chair. "I will bring *desayuno*. We will eat. We will talk."

The shade gave relief from the sun, which was now fully risen above the compound's walls. Mateo returned with two plates heaped with a scrapple of eggs and tortillas and beans, and Nate now told Mateo to sit while Nate fetched two cups of coffee. Mateo nodded and grunted, and Nate felt a childlike sense of pride that he was catching on to the way things were done.

Nate returned with the mugs of coffee and the two men sat across from each other at the table. They ate. They drank their strong, grainy brew. Mateo did not speak, and Nate did not push him. Mateo had said they would talk today. Nate felt he knew Mateo well enough now to trust that he would keep his promise. He could wait.

When they finished eating and were sipping their coffee, just as they had only twenty-four hours earlier in the rectory, Mateo pulled his chair closer to the table and gracefully gestured for Nate to take in his surroundings.

"Look around," Mateo said. "What you see here is the result of five hundred years of conflict." He looked at Nate. "Five hundred years," he repeated, his eyes dark, his tone somber. "Five long centuries the people have fought slavery. Fought the *conquistadores, colonialismo, dictadores, el gobierno, imperialismo.* And now, this NAFTA." Mateo scowled, took a sip of coffee, glanced at Nate. "You know about NAFTA. We talked during the drive. *Yo recuerdo.*"

"I know a little," Nate said. "Not much."

Mateo turned toward the adults and children going about their chores in the square. "For generations, these people have had nothing. Nothing but the land." He gestured toward the jungle surrounding them. "This land," he said. "The mountains and jungles and rivers. This is their land. All of it. It is theirs by birthright and by the sweat of their labor. But much of it has been taken from them. Seized. Destroyed. Exploited. And they are made to work like slaves, just to feed their children. If they tried to say no, they were massacred and starved. No one cared. No one paid attention. Once, they could go to the government and say, 'Please, my family, our community, we have worked this land for generations,' and the government might say, 'Yes, we honor your claim.' But now, with this NAFTA. . . ."

Mateo shook his head in disgust, and Nate remembered his conversation with Rominko, Chuy's father, in the back of the truck.

"No. Now, they do not even have that," Mateo continued. "Now they have nothing—no land, no food, no work, no doctors, no schools, no plumbing or electricity."

Mateo sighed. He rose and stood with his back to Nate, hands in his pockets, looking out over the camp.

"But now the people refuse to die forgotten. They refuse simply to disappear. Emiliano Zapata was right. *Es mejor morir de pie que vivir de rodillas.* It is better to die on your feet, than to live on your knees."

Mateo turned toward Nate.

"It is time to stand up, my friend. Time to say enough. *No más.* The fight is coming. Justice will be ours."

Nate leaned back in his chair and looked at Mateo.

"Ours? Since when is this your struggle?"

Mateo turned away again. "Since Elba."

Nate looked down, nodded, turned his coffee mug in his hands.

"I'm sorry about Elba, Mateo." Nate looked up at his burly companion. "But what does her death have to do with... with this?"

"She was helping," Mateo said simply. He sat down heavily. "Elba and Xoc were giving medicines, supplies. That is why they were killed. I told her it was dangerous. But Elba... she was like your Sarah."

"And you *weren't* helping."

"No. Yes. I was also helping." He waved a hand. "But not here. I was a supporter. But I was not a Zapatista, not a member of *el ejército*. I stayed in Mirador, near Elba, waiting...." Mateo's words trailed off.

"For El Pitón," Nate said.

Mateo nodded.

Both men were silent for a moment.

"And now?" Nate said.

"And now I am here."

Nate frowned. "I still don't get it. Why now?"

"I told you. Things change."

"How? What changed?"

Mateo hunched forward, clasped his hands on the table, sighed heavily.

"The demonstration," he said finally. "The shootings." He scowled. "The killings." He looked up at Nate. "That had not happened in Mirador before. We were a quiet village. We thought we were safe."

"You didn't know about it. The march, I mean?"

Mateo shook his head. "No. But I should have." His expression darkened. "I should have." He looked up at Nate. "Some of the *campesinos* were becoming impatient. They saw what the *soldados* and *paramilitaristas* were doing in other villages and they were angry. They wanted to strike back. We tried to tell them we must wait until all is ready. But they did not want to wait...." Mateo's words trailed off.

"And people died," Nate said.

"*Sí*," Mateo said. "And people died." He frowned again. "And then your wife...."

Mateo fell silent. Nate waited. Mateo sighed, swept his hand back and forth across the table, sat back and looked Nate in the eye.

"So now I am here," he said. "And now you are here, too."

Nate turned his face to the sky, his heart filled with aching. *Sarah*.

He closed his eyes, took a deep breath, opened his eyes again and looked around the square.

"And this is it?" he asked, sweeping an arm through the air. "This is all there is? This is your army of insurrection?"

Mateo shook his head.

"No. This is not *todo el ejército*. We are only one small outpost. There are others."

"So, who's the head honcho? Who's running the show?"

Mateo smiled and shook his head.

"Is he here?"

"No."

"Where is he?"

"I do not know. No one knows."

Mateo raised a hand, smiled and fluttered his fingers.

"He is like the wind," Mateo said in a mock breathy tone of voice.

"Have you met him?"

Mateo shrugged off the question.

Nate shook his head.

"Have you seen him at least?"

Mateo did not answer.

Nate was getting annoyed.

"Does he have a name?"

Mateo scowled slightly. "He is not our leader. We have no leader. We have only a *subcomandante*. He is known as Marcos. Subcomandante Marcos."

"Known as? So, that's not his real name. What is it, some kind of *nom de guerre*?"

Mateo frowned.

Nate wanted to laugh, but didn't. "You've never met him. You don't know his real name. How do you know he's real? How do you know he even exists?"

Mateo scowled. "I know," he said slowly. "We all know. We believe."

Nate's mind jammed. He leaned forward, elbows on the table, ran his fingers through his hair and pulled it back tight over his head, trying to make sense of what he was hearing.

"You believe in someone you've never seen," he said, staring down into the table's worn wooden surface. "And I have trouble believing even what I can see."

He dropped his hands, lifted his head and looked out across the quadrangle.

"Can you ever hope to win?"

Mateo was silent for a moment.

"Yes," he said softly. "No. *Quizás*. In any event, we must try."

Nate leaned across the table toward Mateo.

"Look. I admire your courage." He swept an arm through the air again. "I admire all of you. And I wish you success. I really do. But I have to say, I think your chances of winning this fight are pretty slim. And it's your fight. It's not my fight. I'd like to help you, but I'm not a soldier. I don't like guns." Nate sat back in his chair. "So what am I doing here? Why did you bring me here?"

Mateo stared at Nate for a few moments.

"Come. I will show you."

Mateo led Nate back to the small building in the shaded corner of the compound, the one with the gasoline generator sitting outside, and stopped again at the blue-green door.

"Here," Mateo said. "In here."

Mateo opened the door and the two men stepped into a small room about the size of Nate's sleeping quarters, cool and dark inside except for a shaft of light shooting through a small, high window. What Nate saw, when his eyes adapted to the dimness, stunned him. The hut was filled with computer equipment. The newest, the best, the highest of high tech. An anachronism of the first order. Here, in a remote outland virtually devoid of modern conveniences, computer technology had gained a foothold. Nate stood with hands on hips taking it in.

An array of components sat on a crude wooden table stained blue-green like the door. Nate stepped deeper into the room to examine them closely.

"Do you know what this is?" Mateo said.

"Sure. It's an SGI Indigo. Takes its name from the color. Three-D graphics. Telephone modem. This is state of the art." Nate turned to Mateo. "Where'd you get this?"

Mateo didn't answer. He pointed to what looked like a small, box-shaped attaché case sitting open on a second table with a telephone receiver and other electronic equipment inside.

"And this?" Mateo said. "Do you know what this is?"

Nate looked at him. "Do you?"

"I'm asking you."

Nate nodded. "Satellite phone. Inmarsat. The best. You can attach it to that computer and transmit data files over the Internet."

Nate took the telephone receiver in hand and studied it, shook his head in amazement.

"They operate on a network of low Earth orbit satellites. They give you dedicated high speed Internet service."

"Can we use it from this location?"

"Depends on the reception. You're near the top of a ridge, so it should work."

Mateo pointed to another piece of equipment.

"And this?"

"Solar power unit." Nate nodded. "Smart. God knows there's plenty of sun around here."

Nate turned to look at Mateo, standing at the other side of the room.

"This doesn't make sense. This is all top-of-the-line equipment. Where'd you get this stuff? How did you—"

"It does not matter. We have our supporters. But it does us no good sitting here. We need to use it. To get our message out. To let people know. To tell the world."

"You mean you have all this equipment but you don't have anyone who knows how to use it?"

Mateo looked at the ground. "We had someone. From Mexico City. He is *desaparecido*. Four months now. Since the demonstration." He looked up at Nate. "Now we have no one. And the time of the rebellion is approaching." He drew in a deep breath. "We need your help."

Nate stared at Mateo, looked around the small room at the stacks of equipment again, looked back at Mateo. Neither man spoke for a long time. Mateo took a step toward Nate.

"Our army is weak," he said softly. "Some of our people have no weapons at all, nothing but machetes and sticks, hoes. How can we face an army that has modern equipment? We cannot win this battle with weapons, with bullets. We must fight with words. If we can get our message out on the Internet. . . ."

Mateo paused, gazed at Nate expectantly. Nate said nothing.

"We need a website," Mateo continued. "Website. That is what it is called, yes?"

Nate nodded.

"A website, *sí*. We need a website. We need to put our message out on the Internet, and keep getting it out. If we can do that, we can win. Our cause is just. People will see that, and they will support us. They will care. They will not let us be forgotten." He took another step toward Nate. "This is our secret weapon. Our most powerful weapon. Can you help us?"

Nate frowned, put the satellite receiver back in its place.

"Well, yeah, I *can*. Of course, I *can*...." Nate panned the trove of equipment, thinking, assessing. "So this is why you wanted to bring me here."

Mateo nodded. "*Sí*. And then when you came back...."

"No, I meant— Wait. What?" Nate was confused. "What do you mean, when I—"

And then it hit him, and his jaw dropped. Everything fell into place. Nate stared at Mateo, unable to speak, closed his mouth and walked out of the computer room, jaws now clenched, fury rising. Mateo followed him. Nate walked to the center of the square, stopped, looked around at the life going on around him, turned to face Mateo.

"Now I get it," Nate said, his manner calm. "This is what you had in mind from the beginning. To get me here. To build your website. To get you on the Internet."

Mateo drew himself up to his full height.

"To help us. *Sí*."

Nate pressed the palms of his hands to his temples. The truth in his own words knocked the wind out of him. An avalanche of deduction overtook him. He went cold.

"That's why you and Pastor Tom didn't care that Sarah was a nurse. Because it wasn't Sarah you were interested in getting down here." He looked Mateo in the eye. "It was me."

Mateo returned Nate's gaze. Said nothing.

Bitterness rose up in Nate's gut and throat like a geyser.

"God! No! You...."

He started pacing like a caged animal, stalking and turning, stalking and turning, pounding his forehead with the heels of his hands, cold sweat drenching his face. Mateo stood his ground.

Nate wheeled on him. "You must have laughed your ass off at how gullible we were," he said, his voice shaking with rage and indignation. "You put on a little act about how poor you are, how much you need help. And presto! We hop on a plane and head south."

"We told the truth," Mateo said calmly.

"But not the whole truth."

"There was no reason. We did not know you would come."

"You just got lucky, huh?"

Mateo looked Nate straight in the eye. "*Sí.* We got lucky."

Nate threw back his head and laughed out loud, then glared at Mateo.

"And then... this is the best part. You get my wife killed. And what do I do? I come back. You didn't even have to lure me this time. I came back on my own."

Nate closed in on Mateo as another piece of the puzzle snapped into place. "And you knew. You knew I was coming, didn't you? Because Pastor Tom told you. The only person I told, told you."

"He is a friend."

"Yes, of course. And a very persuasive friend, isn't he? He certainly persuaded Sarah. Quite the charmer, he is. You, too. Sarah was taken with both of you. I hope that makes you happy."

Nate closed his eyes, pounded his temples with the heels of his hands.

"That liar," he snarled. "That fucking liar!"

Mateo did not respond.

"And now... after what you've done... you have the gall to ask me to help you?"

Mateo took a step toward Nate, his back board-straight.

"We do what we have to do," Mateo said, stone-faced. "We cannot afford the luxury of good manners. We are fighting for our survival."

"Go to hell! I don't give a damn whether you survive or not!"

Nate had an impulse to fling himself at Mateo and pummel him with his fists. Instead, he wheeled and stormed away, not sure where he was going and not caring. Mateo followed and took him by the arm. Nate jerked free.

"Get away from me!" Nate barked at Mateo. "Get away! How could you do it? You son of a bitch! How could you do it?"

Around them, people looked up from their chores.

Nate turned to stomp off again. Mateo sprang ahead of him and blocked his way.

"What?" Nate said, stopping in his tracks. "Am I your prisoner now? Is that the next little surprise? You're going to lock me up?"

Mateo put his hands on Nate's shoulders, bowed his head.

"I am sorry," he said. He looked up, his expression solemn. "I never meant for your wife to be hurt. I never imagined that would happen."

"But you were willing to risk it. You were willing to take that chance." Nate shook his head in disgust. "Why am I even talking to you?"

Nate turned and started to walk away again, and again Mateo moved in front of him. Angry himself now and seemingly impenitent, Mateo planted his feet wide apart and grasped Nate by the shoulders, pinning him in place. When Nate fought to free himself, Mateo let go and pushed him back. Nate lost his balance and sat down hard.

"*Basta!*" Mateo thundered, hulking over him, his face filled with scorn. "Children! You are children! You *gringos* come down here for a couple of weeks. Take a little vacation to Mexico. Lay a few bricks on an old church. Say a few prayers. Then you go back to your houses, your cars, your country clubs and feel good about all you have done to help the poor *campesinos*. But the truth is you do nothing! You want to help us? *This* is how you help us! You must help us bring our fight to the world!"

Nate came to his feet in a fury, brushed himself off and put his face inches from Mateo's face.

"I never said I wanted to help you," he seethed. "I never even wanted to come to this godforsaken place. I came because of Sarah. She's the reason I came the first time. And she's the reason I'm here now." Nate waved his arm around. "You want to go to war? Get slaughtered? Fine. Go for it. Kill each other all you want. Just leave me the hell out of it. This isn't my country. You're not my people. This isn't my fight."

"Not your fight?" Mateo repeated, putting his knuckles on his hips and raising an eyebrow. "Maybe it wasn't before. But it is now, my friend. El Pitón murdered your wife just as he murdered mine. I did not stop him. You did not stop him. I was not there when they took my Elba. But you..." Mateo looked Nate up and down with contempt. "You were there when he killed your wife. And still she died."

Gutted by Mateo's words, Nate stumbled back a step, turned away, blinded by nightmare images. Sarah, being thrown to the ground. Sarah, on her knees in front of El Pitón. Sarah, lying dead in the mud, blood spouting from the bullet hole in her head. It all came back in a torrent.

"You saw what happened when we went to *el comandante,*" Mateo continued, talking to Nate's back, showing no mercy. "They will treat your wife's murder the same way they treated my wife's murder. They will do nothing. There will be no justice." He was silent a moment. "We had someone to help us build our website. *Muy intelligente.* You would have enjoyed meeting him. Now, he is gone, too. And there will be no justice for him, either."

Nate covered his ears with his hands. He didn't want to hear anymore. No more!

But Mateo wasn't finished. He came around to stand in front of Nate again, looked him hard and long in the eyes. "You say this is not your fight. *Bueno.* We will not force you to stay. We need men who want to be here, real men." Mateo pounded his chest twice with a fist. "*Hombres verdaderos.*" He stepped closer to Nate. "But tell me, then. Why *are* you here? Why did you return to Mirador if this is not your fight?"

Nate looked around and, only half-seeing, found his way unsteadily to the wooden table where he and Mateo had sat eating breakfast only a short time before. He sat down, put his head in his hands, felt Mateo sit down across from him. The two men sat in silence as, around them, people returned to their chores and the chatter and hum of activities in the central square resumed.

Nate's thoughts tumbled and raced. *Mateo didn't know it would happen. It's true. He didn't want her to die. And he's right. I did nothing. But he lied! He tricked us! And Pastor Tom lied, too! They both lied! If we'd known, we never would have come. No, that's not true. Sarah would have wanted to come. We would have come anyway. And she would have died anyway....*

Nate pounded his forehead with his fists, sat up, let out a cry of agony and rage. He looked around at the square, the people, the children, who had all stopped to stare again. Nate hardly saw them. He looked up at the jungle canopy, the sky.

Sarah! Sarah! Forgive me! Can you ever forgive me?

Nate closed his eyes, took a deep, ragged breath, opened his eyes and looked at Mateo, who sat watching, waiting.

"Will you help us?" Mateo said again calmly.

Nate rubbed his forehead. "And if I say yes?"

"There will be danger in it. I promise you that. I do not know how or when you will be able to go home. But we need your help. Will you help us?"

Nate did not answer immediately. He turned and gazed out over the square instead, taking in the morning, drinking in the sun.

"El cazador," he muttered under his breath.

Mateo cocked his head. *"Qué?"*

Nate looked at him. "Lourdes called me *el cazador."*

Mateo nodded. *"Sí.* The hunter."

Nate looked away again, thinking about his new name, his old name suddenly imbued with new meaning. Mateo waited. Finally, Mateo reached across the table and put a heavy hand on Nate's arm.

"My friend. Will you help us?"

Nate looked at Mateo's hand, lifted it from his arm, looked at Mateo with cold eyes.

"I'm not your friend. Don't ever call me that. Ever. I am not your friend, and you are not mine."

Mateo stared at Nate, nodded.

"Very well, Nate Hunter. Will you help us?"

Nate took a deep breath, exhaled slowly.

Sarah. I do this for you. Only for you.

"Yes," he said. "I'll help you. But only until El Pitón is dead."

Mateo nodded as, across from him, Nate took a silent oath and set his seal to it, swearing God's own vengeance on the man who murdered his wife. And then Nate looked across the table at Mateo, his eyes daggers.

"But I will never forgive you. Never. And when this is done, I may just come after you."

Mateo straightened and returned Nate's cold stare.

"Do not worry, Nate Hunter," he said. "I will not be hard to find."

CHAPTER 19

The Waters of Uncertainty

Nate spent the next few hours giving the hardware a thorough going-over. Taking pleasure, despite himself, in resurrecting his consummate skills and expertise in all things having to do with the brave new world of telecommunications and information-sharing, he organized and assembled the basic computer components, connected them to the jenny outside, and soon had the system up and running.

By the dim light of the monitor and a single lightbulb dangling from a cord overhead, he located the software discs he needed and began loading the programs onto the hard drive. The process of building a website was underway.

"What do you want to call it?" Nate asked Mateo, who stood off at a distance, watching him work.

"We have decided that," Mateo answered. "We are the *Ejército Zapatista Liberacion Nacional*, the EZLN. Our cry is, *'Basta! Ya basta!'"*

Nate nodded and went back to clicking keys. Later, absorbed in his work, he only gradually became aware of the sound of footsteps and scuffing on the roof and men's voices overhead and outside. Oscar and Sebastiano were positioning the phone's satellite dish with Mateo supervising.

"Okay!" Mateo called in to Nate when they were finished. Nate connected the cable and picked up the phone. He switched it on, punched in a series of numbers, and waited. At first, there was only static. Then Nate heard the familiar, satisfying series of beeps and whirs that signaled an attempt to connect. Then, after more static, the even more satisfying sounds and screen information indicating a successful connection. Nate clicked tabs, selected options and filled in the technical data required for an initial sign-on, and the computer screen came alive. Images and lists of websites sorted by categories appeared before him.

For a while, staring at the screen, tapping keys and clicking windows, Nate lost all sense of place and time. He could have been sitting at his desk, in his office, at his job back in the States. And then he came out of his self-induced trance and was back in real time, sitting in this little hut, in this compound somewhere deep in the jungle. And Sarah was dead. The stark reality hit him all over again with the force of a kick to the solar plexus. His heart pounded. His hands trembled. Sweat glazed his face. He felt short of breath. What was he doing here? *Think, man. Think!* From where he sat, in a tiny hut within the walls of a rebel camp, lost to the world in a dense tropical rain forest, he could assemble the words and construct the graphics that would help launch a peasant revolt. He could put a match to a keg of gunpowder. He could call the world's attention to an oppressed people's battle for freedom and dignity. Or, he could say *Screw it,* make a couple of quick phone calls, turn informer and book a flight home.

Lost in thought, hands poised on the computer keyboard, Nate became aware of a new sound inside the hut, coming from somewhere behind him. A continuous, low tonal buzzing, like a feline purr. And a smell. A feral smell. He sniffed it in. Cat breath? He flashed on the amber eyes he was certain he had seen watching him from the brush by the river, the creature he had felt stalking him during the trek to camp. He froze, turned his head slowly, ever so slowly toward the sound. Nothing. He was alone in the hut. *You're imagining things. There's nothing there.* He tried to go back to work, but the flood of fear and the wave of relief had left him drained. *I need air.*

Pushing back his chair and turning to rise, Nate saw a small, oddly shaped figure standing in the half-open doorway, backlit by bright afternoon light. Nate squinted, not sure who or what it was. And then he recognized Rafael, the one-legged boy from the rectory. The skinny sprout of a kid leaned on his crutches, silent, motionless, watching. How long had he been standing there? Nate shook his head. Rafael was here, too? It seemed to Nate as if the whole village of Mirador had come to this jungle outpost, or at least everyone he had met there. Except the old priest. Nate hadn't seen him yet. But, for all he knew, Tatic was here, too. He snickered to himself. *How hidden can this so-called secret camp be if everyone's here? How secure can it be if even a one-legged boy can get to it?*

Nate mopped sweat from his forehead with his shirtsleeve and studied the boy, the tempest of confusion and fear within him calming. He sighed.

"*Hola,*" he said.

The boy did not answer.

"*Hola,*" Nate repeated.

Still no answer.

Oh, that's right, Nate thought. *He doesn't speak.*

Nate tried a combination of spoken English, hand gestures, and facial expressions.

"Want to come in?" he said, smiling, raising his eyebrows and making a beckoning gesture with one hand. No response. "Are you... do you... uh... are you... interested in computers?" he said, still smiling, eyebrows still raised, pointing from the boy to the computer and back to the boy.

The boy still did not move or answer. But despite his tensed, hunched posture and the cautious expression on his face, his large bright eyes betrayed eager curiosity.

Nate rose and looked around the room. In a corner he spotted a small, wooden camp stool. Stumbling slightly, he crossed the hard-packed dirt floor, picked it up and set it next to the chair.

"I'll just put this here," he said, patting the stool. "That way... " He sat down in his chair. "... If you want to come over and help... " He smiled, made another beckoning gesture and patted the stool again. "... Or just watch... " He turned back to the computer and mimed working and talking to someone sitting next to him. "You can." He smiled at the boy again. "You don't have to. But you can... if you want to."

Nate laid his hands on the keyboard, took a deep breath and released it through pressed lips, puffing his cheeks and pushing out a series of Ps—puh-puh-puh-puh-puh—like blowing bubbles. The boy intrigued him now, and with a sidelong glance, Nate took his measure. Rafael stood unmoving. He still said nothing. But Nate could see that he was watching.

Nate ordered his thoughts and went back to work. His agile and experienced fingers danced around the keyboard. His right hand jumped back and forth from keyboard to mouse, sliding and clicking. Letters and symbols flashed on the screen in time to the clicking of keys as he immersed himself in the labor of birthing a website. The wash of light from the monitor alloyed with the dim glow of the overhead lightbulb and scraps of sunlight seeping in through the partially open door gave the room a blue-green hue.

After a few minutes, Nate sensed movement and heard Rafael ease forward a few steps. He refrained from turning to check for fear of frightening the puppy away. He kept his fingers on the keyboard, eyes on the screen.

Inch by inch, the boy tottered across the floor, making his way slowly toward Nate and the computer. He stopped and positioned himself behind Nate's right shoulder, watching him work, watching his fingers fly, watching letters and images appear on the screen, disappear, reappear, change position. When Nate hit a wrong key and the computer responded with a sudden electronic beep and boing, the boy jolted and gave up a fragment of a laugh. It came like a sudden gust of wind, and as quickly died away.

The silence that followed, disturbed only by the dull click of computer keys and slide of mouse on the mouse pad, filled Nate with a sense that something important was happening with the boy beside him. Resisting the urge to turn and smile, Nate continued his purposeful tapping of keys.

Entranced, Rafael moved closer, leaned his crutches against the table and slid onto the stool, his eyes never leaving the monitor. Nate forced himself not to react. He didn't turn toward the boy, didn't acknowledge his presence. He simply kept on tapping.

Wanting to engage the boy, Nate searched out a university website and scrolled and clicked until he found a link to a page about the Lacandon Jungle. He clicked the link, and Rafael gave out a low gasp as photographs of familiar nature and wildlife appeared on the screen—birds and butterflies, green jungles and blue rivers. The boy sat wide-eyed, mouth agape. Nate understood what he was experiencing. He had experienced it himself. With no forewarning, the boy had had his first glimpse of the infinite world of words and images, knowledge and information that the Internet made instantly accessible even to a boy living deep in the jungle in the midst of a rebel camp. Rafael had witnessed the power and magic of this new technology, and it had shocked and thrilled him, filled him with awe. Which spoke well of him, Nate thought. *He might not be educated, but he's bright. Filled with curiosity, a hallmark of intelligence.*

Nate tapped a key, trying to go to a second web page of images and information, and the computer beeped and boinged again. Raphael laughed. Nate tried again, with the same results.

"Hunh," Nate grunted. He searched the table. "Guide, guide, where's the guide?" he muttered to himself. "It's got to be here somewhere."

Leaning on his good right leg, Rafael reached behind the computer and handed Nate a thick booklet with the words Owner's Guide printed on the cover.

Nate was surprised.

"*Gracias*," Nate said.

"*De nada*," the boy responded in the merest of whispers.

Another surprise. The boy spoke.

"So you can read," Nate said casually, paging through the manual. "And you know some English."

The boy nodded. "*Sí*."

Nate put aside the manual and studied the images and words on the computer screen.

"My Spanish isn't very good," Nate said. He pointed to the caption under a photo of a river. "Can you read this for me?"

Rafael leaned forward.

"*La Selva Lacandona*," he read aloud softly, "*es una región tropical localizada en el estado de Chiapas*."

Nate nodded. "I understand what *La Selva Lacandona* means," he said. "But the rest...." He shrugged and turned up his palms.

"It says the jungle is in Chiapas," Rafael said softly in an accent Nate had come to recognize as a mix of Spanish and some indigenous language. Tzotzil, he remembered. *Tatic said he's Tzotzil*.

Nate nodded. "*Gracias*."

"*De nada*."

Nate picked up the computer guide, leafed through it.

"Can you read this?" Nate asked, pointing to a word in big type at the top of the chapter listings.

Rafael leaned closer to Nate, looked where he was pointing, nodded. "Contents."

Nate flipped through a few pages. "And this?"

"List of figures."

Nate stared at the boy, this skinny kid with one leg.

"You read well, Rafael. In English and in Spanish."

The boy nodded solemnly.

"Where did you learn?"

"I was in school. . . in my village. . . . " Rafael looked down and went silent for a while. Nate wanted to lay a hand on his bony shoulder. He resisted the urge and waited. Rafael looked up. "Now Tatic teaches me," he said, offering a small smile. "And Mirasol. And Quina."

"They must be proud of you. You are a good student, *sí?*"

Rafael nodded vigorously. "*Sí, sí. Me gusta aprender.*"

He leaned across Nate to study the keyboard, frowned and pointed to the keys. "*Se mezclan,*" he said, making a churning motion with his hands. "*Las letras.* They are mixed. But you. . . " He held up his hands and wiggled his fingers in an imitation of typing. "*Y aquí,*" he pointed to the monitor. "*Palabras. Fotografías.*" He looked at Nate. "*Cómo lo hace?*"

Nate gazed at the boy, impressed. He had watched Nate closely, seen something that intrigued him, and instead of just sitting and scratching his head, he had spoken up, formulated a question, expressed a desire to learn. Rafael reminded Nate of himself at around the same age. Smart. Eager. Fascinated by technology. Full of talent and abilities with nowhere to apply them and no one to encourage them.

"You know, I could use some help with this," Nate said. "Would you like to help me?"

The boy's eyes lit up.

"I can teach you about computers," Nate said, pointing from Rafael to the monitor and miming typing. "And you can help me," he said, pointing from Rafael to himself, "with my *español.*" He raised his eyebrows. "Okay?"

Rafael smiled and nodded, eyes shining. "*Sí.* Okay."

"Okay," Nate repeated. He slid his chair to the left and helped Rafael reposition himself in front of the computer. "We'll start with something simple."

No surprise to Nate that Raphael proved a fast learner. He quickly grasped what a cursor was and how to move and position it using keys or the mouse, how to make a page displayed on the monitor shift up or down, left or right. They were working on backspacing and deleting when Mateo appeared in the doorway.

"Come," he said calmly but forcefully, somewhat out of breath. "We must go." ▲

CHAPTER 20

Prelude to War

"Come," Mateo said again, beckoning impatiently when Nate didn't move. *"Rápido, rápido!"*

"What? Why? What's happening?"

"Army patrol. We must go. Now."

Through the open doorway, Nate could see people rushing around in the square.

Nate looked around the room.

"What about all this?"

"Leave it. We must go."

Nate hesitated.

"Come! Hurry!"

And then Mateo was gone. Nate pushed back his chair, saw Rafael reach for his crutches as Mateo called again from a distance. "Come quickly, Nate Hunter! Quickly!"

Rafael's crutches clattered to the floor, and the boy began the awkward process of retrieving them.

No time for that now. Nate grabbed the boy under his arms and swung him onto his back. Rafael wrapped his arms around Nate's neck, pressed his good right leg and left stump against Nate's sides and held on tight as, carrying the boy piggyback, hands clasped behind him under the boy's bottom, Nate walked quickly out the door and into the quadrangle.

The camp churned with activity. Men raced about collecting weapons and ammunition. Women doused fires, gathered up children and belongings. There was no panic, no shrieking. Only rapid, efficient, purposeful movement accompanied by the sounds of scuffling feet, rustling skirts, clanking of pots and pans, horses whickering and stamping their hooves, mules and burros braying, babies whimpering, weapons being gathered, rifle bolts being slammed.

Nate saw Mateo and Oscar in the middle of the square, both with weapons in their hands, walking toward the entrance gate, motioning for Nate to hurry.

"What are we doing?" Nate said, catching up with them. "Where are we going?"

"Into the jungle," Mateo answered.

"But the computer—"

"No time. Some of the men will try to draw the soldiers away. Others will stay with those who cannot run. The rest of us will hide in the jungle and hope the *soldados* do not find this place. If they do not, we will come back. If they do, we will find another place. Come. Leave the boy. The men who stay will look after him. We must hurry."

Nate hesitated. Mateo stepped behind Nate to help Rafael down. Nate felt Rafael tighten his grip around Nate's neck.

Nate hitched the boy higher on his back, tightened his own grip under him, turned and squared himself to Mateo.

"No. He comes with me."

"*Por favor, amigo,*" Mateo said, exasperated. "We do not have time. The boy understands." Mateo stepped sideways to address the boy on Nate's back. "Rafael, *basta,*" he said sternly.

"I told you, I'm not your friend," Nate said. "And I'm not leaving him."

Mateo started to protest, but checked himself.

"All right. All right then. *Vámonos.*"

"What about Lourdes? And Quina?"

"They have already gone. Come. Hurry."

The square was emptying as the men and women leaving led children and animals out through the compound's massive wooden doors and those remaining retreated into their hiding places. Mateo looked around, checking for strays and stragglers, saw none, motioned to Oscar, and, together, they led Nate and his charge through the doors of the compound and northeast up the ridge into the jungle.

"*Gracias,*" Rafael whispered into Nate's ear as the men climbed.

The traveling party followed a trail at first, then veered southeast near the top of the ridge into an area of thick vegetation. They moved in swift silence for a good twenty minutes or so by Nate's reckoning, putting as much distance as possible between themselves and the compound. Every few minutes, Oscar held up a hand and they stopped, listening for movement, voices, gunfire, anything that might signal the approach of soldiers. Hearing nothing unusual, nothing disrupting the chatter and buzz and trill of jungle sounds, they continued, walking swiftly in silence, stepping carefully, trying to avoid even the crack of a twig. And then, at a series of hand signals from Oscar, they knelt among a stand of tall, thin saplings. Nate slid Rafael from his back and set him on the ground. The men breathed heavily but silently through their mouths. Even Rafael knew to keep still as men and boy scoured the brush with their eyes, looking for any sign of movement, listening for any unnatural sound.

Nothing.

Nothing.

Nothing.

Nate turned to Rafael, sitting silent and unmoving beside him, eyes large with fright. Nate winked. *I think we're okay.*

And then they heard voices in the distance. Men's voices. Soldiers' voices. Nate watched Oscar and Mateo confer in whispers. Then as Oscar kept a sharp watch, Mateo signaled Nate to follow him deeper into the vegetation. Nate nodded, picked up Rafael, propped the boy on his hip and followed as quietly as possible, crouching, stooping, bending to make his way. At another signal from Mateo, Nate stopped, lowered Rafael to the ground again and sat down behind him. Positioning the boy between his legs, he pulled up his knees, pulled the boy's back against his chest and folded Rafael's good leg into the protective fortress Nate had created.

"Stay here," Mateo whispered. Nate and Rafael nodded, and Mateo began concealing them behind a curtain of overhanging vines, arranging undergrowth in front of them for maximum cover. *Like he covered the bus,* Nate thought. As Mateo was about to position the last vines over them, he leaned down and put a finger to his lips. Nate and Rafael nodded again, and Mateo closed the curtain.

Nate heard the faintest squish of undergrowth as Mateo moved off. And the jungle fell silent. No chirping or chattering, no trilling or buzzing. Nate thought of the amber eyes in the brush on the riverbank. *No. Stop it.*

Nate and Rafael waited. The voices of the soldiers seemed to move off, fade away. Nate felt Rafael trembling, wrapped his arms around the boy, held him tight. A heavy silence lay over them.

And then they heard voices again. Soldiers coming closer, then closer still. *How can this be?* Nate thought. *How in the midst of this vast jungle can they manage to come so close?* Nate lifted a hand and touched his index finger to Rafael's lips. The boy nodded but otherwise did not move or make a sound.

Out of the corner of his eye, Nate caught movement in the grass off to his left. In their hidden sanctuary, an unexpected but not altogether unfamiliar foe appeared. A snake. Tan and brown diamond pattern. Spade-shaped head. The serpent seemed to stretch a good four feet in length and was as big around as Rafael's forearm. *Rattlesnake?* Shiny, even in the filtered jungle light, it moved toward them, tongue flicking, eyes unblinking, sliding silently, effortlessly over leaves and sticks, coming closer. Nate did not move or make a sound or tighten a muscle or shift his weight, even in the slightest. Rafael saw the snake, too, now. Nate felt the boy tense but remain absolutely still.

The snake reached Nate's mud-and-grass-stained left sneaker. There, it paused. Nate grimaced but did not move. Then, as if encountering a fallen branch or mound of earth, the snake moved up, onto and diagonally across the front of Nate's sneaker and down into the grass. Nate could feel the weight of the snake's body through the thin canvas as the creature slithered across his toes, all four-plus feet of him, distinctive tail last. Nate's right eyelid twitched. His lips quivered. He had guessed right. It was a rattler.

When the snake disappeared back into the vegetation, Nate breathed again. He patted Rafael's shoulder, feigning calmness, but his upper lip trembled. He opened his mouth wide and pulled his lips back over his teeth, stretching out the nervous tic, silently took in a deep breath, then exhaled as if he were blowing out lungfuls of smoke. Rafael leaned back and rested his head against Nate's chest. Nate could feel the boy's body trembling.

Nate breathed slowly and deeply, trying to calm himself. The jungle was quiet. Maybe the soldiers were gone. He closed his eyes, concentrating on his breathing, slow in and slow out, slow in and slow out, until a sudden loud thrashing in the brush somewhere directly in front of them jolted him upright. The wild thrashing grew louder, came nearer, mixed now with angry scraping and scuffling, guttural grunts and groans, the rattle of metal, dull thud of fists connecting with flesh and bone. The sounds of men brawling, of hand-to-hand combat. No shouts, though. No loud cries.

Nate held Rafael firmly by the shoulders to reassure him, then reached past the boy, opened a peephole in the drapery of vines with his fingertips and peered through. A short distance away, in a small clearing, he saw Oscar locked in mortal combat with a soldier in green fatigues, the two men slugging, grabbing, choking, butting, elbowing, grunting, gasping. Oscar turned and twisted, throwing the soldier off balance, and the two men went heavily to the ground, rolling, punching, kicking, bodies heaving and twisting, arms and legs entangled, grabbing at each other's necks. Oscar gained the advantage, started rolling on top of the soldier. And then he was on his back, and the soldier was on top, pinning him to the ground, his hands at Oscar's throat, gripping, squeezing, snarling, the muscles of his own neck straining as Oscar kicked and writhed, coughed and gasped, fighting to throw the soldier off, pry loose the soldier's death grip around his neck.

As if in an altered state, mind blank, Nate rose slowly to his feet, signaled for Rafael to stay silent and hidden and slipped out through the curtain of vines. He circled around behind the two men wrestling and grunting on the ground and crept forward. He cast about for a weapon, spotted the soldier's rifle and helmet on the opposite side of the clearing.

No. Too far.

His gaze fell on a branch lying near his feet. Solid-looking. Thick. Long.

Pick it up! Pick it up! Do it!

Nate looked around desperately. *Mateo! Dammit! Where are you?*

The soldier was still on top of Oscar, choking the life out of him. Gurgling sounds came from Oscar's throat. His arms flailed, his legs kicked and twitched.

Nate picked up the branch, heart racing. He examined it, weighed it in his hand. Found it hard and heavy, like a baseball bat. He crept closer, set his jaw, gripped the branch in both hands and, mustering every ounce of courage within him, raised it high over his right shoulder and brought it down hard against the soldier's head. Not the mightiest or truest of blows, the cudgel glanced across the soldier's skull but had enough power to knock the man sideways off Oscar and send him tumbling to the ground, eyes rolling white in their sockets.

At Nate's feet, Oscar writhed in pain, clutching his throat, gasping for air, waving an arm toward the soldier and calling to Nate in a hoarse whisper.

"*Mátalo! Mátalo!*"

Dazed, not understanding, Nate turned to see the soldier coming to. The man in the green fatigues rolled onto his left side and pawed at the holster at his right hip, going for a pistol as Oscar, flat on his back and struggling to breathe, groped frantically to find and raise the rifle still strapped across his chest.

"*Mátalo!* Kill him!"

Nate looked at the club still in his right hand. *Do it! You have to do it!* The soldier had drawn his pistol, was rolling onto his back, lifting himself on his left elbow, raising his right hand. Nate brought his arm back. *Do it! Now!* And then the club was being snatched from Nate's hand, and in a silent blur of movement Mateo brought it down with a mighty crack on the soldier's head, staving in his skull. The soldier collapsed to the ground, his body jerking and convulsing. Mateo stood over him and clouted him again. The soldier's body stilled. Mateo tossed the club aside and went to Oscar. Kneeling at his side, he helped him pull himself into a sitting position. Oscar gripped his arm.

"*Gracias, amigo. Gracias.*"

Nate looked down on the soldier's lifeless body, hideously disfigured head, blood running from his ears. He felt bewildered by what had just happened, what he had done and failed to do, stunned by the grisly affair he had just witnessed and astonished by his own part in it.

Oscar came to his feet and massaged his injured throat. He gave Nate a grudging look. "*Y usted también. Gracias.*" Nate stared at him without expression. He had no idea what to say.

Together, Oscar and Mateo dragged the body into the undergrowth, kicked dirt over it, and covered the trail of blood and brain matter. Oscar recovered the soldier's rifle and helmet and started walking away, clenching his jaws, shaking his head. Mateo followed, stopped and turned to Nate.

"*Vamos,*" he said.

"Where are we going?"

"Back to the compound."

"We're going back?"

"*Sí.*"

"But what about the patrol?"

"They are gone."

"But won't they come looking for... I mean.... "

"Maybe yes, maybe no."

"But won't they suspect.... "

"The jungle is a dangerous and unforgiving place. People disappear. Soldiers disappear. It is not always possible to know why. Sometimes it is enough that you are not one of them. Come. We must go."

Nate nodded. "I'll get Rafael."

Nate returned to their hiding place. When he parted the vines and knelt to lift the boy, Rafael studied Nate's face, then put a finger to Nate's right cheek. It came away bloody. Nate swiped his cheek with his own hand. His fingers came away bloody, too. Man and boy held their reddened fingers in front of them, hands almost touching, stared at them in silence, looked at each other. Then, without a word, Nate gathered the boy in his arms, shifted him to his back, and fell in behind Oscar and Mateo.

Walking in customary and now familiar silence, Nate tried to order his thoughts and feelings. Here, on this jungle battlefield, his mettle had been tested again and found wanting again. Nate felt confused and ashamed. He had just struck a man in the head with a club. It was the most violent act he had ever committed. And yet when the moment had come to kill or be killed, he had hesitated. If Mateo hadn't appeared, Nate knew, he and Oscar would now both be dead. He felt sobered and ashamed. He owed Mateo his life now. Or maybe not. He had saved Mateo from the river. And now Mateo had saved him from a bullet in the chest. Maybe that made them even. The thought made Nate feel a little better, a little less beholden. But one thing he knew for sure now: He had not undergone any profound transformation on *El Río de la Revancha*. He was still Nate Hunter, not *el cazador*. He was not a Zapatista, wasn't a rebel, wasn't even much of a fighter. He had changed, certainly, into someone who could wield a club at another man's head. But what did that mean? Maybe he wasn't a total coward. But he was no hero either. No, *hombre verdadero*. To the contrary, he saw himself, perhaps more clearly than ever, as just a man. A mere man. How much of one, he did not yet know. ⛰

CHAPTER 21

A Door Opens

The secret of the stronghold called La Libertad held. The soldiers did not discover it.

Nate and Rafael returned to the computer room. Nate set the boy on the stool and handed him his crutches. Looking down, Nate saw that his hand, where he had wiped his cheek, was still slaked with blood. He held it out to examine it. Rafael saw it, too, and held out his own bloodstained finger in response. "Come on," Nate said. "Let's get cleaned up."

They were standing at a washbasin in a row of washbasins set up in the northwest corner of the quadrangle, scrubbing their hands and faces with water when Mateo appeared with a bar of soap and a set of clean clothes.

"Here. Use this," he said, handing Nate the soap. "Wash and then put these on." He handed Nate a large, worn but clean pair of black army fatigue pants, frayed canvas belt, and a band-collared, button-front shirt, hand-sewn from unbleached muslin. "Leave your other clothes in your room for now. You can wash them tomorrow."

Nate examined the clean clothing. It would do nicely. "Thanks."

"I will try to find you some *huaraches,*" Mateo said, nodding at Nate's filthy sneakers. "But, as you see, many here have no shoes at all."

Nate nodded.

Mateo looked from Nate to Rafael and back at Nate.

"I see you have made a friend," Mateo said.

"He's a smart young man," Nate said, glancing at the boy. "He's helping me in the computer room. Aren't you, Rafael?"

"*Sí,*" Rafael said shyly. "*Estoy ayudando.*"

Mateo raised his eyebrows, impressed. "You *have* made a friend," he said. He put a hand on Rafael's shoulder. "You were very brave today, Rafael. You should be proud." He smiled. "And you must be hungry." He patted the boy's shoulder. "Finish washing, then go and eat."

Mateo turned back to Nate. "And you, too, Nate Hunter. You did well. You saved Oscar's life."

Nate frowned and shook his head. "No, I didn't."

Mateo patted his shoulder. "It will be dark soon. Wash. Change. No more work today. We will eat. Then we will rest. It has been a hard day for all of us. We will start again in the morning."

Nate and Mateo sat together that night at Lourdes's cookfire, as they had the night before. Too weary for talk, the two men ate in silence, concentrating on their meal. Glancing sideways at Mateo as he reached for his cup of water, Nate saw Mateo staring into the darkness, deep in thought.

"Are you thinking about the soldiers?" Nate asked.

Mateo shrugged noncommittally, gazing into the dark.

"Will they come back?"

Mateo shrugged again. "*Tal vez, sí. Tal vez, no.*" They may suspect we are somewhere in the jungle but they do not know where. The Lacandon is a vast place. We were lucky today. Next time..." Another slight shift of the shoulders. "Who can say?"

Mateo hadn't so much as glanced at Nate. Nate looked where Mateo seemed to be staring and saw that he was watching Oscar, sitting at another cookfire with Quina. Mateo scowled. Then, realizing Nate was watching him, he shook his head.

"Oscar..." Mateo said, gesturing with a nod. "He is a good man. A good fighter. But this..." He flicked his eyes toward the jungle where they had left the dead solider. "This did not have to happen." He was silent for a moment, as if weighing how much to tell. "Last year," he continued. "The *soldados* came to Oscar's village, looking for him. He was not there." Mateo frowned. "But his brother was there." Mateo looked at Nate. "The *soldados* took his brother. They left him with a bullet in the back of his head." Mateo looked down, lifted his gaze to Oscar. "Now, he has a score to settle. All he wants to do is kill *soldados*. The soldier today, he would not have seen us. He would have passed by. But Oscar could not let him."

Mateo sighed heavily, went back to eating. Nate found himself staring at Mateo's hands, the meaty paws that had ripped a club out of his grasp and beat a man's skull to pulp just a few hours before. Sitting near the fire next to this man in gathering darkness, Nate felt like he was lost in a dream, or a nightmare. He began to think that none of what had happened in the jungle had really happened. Because if it had, how could he be sitting here now, sharing a meal with Mateo and feeling so calm about it? Feeling nothing at all.

Later, lying on his cot, staring into pitch blackness, Nate replayed the entire jungle crucible in his head, starting with the moment he crept out and picked up the branch. *And then what? What happened next? I picked up the branch and then... I swung it at the soldier's head. No. That wasn't me. It couldn't have been.* The man Nate knew himself to be, the man he used to be, could never have done such a thing. Was incapable of it. But he had done it. Nate Hunter, computer engineer, former up-and-coming young professional from Dallas, Texas, had intentionally bludgeoned a man with a club. *So what does that mean?* He couldn't figure it out. *Who am I now? What's happening to me?* Trying to make sense of it was too hard. He was too tired. So tired. Bone-weary, Nate closed his eyes and descended into sleep.

Next morning, with nothing else to occupy him and needing a distraction from his thoughts, Nate returned to the computer room and the challenge of setting up a working website in the middle of the jungle. By midday, with Rafael at his side, learning and helping, Nate had a simple template built. Now it needed content. Nate knew himself to be a more-than-decent writer. He had no false modesty about that. He was confident of his ability to formulate any kind of statement, press release or communiqué once he knew its substance. He needed help with the substance.

"You're in charge until I get back," he told Rafael and went out to look for Mateo, who was walking across the quadrangle toward the computer hut.

"I will teach you the history," Mateo said, seating himself on a crate inside the doorway as Nate settled back at the computer with Rafael at his side. "I will explain our cause, give you the message, and you will write it. I will tell you. You will tell the world. Make people understand. Make them care."

Nate gave him a skeptical look.

"I can tell them. I can't make them care."

"Timing is important," Mateo said, ignoring the remark. "NAFTA will probably go into effect early next year. The government will open up the Lacandon to multinational corporations. Already, they have ended communal land holdings. Once again, the giants of the world will grease the gears of their machines with the blood of poor people." He looked hard at Nate, who was staring back at him, remembering how Mateo had held forth about the suffering of los indígenas during the drive to Mirador. *I should have known then,* Nate thought.

"We must be ready," Mateo said now. "We must strike at the right time."

Nate almost laughed.

"Strike how?" he said to Mateo. "With words? With the weapons I've seen in this camp? No offense, but what kind of blow can a ragtag bunch of *campesinos* deliver?"

Mateo pulled his crate closer to Nate.

"We can resist. The people of the world will take notice."

"But—"

"They will take notice," Mateo repeated with conviction. "We will be heard. We will have a voice. People will listen. And they will see the injustice. They will want to help."

Nate shrugged. "Okay, if you say so."

Mateo sat upright.

"*Sí.* I say so." He put a fist to his heart. "*We* say so."

Mateo stood and dragged his crate over to the computer, squeezed in next to Rafael, took a folded piece of paper out of his shirt pocket and unfolded it. It was covered with handwriting. He studied it for a few moments.

"Begin with this," he said. "*Hoy decimos basta. Ya Basta.*" He looked up at Nate and translated. "Today, we say enough. Enough is enough." He tapped the paper. "Here, it is written in Spanish. You can copy it, yes?"

Nate nodded. "Rafael can help me," he said, nodding toward the boy who had been silently listening. "But what are you going to do? Declare war on the entire world?"

Mateo smiled.

"No. Just the Mexican government, the Mexican army, the paramilitaries."

"That's all, huh?"

"That is all."

"Do you want to take over the country?"

"Ha. No." Mateo frowned and shook his head vigorously. "All we want is to be at home in our own country. We are reclaiming our rights under our own constitution. We are waging a war against forgetting... against being forgotten. We fight so the world will not forget us."

Mateo looked back over his right shoulder, through the open door leading out into the compound, watched the men, women and children passing by. He turned back to Nate.

"Our cause is just," he said matter-of-factly. "You know that. This fight is our last hope, and you are part of it now. We both are." He leaned forward, forearms on thighs, hands clasped. "We did not ask to be part of it, you and I. We were brought here, both of us. God put us here, my friend."

Nate stared at the computer screen.

"I am not your friend," he said quietly.

Mateo shifted his weight, dropped his head and sighed. Nate fixed him with a harsh gaze, felt a strong urge to remind this man that it was not God who had brought him here. It had been Mateo's deception, his and the pastor's, that had sucked Nate into this war.

Mateo looked up at Nate with tired eyes, nodded and sighed.

Having made his point, Nate gazed past the man and out through the open doorway and into the life bustling in the compound, at the people who had dedicated their lives to the Zapatista cause, who were ready to die for it. The two men sat in silence for a while as Rafael sat between them, looking from one to the other.

Nate sighed. "I did an inventory," he said, pointing to a stack of large cardboard boxes in a corner of the room. "The labels on those boxes. They look like Cyrillic." He looked at Mateo. "I have to ask you. Where did you get this stuff?"

Mateo peered up at him. "Does it matter?"

"It might. Are you communists? Hell, I don't even know for sure what a communist is. But is that what you are?"

Mateo shook his head. "I know only that we are *Tzoque, Tzotzil, Tzeltal, Choles.* We are *los indígenas y los mestizos y los campesinos. Y todos somos Zapatistas.*" Mateo turned to Rafael. "*No es verdad?*"

Rafael nodded, "*Sí.*"

Mateo patted the boy's shoulder, turned his attention back to Nate.

"We are all Zapatistas. Where we get the weapons for our struggle does not matter."

Nate raised an eyebrow.

"Nothing's ever free, you know. Someday your benefactors might try to claim your country, claim your people as their own. They might just want to be the next guy that greases the wheels of his machines with your blood."

"Then we will fight them, too. We will fight anyone who tries to oppress us."

"So that will be your next revolution. A new one."

"There is never a next revolution. There is only one. The same one everywhere, all over the world, year after year. It never ends."

Nate sighed and smoothed back his hair with his hands. He leaned back in his chair, laced his fingers at the nape of his neck, and let his gaze drift, pondering Mateo's words.

"So, we're the good guys? And we're doing something heroic here?"

Mateo shook his head in exasperation. "Ahh...the good guys. *Norteños* always think in terms of good and evil. Are we the good guys? Are they the bad guys? I am afraid the world is not painted in black and white. It comes only in shades of gray. Such questions should not be asked."

Nate lowered his arms, pushed back his chair and turned it toward Mateo.

"No. You're wrong. Such questions must be asked."

He turned to Rafael, put a gentle hand on the boy's bony shoulder. "Rafael, *por favor*. We will start again tomorrow. Okay? Mateo and I need to talk."

Rafael nodded. "Okay."

When the boy was gone, Nate extended his legs, crossed them at the ankles, folded his arms across his chest and fixed Mateo with a steady gaze.

"When I was a kid, my father was very hard on my mother. He drank a lot. And when he drank, he got mean."

Mateo raised a hand and looked down, signaling Nate that he need not go on. But he did go on.

"We tried to stay out of his way when he was drunk. We'd leave the house if we could. But we couldn't always. And, then, as his drinking got worse, we never knew if he'd be coming home or not. Sometimes he didn't, which was better, actually. Other times, he'd come home in the middle of the night, and I'd lie in bed, listening to them fight. Yelling, screaming. I'd hear him say awful things to her. Awful things." He paused. "And then she'd say awful things to him. And then he'd get violent and hit her, and I'd hear her cry out and fall.... "

Mateo sat hunched over, forearms on thighs, head lowered, hands clasped.

"I'd jump out of bed and run to their bedroom and try to open the door, but it was always locked. So I'd pound on it and yell, 'Stop it! Stop it!'" Nate shook his head. "And it would stop," he said, shrugging.

"But it never really stopped. She'd get her pound of flesh the next morning, and the cycle would begin again."

Nate stared vacantly, overcome with memories. His eyes started to burn.

"I'd tell my mother that we should leave. I'd get a job. I'd take care of her, protect her." He looked at Mateo, whose head was still bowed. "But that didn't happen."

Nate shook his head

"She wouldn't leave him. Wouldn't, couldn't..." He shrugged. "One or the other." He fell silent for a few moments, inhaled and exhaled deeply. "So I finally gave up," he said, "and decided to just save myself."

Mateo put a hand on Nate's knee. Nate ignored it. He didn't know why he was telling Mateo all this. He'd never told it to anyone, except Sarah. He looked down, stared at his feet.

"I was a smart kid. Teachers encouraged me. I got a college scholarship. Full ride. Left home and only came back when I had to."

He fell silent again, remembering.

"First person in my family to go to college," Nate said, glancing up at Mateo, who was gazing at him with kind eyes. "My folks were proud. They really were."

He shook his head, pulled in his feet, hunched forward, forearms on thighs, head lowered, hands clasped, mirroring Mateo's posture.

"But every time I came home, my dad was drinking more, and my mother got sadder and sadder, more and more broken.... "

He stopped talking, his throat constricting, choking on a flood of grief, anger and pain. He swallowed them back down hard.

"She was always small, but she just seemed to get smaller and smaller...."

Nate took a deep breath, let it out slowly.

"And then the summer between my freshman and sophomore year in college, I had this office job at a mattress factory and I came home one day, and she wasn't in the kitchen, where she always was, so I went to look for her...." Nate took another, deeper breath. "I found her in the garage." Nate gathered himself, forced himself to continue. "She was in the car. Engine running." He looked at Mateo. "I guess she just couldn't take it anymore."

Mateo looked down and away, and for a little while there was silence. Nate was grateful for that.

"You were a boy," Mateo said, looking up with sad eyes. "You tried to save her. It was not your fault."

Nate chuffed. "Yeah. That's what everyone said. I had an older brother who'd died a few years before...."

Mateo grimaced.

"Jack," Nate said. "That's what people blamed it on. They said she never got over losing Jack." He shook his head. "But I should've done something. Told someone. Gone to the cops. *Something.* But no... that's not me. I hold back. I think...." He tapped a finger to his temple. "But I don't act. I play it safe. I always have."

Nate looked down at his hands. "On the road, when we were all lined up against the bus. I thought about going for El Pitón's knife." He snorted, shook his head in disgust. "Thought about it. But I didn't do it."

"But in the jungle," Mateo said. "The *soldado*...."

"But then I froze. If you hadn't shown up...."

Nate shook his head again. "I have to be sure, you see?" He tapped a finger to his temple again. "Think before I act. I need to know I'm doing the right thing."

Nate lifted his head and looked deep into Mateo's eyes.

"So, I ask you again. Are we the good guys?"

Mateo dropped his gaze, furrowed his brow. After a long silence, Mateo looked up.

"*Sí*, Nate Hunter," Mateo said. "We are the good guys. Our cause is just. And so is yours."

Nate studied him. This large, rough man of many identities who had bashed in a soldier's skull the day before. This man he still held responsible for Sarah's death.

"How can I know what you're saying is true?"

Mateo sat up, arms straight, hands on thighs. "You cannot."

"Then why should I trust you?"

Mateo shrugged. "I cannot answer that. Only you can answer that."

The two men stared at each other.

Swear it, Nate wanted to say. *Swear before God that if I help you, I will be doing something noble. That if I pledge myself to your cause, my sins will be absolved. Swear it!* But there were no guarantees. Nate knew that now. And trying to think things through before he took action— where had that gotten him? And, what difference did it make, really? He'd lost everything when he lost Sarah. Nothing meant anything to him anymore. These people, on the other hand, were willing to die for something they believed in. They needed him. He could help them. It was something. It was all he had.

Mateo waited, watching Nate wrestle with his thoughts.

"And now I ask you again," Mateo said finally. "Will you help us? Will you see this through?"

Nate sat up, hands on thighs, again mirroring Mateo's posture. He looked around the room, out into the compound, back at Mateo. Sarah would have been all in, he thought. Sarah, who was always so quick to act, to speak up, to speak out against injustice. Nate sighed. This wasn't his fight. These weren't his people. But one of the people they were fighting had killed his wife.

"Yes," he said. "I'll help. As I said before. Until El Pitón is dead. For as long as that takes." He fixed Mateo with a steely gaze. "And then...."

Mateo nodded.

CHAPTER 22

Transfiguration

In the days to come, Nate and Mateo would talk regularly—about the cause, about computers, about the absence of seasons in the jungle. They shared meals, strolled the compound at dawn and dusk, spent hours in the computer room, usually accompanied by Rafael, uploading images, writing content, crafting the website. They became more than comrades in arms, but less than friends. *No, not friends*, Nate thought. More like close associates who regarded each other with equal measures of respect and reserve. Still, to Nate's surprise, he sometimes found himself interacting with Mateo as if he had no reason not to be friends with the man, no reason not to trust him. Found himself sometimes briefly forgetting the deception that had brought him and Sarah to Chiapas, and cost Sarah her life.

Little by little, day by day, Nate fell in with the life and rhythms of La Libertad and began adapting to the rebel way of life. Conditions were Spartan but not primitive. There were, for example, working latrines. A campesino named Gustavo, a plumber and a carpenter, had constructed pit toilets with hinged wooden seats—one group of three for men, another for women—complete with plywood walls, plank doors and inside hooks and latches for privacy. Nearby, he had also built three camp showers, separated and shielded by hanging tarps. Each featured a galvanized steel tub of water positioned high atop a tall trestle to take advantage of solar heating, and a garden hose equipped with an in-line ball valve running from a bunghole near the bottom of the tub to a showerhead made of a perforated fruit can. Men and women could shave and wash up at the six enameled washbasins set in the long, waist-high wooden washstand and could wash clothing at the camp's laundry: four tubs set up on wrought iron stands over open wood fire—two for washing, two for rinsing—and two clotheslines for drying. Nothing was fancy. Everything served a purpose. There was even a small one-room library—"*La biblioteca*," Rafael translated—containing mostly Spanish-language children's books but also a few novels and nonfiction books in English and Spanish. Before long, Nate started wondering why anyone needed anything more.

Everyone worked at La Libertad. Children and adults all had their assigned tasks and were expected to pitch in wherever help was needed. Nate worked in the computer room and began taking on other chores—drawing water from the well for Lourdes, helping a campesino named Severino feed and tend the livestock, practicing Spanish with Rafael, teaching the boy about computers and the Internet.

"He learns fast," Nate said to Mateo one afternoon as the two watched Rafael sitting in front of the computer, one hand poised over the mouse, totally engrossed in something he was reading on the screen.

"He is a bright boy," Mateo responded. "Tatic was teaching him. Now it is your turn, eh?"

Nate thought about this lying on his cot that night, slapping at mosquitoes. Maybe it was his turn, even his responsibility. Maybe he had more reason to be here than he had thought. The Internet was still in its infancy pretty much everywhere, Nate knew—even in the United States. Yet here he was, in a rebel hideout somewhere deep in the Lacandon Jungle, teaching a bright young boy about the reach and power of this new technology and helping a ragtag group of revolutionaries prepare to use it to call attention to their cause. It was a powerful weapon to hand them for waging a war against forgetting. Nate began to wonder if ending up in this place at this time under these circumstances was his destiny, if maybe this was the work he was meant to do. He didn't sugarcoat his circumstances or lie to himself about how he'd ended up here or the consequences of the choice he made to adopt the Zapatista cause. People would die in this fight. Already had. The bloody encounter in the jungle was still fresh in his mind. And grief and guilt over Sarah's murder continued to dog him. But staying busy with chores and computer work helped with that. When painful images and feelings did threaten to overtake him, he was getting better at hazing them into a remote corner of his mind and locking them in. They weren't erased or banished. He didn't kid himself about that. They were still there, he knew, skulking and brooding like a madman locked in the basement, waiting to break loose.

As days turned into weeks and the residents of La Libertad realized that the *Norteño* was there to stay, Nate was given more responsibilities. He started taking his turn standing watch on the fortress wall. He went on missions outside the walls with other men to gather firewood. From time to time he saw a detail of men leave the compound with a string of pack burros outfitted with empty panniers. They would return a few days later, with panniers filled with an argosy of food, toiletries, textiles, tools, and other supplies. Did the men go all the way to Mirador? To some other closer village? Was there a land route? Or were they meeting supply boats on the river? Nate didn't know and didn't probe. Nor did he ask to join a run. He was content to remain where he was, and this surprised him. He began to realize that he enjoyed his physical labors around camp as much as his mental labors in the computer room. There was something liberating about hauling water for Lourdes, helping Gustavo with repairs, helping Severino tend the animals, hauling buckets of feed and water, cleaning out pens.

Sometimes, as Nate went about his chores, he caught sight of Quina. Walking across the quadrangle with a group of women. Drawing water at the well. Brushing her hair outside her quarters, sitting with Mirasol, books in their laps, surrounded by children. Eating at a cookfire in the evening, often with Oscar at her side. Were they a couple? It seemed to Nate that Oscar might be interested in Quina, which made sense. She was a beautiful woman. But there was nothing in Quina's manner to suggest she was interested in Oscar. Sometimes she would glance up and see Nate watching her. Their eyes would meet for a moment, and Nate would feel something stir inside him. And then Quina would immediately drop her gaze or turn away.

Nate's skin darkened under the searing sun. His hair lightened. His hands became rough from his labors. He grew stronger and more resilient. Went hours sometimes without thinking about the soldier in the jungle... or Sarah. Caught himself whistling one day as he cleaned the stalls. He hadn't whistled since he was a teenager, when he'd go for long walks through the fields around his house, just to get away. Jungle heat and humidity no longer felt oppressive, and he came to think of the scorching sun as more friend than foe, as a source of energy for growing food, hot showers, and powering the computer and satellite phone. Being in La Libertad, surrounded by jungle, with no clear fix on his location no longer filled him with a sense of lostness and uncenteredness. Now, he savored the isolation and concealment that allowed him to do his work, the long stretches of peace and silence that had been so hard to come by in his old life, at his old job. The conditions that had felt stressful and burdensome now seemed advantageous. Nothing to disturb or distract.

In Nate's homeland north of the Rio Grande, he knew, the season would soon be changing. The air would chill. Leaves would turn red and gold and fall to the ground to be swept up by the wind into brittle swirls and corner piles. But, except for periods of more intense rains, the jungle had no seasons. It remained the variegated greens of the lush vegetation that threatened constantly to devour every manmade structure within it. In the jungle, there was only an endless stretch of hot, humid days filled with work and preparations for war.

Every day in the computer hut, with Rafael at his side, Nate took a form of dictation on the computer, typing notes as Mateo talked to him about the Zapatista cause—*la causa*—and the struggle against oppression—*la lucha*—and the message—*el mensaje*—he wanted Nate to communicate to the world. In these long, slow days of talking and listening, questioning and arguing, learning and thinking, living with these members of the rebel army and getting a deeper sense of their strength and courage, their richness of spirit, *la causa* began to find its way into Nate's empty, aching heart and take root there. *They have so little*, Nate found himself thinking. *And they are asking for so little. Just a little respect and recognition. A little fairness. The right to work their land and feed their families and live in peace. And still they have to fight. Even for that.* Sarah wouldn't have stood for it, Nate knew. *She would have been so angry.* He could see her, feel her anger, and her anger became his. The injustice, once he began to see it, understand it, was too appalling not to get angry. It was so obscenely extreme, so entrenched. Every person in the camp, it seemed—man and woman, old and young— had a story to tell, or a story Mateo told for them, of land being seized, crops being destroyed, livestock being stolen, husbands and sons and fathers being taken away and found dead days later or never found at all, clinics being bombed, schools set on fire, soldados and paramilitaristas descending on villages, firing rifles into people's homes.

And now, with NAFTA, it will get worse, Nate thought. *And no one will know or care. Unless we make them care. Mateo is right. The world needs to know.*

And so Nate took up *la causa,* and joined *la lucha,* became an Internet warrior. The gringo from a land most of the rebels had never seen and never would visit would help them make their cry of *Basta!* heard throughout Mexico and possibly around the world.

Why not? Nate thought. *Why the hell not?* Their cause was just. Mateo was right about that. Nate had the skills. And he had nothing, absolutely nothing, to lose.

Little by little, Nate found himself looking forward to his sessions with Mateo, enjoying the exchange of ideas and, eventually, the sharing of skills. Mateo was an educated man, after all. He grasped the power of the Internet. So it was inevitable, as Mateo saw Nate teaching Rafael, that he would ask Nate to instruct him, too. That meant spending even more time together in the computer hut with Nate now in the position of educator. Mateo didn't catch on as quickly as young Rafael did. But he was determined, tireless, and always quick to laugh at himself and encourage Nate and Rafael to laugh with him when he made mistakes. He also made sure Nate knew how much he valued Nate's expertise and instruction. Never once did he leave the hut after a lesson without saying, "*Gracias,* Nate Hunter. We are fortunate to have you here." These repeated expressions of appreciation and respect got to Nate, began eroding his anger and distrust, like the slow, steady flow of a river carving a channel through stone. Despite himself, without willing it, Nate felt a subtle bond begin to form between himself and Mateo. He felt them becoming friends, after a fashion.

Nate and Rafael were becoming all but inseparable. They spent hours together in the computer hut, and Rafael often sat beside Nate during meals. After waking up one morning to find Rafael curled up asleep on the floor in Nate's tiny room, Nate squeezed another cot into his cubicle, and now the two spent most nights as bunkmates.

The fact that Mateo and Rafael both spoke English made Nate's work inside the computer hut that much easier. Outside the hut, his lack of language skills was a serious handicap, and he collapsed on his cot night after night with his head throbbing from trying to communicate and understand. But he kept at it and his efforts began to pay off. Listening to Mateo and Rafael talk in Spanish and Tzotzil and asking them to translate, walking and talking with Mateo in the mornings and evenings, standing nearby as Mateo conversed with the other men in camp, sitting at Lourdes's cookfire and asking her how to say things in her language, trying to ask questions, understand instructions and return greetings as he went about his chores.... Nate's language skills improved, slowly at first and then more swiftly. With the help of a camp full of patient and willing teachers, and always following Mateo's example of laughing at his own mistakes, Nate's everyday speech morphed from mostly English with a smattering of Spanish to a nonstandard blend of three tongues, a provincial patois that transcended borders, class, and time.

Sometimes, when Nate saw Mirasol sitting at a table with a youngster, reading a Spanish-language book, he would ask to join the lesson and was always welcomed. He never did that with Quina, though. He never approached her.

Sometimes he wouldn't see her for a week or more. And then, there she'd be, sitting at a table with a group of children, carrying water from the well, helping Lourdes or another old woman named Tulita cook and carry food to the elders in the camp. Their eyes caught often, and each time, Nate felt a vague stirring. Then he or Quina would look away.

Sitting with Mateo at Lourdes's cookfire in the evening, Nate sometimes watched Quina having her evening meal at Tulita's fire. When Oscar was around, which he sometimes was and sometimes wasn't, he would appear and take a place next to Quina—without asking, Nate noticed. When Quina was busy helping Tulita or Lourdes prepare meals, Oscar would sit with Mateo, and Nate would watch him watch Quina, too.

One evening, as the three men sat eating together, Lourdes casually addressed Nate by the nickname she had given him.

"*Cazador,*" she said, handing him a plateful of beans.

Nate saw Oscar freeze a moment, mug halfway to his lips, smile and shake his head in amazement.

"*Gracias,* Lourdes," Nate said, accepting the plate from the old woman. "*Kolaval.* But please. *Abokoluk. Ja'jbi* Nate. Call me Nate."

Lourdes shrugged, and Nate saw Oscar shake his head again. He didn't blame the man. The name Lourdes had given him carried with it an implication of boldness that made Nate uncomfortable, given what Oscar, Mateo and Nate all knew about his performance in the jungle... and what he and Mateo also knew about the way Sarah had died. Some of the other residents of La Libertad had picked up on the nickname and occasionally used it, too, but when they did, Nate lowered his gaze and walked on as if he didn't recognize it. He did not want to encourage any misconception that he considered himself more than the most ordinary of men, for he knew now with perfect assurance that he was not. He had certain skills that had a certain value, but so did everyone else in camp. Everyone contributed. Everyone played a role. Nate was nothing special, nothing special at all.

Preparations for war proceeded apace. Every day, on his way to and from the computer hut, fetching water from the well or feeding the livestock, standing watch or gathering firewood, Nate witnessed the seriousness of that effort. Every day, an assigned detail cleaned and oiled weapons in a tireless effort to guard them against the ravages of rust brought on by heat and humidity, while another contingent augmented the army's arsenal with homemade weapons: booby traps and incendiary devices. Land mines made from fertilizer. Nail grenades. Pipe bombs. Glass bottles of gasoline stoppered with rags.

Every morning, brothers and sisters in arms, young and old, Quina often among them, some carrying rifles, some carrying sharpened bamboo stalks, formed ranks at the command of their chosen leaders to practice exercises and drills. Push-ups. Sit-ups. Marching, running with heavy packs. Negotiating an improvised obstacle course. Hand-to-hand combat. Disassembling and reassembling their rifles. Proper shooting stance—prone, kneeling, standing—proper sight picture. All to the shouts and imprecations of their leaders. "*Más rapido! Más rapido! Carajo! Maldita sea!*" Little by little, day by day, Nate saw the ragtag bunch of rebels transform itself into a trained and disciplined army, prepared for war.

Each day, while the fighters trained and other camp residents tended the arsenal, still others—mostly old women and mothers with small children—sat in sewing circles on the ground, stitching and mending clothes for their fighting ranks. They made simple uniforms—shirts and trousers—out of coarse brown fabric, altered and patched cast-off or stolen army fatigues. They sewed red bandanas for the rebels to tie around their foreheads, over their mouths and noses, around their necks. Soon, all the men, women and children in the camp were wearing and using these versatile red scarves. Nate wore one, too.

The population of La Libertad was both stable and fluid. Nate counted a core group of more than one hundred men, women and children, including five infants born in camp, one a month after Nate arrived. Other people came, they stayed, they left, they returned.

"Where does all this stuff come from?" Nate asked Mateo one afternoon as they watched Sebastiano and another young man named Fulgencio, just back from a supply run, unpacking boxes of nails, bags of fertilizer, bolts of cloth and other goods from their burros' panniers.

"We have friends," Mateo said.

"In Mirador?"

Mateo nodded. "And other places."

"That's what you were. A friend."

Mateo nodded. "*Sí.*"

"And Tatic?"

Mateo didn't answer.

"Oscar comes and goes a lot," Nate said. "Is he the main contact?"

Mateo raised an eyebrow. "You are observant, Nate Hunter."

Nate shrugged. "I just know what I see."

"He is a good man," Mateo said. "One of our best men."

"And those two?" Nate said, nodding toward Sebastiano and Fulgencio.

Mateo turned to him. "We need eyes and ears. We need messengers. Sebastiano and Fulgencio, they have big eyes and big ears. *Ven todo. Oyen todo.* And they are discreet. *Entiendes?*"

Nate nodded again.

"They are cousins, those two. Lourdes delivered them both. They are greatly trusted."

"And Quina?"

Mateo frowned. "What about Quina?"

"I don't know. She disappears sometimes, too."

Mateo was quiet a moment. Then he smiled and patted Nate on the shoulder. "Come," he said. "We will help them unload."

Taking a break from the computer hut the next afternoon to stretch his legs, Nate heard the panicked squealing of a pig coming from a shady corner of the compound. Investigating, he found a heavily whiskered, white-haired old man named Guillermo preparing to slit the pig's throat. When the deed was done, he hung the pig by its hind legs, trussed up between two bamboo stanchions, with a pan under it to catch the blood. Nate thought Guillermo was bleeding the animal for some reason before cooking it. Instead, Guillermo strained the coagulating fluid through a cloth into another container, mixed it with gasoline, added salt, stirred, and poured some of the gel into an empty, dark glass bottle. As Nate watched, Guillermo stoppered the bottle with a rag fuse and carefully laid it on a thick blanket.

"*Qué haces?*" Nate asked in his now more-than-passable Spanish as the old man reached for a second empty bottle.

Guillermo looked up and grinned. "Napalm."

"Napalm?" Nate repeated, unsure he had heard right.

Guillermo nodded and grinned again. "*Sí. Estoy haciendo* napalm."

"Napalm," Nate muttered to himself as he walked away. "Homemade napalm. Amazing."

Lying on his cot that night, staring into blackness with Rafael asleep on the cot beside him, Nate found himself thinking about guns. He had never cared much for guns. Had never owned one. Had done a little target shooting as a kid with a favorite uncle, but that was all. Now, though, after weeks of watching the Zapatistas practice with their weapon—taking them apart and putting them back together—*más rapido! más rapido!*—loading and unloading them, falling to the ground on command and taking quick aim at distant targets—and after seeing how cool, competent and proficient even Quina and some of the other women were with their weapons, Nate began to think that maybe it was irresponsible of him not to learn how to use a gun, too. What if the army patrol returned? What if they found the camp this time? He wasn't sure he could shoot another human being to save his own life. Probably not. But what if a soldier threatened to kill Mateo? Or Lourdes? Or Rafael?

And then, there was El Pitón. The murderer, the monster, who had shot Sarah in the head in cold blood. Given the chance, could he point a gun at the man's head or heart and pull the trigger? He was not sure. He hoped so, but he didn't know. The only thing he did know was that he needed to be ready if and when the opportunity came.

"I want to learn to shoot," Nate announced to Mateo as they sat at a table eating breakfast the next morning.

Mateo stopped chewing his tortilla and raised two bushy eyebrows. "You?" he said.

"Yes. Me."

"*Por qué?*"

Nate looked down into his coffee mug, swirled the dark dregs inside. "In case."

Mateo studied him. "*Estás seguro?*"

Nate was silent a moment. "Yeah."

Mateo stared at him, nodded. "*Bién.* Perhaps we will hunt, Nate Hunter." He smiled. "*Cazaremos, El—*"

A sharp warning look from Nate silenced him.

Nate's training started the next morning. Mateo began by having Nate simply hold an M1 Garand rifle and a 1911 U.S. Army .45 automatic pistol, to get a feel for their weight and balance. Then, putting him through the same basic training as other new recruits, he taught Nate how to load and unload both guns, how to carry them, how to clean them, how to field strip the rifle, tear down the pistol, and put them back together.

"You must know your gun by feel," Mateo told Nate. "You must be able to assemble and load it in the dark. You must know how to take care of it so it can take care of you."

They progressed from there to aiming and firing: proper stance; proper sight picture; how to draw a fine bead on a target; how to squeeze—not jerk—the trigger; how to aim quickly and shoot from any position—on his belly, dropping and rolling, on the run.

To save ammunition, Nate began, like all trainees, by dry firing at hand-drawn targets nailed to tree trunks and hay bales, and at empty cans tossed in the air. The next step was shooting real bullets during practice sessions held far from camp in case the sound of gunfire attracted attention. Mateo proved a good teacher, and, to Nate's surprise, he made a good student. Once he got past his initial distaste of guns and accustomed himself to the report and recoil of the weapons, he learned swiftly and well. He was amazed at how ably he acquired the new skill and how much he enjoyed it.

"You have a gift," Mateo said, clamping a hand on Nate's shoulder on their walk back to the compound after a training session. "Perhaps you really are—"

"Don't," Nate cut him off.

Mateo put his hands up in a placatory gesture and walked on, taking the lead through the brush.

"You sit too much," Mateo said suddenly over his shoulder to Nate.

"What?"

"You sit too much. If you are going to help us, you must stay strong."

Nate laughed. "You want me to start exercising? Is that what you're saying? Doing push-ups and sit-ups? Running with a pack on my back?"

"It would not hurt you," Mateo said gruffly.

Nate took the measure of Mateo's broad shoulders and back as they continued walking single file. *He's serious,* Nate thought.

They walked on.

"I can teach you other things, too," Mateo said after a while.

"Like what?" Nate asked distractedly, concentrating on where he was stepping.

Mateo turned to face him. "Other ways to fight."

Nate stopped and regarded his instructor.

"Like what?"

"How to wrap a wire around a man's throat," Mateo said coolly, grasping his own throat between thumb and forefinger. "How to put a knife blade here," he said, turning his head and tapping a finger to the base of his skull. He snapped his fingers. *"Muñeca de trapo."*

"What does that mean?"

"Rag doll."

Nate looked down at his feet, nodding, thinking, stepped around Mateo to take the lead position.

"Thanks," he said. "I'll think about it."

The next day, instead of heading out again for target practice, Nate and Mateo scouted higher up the ridge for backup satellite phone reception sites and began testing communication with another camp that had recently acquired a phone.

"So, how many camps are there?" Nate asked Mateo as they trudged back down the ridge after a brief and staticky but successful call to the other outpost.

"Enough," Mateo said. He glanced at Nate.

"We may need your help setting up phones at some of them," he said. "Would you be willing to do that? Would you be willing to travel?"

The question took Nate by surprise. Leave La Libertad? The thought hadn't occurred to him since... well, not for a while. And that realization surprised him, too.

Nate hesitated.

"Travel where? When?" He looked at Mateo. "With whom?"

Mateo waved away his questions. *"No sé,"* he said. "I do not know yet." He turned to Nate. "But when I do know, will you go? Will you help us?"

Nate frowned, his cautious instincts kicking in. He had told Mateo he would help. But he hadn't signed on to go traipsing through the jungle, making housecalls at other camps. He didn't want to say no outright. But he didn't want to say yes, either.

"When you know, ask me again," he said. "I'll have to think about it. Maybe. We'll see."

Mateo frowned, started to say something, then stopped himself. "Of course," he said, nodding. "We will see."

The satellite dish went back on the roof of the computer hut, and Nate and Mateo went back to work, creating documents and manifestos to put up on the website when it launched.

"You say you must be ready," Nate said to Mateo a few days later as Nate sat in a corner of the hut, watching Mateo at the computer, typing swiftly with two fingers. "You say the rebels must strike at the right time. But when is that? Do you even know?"

"Soon," Mateo said, his eyes never leaving the keyboard. "Soon now."

"So you do know."

Mateo didn't answer, kept typing.

"But you are not going to tell me."

Mateo kept typing.

"When it is time," Mateo said, finally, "you will know."

Nate thought about Mateo's response and realized he was okay with it, which also surprised him. Normally, he didn't like being kept in the dark. He was by nature a gatherer of facts and information, someone who liked to get the lay of the land and consider his options before making a move. But what did he really need to know that he didn't know already? A date, that's all. Everything else seemed clear. The rebels' cause was just. Nate was convinced of that now. But how many of them were there? And how well trained, armed, and coordinated could they possibly be? Watching Mateo type, brow furrowed in concentration, Nate felt a wave of sadness wash over him. *They will be crushed,* he thought. *Surely, they know that. Many will die. They must know that, too.* To be willing to die for a cause.... Nate shook his head. He understood that he might die in the fighting, too. But it wouldn't be from any act of courage. He had no more delusions about that.

Most likely, it would simply be a matter of wrong place, wrong time. The best he could hope for, he figured, was that he didn't die a coward. But what if he did? Who would know? Who would care?

Nate was now in the habit of leaving Rafael in charge of the computer hut when he was away from camp. The boy was a natural with computers, loved exploring the Internet and was always careful to straighten up and shut everything down before leaving. Returning from weapons training one afternoon a few days after his conversation with Mateo, Nate found Rafael in the hut, as expected, sitting at the monitor, staring at the screen.

"Rafael, *vén*," Nate called from the doorway. "Time to wash up for dinner."

The boy did not answer or even acknowledge Nate's presence. His eyes remained glued to the monitor, hand fastened to the mouse.

"Rafael, *vén*."

Again the boy did not respond.

Strange.

"Rafael, *qué pasa*?" Nate said, entering the room. "*Hay una problema?*"

Stepping behind Rafael to check the computer screen, Nate saw what had the boy entranced. Rafael had stumbled on a photograph of a young Asian man sitting on a bench in an office or clinic, smiling. He wore shorts and a long sleeve shirt. He was missing a leg. Another young man sat on a chair in front of him, also smiling, holding a prosthetic leg at an angle for the young man on the bench to try on.

"Ahh," Nate said.

He laid a hand on Rafael's shoulder and knelt at his side.

"One day you will have one."

Rafael looked at him.

"*Un día*," Nate said, pointing to the screen.

Rafael's expression was solemn.

"*Sí? Verdad?*"

"*Sí*," Nate said. "*Te prometo.*" Nate rose. "Now come. Time to eat."

After being gone for more than a week, Oscar reappeared in the camp and reclaimed his spot next to Quina at Tulita's cookfire. Glancing back toward Mateo as he spoke to her one evening, he caught Nate watching the two of them and held Nate's gaze with cold eyes until Nate looked away.

When Oscar joined Mateo at Lourdes's cookfire a few nights later, he didn't speak a word to Nate, except to snicker under his breath when Lourdes again addressed Nate as *"Cazador."*

Nate didn't care. He and Oscar had never become friendly. The man would greet him when they encountered each other as they went about their chores, but he seemed to veer off when he could to avoid encounters and often broke off talking to Mateo and walked away with a frown when he saw Nate approaching. If Oscar needed to speak with Mateo when Mateo was in the computer hut, he would beckon from the doorway, but he never came inside. It was clear to Nate that the man chose not to associate with him, had no interest in the work Nate and Mateo were doing in the hut, and had moved past being grateful to Nate for clubbing the soldier who had almost killed him to feeling something more like scorn that Nate hadn't seen the bloody business through.

Heading toward the computer hut one morning a few days after Oscar's return, Nate saw Mateo and Oscar standing near the doorway, backs turned to him, having a heated argument. Nate stopped a few paces off, waiting for them to move away so he could get back to work.

"Basta!" he heard Mateo bark at Oscar, raising a hand to cut him off. "He saved your life!"

They were arguing about him.

"No!" Oscar retorted angrily. *"You* saved my life! *El habría dejado que el soldado me matara. Es un cobarde!"*

Nate stood stock-still.

"Basta!" Mateo growled. *"No más!"* With an angry wave of a hand, he turned to stalk off, saw Nate, shook his head and walked past him. Turning to follow, Oscar also spotted Nate and wheeled off in a different direction. Nate watched him go, absorbing and thinking about what he'd just heard and seen. He should have felt insulted, but he didn't. What Oscar had said was true. Nate might have let the soldier kill him. If Mateo hadn't arrived, Nate might also have been killed. Oscar was right to question his courage. If Mateo was half the natural-born leader he seemed to be, he should be having doubts, too.

Oscar was also right to be suspicious of the way he'd caught Nate watching him and Quina. The man had good instincts, Nate had to give him that. For it was true that during his weeks and months at camp, Nate had become increasingly aware of Quina's presence.

Found himself searching for her when he didn't see her, following her when she reappeared. Not literally. He never approached her, didn't even speak to her. It was more the feelings she stirred inside him—a dull ache, like a hunger, when he didn't see her; a warmth, like a fullness, when he did. The way she moved, her form and face, her dark eyes and great mass of dark hair. Watching her help Tulita or Lourdes at their cookfires, practicing drills with other trainees, drawing water from the well, reading and playing games with the children, walking and laughing with Mirasol, standing in the doorway of her room in the morning, brushing and braiding her mane of glossy hair. . . . All of it gave him pleasure.

She was a puzzle to him—a beautiful mysterious puzzle. Sometimes, he'd see her in jeans and a white muslin blouse, hair pulled back in a sleek pony tail, looking like the kind of attractive, sophisticated Latina he used to see every day in downtown Dallas. Other times, were she not taller and more shapely than most of her female comrades, her face more beautiful, her hair more lustrous, Nate would have had trouble picking her out from the other women in her standard-issue green fatigue pants and shirt, red bandana, and long braids. And then every now and then, not often, she'd appear in the evening in traditional Indian dress—dark wool skirt, embroidered huipil, purple rebozo around her shoulders, hair plaited and coiled at the nape of her neck. Why, he had no idea. Always, though, no matter what she wore, she had the look and manner of a woman who knew something of the world, who had seen more of it than most of the other men and women in camp.

Nate was finding it more and more difficult to take his eyes off Quina. Even when she caught him looking—was it his imagination or were their eyes meeting more often? Even when Oscar and Mateo and Lourdes and Rafael caught him looking, too. At night, as he drifted off to sleep, he often found himself thinking of her instead of Sarah. Quina's eyes, her laugh, her physical grace, the sway of her long black hair as she walked when she wore it loose down her back. All this was becoming more vivid to him than the fading memory of his dead wife. . . and that worried Nate. *Sarah.* Quina was not Sarah. Nate loved Sarah. He'd conjure her face, her golden hair, her emerald eyes. But as he drifted off to sleep, Sarah's face would fade and Nate would see Quina's face. He would wake the next morning deeply troubled.

The thought that he might be developing feelings for another woman distressed him. The prospect of being untrue, even in his imagination, weighed on his soul.

One quiet evening after dinner, Nate and Mateo strolled over to the corral, where the camp's small herd of burros, a few mules, and two sturdy horses—one gray, one brown—were feasting on hay and grain. The men leaned up against the fence, rested their crossed arms on the topmost rail, and studied the dutiful equines in the muted light that precedes full darkness. Mateo pointed toward the horses.

"They started in North America, you know."

"Oh, yeah?" Nate said. "I thought the Spanish brought them over."

"They did. But before that, long before, *el caballo* originated in North America. Then it spread to other places and disappeared here. Then the Spanish brought it back."

"Hunh," Nate said. "I didn't know that."

Side by side, the two men lost themselves in contemplating the beautiful beasts, their shapely heads, large dark eyes, powerful shoulders and backs, sleek coats.

"Severino says *los caballos* know more than we do," Mateo said, breaking the comfortable silence. "He says they think less, but understand more. Perhaps, he is right."

Mateo pointed to the gray horse.

"He understands death. I sense that. It is in his nature to understand it. But he has no dread."

"Is he a born hero?" Nate asked. "Born brave?"

"No. He is not a hero, not a coward. He is what he is. He does what he must."

Nate nodded. "He doesn't have to worry about right and wrong, good and evil. He doesn't wonder if there's a God."

"Perhaps he knows without asking."

"Maybe," Nate said, watching the two horses peacefully munching their dinner, lifting and turning their heads occasionally to give Nate and Mateo an indifferent look. "You have to wonder what else they know. Do they worry about the future? Do they remember the past? Do they blame themselves for anything? Have hopes and fears?"

Mateo shrugged.

"*Quién sabe*? Maybe they are simply at peace with their god."

Nate turned to rest his back against the fence and saw Quina across the quadrangle, helping Lourdes and Tulita clean up after the evening meal.

"Ahh... she is beautiful, no?" Mateo said, turning and tracking where Nate's gaze was focused. Mateo smiled. "It is no secret here that she has caught your eye."

Oh, great, Nate thought. *It's that obvious.* Disconcerted, he started to deny it, but stopped himself. It was true. Why lie?

"Is she with Oscar?"

Mateo gurgled a fragment of a laugh that didn't make it out of his throat, shook his head.

"No. No. He dreams of it." Mateo shot him a warning look. "And he is jealous. But she is not with him, no. She is with no one. She has a heavy heart. But who in Chiapas does not have a heavy heart? She says she wants nothing to do with men."

Mateo paused.

"But one can never know about such things. Tatic always says, '*Cuando una puerta se cierra, otra se abre.*' When one door closes, another opens." He gave Nate a probing look, but Nate ignored it.

"There's something different about her," Nate said.

Mateo nodded. "She is educated," he said.

"It's more than that."

The two men watched Quina and Tulita working quietly together.

"She has suffered," Mateo said. "After her husband died, she came to see Tatic. For many days she came to sit with him. They would talk and pray together. Then she started helping Tatic and Lourdes around the rectory, cooking, running errands, whatever needed doing.

"Did she live there?"

"No, no. Only Lourdes and Rafael."

Nate was silent a moment.

"How did her husband die?"

Mateo frowned and stared at the ground. He looked up at Nate.

"Quina is a very private person," he said. "Even at the rectory, she kept to herself. She speaks to Tatic and Lourdes, and a little to me, but only because she knows we will protect her privacy. *Entiendes?*"

Nate nodded.

"Perhaps someday she will feel she can talk to you, too," Mateo said. "I think you would like that, no?"

Nate didn't answer.

"Yes, I think so," Mateo said, gently teasing. "I can see it in your eyes."

With a lazy sweep of his hand, Mateo pointed to his own dark eyes, then at Nate's lighter brown ones.

"*Los ojos son el espejo del alma.*"

Nate smiled and nodded. "The eyes are the. . . something. . . of the soul."

"Mirror," Mateo said. "The eyes are the mirror of the soul." He smiled. "*Muy bien,* my friend. You are learning quickly."

With that, Mateo gave Nate's shoulder a heavy pat and took his leave. Nate stood alone, leaning against the fence, elbows resting on the top rail, letting darkness fall around him, reflecting on what Mateo had just said and wondering how much was visible in his eyes. If he looked in a mirror, would he see what others saw? He pulled a hand across the two days of growth on his cheeks and chin. Maybe he should stop shaving so he wouldn't have to look in a mirror again. He wasn't sure he wanted to see what his reflection might reveal.

Nate searched the deepening darkness for Quina. Like an apparition, she had disappeared, and in the next instant the blackness of night enveloped him. A sudden cool breeze brushed his neck and prickled his skin. Shivering a bit, he folded his arms across his chest and headed to his room. Halfway across the square, he felt a tremor in his legs, and a wave of weakness washed through his entire body.

Not again.

The first time it had happened, four days earlier, Nate had shrugged it off. The second time, two days later, he had tried to ignore it, but it had left him a little spooked. He knew about mosquito-borne diseases. He and Sarah had started taking malaria pills before heading to Mirador, but he'd thrown them away after bringing her home.

The trembling and weakness came at him again, this time full bore. Nate stumbled into his room an collapsed on his cot. ▲

CHAPTER 23

Lost Days

Infirmity came down hard almost as soon as Nate's head hit his pillow. From perfidious jungle darkness, the skulking malady descended. Stretched out on his cot, diamond-patterned blanket pulled over him up to his chin, Nate shivered uncontrollably, teeth chattering, freezing cold and ablaze with fever at the same time. He moaned and whimpered like a motherless child.

Nate heard Rafael shift in his squeaky cot, sit up, and call his name softly. *"Señor Nate?"* When Nate didn't answer, couldn't answer, the boy leaned close and touched his shoulder.

"Señor Nate," he pleaded through the darkness. *"Está bien?"*

"N-n-n-no, I'm sick," Nate managed in a hoarse whisper. "I'm s-s-sick." Struggling hard to speak, he managed one more lockjawed word: "M-m-m-mateo."

The next time Nate opened his eyes, Mateo was leaning over him in the darkness. Then Mateo's face became the face of Lourdes. He felt a leathery hand on his brow, then on his chest. Heard soft talking, what sounded like praying. Felt the shock of cool, wet rags on his forehead, a hand behind his neck, lifting his head. Water brought to his lips. Something else, some bitter concoction. Indistinct faces appeared, disappeared, shifting, changing. Mateo. Lourdes. Quina. Smoke. Incense. Chants and singing. The old woman's hands waving above him.

A short time later, Nate felt someone removing his clothing, smudging a tarry substance on his face and chest. He felt himself being lifted in strong arms, carried and gently laid down somewhere. A small, dark cave. Thick steam. Searing heat. Rocks glowing and hissing, hot fog scented with eucalyptus. He saw Quina. She was naked, face and body shimmering, skin glistening. She was whisking him with palm fronds, whisking her own back and breasts. And then Sarah was there. She was smiling at him. *Sarah.* Nate reached for her, caught her wrist. She pulled away, her face suddenly contorted, covered in blood. *Sarah!* Snakes hissed and slithered over him. Golden jaguar eyes stalked him. Vultures swooped down upon him, huge talons extended, tearing at his heart and lungs, ripping at his bones. A giant black crow perched on his chest, pecked at his eyes, but still he could see. The crow had a human face. Oscar's face. El Pitón's face, half human, half demon. Hideous, distorted. Eyes bulging, mouth agape. He was laughing, jeering. *"Cobarde! Cobarde! No es nada! Nada! Nada! Nada!"*

Powerless, defenseless, unable to fight or escape his tormenters, Nate surrendered. He let go, let it all rise up and drift away, like cookfire smoke. Everything he knew, everything he was, everything he felt. Hopes, fears, beliefs. Love, hate, desire. Past, present, future. He surrendered it all, emptied himself and felt himself disintegrate, get smaller and smaller, until all that remained of him was a single cell, the primal spark of his existence. And then, the cell dissolved. The spark flickered and dimmed.

Now. Yes.

The light died. The wind swept over him and Nate Hunter disappeared. He was no more.

Nate awoke to the sounds of children playing, cookpots clanging, people talking. He opened his eyes to morning light. He was in his room, on his cot, his blanket drawn up to his chest. He tried to sit up, but couldn't. Turning his head, he saw that Rafael's cot was empty. Someone had put a rush-bottom straight-back chair next to Nate's cot and left a hand-painted clay figurine of a jaguar on the small, packing-crate night table. He tried to sit up again, fell back, dizzy, weak as water. He waited until his head cleared, took three slow, deep breaths, summoned his strength, pushed himself upright and lowered his feet to the ground. Dizzy again from the effort, he sat clutching the edge of his cot, letting his head clear. The close air in his tiny sickroom smelled of smoke. He picked up the jaguar figurine and turned it over in his trembling hands. Terracotta color, stippled with black spots and painted with large black eyes. Like the eyes in his dreams. Carefully, he returned it to the crate.

Moving slowly and ponderously, Nate pulled his blanket over his shoulders, gathered his skinny legs under him and struggled to his feet. Using the chair and the wall for support, he tottered, swathed in his blanket, to the open door and propped his long, spindly body against the jamb. Three children, playing a few feet away, looked up at him, round-eyed. They ran away.

Do I look that bad?

He rubbed his jaw, felt his sunken cheeks, the scar under his left cheekbone, and the start of a beard. He realized he had lost track of time.

How long have I been out?

Glancing up, he saw Mateo striding toward him.

"*Buenos días,*" he said. "*Lazarus se levanta de entre los muertos.*"

Nate understood enough to get the reference.

"*Vén. Siéntete,*" Mateo said, retrieving the chair from his room and helping Nate into it. Squinting in the bright light, Nate peered around the quadrangle, getting his bearings. Mateo pulled up another chair and sat down beside him.

"Was I bitten by a snake?" Nate said in a raspy whisper. The sound he made was unfamiliar to him.

Mateo smiled.

"No."

"Did I eat a snake?"

Mateo's eyebrows shot up. "Eat a snake?"

"Yes. I dreamed I ate a snake."

Mateo chuckled. "No. You drank one." He patted Nate's knee. "It is an old Mayan remedy. Lourdes prepared it. It is like a curative tea."

"Snake tea?"

"Snake powder. Made from the dried meat of a rattlesnake. *La serpiente de cascabel.*"

Nate grimaced. "I remember something that tasted terrible. That's what it was?"

"*Sí.*"

"What's it supposed to cure?"

"Oh... many things."

"For me?"

"For you, malaria."

"Malaria," Nate repeated. "That's what it was?"

"*Sí.*"

"How long have I been sick?"

Mateo frowned, counted on his fingers. "*Cinco días.*"

Nate considered that.

"I dreamed I was carried somewhere. It was like the fires of hell."

Mateo nodded. "*El temazcal.*" He pointed across the compound toward the low mud structure he had shown Nate on his first morning in La Libertad.

"The sweat lodge," Nate said.

"*Sí.* Another old Mayan cure. They call it *zumpul-ché.*" For when we are sick. In the body. . . " Mateo tapped his chest. "Or the spirit."

"Or both," Nate said.

Mateo nodded. "*Sí.* Or both."

Nate was silent for a moment. "I think I died."

Mateo shrugged. "*Quizás.* If you did, you came back."

"I saw things. People. Faces. I heard music, too. And some kind of chanting and praying."

Mateo nodded. "*Sí. Sí.*"

"That's all part of the treatment?"

"*Sí.* Sometimes. Yes."

Nate felt unexpectedly moved. "That's a lot."

Mateo nodded but made no other response.

Out near the center of the compound, Nate spotted Lourdes and Quina working around a cookfire. "I saw Quina," he said, recalling the vision of her naked form. Swell of her breasts. Nipples the color of rich earth against bronze skin. Face and body shimmering. The mysterious quality of the light.

Mateo nodded. "Yes, she was there."

"In the sweat lodge."

"*Sí.*"

"And you?"

"In the sweat lodge, no. But, yes, I was there."

"And Lourdes."

"*Sí.*"

"And Oscar? I saw his face. It turned into a mask."

Mateo chuckled. "Oscar. He does not like it that Quina helps you. He is jealous, as a man for a woman. But he also protects her, as a brother protects a sister, *entiendes*? He came to your room many times when she was with you. She would send him away, and he would get angry, but there was nothing he could do." Mateo gave Nate a warning look. "But he did not like it."

Nate nodded. "And he doesn't like me."

Mateo sighed. "Oscar is a brave man. A good soldier. But he is a man of action, not words. He has a quick temper, and he does not understand about this thing called the Internet. He does not trust it."

"And he doesn't trust me."

Mateo sighed again. "No. He does not trust you."

Nate looked at Mateo. "And you. What about you?"

The question caught Mateo off guard. He gripped his knees, remained silent for a few moments, looking pained.

"When you were sick," he said, "I asked God to forgive me. For bringing you here." He took a deep breath, let it out slowly. "For what happened to your wife. And to you."

Nate closed his eyes, lifted his face to the sun. "I saw her, too."

Mateo bowed his head. "You are a good man," he said. "You did not ask for this." He waved a hand. "For any of this." He turned to Nate. "But you are here now. And I am glad you are here." He looked Nate directly in the eye. "I am glad you did not die."

It wasn't everything Nate wanted to hear. But, for now, it was enough. He leaned back in his chair, lifted his left leg, rested the ankle on his right knee, and examined the bottom of his foot. The skin was as thick as shoe leather, burnt-orange in color. He picked at the parfleche edges, then peeled away the entire veneer in one deliberate movement. He cast it aside, like an old tire tread, exposing new skin. Unblemished, soft and fresh as a baby's.

"Would you look at that," Nate said.

He peeled the other foot.

Mateo frowned. "That is too bad, my friend. Now they will have to grow strong again." He patted Nate on the shoulder. "And *you* must grow strong again. Rest now. We will talk more soon."

Now that the crisis was past, Lourdes took charge of Nate's care, waking him from sleep that afternoon to feed him a bowl of soup. As she pulled the chair up beside his cot, Nate noticed that the hand-painted clay jaguar with the penetrating eyes was still on the table.

"*Qué es esto?*" Nate asked, gesturing weakly toward the figurine.

"Para tu protección," Lourdes answered in her deep, soothing voice.

"De tí?"

She shook her head.

"De quién, entonces?"

Lourdes looked up from the bowl in her lap, eyes twinkling. *"Su angelito guardian."*

"Rafael?"

Lourdes shook her head and smiled. *"No."*

Sitting up in bed after Lourdes had left, too tired to rise, too awake to sleep, Nate picked up the jaguar figurine and studied it. When he looked up, he saw Rafael in the doorway, watching him. Nate waved him in, but the boy shook his head and moved off and didn't return that night. He appeared in the doorway regularly the next day to look in on Nate, but Nate could not entice him to enter. *Maybe he's afraid of getting sick himself or doesn't want to disturb me,* Nate thought. He didn't know. But he let the boy be.

Days of convalescence blurred by. During the first days of his greening, as Nate slowly walked the compound, sometimes trailed by a silent, watchful Rafael, he often caught Oscar watching him with his usual pique, his eyes dark with resentment and disapproval. Nate would nod politely. He couldn't change what Oscar thought of him, and he wasn't going to waste time trying. Through the beneficence of the jaguar god or some other power, or the skill of an old *curandera* and her beautiful assistant, or purely by luck and chance, he had survived the malarial siege, and he found himself a changed man. He had endured the assault of the bone pickers and eye pluckers. He had surrendered everything, gone to the brink of annihilation, and had come back cleansed and renewed. The past was still with him, but it was a smaller part of him. Sarah was still a part of him, but Sarah was dead and Nate was alive. Now, as he concentrated on regaining his strength and coming to restored manhood, he felt no need or desire to disguise his deepening interest in the woman with the mysterious dark eyes and quiet ways, the woman of shimmering body and glistening skin, who had helped save his life. Without guilt or subterfuge, he watched her from afar. He couldn't stop thinking about her. Try as he might, he could not help himself. ▲

CHAPTER 24

Maya Blue

Resting on his cot in his darkened room or sitting in the sun outside his quarters, Nate often looked down to find that he had unthinkingly picked up the jaguar figurine and was sitting there holding it, stroking it, turning it over in his hands like worry beads or some kind of talisman or lucky charm. When Lourdes or Mateo came to check on him and saw him with it, they smiled but said nothing. Nate began to wonder if it might have come from Quina. If so, he wanted to thank her for it, and thank her for her healing ministrations during his illness. He had thanked Lourdes so often she finally grew tired of it. *"Basta,"* she said irritably, holding up a leathery hand when he expressed his gratitude yet again after she brought him a bowl of soup. He hadn't thanked Quina at all. He hoped the opportunity would present itself naturally, but Quina seemed to take such pains to avoid him when they saw each other in the compound that it never did. So, one morning about a week after emerging from his sickroom, Nate decided he could no longer leave the matter to chance. Seeing Quina sitting at a shaded table outside her room on the opposite side of the quadrangle with a pile of mending before her, he walked over. By the time she looked up, he was standing in front of her.

"Good morning," he said.

Quina eyed him coolly. *"Buenos días,"* she said.

"I just want to thank you for helping take care of me when I was so sick. *Cuándo estaba tan—"*

"No need for thanks," Quina said, cutting him off and going back to her mending.

"Well, I just—"

"It was necessary. You are the computer man. You will help us tell the world about our cause." She looked up at him. "Yes?"

"That's right."

Quina nodded and returned to her work. "That is why I helped you. We need you to do your job. We must all do our jobs. If we do not, there is no reason to be here."

Nate stiffened.

"Right," he said, mirroring Quina's brusque manner. "I build the website. You keep me alive. Simple. Makes sense."

Quina looked at him, her expression icy and unyielding. Nate felt repelled and yet still obliged to express his gratitude.

"Well, thanks just the same. You did help save my life. And I do appreciate it."

For a few moments the two gazed at each other in silence, each waiting for the other to speak. In those moments, Nate felt a warmth stir inside him and thought he detected a subtle change in Quina's expression, a slight softening. Finally, Quina nodded, a little less coolly, and went back to her sewing. Nate returned the nod, though Quina didn't see it, and left her to her work. He headed toward Lourdes's cookfire for a mug of coffee, aware of feeling oddly pleased. He took Quina's softening as a positive development. A slight but encouraging melting of the ice.

All that day and the next day and for days after that, Quina continued to keep her distance. That was okay with Nate. Despite his pleasant fragments of memory of their shared time in the sweat lodge, he understood that there was no real closeness between them. Nor was he really ready for any. He still wasn't fully recovered. He needed time to regain his strength, put himself back together, do a self-inventory of sorts—figure out which parts of the old Nate Hunter had survived his second brush with death, which had burned away, and what the fire of fever had exposed. He needed time to get some clearer sense of who he was, what kind of man he was now. But he couldn't prevent his gaze from straying in Quina's direction. Nor did he try. The warmth he'd felt after their brief exchange stayed with him, smoldering into incipient desire.

Nate was also aware of Oscar's eyes following him, Oscar watching him watch Quina, not bothering to look away or mask his displeasure when Nate caught him at it. Nate took it in stride. He could understand Oscar's devotion to Quina and his determination to protect her, whether she thought she needed protecting or not. Sarah hadn't thought she needed protecting, either. But she did. More than Nate had realized or had been able to provide. Nate did nothing to rile Oscar intentionally, but he didn't try to placate him, either. If Oscar didn't like the way he looked at Quina, that was unfortunate, but it was Oscar's misfortune, not Nate's. There was nothing Nate could do about it. Or would do.

D ay by day, Nate grew stronger. Walking the compound for exercise, eating wolfishly several times a day, he started regaining weight and muscle. His stamina increased and his mind became clearer, until, a little less than two weeks into his recovery, he finally felt ready to return to the computer room and resume the work Quina had pointedly reminded him he'd been brought there to do. No more than an hour after he'd settled himself in front of the monitor again, Rafael appeared in the doorway. This time, when Nate motioned him in, he approached cautiously and took a seat at Nate's side. It was the closest he had come to Nate since his illness, and even now, sitting beside him, the boy remained silent and withdrawn. Nate had a feeling he knew why. So, after switching on the computer and working quietly for a while, he decided to broach the subject gently.

"You're very quiet these days," he said casually, keeping his eyes on the screen. "Something on your mind?"

Rafael kept silent.

"You can tell me. Maybe I can help."

More silence.

Don't push it, Nate told himself. *He'll speak when he's ready.*

Nate concentrated on the page he was writing. Five minutes passed. Ten.

"I thought you would die," Rafael said finally, softly, staring down at his hands. "I thought you would go away."

It was as Nate thought. He heard the fear and anger in Rafael's words, and he understood. Death had visited the boy before. In an instant, an ordinary day had turned into a nightmare and the two people he loved most in the world had been taken from him. They had abandoned him. Now he had grown close to the norteamericano, and he, too, had almost died. It could happen again.

"But I didn't die," Nate said. "And I won't die. I know it now. I'm strong. And I get stronger every day. You see that, don't you?"

The boy nodded reluctantly.

Nate took his hands off the keyboard and turned to the boy, who was still looking down, wringing his small hands. He put a finger under the boy's chin and gently lifted it.

"*Mirame,* Rafael," Nate said.

Rafael looked up slowly. Nate placed his hands atop the boy's.

"I'm not going to die, Rafael. And I'm not going to leave you. *Te lo prometo.*"

Rafael looked down, then back at Nate, wanting to believe, afraid to believe. Nate saw desire and distrust warring in the boy's dark, shining eyes.

Nate smiled and turned back to the computer. "Come on, now. We have work to do."

But, of course, it was not that simple. Rafael's reawakened fears could not be assuaged that easily. That night, Rafael returned to sleep in Nate's room, but for many nights thereafter, his sleep was troubled—restless, shallow, arms and leg twitching. Some nights, he sobbed in his sleep, called out, uttered desperate pleas Nate could not understand. When Rafael's distress seemed extreme, Nate would wake him and sit with him, stroking his head—"It's okay, it's okay, *está bien, es solo un mal sueño"*—until the boy eased back into a more peaceful sleep. Imagining the horrific images that tormented the child, remembering the nightmares that had plagued Nate's own sleep for years after his own mother's death, that still tortured him about Sarah, Nate's heart broke for the boy. Nate had no choice but to begin again, earning Rafael's trust, gaining his confidence. It would take time, but Nate had plenty of time. More and more, he felt he had all the time in the world.

As Nate recovered his strength and vitality and resumed his full load of duties and chores—standing watch, helping tend livestock, hauling water and firewood—he crossed paths with Quina more often. She still kept her distance, but when their eyes met from time to time, it seemed to Nate that her expression was friendlier, a little less steely, and she held his gaze a moment longer before looking away.

Emerging from his room earlier than usual one morning, before the jungle haze had burned off, he saw Quina, in fatigue shirt and pants, crossing the quadrangle toward the well, carrying two steel buckets. Nate watched her tread carefully over the muddy ground around the well, lower one bucket, haul it up, set it down heavily, sloshing water, and begin lowering the second bucket. Without thinking, he headed over to help, as he always helped Lourdes and Tulita and the other women and girls when he saw them wrestling with heavy loads. He reached the well just as Quina set the second bucket awkwardly in the mud, spilling more water.

"Here. I'll get those," he said, stepping carefully and reaching for the buckets.

Quina slapped his hand away.

"No!"

Nate yanked his hand back.

"I was just trying to help."

"I do not need your help," Quina said angrily. "I do not need any man's help."

"All right. All right," Nate said, putting up his hands.

"Just because I helped you does not mean—"

"Hey. I didn't come over here to argue. I came to help you. You don't want my help. Fine." He waved a hand dismissively. "Forget it."

Nate turned to walk away and, irritated himself now, didn't look where he was walking, lost his footing and went down, face-first in the mud. More stunned than hurt, he lay unmoving in the cool, wet sludge like a toppled statue.

"Hey. Hey," he heard Quina call down to him. "*Está bién?*"

Slowly, Nate rose to his hands and knees, started to stand, slipped again, sat down. Looking up, he saw Quina staring down at him, a frown on her face. And then she began to laugh. She covered her mouth with a hand, but she could not stifle her amusement. Nate rubbed his face to clear his head, realizing too late that his hands were covered in mud. Which meant his face was now also covered in mud. Standing over him, Quina crossed her arms over her chest, put her head back and laughed harder. Soon, Nate was laughing, too.

Quina extended a hand and helped Nate pull himself to his feet.

"*Gracias,*" he said, wiping his hands on his trousers. He glanced at Quina, who was still giggling, eyes crinkled, a hand over her mouth. "And thanks for the laugh," he said, meaning it. "That's the first laugh I've had in a long time."

Quina took in a deep breath and let it out.

"*Yo también*," she said, nodding.

They both reached for the buckets at the same time, hesitated, and then, by unspoken agreement, each took one. Walking comfortably side by side, they carried them back to Lourdes's cookfire.

So it began. A display of clumsiness and a moment of low comedy opened the door. Quina still moved away if she saw Nate approaching, but there was something softer about her manner of leaving, and if Nate did pass close enough to wish her a "*Buenos días*" or "*Buenas tardes*," she responded in kind. Over time, this simple exchange of courteous greetings became more personalized—"*Buenos días, Quina.*" "*Buenos días,* Nate."—and went from there to an exchange of pleasantries.

"*Buenos días,* Quina. It's a beautiful morning, isn't it?"

"Good morning, Nate. *Sí, es una mañana hermosa.* Did you sleep well?"

"*Sí, gracias. Y tu?*"

Quina spoke tentatively, in clipped sentences. But for the first time, Nate was hearing her voice. Rich and tender, sweet and gentle, darkened with sorrow, but firm and resolute. The voice of a woman who had seen much, felt much.

The conversations lasted mere seconds. But they were conversations. And Nate treasured hearing the woman with the raven hair speak his name. "Nate." She called him "Nate." If Mateo or Rafael or Lourdes happened to be near when the two exchanged pleasantries, Nate would see them smile. If Oscar was near, he would scowl and turn red in the face, but say nothing. Nate didn't care, and he was pleased to see that Quina didn't seem to care, either. Clearly, she was a woman who made her own choices.

Sitting around Lourdes's cookfire one evening about two weeks after the encounter at the well, Nate reached to accept a plate of tortillas and beans from Quina. Her hand grazed his and he felt an electrical charge shoot up his arm and through his whole being. He looked up at her and their glances met, the question in his eyes answered in hers.

Did you feel that?

Yes, I felt it.

After the meal, instead of strolling the compound with Mateo as he often did, Nate let Mateo take his leave and lingered at the cookfire, sipping coffee, while Lourdes and Quina cleaned up. One by one, the other people sitting around the fire drifted away, too. All except for Oscar, who remained seated in an unspoken challenge until Quina gently dismissed him.

"*Está bien, Oscar. Gracias.*"

Oscar took a last sip of coffee, set down his cup, glowered at Nate, and left. Lourdes busied herself for a few more minutes, then rested her gnarled hands on her lap and sighed.

"*Basta. Estoy cansada.*" She reached out to Nate. "*Ayúdame, por favor.*"

Nate stood and helped the old woman to her feet.

"*Gracias, Nate Hunter.*" Lourdes still had difficulty pronouncing the name, but she had kindly stopped calling him by the nickname that embarrassed him. She brushed her skirt, front and back, smiled at the two young people. "*Buenas noches. Hasta mañana.*"

"*Buenas noches, Lourdes.*"

"*Hasta mañana.*"

Nate and Quina sat alone at the fire. For a while, neither spoke.

"I love this time of evening," Nate finally ventured. "The blue light, the sounds of the jungle, perfect sky."

Quina nodded. "It is very beautiful," she said. She lifted her face to the darkening sky, closed her eyes and smiled. "Very... peaceful."

They talked easily then, about the weather, the history of the hacienda, the close call with the army patrol.

"It's amazing they didn't find us," Nate said.

Quina nodded. "The jungle is thick," she said. "It holds many secrets."

Nate thought of the dead soldier. He wondered if Oscar had said something to Quina about the incident, if he had told her he thought Nate had behaved like a coward. Nate wasn't going to ask.

He and Quina talked about Rafael, how bright he was, how quickly he learned, his natural grasp of computer technology.

"He has a gift," Nate said. "He reminds me of myself at his age."

Quina looked at Nate gravely. "He was very frightened when you were sick."

Nate nodded. "I know. We talked a little about that. He thought I was going to die. But I told him I'm not going to die and I'm not going to leave him. I made him a promise."

Quina looked down.

"Be careful what you promise," she said softly. "We cannot know what the future will bring."

Nate nodded. "No. That's true."

They both fell silent then, stared into the dying embers of the fire.

"But I'm alive now and getting stronger each day," Nate said, smiling and sitting upright, arms straight, hands on thighs, turning away from his own dark thoughts and hoping to distract Quina from hers.

Quina returned his smile. "*Sí, lo veo.*"

Nate felt a slight thrill. Was Quina flirting with him? Had she just paid him a compliment? He suddenly remembered the terracotta figure on his bedside table.

"The jaguar figurine...." he said.

Quina picked up a stick and began poking at the fire.

"The jaguar god, the god of fire...." Quina said. "He travels through the underworld and returns with the sun." She glanced up at Nate. "To protect and guide you." She looked down again. "To bring you back."

Nate felt his heart flood with warmth. He couldn't speak for a moment.

"*Gracias,*" he finally managed.

Quina nodded.

The fire was out now. Quina scattered the ashes.

"*Es tarde,*" she said, standing and wiping her hands on her pant legs. "*Tiempo para dormir.*"

Nate stood. "*Sí,* time for sleep."

"*Buenas noches,* Nate Hunter," Quina said, turning to face him and looking into his eyes. "Sleep well."

Nate nodded. "*Buenas noches,* Quina—" He realized he didn't know her full name.

Quina smiled. "*Hasta mañana,*" she said, turning and walking away.

"*Hasta mañana,* Quina."

In the days and weeks that followed, Nate and Quina spoke often. In the morning at breakfast. Fetching firewood and carrying water from the well. Washing their clothes side by side at the laundry. When Quina happened by as Nate was feeding the livestock. Lingering at the cookfire after the evening meal.

Oscar would still sometimes sit down next to Quina at the evening cookfire, glare at Nate and monopolize Quina's attention for the rest of the night. Nate shrugged it off. He had no claim to Quina, and whatever else Oscar was or thought of Nate, he had been a faithful friend to her. In any event, Quina knew how to dismiss him when she'd had enough of his company. She made her own choices, knew her own mind.

Even as their own friendship deepened, however, Quina remained a mystery. Nate wanted to know more about her, but he also knew not to ask. When they talked at the cookfire or during chores, he let her steer the conversation, and she always turned it away from herself. They talked about how the website was progressing, how Rafael was doing.

"Better," Nate reported. "He's sleeping peacefully again."

"*Bueno. Me hace feliz.*"

They talked about some of the funny things the other children said and did during their lessons, how big the babies were getting, how well or poorly the elders were holding up under the rigors of camp life. Nate was concerned about Lourdes.

"She works so hard. She's always working. And she looks so frail."

"Do not worry about Lourdes," Quina said. "She is stronger than she looks."

They talked about their favorite foods, music, what instrument they wished they knew how to play—violin for Quina, piano for Nate—what animal they would be if they could be one.

"An eagle," Quina said without hesitation. "To be able to fly so high and see so much...."

Nate nodded. "Yeah, me, too."

Later, as they progressed to sometimes strolling the compound together, Nate began offering up benign bits of his own background and childhood, hoping to prompt Quina to do the same. He told her how much he used to love taking long walks as a kid through the fields around his house. How he'd always wanted to have a horse. "But we didn't have that kind of money." How hot and humid it sometimes got back in Texas. "Kind of like here."

Quina listened, didn't ask questions, didn't offer any information in return. Until she did.

"My father was American," she said, apropos of nothing, as they were strolling the compound one evening.

Nate stopped in surprise.

"He was?"

"*Sí.* Like you." Quina kept walking. Nate caught up. "He was a student," Quina continued. "From Harvard University." She glanced at Nate. "You know Harvard?"

"Yes, of course."

"He was here to study our culture. The Tzotzil Maya. It was a big study. They had a ranch in San Cristóbal. Many people came and went. My mother was a cook."

"And they fell in love?"

Quina smiled. "*Sí.* She loved him very much. And he loved her."

"So they got married?"

"No."

"No?"

"No." Quina looked down. "*Ya estaba casado.*" She frowned. "My mother didn't know. He didn't tell her until their last night together."

"What happened to him?"

"He went back to *el norte,* and my mother never saw him again."

"She didn't tell him.... " Nate let his words trail off.

Quina shook her head. "She didn't know."

Nate was astonished that Quina was telling him all this but was careful not to let his amazement show. They walked on for a while without speaking. Nate's mind buzzed with questions. *Do you know your father's name? Does he know about you? Have you ever tried to contact him? Where is your mother now? Is she still alive? When you disappear, is that where you go?* He didn't ask any of them. He looked up at the dimming sky, breathed in the soft air.

"I don't think I will ever leave here," he said. "There's nothing for me in *el norte*. The only life I have now is here."

Quina shrugged.

"Perhaps. Perhaps not."

They began taking evening walks around the compound fairly often after that. Sometimes, Mateo or Mirasol or other friends joined them. Sometimes, they strolled alone, stopping here and there to listen to men sitting together on the ground, playing guitars and singing, or to chat with other residents sitting by their cookfires or also out walking, enjoying the evening air. On these occasions, Nate had to resist the urge to take Quina's hand in his, fought it off by hooking his thumbs in his belt and closing his fingers. But he could not keep his eyes off her. He caught himself stealing glances. At her strong profile, her long neck and handsome shoulders. The swell of her breasts beneath her shirt. Her rounded hips. Walking close beside her, he would pick up her scent, earthy and sweet. Something was stirring in his blood. It made him want to take her in his arms and bury his face in her hair.

"I am sorry about your wife," Quina said softly one evening as they walked the grounds.

Nate's heart twisted. He couldn't respond.

"She was a good woman," Quina said. "Very beautiful." She glanced up at Nate. "Very brave."

Nate swallowed. "Yes. She was."

It was all he could manage.

They walked on in silence.

"You were married," Nate said after they had walked on for a while.

Quina looked surprised. "How did you know?"

"Mateo told me."

Quina frowned.

"Don't be upset with him," Nate said, seeing Quina's displeasure. "I wanted to know more about you. He told me your husband was a doctor. That he died. But that's all he would tell me."

Quina nodded. "It is true."

Nate waited for her to say something more, but she didn't.

"I'm sorry," Nate said finally.

Quina nodded but didn't respond.

Soon, Nate began feeling that something was developing between him and Quina. A connection. Affection. And with it—Nate could no longer deny it—desire.

Sitting at a table with Quina one evening after dinner, Nate saw Sebastiano on the far side of the quadrangle, walking toward a stand of trees, carrying a guitar. He seated himself against a tree trunk and began idly strumming and singing in a low voice. The pleasant melody sounded vaguely familiar. Nate couldn't make out the words.

"Do you know this song?" he asked Quina.

Quina listened, nodded. "*Es un corrido* of the Mexican Revolution. It is called *La Adelita.*"

Sebastiano's strumming slowed. His singing took on a melancholy tone.

"Sounds like it just turned sad."

"*Sí.* It tells the story of a young woman who is in love with a sergeant."

Sebastiano finished the song. Stillness fell. And then he began strumming and singing the song again, slower, sadder. Nate listened as Quina translated.

"Adelita is in love with a sergeant," Quina said. "The soldiers respect her because she is very beautiful and very brave. And the sergeant loves her very much."

Quina paused, letting Sebastiano's soft playing and singing drift over to them.

"There are different versions of the song," she said finally. "In some, the soldier Adelita loves goes off to battle without her. In others, she follows him to war. In some, he tells her that if he dies on the battlefield, she should cry over his body. In others, he begs her not to cry. 'Never forget me,' he says. 'But if I die, do not cry.'"

"And in this version?"

Quina listened, her face in a shadow.

"He asks her not to cry," she said softly.

Quina fell silent. Nate saw her eyes begin to mist and he wanted more than anything to reach for her hand. But he didn't.

"I do not want to cry," Quina said finally. "*No más.* There has been enough crying."

She stood. "*Es tarde,*" she said. "*Estoy cansada.*"

Nate rose. Their custom was to say goodnight and return separately to their quarters. But Nate wasn't ready to say goodnight.

"Let me walk you back to your room."

Quina hesitated, then nodded. They started slowly across the square, walking, not talking, Nate with his thumbs hooked in his waistband as usual. About halfway to Quina's quarters, Nate felt Quina slip her arm through his. Her touch sent an electric current coursing through him. He walked on, saying nothing, wanting only for her touch, this moment of contact, to last. When they reached her room, she withdrew her arm and turned to him.

"*Buenas noches,* Nate Hunter," she said, looking up into his eyes.

"*Buenas noches,* Quina." Nate still didn't know her full name.

The next day, after the midday meal, as Nate sat alone at a table, reviewing the computer manual again, Quina came up to him, smiling, dressed in a white muslin blouse and fatigue pants, carrying a canteen slung over her shoulder, her hair in one long utilitarian braid. "Come," Quina said. "I want to show you something."

Nate hesitated. Rafael was waiting for him in the computer room. He looked around, saw Mateo sitting at a nearby table, watching them.

"*Está bien,*" Mateo said, waving a hand. "I will tell him."

"*Gracias,*" Nate said. He rose and followed Quina, who was already crossing the quadrangle and heading toward the compound's doors.

Outside the doors, moving through a sultry, gray mist, they made their way to a jungle trail that led up the ridge. After trekking for about a mile by Nate's reckoning, they emerged onto the crest of a small hill.

"Look," Quina said, pointing across a narrow valley. Squinting where she was pointing, Nate saw a small clearing midway up the facing hill a few hundred yards distant and, within the clearing, a breathtaking sight. Barely visible through a thin veil of mist, the gray stone ruins of a Mayan temple stood shrouded in vegetation as if it had issued from the earth itself. It looked like the weary queen of some long lost civilization, stripped of her regal raiment by the passage of centuries and the relentless advance of the jungle.

For the longest time, Nate and Quina gazed across at the temple in reverent silence. Then, a faint sigh of wind, a whisper from antiquity, brushed Nate's cheek and roused him from his meditation.

"It's stunning," he said.

Quina put a hand on his arm.

"Come."

Nate followed Quina down into the valley. They kept to a vague track that led through the jungle and up the far hill, climbing and picking their way through encroaching vegetation until they were standing at the foot of a towering limestone monument, looking up. The structure rose as high as a three-story building. Bushes, shrubbery, and a heavy encrustation of earth and plant life had all but consumed the towering, manmade escarpment. Vines scrawled across the surface and dripped like candlewax from the top and sides. Stone steps, covered in a mat of dirt and moss, climbed steeply up its face.

"Come," Quina said again, moving toward the stairway.

Nate hesitated. The steps were incredibly shallow and steep. He looked at Quina. "You've done this before?"

She smiled. "Like this." She leaned into the steps and began a handhold ascent, keeping her body close to the almost vertical face of the escarpment. Nate followed her lead. Clumsily and cautiously, he began climbing, reaching for a handhold, then a foothold, then stepping and pulling. Quina moved smoothly and steadily above him. After a while, he got the hang of it, and the exercise, the stretch and pull of his arms, thighs and calves, began to feel good.

They grappled their way to a flat, rectangular landing and paused to rest. Above them, the remaining steps faded into green earth, narrowing to a barely negotiable treadway leading up to a platform summit. Atop it stood a small, rectangular porticoed structure, crowned by a formerly grand, now crumbling roof comb. Before Nate could say a word, Quina began climbing again and Nate followed. To the doleful calls of large, swooping birds, they carefully scaled the last of the crumbling steps and gained the sentinel peak. Unaccustomed to physical exertion since his illness, Nate stood breathless for a moment with his hands on his knees, sucking in air. Quina wasn't even breathing hard.

Quina pointed toward the stone chamber before them. Serpentine columns flanked its wide entrance. An entablature of jaguar heads and indecipherable runes adorned the proud facade.

"This is the sanctuary, the station of priests and Mayan royalty," Quina said. "To the ancient ones, pyramids like this represented mountains. They believed that at the top they could be closer to the gods, closer to heaven. This entranceway represents the mouth of a cave, the entrance to the Underworld, the sacred place of creation, of birth and death."

Quina turned to take in the view. *"Mira,"* she said, sweeping an arm out over the jungle. Nate straightened, turned, and stood, hands on hips, pondering the enormity of the Lacandon. From their vantage point atop the ceremonial citadel, beneath an arc of deepening blue sky, they gazed out over the seemingly endless wildlands that surrounded them. An untrammeled verdant expanse, full of danger and uncertainty, lit now by the golden blaze of the afternoon sun.

Quina pointed to a flat stone slab covered in jungle growth in front of the entrance to the sanctuary. Almost waist high, it reminded Nate of a park bench.

"This is the place of death," Quina said. "A sacred place. Here, holy men dressed as jaguar gods cut the hearts out of human sacrifices with stone knives."

Nate stared at the sacrificial altar. Mateo had told him about these sacrifices on the river, but he never imagined he would find himself standing a few feet from where they had taken place. It spooked him a little.

"It was an advanced culture, but a brutal one," Quina said quietly.

"Barbaric," Nate said.

"You think so? When this society was flourishing, Europe was in the dark ages. These people were studying the stars, plotting the courses of the sun and moon, developing higher mathematics. They invented the concept of zero. The concept of nothingness. Did you know that?"

Nate nodded, a little embarrassed.

"I did, actually." It was one of the facts Sarah had shared with him when she'd been deep into her reading, trying to convince Nate to join the mission trip. *Sarah*. He saw her face again, her bright eyes, her brilliant smile.

"Are you all right?" Quina asked.

Sarah's image faded. Nate was silent a moment. "Yes," he said. "Fine."

"The sacrifices were bloody," Quina said. "But across the Atlantic, people were killing each other in feudal wars, burning each other at the stake. Here, people were creating the first three hundred and sixty-five-day calendar."

"And then it all came apart," Nate said.

Quina sighed, let her gaze sweep over the pillars and carvings adorning the entrance to the sanctuary.

"*Sí*," she said sadly. "And then it disappeared."

Nate and Quina turned to gaze out at the Lacandon again. Before them stretched an immensity of green—a seemingly limitless, wrinkled blanket of thick vegetation. Shrouded in a haze of fog, it was vague and mysterious. In the western sky, the sun was liquid gold behind streaks of jagged clouds. Overhead, the sky was a measureless dome of cerulean blue.

"Maya blue," Quina said softly, gazing up.

She smiled at Nate.

"That is what we call it. Maya Blue. It is the hue of the Mayan heaven. A combination of the colors of sky, water, jade, *maíz*, everything precious and sacred."

Quina turned her gaze back to the oceanic sky. "In olden times, Mayan priests and royalty wore that color. It was also the color of offerings to the gods. Sacrificial victims were painted with blue pitch. So were those steps." She pointed to the mossgrown steps they had ascended. "And that slab. All Maya blue."

She walked over to the slab and started pulling away vines and brushing dirt from one edge. "It is a very durable pigment," she said. "Some of the color might still be here." She worked a minute more. "No, I cannot find it. But it is probably still here, somewhere."

Quina turned to Nate, brushing her hands on her trousers.

"Brutal, yes," she said. "A brutality born of fear and superstition. But born of reverence, too. And duty and necessity. And courage, and willingness to sacrifice."

Nate watched her, drinking her in.

"How do you know all this?" he asked.

Quina looked at him. "It is my culture. Why shouldn't I know?"

Nate nodded, embarrassed again.

Quina walked back over to him, sat down on the top step and gazed out over the jungle canopy. Nate sat down beside her.

"They were like us. Wives, husbands, mothers, fathers, children, neighbors."

"Scientists, farmers... " Nate looked around at the stonework surrounding him. "Builders.... "

"Yes. They worked hard. They loved hard.... "

Quina looked down, her face suddenly flushed, fell silent for a long time. Nate watched her. It was all he could do. He couldn't help himself.

Then Quina rose. "We should go back now, yes?"

Nate rose and faced her. They stood like that for a few moments, almost touching, looking deep into each other's eyes. Nate breathed in Quina's scent—sweet, earthy scent. There were no more words.

Nate took Quina's face in his hands and kissed her, gently. She didn't resist, let the kiss linger. Nate pulled back. Quina opened her eyes, gazed up at him. Such eyes, such beautiful, mysterious eyes. The color of polished obsidian. Volcanic mirrors. He kissed her again, more deeply, felt her move closer, lips parting. She laid her hands gently on Nate's chest and then slid them up around his neck as he pulled her to him and wrapped her in his arms. They kissed and kissed again. He pulled back, looked into her eyes. They were burning, shining.

There was no resisting anymore.

Nate gently took Quina's arms from around his neck and, holding her hand, led her into the sanctuary. She went silently, willingly. There, he took her in his arms again, brought her tightly to his body and kissed her again. A long, deep, soulful kiss that raised in her a soft moan.

In the dim light of the sanctuary, with the fire in the western sky now burning in their eyes, Nate sat on the stucco floor carpeted with a layer of rich, electric green moss and drew Quina down beside him. They kissed again, his hands roving her body, exploring her, unbuttoning her blouse, slipping inside it, laying her gently down on the carpet of moss, as he slipped her bra strap down over her silken shoulder, ran his palm over her bare breast, found her erect nipple. Quina moaned again, arching her body, his hands finally settling at the small of her back.

"Nate," Quina whispered, her voice throaty with desire.

Slowly, never completely letting go of each other, they helped each other undress. Quina unbraided her hair, shook it loose and lay back again. Nate's eyes roamed her face and body. Her beauty was almost too much to take in.

"Quina," he whispered.

She reached for him, pulled him down over her. He kissed her again and again, devouring her, consuming her. He held her close, and closer still, and she opened herself to him. He entered her and became part of her, and she became part of him.

Afterward, as dusk gathered, they sat together leaning against the sanctuary wall, Nate's arm around Quina's shoulders, her head against his chest. Nate breathed in her scent again, now mingled with his.

"Tell me your name," he said softly.

Quina was silent a moment.

"You know my name."

"No, your full name."

Quina looked up at him, lay her head back on his chest and settled into silence. Then she pushed herself away from the wall, rose from the mossy floor, stood languorous for a moment, and began getting dressed. Nate watched in a state of wonder and contentment. Quina tucked her blouse into her pants, smiled at Nate. Then, eyes lowered, looking away, she put a hand on his arm and left the sanctuary.

Through the shadowy portal, Nate watched Quina walk to the edge of the outer platform and gaze out over the kingdom of interlocking treetops. Loose from its braid, her raven hair danced in the breeze, free and unrestrained.

She belongs in this world, Nate thought. *She's part of it. She understands it. Its cruelty and injustices, its meager beauty and joy.* Maybe he was wrong about that second part, Nate thought, watching Quina. Maybe this world contained more beauty than he realized. But he was not wrong about the cruelty and injustice or the costs of caring too much, of trying to improve this world. Nate knew that Quina had paid her share of these costs, as he had. And he knew that she had borne her suffering with far more grace and strength. He didn't need to know the details. He could tell. From the way she carried herself. From her dignity and reserve. Maybe because people here were more used to suffering, Nate thought. What was it Mateo had said to him? In Chiapas, everyone has a heavy heart.

And then, Nate's mind suddenly flooded with vivid memories of Sarah. He saw her face again, her beautiful, smiling face, and his soul ached. An old sadness gnawed at his heart.

At that moment, Quina turned, smiling faintly, saw his expression and seemed to read his thoughts. Her smile faded, her own expression saddened, and she looked away.

Oh, Quina.

Nate rose, quietly put his clothes on and went to her, turned her toward him and held her close. They stood together in that sacred place simply holding each other. Then Nate stepped back.

"Are you sorry?" he asked gently, sweeping her raven hair back off her face and watching it fall like silk down her back.

Quina searched his eyes.

"Are you?"

Nate probed his aching heart. Sarah was still there. He still loved her. He would always love her. But she had loved him, too. And she would want this for him. *Yes.* It came like a whisper. She would. She did.

Nate smiled at Quina.

"No," he said. "I'm not sorry. But maybe you—"

"No," Quina interrupted. "No." She laid her head against his chest. "We are the living. And the living need each other to carry on." She lifted her head and took his hand. "Come. It is getting dark. We should get back."

Quina sat down on the platform, turned to face the stone, and started backing carefully down the narrow stepway. Nate sat to begin his descent, lingered in the fading light.

"It won't be long now, will it?" Nate said. "Something is about to happen. I can feel it."

Quina paused, stood erect and looked up at him. She nodded. "*Sí,*" she answered. "It is coming."

"Soon."

"Yes. Soon, I think."

"And many will die."

"Yes."

Nate looked down at her. "Can we win?"

Quina did not answer.

"I do not know," she said finally.

"And that doesn't bother you."

Quina shook her head, resumed her careful descent.

"I envy you, you know that? You, Mateo, the others. You never seem to doubt yourselves. You never question your own courage."

Quina stopped and looked up again. "We do not have the luxury of doubt. We have no life but this one. We have no home but this one."

"But can we win?"

Watching her, waiting for an answer, Nate saw a different kind of fire flash in her eyes.

"Does it matter?"

That question again.

"We must try," Quina finally said, her face both sorrowful and bold. "What else can we do? Now, come. We must go back."

Nate turned and looked once more at the altar, then out across the darkening vastness. The jungle spread out endlessly before him. The wind picked up, and Nate thought he heard voices again. Whispers. Murmurs. The moans of the ancient dead and those about to die. 🔺

CHAPTER 25

A Time to Dance

In camp a few weeks later, under a clear night sky lit by a full moon, a spontaneous fiesta erupted. The tensions, tedium, and weariness of long days of preparing for war exploded in a drunken saturnalia. It began soon after the evening meal when a group of children, under the watchful eyes of their mothers, set about gathering firewood and forming a great cone of dried branches in the center of the quadrangle. Guillermo, the napalm maker, doused the wood with kerosene and, after instructing everyone to stand back, tossed a match onto it. A gasp of ignition followed, and soon, a bonfire. Burning wood crackled and hissed, spewed a tempest of embers skyward. Thousands of tiny, bright specks rose to meet the darkening sky like swarms of fireflies.

The blaze drew a crowd. Three men fetched their instruments—violin, trumpet, guitar—and began playing mariachi music. Guillermo reappeared with a short-necked, full-bodied, six string guitar and began strumming along. Severino, who tended the livestock with Nate's help, strolled over with an accordion. Mirasol joined in on the vocals, harmonizing in a sweet, strong voice. Soon, almost all the residents of La Libertad were assembled around the music-makers or scattered around the bonfire, adults and children, young and old, clapping, laughing, hollering—"*Ooie! Ooie! Aaaha! Aha!*"—dancing, swaying, tapping their feet. The rebels on watch stood their watches. But for one night, everyone else abandoned any concerns about being heard and discovered by patrolling soldiers. The battle was approaching. Everyone felt it. The time to fight would come soon enough. On this night, it was time to party.

In the dim outer reaches of the firelight's halo, Nate sat against a wall with Quina and Mateo, taking in the festivities, one foot drawn in, forearm on knee, dangling from his hand an old beer bottle sloshing with a murky green homebrew the campesinos called *chicha*—a crude sugar cane wine that Nate was beginning to realize, after knocking back a few drinks, packed a punch. On his left, Mateo sat with legs crossed Indian-style, sipping posh from a fist-sized gourd cup. On his right, Quina sat dressed in her wool skirt, embroidered huipil and purple rebozo, smiling, clapping to the music. Nate sneaked glances as he swigged from his bottle, entranced by her noble profile in the flickering firelight, the dancing flames reflected in her eyes.

"These are classic cantina songs," Mateo said, tapping his fingers against his gourd cup in time to the music. "You hear them all over Mexico. They tell of lost love and tragedy and violence. Everyone knows them."

"I recognize some of the tunes," Nate said.

"Of course. *'El Mariachi,' 'El Rancho Grande,' 'Mi Casita.'*"

Then, the musicians struck up a truly familiar tune. Surprised and skeptical, Nate turned to Mateo.

"*'La Bamba'?*" he said.

Mateo shrugged.

Nate put his head back against the wall and barked the laugh of a man fast approaching the limit of his tolerance for the strong spirit. He stole another glance at Quina. She was watching him, amused, eyes sparkling. He wanted her. He hungered for her even more now that they had made love. He could not help himself.

After a while, the music changed, and the crowd moved back, cheering and applauding, as a line of women danced single file into the center of the square, smiling broadly and flouncing their long, full skirts. The crowd cheered and applauded.

"*Baile folklorico,*" Mateo explained to Nate, pointing. He grinned. "*Más o menos.*"

The women moved to the music in practiced dance steps—heels forward, toes back, waltzing to the left and to the right, cross stepping, dipping and turning, spinning about, drawing figure eights in the air with their fists full of fabric, skirts waving and draping over their arms.

The women twirled, bowed, backed away in two lines to the sides of the dance area, and now the men entered, skipping, heel-and-toe-tapping, into the center of the square. Arms akimbo with hands on hips or clasped behind them, they danced with backs erect, skipping and tapping forward and back, side to side, bending and dipping and turning. A few men loosed their red bandanas from their necks, shook them out, stretched them taut between both hands and lifted them high overhead as they danced and tapped, then lowered them, released one end and twirled them around, tapping and stomping, arms outstretched, strips of cotton fabric streaming in the air.

The crowd erupted in applause, the men bowed, still dancing, the women moved forward again, and now men and women danced together, twirling and bowing and hopping and skipping, waving bandanas and skirts in the air.

Nate laughed. "Men don't dance like that where I come from," he told Mateo, tapping his bottle of home brew against his shin in time to the music. "Women, either, for that matter."

"It is the Mexican way," Mateo said. "For us, a fiesta is an expression of both sorrow and joy. The two come together. The poet Octavio Paz—do you know him?"

"I know his name," Nate said. "That's about all."

"He says a fiesta is a 'multicolored frenzy that evaporates in smoke, ashes, nothingness.' He calls it 'the lodging place of death.'"

"Well, that's a happy thought," Nate said in good-natured, half-drunk mockery. "Thank you for sharing that." He raised the bottle in salute.

"No. No. *Es verdad*," Mateo insisted. "The poet understands. There is nothing so joyous as a Mexican fiesta, but there is also nothing so sorrowful. Life and death, joy and sorrow, endings and beginnings, music and mere noise. . . they all collide."

Nate listened with head down, arms on two bent knees now, bottle dangling between his legs.

"Thank you, professor," he said, waving his bottle in Mateo's direction.

Glancing up, Nate saw a stout, older woman he knew as Blanca approaching their group. About half Nate's height and twice his girth, she stopped in front of him and struck a playful, coquettish pose, flashing a few missing teeth, then clasping her hands in front of her, lowering her gaze to her battered bare feet and looking away. Nate stared at her. Was she asking him to dance? Him? He lowered his gaze and studied his bottle, hoping Blanca would shift her attention to Mateo, who was smiling up at her. Nate had never been much of a dancer, and the chicha in his belly had staked him to the ground.

Mateo nudged him with an elbow. Nate shot him a look and Mateo cocked his head up toward Blanca. Nate did not move. Mateo nudged him and gestured again. Nate still didn't move. Blanca was still standing there.

"Go on," Mateo whispered without moving his lips, still smiling at Blanca. "She wants you to ask her to dance. If you do not, she will be offended."

Nate glanced at Blanca, then turned to Quina for deliverance. But Quina seconded Mateo.

"*Blanca quiere bailar,*" she said, dark eyes sparkling in the firelight, a smile flirting at the corners of her mouth. Mateo jabbed Nate in his ribs again, harder this time.

"Okay, okay," Nate whispered, grimacing and jerking away. He looked up at Blanca, converting his grimace into a gracious smile. More than slightly in his cups, he took a deep breath and nodded to himself. *All right. I can do this.* He handed his bottle to Mateo, who was grinning now, and rose unsteadily. When he was sure he had his feet under him, he bowed at the waist.

"*Quieres bailar?*" he said.

Blanca laughed and nodded vigorously. "*Sí! Sí!*" Of course, she did.

Okay, here we go. Nate offered his arm. Blanca took it, smiling broadly, and, together, they walked toward the center of the square to join the other dancers. Before Nate had a chance to get his bearings, he was swept up in the swirl of music and dancing, shouting and clapping, women stepping and twirling, waving their skirts, men kicking and turning and stomping, all moving in circles and lines—dipping and bobbing, skipping and hopping—in some pattern of steps that was indecipherable to the interloping norteamericano.

Blanca, Nate noticed when he caught sight of her among the swirling dancers, was impressively light and graceful on her feet. Dancing made her happy. He could see that, and he was glad now that he'd asked her to dance.

"*Bailas bien,*" he called out to her the next time she danced near. Already smiling from the joy of dancing, Blanca lit up in a way that let Nate glimpse the pretty young woman she had once been.

Nate Hunter, computer wiz, on the other hand, was no hoofer. But he was drunk enough not to let that stymie him. He tried to copy the exuberant moves of the men capering round and round the fire, the children gamboling along with them, but everyone was moving too fast. He managed to keep pace with the circling but not the steps, seemed always to be kicking when the other men were spinning, skipping when they were bobbing. He finally gave up and began improvising his own moves to a dance he decided to call *Baile Bacchanal*. He caught glimpses of Blanca smiling at him, heard whooping, laughing and clapping, people shouting his name. This was good, Nate decided. The best he could hope for was that the other dancers and people watching would get a kick out of seeing him make a mighty drunken fool of himself, that it would give them all a good laugh.

Looping the fire again, Nate spotted Mateo and Quina at the edge of the circle. Quina was covering her mouth with her hands, trying to contain her amusement, but her crinkled, sparkling eyes gave her away. Mateo was holding his sides, he was laughing so hard.

Oh, yeah? You like that? Wait'll you see this. The music, laughter and chicha had freed him of all inhibition, and he was now thoroughly enjoying performing his wild rigadoon and of no mind to stop.

Falling into line with the other men circling left while the women circled right, Nate saw Rafael a little way ahead, propped on his crutches, watching, clapping and laughing. Without breaking stride, Nate snatched the boy up as he passed, letting his crutches fall to the ground, positioned the boy on his right side, pulled a scrawny arm around his waist, grasped him firmly under his right armpit, and kept moving. Even a one-legged child could do this dance. Rafael laughed aloud in astonished glee, flying through the air at Nate's side, his good right foot only occasionally touching the ground. When the circling stopped and the women and men began twirling in place, Nate swung Rafael in circles in the air. The boy laughed and squealed with joy. Spectators cheered and clapped.

When the dance ended, to more laughter and applause, and the music began again, Nate shifted Rafael to his back, bowed to Blanca, who grinned and curtsied, retrieved Rafael's crutches and deposited the boy at a table with Mirasol. Then he found Mateo and Quina, who greeted him with smiles and applause, and the three returned to their place against the wall, where Nate virtually fell to the ground between them.

Sweating and out of breath, Nate wiped his forehead with the back of a hand and took a long pull on his bottle of joy juice.

"I did not know you were a dancer," Mateo said, his eyes crinkled with amusement.

"I'm not," Nate replied calmly. "I'm a drinker."

Taking a break from playing, old Guillermo now approached Quina, smiling and holding his hat in his hand. *"Señora?"* he said, bowing. Quina smiled back, and the old man extended a hand to help her to her feet. Nate watched her go, then sucked in a deep breath and turned to Mateo. He exhaled and cleared his throat.

"Tengo una pregunta," he said, with drunken purpose. "Tell me the truth. Who is this Subcomandante Marcos who's supposed to be leading the rebellion?"

"He is not our leader," Mateo said evenly. "I told you. We have no leader."

"Okay, your chief coordinator then or whatever you want to call him. Who is he? And where is he?"

Mateo didn't answer immediately. Gazing out at the revelry in the square, he drained his gourd cup, then turned to Nate.

"A palabras de borracho," he said slowly, *"oídas de jicarero."*

Nate angled his head and gnarled his face a bit.

"There you go again... speaking in riddles. Something about words of a drunk." Nate lifted his bottle. "I got that part. I missed the rest."

Mateo leaned in and raised a finger in an instructive fashion.

"A drunk will tell you everything on his mind. Ignore him."

Nate snickered and looked away into the darkness. He still didn't understand. Whose drunken words did Mateo mean? Mateo's? Nate's? He shrugged and turned to Mateo again.

"Come on. *Dime la verdad.* You've really never met him—*el jefe?* You've never seen him? Not even once?"

Mateo shook his head.

"No. I have never seen him. No one here has seen him."

Mateo raised his eyebrows and canted his head as if to say, *Strange, isn't it? Yes, I understand why you would find that odd.*

"You've never seen him," Nate repeated. "But you know he exists?"

"Sí, cómo no."

"But how? How do you know if you haven't seen him?" Nate had a thought. "Have you spoken to him? Talked to him on the phone?"

Mateo looked away and shook his head. He turned back to Nate.

"You pretend to believe only in things you can see. But that is not true, Nate Hunter. You do not say Asia does not exist just because you have never been there."

"That's different," Nate argued back. "You can't compare—"

"You do not deny your mother gave birth to you just because you do not remember it."

"Oh, come on. That's not what I'm—"

"You do not deny the existence of God because you have never seen his face."

Nate's mood darkened. "No. I deny God because I can't believe in a God who let that piece of shit murder my wife. And your wife. If this God does exist and I ever see his face, I swear I'll, I'll. . . . "

Mateo laid a calming hand on Nate's arm. "I am sorry," he said gently. I should not have said that. You see? *A palabras de borracho. . . . "*

Both men fell silent.

"Faith, my friend," Mateo said finally. "We do not have much, but we have faith."

Nate did not respond. He hoisted himself unsteadily to his feet.

"And I . . . have to piss. You have faith and I have a full bladder. But fear not. I shall return and we shall resume our repartee."

Saluting with the bottle of chicha, Nate turned and headed into the darkness. The reel of the party still in his legs, drunk as an English lord and unable to keep a straight line, he made his way to the nearby animal pens to relieve himself rather than risk the longer walk to the latrines. While he was making water, he heard a voice in the darkness.

"Hey, *borrachon,"* someone called to him. A man's voice. Nate squinted and saw Oscar sitting alone against a corner post of the pen, his own bottle in his hands. "Tonight you do the dance of the dead, eh? You fill your belly with *aguardiente* and dance because soon you will be dead."

Nate watched Oscar take a swig from his bottle. He sounded drunker than Nate. Nate decided to ignore him, finish his business and leave.

"You will be dead, and I will be dead," Oscar continued, slurring his words, his tone one of resignation and acceptance. "All of us . . . pffffft." He waved his bottle in the air. "*Muerto.*" He peered up at Nate. "Time is running out, *amigo.* The end is near."

Nate hitched his pants, picked up his bottle and turned to rejoin the festivities.

"*Sí*. Go. Dance," Oscar called to him. "Maybe you will dance with the right woman, eh?"

Nate stopped and looked up into starry darkness overhead, lifted his bottle to his lips and polished off the last three fingers of chicha.

"One dance before you die. Before you die, I die, she—"

Nate wheeled and hurled his empty bottle at Oscar. It hit the ground a few feet in front of him and exploded into pieces. Oscar jerked back, shielding his head and face with his arms, then leaned forward again, sneering.

"You do not like this talk of death, I think," he said, waving his bottle at Nate. "*Qué lástima. Qué triste.* Because we all must die, *amigo*. But maybe you are afraid to die. Does it frighten you, *El Cazador?*" Oscar leaned back against the pen, chuckling. "*El Cazador*," he repeated, shaking his head. He laughed and laughed.

Nate stood like a stone in the darkness until Oscar ran out of laughter.

Oh, yeah? Nate thought. *And what about you? What about the way you begged and squealed for me to kill the soldier who was killing you? What about how scared shitless you were of dying then, Mr. Hombre Verdadero?*

Nate sniffed, hitched up his pants again.

"Fuck you, Oscar," he said.

Oscar looked up at him. "*Qué?*"

"You heard me. *Chinga tu madre.* Fuck you."

Having said his piece in what struck him in the moment as fine form and few words, Nate headed back toward the square thinking that Oscar had one good idea. Nate was going to find Quina and ask her to dance. Not spotting her or Mateo at their place against the wall, Nate headed into the square, and was just approaching the outer edges of firelight when the music and dancing suddenly stopped. Silence fell abruptly. Then came murmuring, whispering.

"*Cómo?*" someone asked. "*Qué es?* What is it?"

"*Qué? Qué pasa?*"

"*No sé. No puedo ver. Qué pasa? Quién es?*"

"*No sé. Personas están llegando.*"

And then, "No. Oh, no. *Por favor*, no."

People began streaming toward the hacienda's massive front gate.

Making his way forward, Nate saw from his height advantage that the gates had been slightly opened and a haggard-looking group of some dozen men and women were shuffling in, silent and grave, most of them in tattered bandages and bloody clothes. Camp residents rushed forward to aid the travelers, walk them to the fire, ease them to the ground, bring water, fresh bandages, food and drink. The last two men to come through the gates carried someone on a canvas litter. Nate recognized Fulgencio at the front of the litter, Sebastiano at the back. The person they were carrying lay unmoving, covered with a blanket up to his chest, arms crossed atop it, face turned away. Nate couldn't make out who it was.

"Tatic!" someone gasped. "Tatic! No!"

"*Sí! Sí! Es* Tatic!"

"*Madre de Dios, no!* Tatic!"

Fulgencio and Sebastiano moved close to the fire and eased the litter to the ground. Mateo pushed through the welter of people gathering around them, followed closely by Quina, and the two knelt on the ground next to Tatic, Mateo on his left, where Tatic could see him, Quina on the right. Shocked into instant sobriety, Nate saw Lourdes making her way to Tatic, and went to assist her, taking her arm and escorting her through the crowd. The old woman seemed oblivious to Nate's presence, so focused was she on reaching Tatic. Nate grabbed a chair, pulled it up next to Quina and helped Lourdes into it. In the light of the fire, he saw that Lourdes was crying silently, tears coursing down her leathered face. And now he saw that Tatic's blanket was soaked with blood.

"*Padre*," Nate heard Mateo whisper as Nate stepped back into the circle of people surrounding Tatic's litter. He felt a pressure at his side and looked down to see Rafael leaning into him. The boy looked up with large, frightened eyes. Nate put an arm around his shoulders and drew him close.

"*Padrecito*," Mateo whispered again. "Tatic," he pleaded softly, leaning closer and gently touching the priest's shoulder. "*Padre. Mi amigo querido. Me oyes?*"

The old man's chest heaved, sending soft cries and murmurs through the camp. Tatic turned his head slowly, opened his dark eyes and gazed up at the heavens. His gaze shifted to Mateo, and he moved his mouth as if to speak. But Mateo put a gentle hand to the old man's lips.

"No. No. *Quieto*," he said softly. "Be quiet now. Do not speak."

"*Tatic, estás seguro*," Quina said softly, putting a hand on the old man's arm. "*Estamos aquí contigo.* I am here. And Lourdes. And Rafael." Quina looked around, saw Rafael standing with Nate a few feet away.

"*Ven*," Quina said, gently beckoning the child forward. "*No tengas miedo.*"

The boy looked to Nate. Nate nodded and put a hand to his back, and the boy slowly moved forward on his crutches.

"Here," Quina said, easing him down onto her lap. "Where Tatic can see you." Then, speaking again to the priest, "*Tatic, Rafael está aquí. A su lado.*"

The old man turned his head slowly. Nate watched his eyes search first for Lourdes—"*Estoy aquí, Tatic,*" the old woman murmured—then for Quina, who met his gaze with a gentle smile—and then, finally, for Rafael, who sat pressed against Quina's breast, staring at Tatic with huge, frightened eyes. And even from where he stood Nate could see the love in the priest's eyes for all three of them, but especially for the boy. His lips moved, forming silent words, and then his gaze went back to Heaven.

"Tatic, stay with us," Mateo urged softly. He looked up at Lourdes, and Nate realized that the old woman had not moved, was not calling for bandages or water. Lourdes shook her head. She crossed herself, leaned forward and put a gentle, leathery hand atop Tatic's hands. The priest did not turn his head or shift his gaze from the night sky above, but Nate thought he saw a faint smile cross his lips at Lourdes's touch. He showed no fear. He did not look sad. If he was in pain, he had transcended it. There was a calmness about him. A look of quiet and peaceful acceptance. And something else. Nate thought he saw joy, a look of hopeful expectation.

And then the old man's dark eyes half-closed. His chest rose and fell heavily, and was still.

Mateo waited, and waited. Finally, he put three fingers to the side of Tatic's throat, held them there a few moments, lowered his head, and then reached up with his other hand and closed Tatic's eyes. He made the sign of the cross over the priest, bowed his head again and said what looked like a brief prayer under his breath.

Moans and whimpers filled the camp. People began crying. Lourdes's eyes were dry now. She sat with her head bent, hand still atop Tatic's, saying her own silent prayer. Rafael buried his face in Quina's neck and began to sob. Quina held him close and stroked his hair, tears streaming down her face.

After a few moments, Mateo wiped his own eyes and hauled himself slowly to his feet. He turned to Sebastiano, who was still standing at the foot of Tatic's stretcher, exhausted and filthy, head bowed.

"*Qué pasó?*" Mateo asked, his dark eyes shimmering with anger and tears.

Sebastiano shook his head sadly, but did not answer. Mateo took a step toward him, fists clenched.

"*Qué pasó?*" he thundered.

Sebastiano lifted his head and spoke a name.

"*El Pitón.*"

PART THREE

EL PITÓN

CHAPTER 26

The Place of Fright

S ebastiano began his story. There had been rumors, he reminded Mateo, that El Pitón and his men were planning to return to Mirador. But nobody knew if the rumors were true. The paramilitaristas had not been seen in the area for months and months, not since heading to the mountains after the demonstration "and the killing of the American woman." Mateo shot Nate a look when Sebastiano said this, but Nate signaled with the wave of a hand for Mateo to let it go. Sebastiano didn't know.

The rumors were true. "*Hace una semana, regresaron,*" Sebastiano told Mateo, triggering murmurs and gasps from other camp residents who had drawn nearer to hear what Sebastiano had to say.

Hungry and wild after staying so long in the mountains, unrestrained by conscience or the Mexican Army or the State Police, El Pitón and his men had set upon the campesinos and villagers, seizing food and livestock, kicking in doors and ransacking homes for money and valuables. Whoever resisted was punished. Men were beaten in front of their wives and children. Three campesinos and two villagers disappeared. When Tatic went to El Pitón and begged him to have mercy on the people, El Pitón laughed, Sebastiano told Mateo.

"Tatic spoke with El Pitón?"

"*Sí.*"

"Where?"

"In the old barracks. They have taken it over."

"You were there?"

"*Sí.* I did not think he should go alone."

"And this happened?" Mateo roared, sweeping a hand toward Tatic and stepping closer to Sebastiano.

"No! No!" Sebastiano protested, stepping back and raising his hands. "*Déjame hablar, por favor.*"

Mateo clenched his fists, pressed his lips together and exhaled hard through his nose. "*Bueno,*" he growled. "*Dime lo que pasó.*"

Sebastiano resumed his story. He had suspected that no good would come of the priest's decision to appeal to El Pitón, but he had been unable to talk Tatic out of it. "So I went with him."

"And?"

El Pitón made them wait outside the barracks in the midday sun for almost an hour, Sebastiano said. "Then, when he did see us, he would not let Tatic sit. He was sitting behind a desk smoking a *puro*, with his feet up in those big shiny boots he wears. You know those boots?"

Mateo nodded.

"But he made us stand. When Tatic said he came to ask mercy for his people, El Pitón laughed. He said he was only doing what he had to do to keep law and order. He said it was a dangerous job and the people should be grateful to him and his men and should be happy to give them what they need. *Dijo, 'Pero si no, tomaremos lo que necesitamos.'*"

"*Y qué dijo Tatic?*"

He said, '*Pero, por favor, Señor.* The people are poor. They do not have enough food to feed themselves. And they are good people who have done you no harm."

"*Y qué dijo El Pitón?*"

"He became very angry then," Sebastiano said. "He took his boots off the desk and stood up and said, 'No! *No es verdad!* We have already seen trouble in Mirador. Stupid peasants carrying signs.' He leaned across the desk and said, 'I do not tolerate troublemakers. I do not care who they are, *entiendes?* If they make trouble, they die.'"

Mateo grimaced. "*Bastardo,*" he growled.

Tatic realized that his visit had been in vain, Sebastiano said. So he nodded and thanked El Pitón for his time and turned to go. But El Pitón stopped them.

"*Dijo, 'Espere un momento,'*" Sebastiano said. Then El Pitón said that he had heard rumors of guerilla bands forming in remote regions of Chiapas, of secret rebel camps in the jungle and countryside. He had heard talk of an uprising.

Mateo frowned at this.

"What else did he say?"

"He said that *los soldados* have been searching the Lacandon, but so far they have found nothing. He said Colonel Delgado is satisfied. He does not believe the rumors."

Mateo grunted and nodded.

"But El Pitón does not agree with *el comandante*," Sebastiano said. El Pitón came around the desk then, stood in front of Tatic, took a puff on his puro and slowly exhaled a stream of smoke in Tatic's face.

"No, I do not dismiss the rumors," El Pitón said. "I listen," he said, raising a finger to his right ear. "And I watch," he said, tapping the corner of his right eye. "And if I see trouble, I strike. And if someone tries to stop me, he dies."

El Pitón stared hard into Tatic's eyes, Sebastiano said. "And Tatic..." Sebastiano's voice broke. He looked down, wiped a tear away, looked back up at Mateo. "Tatic, *que Dios lo bendiga,* he stood *como un estatua, como un ángel.*" Tatic stood there, calmly, unflinching, and calmly returned El Pitón's gaze. Sebastiano shook his head and smiled, his eyes filled with tears. "*El Pitón no le gustó,*" he said. "*Y yo... yo tenía miedo.* I did not know what El Pitón would do, and I did not have my gun or my knife."

Finally, Sebastiano said, El Pitón took a step back, sneered and spit half on the floor, half on Tatic's sandaled left foot.

"Nobody stops El Pitón," he said. "*Me oyes?*" He looked from Tatic to Sebastiano and back to Tatic. "No one."

"And El Pitón killed him because of that?" Quina whispered, shocked and grief-stricken. "Because he did not look away?"

"No," Sebastiano said softly. "That was on Thursday. This... " Sebastiano nodded sadly toward Tatic and swept a hand to take in the other injured refugees being tended and fed near the fire. "He did not do this terrible thing until the next day. Yesterday.... " Sebastiano glanced warily at Mateo. "In the church."

"No! No! *Madre de Dios!*" The whole camp erupted as one, keening, wailing, calling out. "*No en la iglesia!* What is he saying! Not in the church. No! No! *Por favor!* It cannot be!"

Mateo stumbled back a step. Someone brought him a chair, and he sat down heavily, tilted his head back and stared at the dark heavens. Quina remained kneeling at Tatic's side, rocking Rafael in her lap as he sobbed, arms wrapped around her neck, face pressed against her breast. Nate's heart went out to the boy. So much loss, so much violence, at such a young age. Lourdes sat hunched forward in her chair, bent over Tatic, one hand resting tenderly atop his folded hands, lips moving in silent prayer. The cries and moans gradually subsided into soft weeping. Mateo took a deep breath, sighed and turned his attention back to Sebastiano.

"Tell us," he said. "How did this happen?"

It happened on a Friday. Unable to sleep after the meeting with El Pitón, Sebastiano had risen at the sound of the church bells and headed over to *La Iglesia de la Ventana de Luz* to check on Tatic. "I have not been to church in many months," he said. *"Más de un año."* Standing inside the church door, Sebastiano had watched the faithful congregate, pressing together on the wooden benches, praying in low voices, many with long, thin, flickering candles in their hands. He had watched Tatic wander among them, offering greetings and blessings, words of reassurance, laying a comforting hand on bent foreheads, patting shoulders and cheeks.

"El padre was a man of strong faith," Sebastiano said, frowning. "I do not have faith." So, instead of taking a seat on one of the benches as Tatic made his way to the altar to begin Mass, Sebastiano headed to the square to have breakfast and collect the news. Wandering here and there, munching on a tortilla, he spotted a pack of rowdy men gathering in a dusty alleyway, shouting and laughing, heard the unmistakable sounds of roosters shrieking and flapping. A cockfight. Approaching to investigate, he saw soldiers in the crowd, recognized a few of El Pitón's men, including his *segundo,* the one called Chuy. "So I decided to stay... to watch," Sebastiano said, tapping the corner of his eye, "and listen," he said, tapping his ear.

Drawing closer, he saw El Pitón himself standing inside a circle of men, chomping on a cheroot, cradling a white rooster in one arm. Across from him, another man held a black rooster. Sebastiano worked his way to the front of the circle just as the men knelt and, at a signal from the *árbitro,* released their cocks.

It was the usual violent spectacle, Sebastiano said. The birds tore into each other, stabbing and slashing, screeching and flailing, throwing up clouds of dust and gusts of feathers, as the drunken spectators who had bet on the outcome, shouted and cursed, urging them on, until finally the combat ended with one cock, *el negro*, lying bleeding and dying in the dust.

Grinning and clenching his cheroot in his teeth, El Pitón picked up his white champion, smoothed its feathers and tucked it back under his arm. After collecting his winnings, he stepped up onto a packing crate and held the bird in the air like a trophy as the winning gamblers hooted and cheered.

Then, just as El Pitón was stepping down off the crate, a gunshot rang out, sending men diving into the dust, and a bullet exploded off the wall right behind where El Piton's head had been a moment before. El Pitón jerked his pistol from his belt and wheeled toward the mouth of the alley, where the shot had come from, as his men also spun and raised their rifles, taking aim. But then they all lowered their guns, looking confused, Sebastiano said. "Even El Pitón." When Sebastiano edged forward to look up the alley, he saw a young girl standing alone at the entrance. "The girl called Itzel," he said. No one had seen her since El Pitón had taken her away to the mountains months before. Many had thought she was dead. Now, there she stood, thin and wan, hair and clothes disheveled, arms extended straight out in front of her, holding a pistol pointed at El Pitón.

Quina gasped. Nate thought he had misheard.

"*Cómo?*" Mateo said, sitting up straight at the edge of his chair. "*Qué estás diciendo? Itzel le disparó a El Pitón?*"

"*Ojalá fuera verdad,*" Sebastiano said. "*Pero no.*"

El Pitón remained calm, Sebastiano said. He smiled a slow smile, returned his pistol to his belt, and began walking slowly toward Itzel, reaching out his arms to her like a lover, crooning her name. "Itzel, *querida, mi amor....*" At first, Sebastiano said, Itzel did not respond. She didn't move or lower her gun. Then, as El Pitón kept walking toward her, she cried out, dropped the gun and ran north in the direction of the church.

El Pitón's smile vanished, and he and his men took off after her.

"I knew what they would do if they caught her," Sebastiano said. "So, I went around the other way. I thought if I could reach her first I could hide her in the jungle." Sebastiano hung his head. "But I was not fast enough."

"What happened?" Mateo asked.

Sebastiano shook his head. "*No sé.*"

"What do you mean you don't know!" Mateo bellowed.

"I told you! I wasn't fast enough!" Sebastiano said, becoming distraught. "By the time I got to the church, they were shooting."

"Shooting!" Mateo roared, incredulous.

"*Sí.*"

"In the church!" Mateo smashed a fist down hard on his thigh.

"*Sí.*"

"How? *Madre de Dios.* How did this happen?"

"I told you! I don't know!"

"I know," came a calm voice from among the travelers being tended near the fire. A stocky man with sad, dark eyes, leathery skin and a bloody bandage over the left side of his forehead stepped forward. "I am Eliad," he said simply. "I was there. *En la iglesia. Fue una massacre. Muchos fueron heridos. Muchos murieron. Hombres, mujeres, niños.*"

Another collective cry went up from the camp. Mateo collapsed forward in his chair, elbows on thighs, head in hands, and sat silent and still. Then he dropped his hands, stood slowly and motioned for Eliad to take his chair.

"You are hurt," Mateo said. "You are tired. "*Siéntese, por favor.* You do not have to speak."

"*No, gracias,*" Eliad said, drawing himself up. "I will stand. I will speak. You must know." He looked around at the people who had drawn close to hear. "*Todos deben saber.*"

Mass was in progress and Tatic was preparing to serve Communion, Eliad said, when one of the church's heavy double doors banged open and a girl came running up the center aisle, calling his name.

"Tatic! Tatic! *Ayudeme! Ayudeme!*"

The priest put down the cup he was holding and came around the altar and hurried down the aisle toward her. When they reached each other, the girl fell to her knees, clutched at his robe, looked up at him and cried out again.

"Tatic! Tatic! *Ayudeme! Ayudeme!*"

Eliad saw terror in the girl's eyes.

Before the old priest could do anything, the second heavy door banged open and los paramilitaristas swarmed in, fanning out along the walls, automatic rifles raised and pointed, ready to fire. At the sight of them, Eliad said, people began crying, whimpering and cowering. Mothers clutched their children, men hugged their wives.

Then, El Pitón appeared in the entranceway, Eliad said, and things happened very quickly after that. Snarling, red-faced, El Pitón stomped up the aisle toward the girl and put a hand on his pistol. Tatic quickly stepped in front of her and opened his arms wide to the man coming toward them. *"En el nombre de Dios,"* Eliad heard Tatic say just as El Pitón jerked out his pistol and shot Tatic in the chest. People began screaming and running for the door, and El Pitón's men opened fire, spraying bullets everywhere. The priest crumpled to the floor, the girl threw herself on top of him, and El Pitón stood over her and fired his pistol again, shooting her in the back.

The church became a slaughterhouse, filled with the sounds of rifle fire and screams, haze of gunsmoke and stench of blood as los paramilitaristas kept shooting and shooting, and men and women and children fell onto the benches and the floor or clambered and stumbled over the dead and wounded, desperate to escape.

"That is when I arrived," Sebastiano said softly, shamefaced. "I heard the shooting. People were running out of the church. Many were hurt. I took them to the jungle."

"You did well," Eliad said to Sebastiano. He turned to Mateo. "He saved lives." He bowed his head. *"Fue terrible. Terrible."*

When the gunfire finally stopped, Eliad said, a great many people lay fallen over the benches and on the floor. El Pitón and his men walked among them, shooting anyone who moved or made a sound. Eliad had been knocked against a bench and down to the ground by a big man who had been shot while trying to push past him. The man fell on top of him. "I did not move or make a sound," he said. "That is how I lived."

When all the moans had been silenced with gunshots and all movement stilled, Eliad heard El Pitón call to one of his men.

"Chuy! *Mi rifle!"*

He heard one more eruption of gunfire, bullets spraying the back wall of the church, and then something heavy crashing to the floor. *"El crucifijo,"* he said, shaking his head sadly.

And then the shooting stopped and El Pitón and his men left and stillness descended. A silence like no other. The silence of death.

Eliad stayed down, not moving, barely breathing, until he was sure the murderers had gone. Then he rose and went up and down every row of benches, from person to person, to every man, woman, and child, looking for others who were still alive. "There was no one," he said.

Sebastiano, meanwhile, had led those who escaped into the jungle and was still helping people find hiding places when he heard El Pitón and his men coming after them, tracking the sounds of whimpering children and crying babies.

"Again, I was not fast enough," Sebastiano said. "And I did not have a gun." Armed only with a blade, he circled back and managed to jump and kill one paramilitarista as he dragged a screaming boy from his hiding place and pulled another off a woman he was raping and left him bleeding on the ground, as good as dead. "I did what I could," he told Mateo. "But it was not enough."

"No, my friend," Mateo said, laying a heavy hand on Sebastiano's shoulder. "Eliad is right. You did well. You saved lives."

"Some," Sebastiano said. "Not enough."

For what seemed an eternity los paramiliaristas searched the jungle. "They found some of us, but not all of us," Sebastiano said. "We heard gunshots, screams. Many men fought to protect their families. But we did not have weapons. There was nothing we could do but try to stay hidden, to live to fight again."

Mateo nodded, "You did the right thing."

When the paramilitaristas were done, when they were gone, Sebastiano and a few other men searched for survivors—and found more death. One woman had hidden with her infant in a pouch-like defilade at the base of a large tree. A gunman had found her, thrown her infant into the brush, raped and beaten her, then put a bullet in her head.

Another gunman, or perhaps the same one, had dragged a pregnant woman out of her hiding place, cut out her unborn child with a machete, then hacked the mother and the baby to death.

"*Basta!*" Lourdes cried out, lifting her hands in the air in a gesture of surrender, tears streaming down her face. "*No más! Por favor, no más!*" The old woman covered her face with her hands and bent forward, sobbing. Nate saw Quina gently put Rafael down on the ground beside her and rise up on her knees to embrace the old woman, her own face ashen and streaked with tears. Nate wanted to go to her, but some instinct told him not to intrude.

"*Lo siento,*" Sebastiano said softly, bowing his head toward the two women.

"*Está bien,*" Mateo said. "We need to know. We need to hear."

Sebastiano nodded. He sighed heavily. "These people," he said, turning a weary hand toward the other men and women who had straggled into camp with him, who were now spread out on the ground around the fire, sipping posh and chicha as others tended their wounds. "They were there, too. Now they are with us."

Mateo studied the new arrivals, nodded, looked down at the ground, then back at Sebastiano.

"How many?" Mateo asked.

"*Aquí?*" Sebastiano said.

"No." Mateo gazed down at Tatic, his eyes filled with grief and love. He looked back at Sebastiano. "How many?"

Sebastiano nodded. "*Veinte dos.* Twenty-two. Mostly women and children."

Still on her knees bent over Lourdes, Quina straightened, closed her eyes, took a deep breath as if bracing herself and looked up at Sebastiano.

"Alegra?" she asked in a hoarse whisper. "Teresa?"

Lourdes sat up as Quina spoke the names and took her hand.

"No," Sebastiano said. "*No estaban en la iglesia.* They are well."

Quina's eyes flooded with tears. "*Gracias a Dios, gracias a Dios,*" she said, sobbing and collapsing into Lourdes's arms.

Alegra? Teresa? Nate thought. *Who are they?* In all Nate's days in camp, he had never heard Quina mention them. And yet, she had asked about them first.

Sebastiano turned back to Mateo. "There is no going back now," he said. "There must be blood for blood. Death for death."

"*Sí,*" Eliad seconded. "*Debemos luchar.*"

"*Sí! Sí!*" others began shouting. "We must fight! We must fight!" people chanted, pumping their fists in the air.

"*Sí! Sí!*" Mateo said, putting his hands up to quiet the crowd. "Yes, we must fight! But we must be ready! We must strike when the time is right!"

Distracted by the outburst, Nate turned back to check on Quina, but she was gone. Scanning the square, he saw her disappear into her quarters. By the time he reached her doorway, she had changed into green fatigues and was stuffing clothing and gear into a knapsack. He watched in silence, waiting for her to notice him, but she didn't look up.

"What are you doing?"

No answer.

"Quina, what are you doing?"

She continued packing.

"I am going to Mirador," she said finally, without looking up.

"What? What are you talking about? You can't go to Mirador. Weren't you listening? It isn't safe."

Quina stopped packing and looked up at him. "Yes, I was listening. That is why I must go."

She closed the knapsack, slung it over a shoulder, and turned toward the door. Nate blocked her way.

"What do you mean you must? Why must you go?"

Quina did not answer. She averted her eyes. Nate ducked his head into her line of sight, seized her gaze and held it.

"Is it because of Alegra?"

Quina inhaled sharply. She looked away. Nate put a finger to her chin and gently turned her face back toward him, waited until she looked up.

"Quina, who is Alegra? You never—"

"She is my daughter."

"Your—"

Quina stepped around Nate and out the door. Nate spun and took her arm.

"Quina, wait."

She stopped and turned to him, looking impatient, angry, determined. In the middle of the square, people were still gathered around the dwindling light of the expiring bonfire, tending the injured, debating what to do about the horrible news they had just received.

"I didn't know you had a daughter," Nate said to Quina, keeping his tone calm.

"Yes. Her name is Alegra," Quina said. "She is six years old. She is with Teresa."

"Who's Teresa?"

"Her grandmother."

"Your mother?"

"No."

Nate nodded

"So, she's there and you're here."

"Yes."

"I don't—"

"I thought she would be safer there. But now...."

She turned and began walking again, and again Nate put a hand on her arm and stopped her.

"Quina, wait. You can't go tonight. Wait until tomorrow. I'll go with you."

"No," Quina said, pulling free. "I must go now."

"Quina, be reasonable," Nate said, taking her arm again. "It's pitch black out there. You can't go walking through the jungle at night."

Just then, the last charred and glowing stack of branches on the bonfire collapsed, belching sparks skyward, and Nate saw Oscar and Mateo walking briskly toward them. Mateo looked angry. Oscar looked ready to pounce.

They think we're arguing.

"*Qué pasa aquí?*" Mateo demanded, and then, noticing Quina's knapsack, "*A donde vas?*"

"*A* Mirador," Quina said, hitching up the knapsack.

"*Ahora?*" Mateo looked surprised.

"*Sola?*" Oscar said, incredulous. "*Por tí mismo?*"

"Mateo, tell her not to go," Nate said. "Tell her to wait until tomorrow at least."

Quina set her jaw and narrowed her eyes.

"No one tells me what to do," she said. "I am going."

"*No puedes,*" Oscar growled.

Quina glared at him. "*Sí, puedo!*"

"Okay, okay," Mateo said, raising his palms in surrender. "Go if you must go. But go quickly. Time is short."

"No!" Oscar protested.

"Oscar, she must," Mateo said. "*Su hija....*"

Nate looked at the two men in astonishment. They knew about Alegra. Of course, they did. Only he hadn't known. The gringo. The outsider. The norteamericano Oscar was always telling Mateo not to trust. The realization stung. But there was no time for that now.

"All right. All right," Nate said, mimicking Mateo's gesture. He turned to Quina. "If you're going, I'm going with you."

"No!" Oscar protested. "No! I will go!"

"*Basta!*" Quina said angrily, waving her hands in front of her face as if to make all three men disappear. "I am going!"

"No, wait!" Nate pleaded, taking her arm again. "Quina, please! I'm coming with you."

"No, Nate. You are needed—"

Nate held up a hand to silence her, looked Oscar in the eye, daring him to speak, then turned to Mateo.

"Look, the website is in good shape. The pages are ready to be uploaded. Rafael knows how to do that, and you know most of it. He can teach you anything else you need to know. There's really not much for me to do now until we're ready to go live, and unless that's happening in the next few days and you just haven't told me"—Nate couldn't resist the dig—"I'm guessing we can be back in time for that."

"*Es loco!*" Oscar protested. "*Loco!*"

Mateo rubbed his chin, turned to Quina.

"Two are safer than one, *no crees?*"

"But you need him here."

"No, he doesn't, Quina," Nate said.

"No, he is right," Mateo said, nodding. "We can spare him." He gave Nate a hard look. "But not for too long."

Nate nodded.

Quina shook her head. "Nate, you do not have to do this."

"Yes, I do, Quina. I want to. Let me. Please."

Quina looked down, considering. "Okay," she said. She looked up at Nate, her expression softened. "But we must go quickly."

"*Mierda!*" Oscar exploded, throwing his hands in the air. "*Él no puede protegerla! Yo puedo protegerla!*"

Nate shrugged off the remark, but Quina got angry.

"I do not need your protection," she shot back. "I can protect myself."

"*Calmate! Calmate!*" Mateo said, raising his palms in the air. He turned to Oscar.

"*Sí*, Oscar, you could protect her," he said, putting a hand on Oscar's shoulder, trying to calm the woman and reason with him. "But you are needed here. Time is short, and there is much to do. We must prepare for the coming fight, train the new fighters. We must decide how to respond to the massacre." Mateo fell silent and both men lowered their heads. Mateo looked up. "You are the best at tactics, Oscar. *Y usted es nuestro major luchador y maestro, no es verdad?*"

Oscar seethed, but he did not argue. Mateo patted his shoulder.

"It is best, *sí*. We can spare these two. But we cannot spare you. You are needed here."

Knowing he'd been out-argued and making no effort to conceal his anger and his jealousy, Oscar let fly a rapid, indecipherable string of Spanish curse words and stomped away.

Mateo turned to Quina. "You have all that you need?"

Quina patted her knapsack. "*Sí.*"

Mateo gave Nate a once-over. "You have no weapon."

Nate fished in his pocket and produced a small folding knife one of the other residents had given him.

Mateo shook his head in sad amusement and removed the web belt from his waist. On it hung a brown leather holster with a .45 automatic pistol and a leather pouch containing two full magazines. He fastened the buckle and handed the rig to Nate.

"Here," he said. "Take this. You know how to use it now and you may need it."

Nate took the belt. He slipped his arm through the loop and let it rest on his shoulder.

Mateo squinted up at the night sky. "A clear sky," he said. "We will use the satellite phone to arrange a boat. Quina, you know the place, *sí*?"

Quina nodded. She turned to Nate. "*Listo?*"

"One second," Nate said, looking around for Rafael. He saw the boy standing a few feet away leaning on his crutches, watching them, silent and wide-eyed.

"Rafael, *ven acá*," Nate called.

The boy approached reluctantly. When Nate squatted in front of him, he saw hurt, fear and anger in the boy's luminous eyes. Nate put his hands on the boy's shoulders.

"I'll be away for a few days. You're in charge of the computer hut while I'm gone, okay? No one touches anything unless you say so. Not even this guy." He jerked a thumb up at Mateo, who nodded obedience. "You're the boss until I return, okay?"

Rafael looked down at the ground.

"Okay?" Nate repeated, ducking his head to find the boy's eyes. "I'm depending on you, Rafael. I need you to take care of things while I'm gone. Will you do that for me?"

The boy looked down, frowned, looked up again into Nate's eyes. "Where are you going?"

"To Mirador."

"I want to go with you."

Nate's heart stirred.

"And I'd like to take you with me. But I can't, Rafael. I will miss you. But I'll be back soon."

"When?"

"Soon."

The boy's look was one of disbelief.

Nate slipped his arms under the boy's armpits and lifted him in a warm embrace. Rafael dropped his crutches and wrapped his arms and one good leg around Nate's neck and back. Nate held him tight, then knelt, patted the boy's back, picked up his crutches, gently removed the boy's arms from around his neck and got him standing again. He stood and rested his hands on the boy's shoulders.

"Look at me, Rafael." The boy looked up. "I will be back, okay?"

The boy lowered his eyes and nodded sadly.

"Okay?"

The boy nodded again. "Okay," he said softly.

"Okay." Nate tousled the boy's thick, silky hair. "Will you walk us to the gate?"

Rafael nodded, and Nate turned to Quina.

"Okay. *Listo.*"

Mateo and Rafael walked them to the front of the compound. When they reached the gate, Mateo gave Quina a quick, hard hug, then wrapped his huge arms around Nate and pulled him into a crushing embrace. He let go, pushed back and rested his hands on Nate's shoulders, just as Nate had done with Rafael a moment before.

"Goodbye, my friend. *Vaya con Dios.*"

Nate tried to come up with some appropriate response, but his Spanish and even his English failed him, and Quina was already heading toward the gate. So he simply nodded. Then, without ceremony, he turned and followed Quina through the arched doorway and into the darkness. ▲

CHAPTER 27

Return to Mirador

Nate and Quina walked through the night, sweating along a narrow jungle trace. Quina led the way, bolstering the light of the full moon with a flashlight, moving in long, steady strides, hardly speaking at all. When a steep climb or tricky descent left Nate winded, he called to her softly, "Quina," and she would stop, allow a few minutes of standing rest, a sip of water, then move on. Nate gradually became aware that he wasn't experiencing fear during this nighttime journey, wasn't watching for snakes or imagining jaguars stalking him in the brush. Because he was with Quina? Because the jungle was no longer such an alien place to him? Because he had changed somehow? Nate wasn't sure. He just noted the difference and kept moving.

They reached the river before daybreak. "We wait here," Quina said. She pulled a small tarp from her knapsack, spread it on the ground in front of a house-size boulder and sat down to rest. Nate sat next to her, leaned back against the rockface and closed his eyes. When he opened them again, the light was returning, and Quina was standing on the riverbank, looking downriver toward the sound of an engine working its way up channel. By the time Nate stood and gathered up the tarp, a small motorcraft was edging toward shore. The young man at the tiller idled the engine while first Quina, then Nate, climbed in. Then he backed the boat into the river, brought it around, and throttled up against the current.

They encountered no rapids during their trip upriver, but the current was strong—impossible to paddle against, Nate realized—and the boatman hugged the shore as much as possible to avoid it. Every now and then the young man and Quina exchanged a few words in a language that sounded like Tzotzil, but, other than that, they were silent, and Nate followed their lead. When the sun was almost directly overhead, the boatman steered the small craft to the river's edge, where two other men stood in a clearing next to a beaten-up truck. Nate thought he recognized the spot as the place where he and Mateo had put into the river months before, but he couldn't be sure. Either way, he thought, he was coming full circle, back to where his journey had begun.

As soon as Nate and Quina stepped out of the boat, the silent helmsman swung the vessel around and disappeared downriver. Quina and the two men on shore walked off a few paces to confer. One of them eyed Nate suspiciously as they talked. Nate met his eyes with a steady gaze, and the man looked away. Nate decided to look around and see if he could find the old church bus in the brush, but, just then, the huddle broke up. The men got into the cab of the truck, and Quina motioned for Nate to climb in the back with her.

"They cannot take us all the way," Quina said as they settled themselves against bags of flour. "It is too dangerous now."

Nate nodded. He wanted to ask Quina about Alegra and Teresa. Is that where Quina went when she disappeared from camp? Why did she go off to train with the rebels when she had a daughter to protect? Did it have to do with her husband? What was his name? When did he die? *How* did he die? Had the soldiers killed him? The paramilitary? El Pitón himself? Nate's mind reeled with questions. But the ride was bumpy and the engine noisy, and he was exhausted and wrung out from drinking and dancing—*Was that really only last night?*—and he was glad just to be off the river and back on solid ground.

After about an hour, the truck pulled to the side of the road and Quina and Nate climbed out.

"A few more miles," Quina said, setting off as soon as her feet touched the ground. Nate tried to get his bearings, but this road wasn't familiar. Again, he fell in behind Quina, following her lead.

They kept to the side of the road when the brush edged close enough to offer quick cover and moved off the road and nearer the brush when it receded. They walked at a natural, almost casual pace so as not to attract attention, but they moved continuously with only brief respites.

They walked for hours, single file, not speaking, and reached the outskirts of Mirador after dark. When the lights of the hamlet hove into view, Quina raised a hand and they halted.

"Listen," she whispered.

Nate listened. He heard nothing. The night was strangely silent, devoid of the usual jungle sounds and the distant sounds of village life. No night birds calling or music drifting on the night air. No distant laughter or murmur of conversation. Not even the barking of a dog. It was as if the whole community had hunkered down and withdrawn into itself, Nate thought. Like some wounded animal hiding from a predator, waiting to die.

Nate and Quina stood quiet and still a while, gazing down warily at the lights of the silent village. Then they looked at each other.

Ready?

Ready.

They resumed their trek.

As they walked, it started raining, and they found themselves moving through a steady, relentless mist just heavy enough to soak them. Quina paid it no mind. She didn't lower her head or turn up her collar. She never broke stride, even as the road turned muddy. If they heard a car or a truck approaching from either direction, they crouched in the dripping undergrowth until it passed. But before the taillights disappeared, Quina was up again and walking steadily, increasing her pace as they neared their destination.

Rounding a bend at the edge of the village, they saw the smoky, eerie glow of what looked like a bonfire at the side of the road ahead of them. Drawing closer, they were able to make out the skeleton of a boxy vehicle engulfed in flames, burning unattended, smoke rising and swirling. Quina stopped for a moment, looked silently at Nate, moved on. Through a gap in the lashing flames, Nate glimpsed a large, round VW emblem on the front of the burning vehicle. He stopped and held still. It was the church van, the broken-down rattletrap that had carried the missioners to Mirador and carried Sarah's coffin to San Cristóbal, the van Nate had thought might still be hidden by the river.

Nate's heart shattered all over again. *Sarah. Can you ever forgive me?* He lifted his face to the dark skies and falling mist. *If there is a God, let that bastard El Pitón still be here so I can hunt him down and kill him like a dog. I can die, too. I don't care. As long as I get to watch him die first.*

Looking up the road, Nate saw Quina standing off a few paces, watching him, waiting. He readjusted his belt and holster and walked on.

As they entered the village, the rain let up and the full moon broke through the clouds, its light glistening on glazed cobblestones, awakening sleeping shadows and launching a pandemonium of them against walls, conjuring spectral figures that seemed to trail Nate and Quina, matching them stride for stride. Nate could smell the moist earth and wet stones.

Teresa lived in a part of Mirador Nate had never visited. Quina led the way silently down a narrow street, through an alley, and around a corner, where a snarling dog leaped at them—teeth bared, ears flattened—and was yanked sideways by his tether, just as Nate pulled Quina away from his snapping jaws. They collected themselves and kept going.

Nate was just beginning to wonder how much farther it would be when Quina finally stopped at the gate of a low fence surrounding a small shack with a tin roof and wood-plank walls. The fence was fashioned from sapling stalks and branches. The gate was made of bits of plywood and linoleum flooring.

"This is it," Quina whispered.

Where Nate came from, this tumbledown structure would have trouble passing for a shoddily built boys' clubhouse and would probably be torn down as a public eyesore. Here, it was someone's home.

Quina unlooped a string latch from a nail in the fence post and slowly pushed the gate open. With Nate close behind, she silently crossed the yard and opened the door to the shack little by little, just wide enough to peek in. Peering over her head, Nate saw an old woman with a thick white braid over her shoulder sitting at a small wooden table, reading what looked like a heavy black Bible by the light of a smoky kerosene lamp.

Quina pushed the door open a little wider. It gave with a scrape and squeak, startling the woman up out of her chair, a look of terror on her face that transformed instantly into joy at the sight of Quina. The two women rushed into each other's arms as Nate stepped quietly inside and closed the door.

"*Gracias a Dios! Gracias a Dios!*" the old woman murmured huskily, taking Quina's face in her hands and kissing her on each cheek and on the forehead. *"Tu has venido! Benditos los ojos que te ver. Cuánto esperaba que vinieras. Gracias a Dios. Gracias."*

"Sí, he venido. He venido," Quina whispered, wrapping her arms around the woman. *"Estoy tan dichoso de verte."*

While the two women hugged and kissed, Nate looked around the tiny, tidy hut. The small wooden table occupied the center of one side of the room. Four straight back chairs with chipped and weathered blue-green paint were arranged around it. A child's drawings adorned the rudimentary walls—pencil sketches on white paper of a smiling lady with long dark hair, another smiling lady with a long braid, a dog. In a corner, a soot-stained coffee pot rested on a Coleman propane camper stove. Above it, a row of clay pots of varying sizes sat on a narrow shelf, one containing a clutch of yellow and red wildflowers. A pale blue bureau with a missing bottom drawer partitioned off a sleeping area furnished with a single cot. A wooden crucifix, perhaps twelve inches high, hung on the wall above it. A large, beaten-up packing trunk was pushed against the far wall. On the floor next to the cot, a little girl with long dark hair and thick eyelashes lay sleeping on a pallet of quilts. She wore a pale nightgown that looked at least a size too small, the skirt barely covering her knees.

Quina released herself from the old woman's embrace and turned to Nate, one hand resting on the woman's shoulder.

"Nate, this is Teresa, mother of my husband, Amador," Quina said softly.

Amador, Nate thought. *Finally, his name.* Nate gave Teresa a respectful bow. *"Con mucho gusto,"* he said in a voice just above a whisper.

The woman nodded back, a questioning look in her eyes.

Quina turned to Teresa. "Teresa," she said softly. "This is Nate Hunter. *Es un amigo. Él nos está ayudando."*

The introduction unsettled the old woman, Nate could see. She clasped her hands and kneaded her fingers, studying him with a worried expression. But then he saw her try to collect herself, as if remembering that Nate was her guest.

"Hoon-tare," she repeated graciously. *"Ahh. El cazador."*

"No," Nate said, smiling, shaking his head and raising a hand. *"No soy—"*

"Sí," Quina said, cutting him off. *"Sí, el cazador."*

Quina gave Nate a look that silenced any protest and went to the sleeping child. She knelt beside her, eased her silky dark hair from her face with a gentle sweep of a hand and softly kissed her cheek. The child stirred and opened her eyes. She blinked, fluttering her long lashes, and squinted at the face so close to hers.

"*Mami?*" she said in a hoarse whisper.

"*Sí, mi niña. Soy yo.*"

"*Mami!*" The little girl cried, sitting up and throwing her arms around Quina's neck. "*Mami! Mami!*"

Tears glistening in her eyes, Quina gathered the child in her arms.

"*Sí, mi corazón. Estoy aquí.*"

Quina rose and lifted her daughter in her arms, holding her close, smothering her with kisses. The girl wrapped her legs around her mother and buried her face in her neck. "*Mami. Mami. Estás aquí. Estás aquí.*"

Quina leaned back, swept away her daughter's sleep-tangled hair again and studied her face , smiling, eyes filled with love.

"*Tan hermosa,*" Quina crooned. "*Tan adulta.*"

Quina shifted Alegra to a hip and carried her to Nate. Easing the girl's hair from her face one more time, she introduced them.

"*Alegra, mi corazón, se trata de Nate Hunter.*"

Nate smiled warmly and made a slight bow.

"*Con mucho gusto.*"

She was a beautiful child, with her mother's dark hair and eyes, a heart-shaped face and perfect sepia-toned skin.

The child smiled shyly, then buried her face in her mother's shoulder again.

"*Ahh,*" Quina said. "*Alegra tiene miedo. No tengas miedo, mi niña. No tengas. Él es un amigo.*"

But Quina's attempt at reassurance failed. The child clutched her neck tighter and would not raise her head. Quina looked at Nate and shrugged, then turned to Teresa.

"*Está bien?*" she inquired about her daughter.

"*Sí. Está bien,*" Teresa assured her. "*A veces, un poquito tímida....*" She darted her eyes toward Nate.

Quina smiled, hitching her daughter up on her hip and stroking her hair. She turned back to Teresa, her expression serious.

"*Y tú, Teresa? Estás bien?*"

"*Sí. Estoy bien,*" Teresa said, dismissing the question with a wave of

a hand. She returned to the wooden table and sat down wearily. *"Pero
...pero....."* She bowed her head and shook it slowly. She looked up
at Quina with eyes darkened by sadness, and fear. *"Oíste lo que pasó?"*
she whispered. *"En la iglesia?"* She put a gnarled finger to her lips and
pointed to Alegra.

Quina nodded. *"Sí. Hemos oído. Sabemos."*

Teresa nodded, wiped her eyes and looked up at Nate.

"Perdóname," she said. She pointed to the chair across from her and
waved her hand down in a sitting gesture. *"Siéntase, por favor.* Please. Sit."

Nate pulled out the chair and sat. Quina took the chair between
them and arranged Alegra on her lap. The child was falling back to
sleep in her mother's arms.

Teresa closed her Bible and drew it close, stroking the cracked leather
cover as if for comfort.

"Fue terrible, terrible," she murmured. *"Una gran tragedia."*

Quina nodded sadly.

"Muchas fueron assesinadas," Teresa continued. *"En la iglesia. En la
selva. Y Tatic...."* She shook her head.

After los paramilitaristas finally left, Teresa said, Sebastiano and Fulgencio wanted to try to get Tatic to a doctor in San Cristóbal, but they
could not find the church van. It was gone. And Tatic refused to go.
He wanted to be taken to La Libertad to say good-bye to his children,
and to give them one last blessing. *"Eso es lo que él dijo,"* Teresa said
quietly. *Quería decir adios."* She stroked the cover of the Bible again,
then looked up at Quina, her eyes wet with tears. Quina sat quietly,
meeting her gaze.

"Lo hizo?" Teresa asked softly. *"Vivió para decir adios?"*

Quina nodded slowly.

"Y...ahora?"

Quina bowed her head.

Teresa put a hand to her mouth and let silent tears flow.

Quina leaned toward the old woman and put a gentle hand on
her arm, and Nate and the two women sat in silence for a moment,
mourning Tatic.

"Estos son los días de tristeza," Teresa said finally, laying her hands
atop her Bible. *"Muy malo. Muy malo."*

There had been no Mass since the massacre, Teresa said. The victims died without receiving the Last Rights and were buried in the

cemetery behind the church with no priest to pray over them. Itzel and her mother, Maria, were buried next to each other. Maria had been in church when El Pitón killed Itzel, Teresa said. When she screamed out and tried to make her way to her daughter, El Pitón's men killed her, too.

Nate felt numb. Sarah had put her life at risk to protect Itzel and Maria from El Pitón. Now Sarah was dead. And they were dead, too.

"*No puede durar siempre,*" Quina said fervently, squeezing Teresa's arm. "*No puede.*"

"*Sí,*" Teresa said sadly. "*No puede. Pero tenemos que continuar. Qué más podemos hacer?*"

Quina sat back, sighing. She checked her daughter. Alegra was asleep. Quina carried the girl back to her pallet and laid her down gently. She covered her with a thin quilt, kissed her cheek, smoothed her hair again and returned to the table. Watching Quina, Nate saw her expression turn grave. Sitting down again, she leaned toward Teresa and took the woman's hands in hers.

"*Y El Pitón?*" Quina said. "*Donde está? Todavía está en Mirador?*"

Teresa frowned and shook her head. "*No. No está aquí. Se fue.*"

"*A donde? Sabes tú?*"

"*No sé. Nadie sabe. No está aquí. Eso es todo lo que sabemos. Dicen que regresó a las montañas.*"

Quina turned to Nate.

"He is gone."

Nate nodded. "Yes. In the mountains again."

"Yes. After the massacre, he will probably lie low for a while."

"What about Delgado?" Nate asked Quina. He turned to Teresa. "*Los soldados,*" he said. "*Están....*" He turned back to Quina. "How do you say 'looking for'?"

"*Buscando.*"

"Ach!" Teresa said, grimacing and flicking a hand derisively. "*Los soldados no hacen nada. Nada!*"

Nate nodded, not sure how he felt about this piece of news. It made him sick that El Pitón and his men were getting away with even more murders. But if the bastard's retreat to the mountains meant he and Quina would be able to get Alegra and Teresa back to La Libertad safely, he was glad for that.

Teresa sat up and put her hands in her lap. "*Perdóname. Debes tener hambre.*" She stood and went to her cookstove. "*Es bueno que hayas venido esta noche,*" she said as she began preparing a simple meal. "*Mañana es Día de Muertos.*" She gave Quina an expectant look. "*Recuerdas?*"

"*Ah, sí, por supuesto,*" Quina said, nodding. She turned to Nate. "Tomorrow is our Day of the Dead celebration. Perhaps you have heard of it."

"I've heard of it. Is it like our American Halloween?"

"I do not know much about your Halloween, but I think so, yes. It is the time when we remember and honor our dead. It is a big celebration."

Teresa reached over and gave Quina's hands a quick squeeze.

"*Mañana nosotros decorémos las sepulturas de los muertos,*" she said, her eyes shining. "*La sepultura de Amado....*" She bowed her head. "*Y los otros. Las víctimas....*"

"*Sí,*" Quina said softly. "*Mañana.*"

Nate understood enough to get antsy.

"We should get back, Quina," he said, giving her a warning look. "All of us. As soon as possible."

"*Sí, sí,* I know. But tomorrow is an important day. We will stay one day. Then we will go. All of us."

Nate experienced a sudden, unsettling sense of déjà vu. One day. That's what Sarah had asked for. One day, just one day. Was this really happening? Here he was again, in Mirador, arguing with a woman he cared about deeply, trying to convince her to leave, unable to force her, unwilling to go without her. He tried to shake off his creeping sense of dread. *Stop it,* he told himself. *You're being superstitious.*

Teresa served a simple meal of beans and tortillas and a warm cornmeal porridge that Quina and Teresa called *pinole.* When they had finished eating, Teresa tried to get Quina to take her sleeping cot, but Quina refused. So Teresa folded blankets into two sleeping pallets on the floor next to Alegra. Nate hung his gunbelt on a high nail and collapsed on the outer pallet, exhausted and pleasantly full. When Quina knelt on the middle pallet to check on Teresa, the child stirred and woke. Quina bent close and shushed her gently until she closed her eyes again, tucked the thin quilt over her and kissed her cheek. Then she lay down on her pallet next to Nate's as Teresa cleared the dishes. Turning his head to gaze at Quina, Nate saw Alegra lying on her side, watching him, taking careful stock of this strange-looking, light-skinned man. Nate smiled, lifted a hand and gave a little wave goodnight with a finger. Alegra turned away.

When she finished clearing the dishes, Teresa moved the kerosene lamp from the table to the bureau, sat down on her cot and turned her back as she slipped out of her clothes and into her nightdress.

Nate and Quina lay within inches of each other not touching, looking into each other's eyes. The shadowy beauty of the woman backlit by flickering lamp light stirred such deep feelings within him that he had to look away. He interlaced his fingers behind his head to keep from reaching for her, took a deep breath and let it out slowly.

"Tell me about Day of the Dead," he whispered, turning to look at her again.

Quina smiled. "We will talk in the morning," she murmured. "It has been a long journey. Sleep now. Tomorrow will come soon enough."

Quina looked once more at Alegra, who was asleep. Teresa extinguished the lantern flame and the room went dark.

"*Que duerman bien, hijos míos,*" Teresa said softly.

"*Y tú, Teresa,*" Quina whispered.

Teresa's cot creaked as she lay back and pulled up her quilt, and then all was still.

Nate turned again to Quina. Her eyes were closed. In the moonlight slanting in through gaps in the hut's plank walls, he tried to memorize the dim outline of her face. She was sleeping. He listened to her breathe. ▲

CHAPTER 28

Day of the Dead

When Nate awoke, Alegra was standing over him, smiling. For a few seconds, he watched her through one slitted eye, then forced the eye open all the way. The other eye came open grudgingly a moment later. Nate yawned and rose up on an elbow, rubbing his bristly chin. Bringing Alegra into focus in a pool of sunlight, he saw she was already dressed in a simple, blue smock.

"*Buenos días*," Nate said.

"*Buenos días*," Alegra answered solemnly in a delicate, sweet voice.

Progress, he thought. *She's shy, but not as shy as Rafael.*

Nate glanced around the room. No sign of Teresa or Quina. Teresa's cot was neatly made up, and Alegra and Quina's sleeping pallets were folded and stacked atop it. Nate looked up at Alegra again and noticed she was holding a piece of white paper in one hand.

"*Qué tienes?*" he said, yawning, motioning to the paper.

No response. Alegra simply stood there watching him.

Nate pointed to the paper.

"*Qué es?* In your hand? *En... la mano?*"

Alegra extended her arm, offering the paper to Nate.

"For me?" He pointed to himself. "*Para mí?*"

Alegra nodded.

"*Gracias*," Nate said, accepting the paper. It was a surprisingly good pencil sketch of the head of a jaguar. The cat's eyes held a set stare, as if locked onto prey and preparing to attack. In a puzzling clash of images, the cat was clutching a flower sideways between his teeth, the blossom protruding from one side of its mouth, the stem from the other. Alegra had worked hard to fill in the petals. It looked like a black orchid.

"*Ahh...*" Nate said. "*El jaguar.*"

"*El cazador,*" Alegra answered, pointing to Nate.

Nate stifled the impulse to correct her. Instead, he pointed to the flower.

"*Por qué—*"

Before he could say more, the door to the hut scraped open and Quina came in. She was dressed in a clean pair of brown pants and an embroidered blouse, her lustrous hair tied in a ponytail at the nape of her neck. Alegra ran to her and leaped into her arms. Quina hugged her daughter, smothered her with kisses and then shifted the child to a hip.

"I see Alegra gave you her present," she said, noticing the paper in Nate's hands.

Nate nodded and held out the drawing.

"A jaguar. Well done, too. *Muy bonito, Alegra. Me gusta mucho.*"

Quina looked at her daughter. "*El Señor Hunter dice que le gusta, Alegra. Que dices tu?*"

The girl peered up at Nate over her own upper arm. "*Gracias,*" she said shyly.

"*Gracias qué?*" Quina prodded her.

"*Gracias, Señor Hoon-tare.*"

"*Muy bien,*" Quina said, smiling and kissing Alegra on the cheek. "She drew it this morning while you were sleeping," she said, turning to Nate. "She said it was a picture of you. She said she had a dream about you. This is what she saw."

Nate studied the portrait again, searching for some resemblance to himself, something in the eyes, the shape of the face. He shook his head.

"I'm afraid I don't see it."

"She does," Quina said. "Some things only a child can see."

"Come," Quina said, taking Alegra's hand and extending her other hand to Nate. "Teresa has prepared breakfast. It is *Día de Muertos*. We have much to do."

Nate looked down at his dirty, rumpled clothing, ran a hand over the stubble on his face.

"I should clean up," he said, and then he remembered he had no other clothes.

Quina studied him. She took a step back, shifted her gaze to the packing trunk against the wall and stared at it, lost in thought. She turned back to Nate, pressed her lips together as if debating something, then crouched in front of her daughter and took the child's hands.

"*Mi hija*," she said to Alegra. "*El cazador necesita ropa limpia. Le daremos algo para llevar? Qué piensas?*"

Alegra looked at Nate, up at his messed and dirty hair, down at his dirty clothing. She turned back to her mother and nodded seriously.

"*Sí?*" Quina prompted her.

"*Sí,*" Alegra said, nodding again.

"*Bueno,*" Quina said softly, kissing her daughter on the forehead.

Quina stood, went to the trunk, knelt beside it and opened it. She sank back on her heels and sat silent for a while, hands resting in her lap. Then she came to her knees again, bent over the open trunk, reached in, seemed to move things around and came out with two folded pieces of clothing, one black, one white, and two small items Nate couldn't make out. She lay the clothing on her lap and smoothed it tenderly with both hands. Then she stood, closed the trunk and placed everything on top of it.

"There is a washbasin out back," Quina said softly, turning toward Nate but avoiding his gaze. "We will be in the yard." She returned to Alegra and took her hand. "*Ven, cariña.*"

Alone in the hut, Nate rose, folded his bedding, placed it neatly on Teresa's cot and crossed to the trunk.

Black trousers. A white shirt. A razor. A comb. Nate picked them up carefully, remembering what Quina had said that evening at the Temple. *We are the living. The living need each other to carry on.*

Nate went out back, washed and changed, combed and shaved. The trousers were a little short but otherwise the clothes fit. Amador must also have been tall and lean. Nate rinsed his dirty clothes in his used wash water, hung them on a tree branch and walked around to the small side yard, where Teresa, Quina, and Alegra were sitting on the blue-green chairs at a blue-green table under the low-hanging branches of a cedar tree. Alegra was kneeling on her chair, hunched over a thin tablet of paper on the table in front of her, pencil in hand, working on another drawing.

Quina and Teresa both stared at Nate as he approached. He stopped and looked awkwardly down at himself, the clothes he was wearing.

"*Por favor, siéntese,*" Teresa said finally, kindly, motioning for Nate to take the fourth blue-green chair.

Nate looked at Quina and saw sadness in her eyes. Then, slowly, the sadness softened and warmed, and if she had been seeing a ghost before, now, Nate knew, she was seeing him. Their gazes held, and Nate felt the heat of desire rise between them. Quina smiled slightly, then lowered her eyes and furrowed her brow, and Nate realized that Teresa was observing him discreetly but closely.

"*Sí, siéntate,*" Quina said, blushing slightly. "Sit. Eat."

The table was set with four mugs, a coffee pot and a small, round loaf of bread. Teresa filled Nate's mug with hot brew, and the three adults sat for a long time without speaking, drinking coffee, eating bread, listening to the sounds of morning, looking at the sky, breathing the air, enjoying the cooling breeze. In the distance, the church bells tolled.

Nate turned to Quina in surprise.

"Who—"

"Someone," Quina answered with a small shrug. "Today is *Día de Muertos*. The bells must ring."

Nate tore off another piece of bread. "So tell me about *Día de Muertos*. I don't really know much about it."

Quina set her cup on the table and laced her fingers around it, assuming a teacherly pose.

"In Mexico death is not something we fear," she said. "We honor it. We believe it is not the end—only a stage in the cycle of life. When people die, they are not gone forever. They move on to a different place, but they can come back to visit. Today is the day the souls of the dead return. So for us, it is a happy occasion. A day for a fiesta."

"Our Halloween is a big party, too" Nate said. "But it's not about honoring death. Where I come from, death is sad."

"It is sad for us, too."

"I mean it's not an occasion for a party."

"In Mexico, everything is an occasion for a party. How else can we bear the pain of living?"

Nate chuckled. "That sounds like something Mateo would say."

Quina smiled. "It does, it is true. But he is right. It is our way of facing death. We honor it, but we also laugh at it. My people have done this for hundreds of years, since long before the Spaniards came."

Nate took a bite of his bread. "This is good," he said, holding up the crust.

"*Pan de muerto*," Teresa said, smiling.

"Bread of the dead," Quina said, automatically translating. "It is round to symbolize the endless cycle of life and death."

Quina gazed at her daughter, absorbed in her drawing.

"We believe that today the souls of the dead are with us once again," she said softly. "So our sadness turns to joy. But only for a while. It is... "

She hesitated, lifted her eyes to the puzzle pieces of blue sky carved out by the green latticework of the branches overhead.

"It is... " She looked at Nate. "What is the word?"

"Transitory?" Nate suggested.

Quina nodded. "*Sí*. Transitory."

Nate took another sip of coffee, then put down his cup and stared at it, visions of Sarah suddenly rushing back, flooding him with feelings of pain and loss.

"I wish it were true," he said, talking to himself.

"*Qué?*" Quina asked gently.

Nate looked up at Quina, back down at his cup. "That the dead could return," he said, "even for a day, and you could tell them.... " His words trailed off.

Quina turned her face to the sky again, closed her eyes and breathed deeply. She looked back at Nate, her expression tender.

"Who is to say it is not true?" she said softly, her eyes shining with the hope and belief of an innocent child, open to the possibility of anything. And for a brief, unprotected moment, Nate allowed himself to believe, too.

But we are the living, the breeze seemed to whisper. And in the next instant, before he could stop himself, Nate was imagining creating a life with this beautiful woman sitting across from him. A peaceful life, after the rebellion—right here in Mirador. They could build their own small house near Teresa's, or he could repair and expand hers. They would live together, the four of them....

Quina rose.

"Come."

"Where?"

She frowned and shook her head. "Gringos," she said, in mock annoyance. "You always want to know everything first. Where? Why? How? Just come. Come with me."

Alegra looked up suddenly from her drawing. *"Mami! A donde vas? No te vayas!"*

"Está bien, querida," Quina assured her daughter. *"No te preocupes. Voy a regresar en una hora."*

Alegra looked at her mother gravely. *"Me lo prometas?"*

Quina gave her another reassuring hug and kiss. *"Sí, te lo prometo."*

Quina led Nate back along unfamiliar streets and alleys until they emerged on the north side of the main square, where a scattering of vendors were setting up their stalls and arranging their wares for the celebration. Memories of exploring the same market with Sarah during another celebration came rushing back, and Nate was saddened by how much the market seemed to have changed. The vendors were fewer, the atmosphere more subdued.

Quina turned east, toward the church, pausing to buy a bouquet of yellow and white lilies from a vendor.

"Are we headed where I think we're headed?" Nate asked as Quina paid for the flowers.

She glanced up at him.

"I am going to *la iglesia,"* she said, gesturing for the vendor to keep the coin of change he was holding out to her. He nodded his thanks. She nodded back and turned to Nate, lilies in hand. "You can come or not come," she said calmly. "It is up to you."

Nate did not want to come. The only time he had been in the church had been with Sarah, on the day she died. It had been a beautiful, if decaying, place of peace, prayer and refuge then. Now... Nate did not know what grotesquery might await.

The church doors were partially open. As Nate and Quina approached, they heard activity inside. Nate reluctantly followed Quina into the echoing nave. What he saw shook him.

The church was mostly empty. Some half dozen or so campesinos sat scattered on benches, praying and weeping. Another dozen or so women were on their hands and knees, scrubbing the stone floor where blood stains were still visible. A few of the women looked up as Nate and Quina entered, then bent to their work again, the sound of their scullery brushes and sponges scraping and sloshing across the paving stones providing a rhythmic accompaniment to the soft keening and praying of the few faithful. Two men were up on stepladders propped against the side walls, patching bullet holes in the faded and peeling frescoes, filling them with plaster and smoothing the patches with trowels.

Nate looked around. The walls were riddled with holes, splotched with white patches. The rows upon rows of burning candles were gone. Piles of brass shell casings, broken pottery, and shattered glass were swept into corners that had been crowded with tall, flower-filled clay pots before. There was no scent of pine needles, incense and candle smoke, no music playing on an unseen radio or cassette player. There was only the smell of lye soap and wet plaster and the sounds of praying and weeping mixed with scrubbing and brushing. The bare altar was heaped with flowers, fresh blossoms piled atop browning bouquets. The wooden crucifix had been rehung on the wall behind the altar. Jesus's right arm had snapped off when the crucifix crashed to the floor. It had been reattached with wire.

Quina put a hand on Nate's arm, signaling for him to wait, and walked up the center aisle to the altar. She added her bouquet of lilies to the pile, made the sign of the cross, folded her hands low in front of her and bowed her head in prayer. Then she crossed herself, turned and walked back to Nate, tears welling in her eyes and threatening to spill down her cheeks.

"A day the angels wept," she said in a low, reverent tone, her voice breaking. She wiped her tears. "Come. Teresa and Alegra are waiting."

When they left the church, Nate was surprised to see that the square had become more crowded and the market more lively. He heard music. Laughter. The mood now felt almost joyful. In the streets, men fired small, homemade skyrockets that Quina told him were called *cojetes*. In the market, artisans were making and selling Day of the Dead handicrafts—paper cutouts of skeletons, skeleton puppets, small dolls with skeleton faces, sugar-candy skulls called *calaveras*. Women baked pan de muerto in outdoor ovens. Pitchmen hawked charcoal-broiled ears of corn rubbed with salt and lime and chili powder. Flower vendors were now everywhere, their stalls brimming with red and pink gladiolas, yellow and white daisies, purple cockscomb, and buckets upon buckets of golden-orange marigolds.

"Why all the marigolds?" Nate asked.

"We call them *cempasuchitl*," Quina said. "For us they are the flower of the dead. We scatter them to mark the way back for the souls who are returning, so they can follow their color and fragrance."

Nate looked around in wonder. "It's amazing," he said. "It's only been..." He counted on his fingers. "Three days." He shook his head. "And you look around... you almost wouldn't know."

"It is Day of the Dead," Quina said simply. "It is our tradition. We do not have many chances to be happy. Each one is precious. We cannot let sorrow rob us of them. For us, what happened..." She looked down. "It only makes this day more special." She turned her dark, shining eyes on Nate. "Can you understand that?"

Nate thought, nodded. "Finding joy in the midst of suffering," he said. "Yeah, I can understand it. And I admire it. But I don't think I could do it."

Quina gave him a wry smile. "If you lived here, you would learn."

Back at Teresa's hut, Quina helped the old woman bake corn cakes while Nate watched Alegra make paper cutouts to decorate her father's grave. Around noon, Nate, Quina and Alegra returned to the market to purchase flowers for more decorations. The square was bustling now. Children running and playing. People talking and laughing. Musicians playing their instruments—mostly drums and slender pipe whistles Quina called *tambor y pito*. Vendors selling foods, flowers, trinkets and wares.

Quina bought three large bunches of cempasuchitl and handed them to Nate, then slipped her left hand through his arm and took Alegra's delicate hand in her right. Nate said nothing, not wanting to call attention to Quina's casual intimacy, just wanting to prolong it, enjoy it. "Joy in the midst of suffering," he muttered to himself.

Quina glanced up at him.

"*Sí*," she said, smiling. "It is the way life conquers death, the way we escape our pain... for a little while. But that does not mean we do not feel the pain. And the anger." She looked up at Nate again. "Make no mistake. We do."

Teresa was waiting for them with a basket of supplies at the entrance to the cemetery, standing with other villagers in the dancing green shade of towering cedar, ceiba and zapote trees. Nate thought Quina might withdraw her arm from his as they approached, but she didn't. Nate watched Teresa register their linked arms, then turn a penetrating gaze on Nate. She studied him, searching his eyes. He stood quietly, submitting to the scrutiny. She made a small sound, like a humph, and nodded. Nate offered to carry her basket. She nodded again, handed it to him and took the flowers.

They passed through the double wrought-iron gate with a stream of other villagers carrying bunches of flowers and baskets of supplies, arriving to tend other graves. Inside the cemetery, Nate followed the three generations of women along a graveled path that wound through a field of assorted grave markers: flat and upright headstones, wood and stone crosses, carved statues, domed and peaked structures that looked like small chapels painted in bright colors—pink, sky blue, turquoise, deep yellow, red—with crosses or religious icons on top. Each one a shrine to a lost loved one.

There was no shrine for Sarah. Nate suddenly regretted that. If things worked out, he thought, if he stayed in Mirador, he would see to having one built.

The women stopped and stood in front of two simple white headstones, one newer and whiter, the other older and more worn. The inscription on the newer one read, *Amador Cárdenas del Río—médico, esposo, padre y hijo.* The inscription on the older stone read simply *Jorge Cárdenas del Río.* Neither contained any dates.

"They are plain markers," Quina said apologetically. "We have not had time or money for more." She pointed to the older stone. "Amador's father. Teresa's husband. I never knew him. He died long ago."

Teresa put down the flowers and gestured for Nate to set the basket down beside them. The women and little girl stood quietly before the markers for a few moments, then crossed themselves and prayed softly. Nate took a step back and stood with his head lowered and his hands folded in front of him.

"*Esta es la tumba de mi papá,*" Alegra said to Nate when the women had finished praying.

Nate smiled and nodded.

Then, without a word, maintaining their solemn manner, grandmother, mother, and daughter set about cleaning and decorating the graves. They whisked away leaves and dirt, pulled weeds. Alegra was sent to purchase a tinful of water from an enterprising boy passing among the families with a large pail and ladle. When she returned,

Teresa and Quina pulled brushes and rags from Teresa's basket and commenced scrubbing the stones.

"Can I help?" Nate asked, feeling extraneous.

"*No, gracias*," Teresa said, nodding kindly. "*Está bien.*"

All around them, Nate saw other villagers, mostly women and girls, hard at work tending other graves, sweeping away fallen leaves and twigs, scrubbing simple stones and more elaborate markers with soap and water. They festooned tree branches with paper streamers that dangled almost to the ground—pink, deep yellow, turquoise, sky blue to match the colors of the chapels. They scattered marigolds, baby's breath and purple cockscomb along the pathways and lined them with wax and tallow candles.

When Teresa and Quina were through cleaning and scrubbing, Alegra took a picture frame out of the basket. "*Papá*," she said softly. She kissed the glass and set the frame atop her father's stone. It contained a photograph of a handsome young family: smiling, intelligent-looking, black-haired young man in a dark suit and tie, holding a laughing little girl in the crook of his left arm; a beautiful, smiling, dark-eyed young woman in a pale dress on the man's right side, long black braid over her right shoulder, caressing his arm, pressing in close. Amador, Alegra, Quina.

Women and child stepped back and gazed at the photograph in silence. Nate stood to the side, studying it. Alegra looked about a year old in the photo. Amador was alive then. When had he died? How had he died? Perhaps someday, as they got closer, if they got closer, Quina would tell him. He wanted so much to know. But he would not ask. He knew only this: The photograph made his heart break for Quina, and for Alegra and Teresa. They had lost so much, endured so much. And yet, they persevered.

Quina sighed, rubbed her hands on her pant legs, reached down, took two bottles of beer out of Teresa's basket and set one on each headstone. She looked at Nate.

"They will be thirsty after their long journey," she explained.

She put out two small loaves of bread.

"And they will be hungry. Later, we can share what is left."

Nate was allowed to help Alegra drape the headstones with her paper cutouts as Teresa and Quina decorated the graves with flowers and spiked small, white candles around the perimeter. Teresa stoked a clay censer with balls of pine resin incense that she called *pom* and Quina called *copal.* They would light it later, Quina said, and it would burn all night.

"The candlelight and incense will guide them," Quina said. "Help them find their way."

Nate marveled at the complexity of this woman who was beginning to mean so much to him. The more she revealed herself, the more fascinating she became. College educated, clearly sophisticated, seasoned by hardship and loss, and yet respectful and observant of the ancient rituals and traditions of her people, proud to honor them, and determined, it seemed, to find some small measure of comfort in them, some element of joy, some quiet eddy of peace in a world of turbulent madness. Nate looked around at the many other families busy tending and decorating other graves. Did they really believe what the ancient stories told them? Did they really think that death was not an ending, that the souls of the dead could return? He watched Quina helping Teresa arrange the last flowers around the older grave. Did Quina also believe? Was that her secret? Nate wondered: Could it be true? And laughed to hear himself answer as Mateo might have: Does it matter? No, it didn't. If believing brought comfort, that's what mattered. The rest didn't matter at all.

When they were finished cleaning and decorating the graves, the people of Mirador returned home to eat and rest before the evening procession. After an early, simple dinner, Quina and Teresa changed into brightly colored skirts and traditional red-and-white brocaded *huipiles,* and Quina braided Alegra's hair with blue ribbons to match her frock. Then Teresa and Quina packed two baskets with blankets, shawls, and Alegra's pad and pencil, and they all returned to the square to join the celebration.

The square was filling up with people by the time they arrived, and the mood again was festive. Many women wore the same red-and-white tunics and colorful skirts that Teresa and Quina wore. Men were turned out in their best pressed pants, clean shirts, and crisp hats. The breeze was fragrant with the scents of baked bread and pine incense, candle smoke and flowers. Masked mummers, costumed as death itself, summoned townspeople to join the revelry. Children in homemade costumes, masks and facepaint danced about, mocking death, as bands of minstrels wandered the square, filling the air with the music of accordions and guitars, horns and flutes, drums and a strange percussion instrument Nate remembered seeing at the carnaval his first day in Mirador—a tortoise shell drum and drumstick made of a deer antler.

The reminder of that day and that procession sent a chill down his spine—and made him suddenly question the wisdom of joining this one. He looked around at Teresa, Quina, and Alegra, all the other men, women, and children crowding the square, talking and laughing, waiting for the procession to the cemetery to begin. Did they not remember? Surely they remembered that slaughter, too. People had died. Sarah had died.

Fine, he thought. If this procession did draw soldiers, if it drew the paramilitary, if it drew El Pitón himself, so be it. All Nate asked was that Teresa, Quina, and Alegra not be hurt, and that he have time to retrieve his gun from Teresa's hut and kill El Pitón.

At the rising of the moon and the fall of blue dusk, volleys of rockets streaked and whistled across the sky and exploded in bangs and pops, raining down showers of brilliant sparks and kicking off the procession. An ensemble of child mummers and musicians led the way. Nate, Quina, Teresa, and Alegra all fell in with the other celebrants, walking side by side as the parade snaked through the streets of Mirador toward the cemetery gates. The procession wound past vendors selling calaveras and other candied treats, skeleton puppets, hollow-eyed dolls. Strung on wires stretching rooftop to rooftop across the streets, paper cutouts of skeleton mariachis and skeleton brides and grooms snapped and fluttered in the breeze. Carved and glowing jack-o'-lanterns grinned from doorways and windows. Seeing them, people pointed and laughed the more.

For Nate, the whole event had a surreal, dreamlike quality. He could not stop marveling at how the townspeople were able to resolutely put aside all thoughts of the killings, the tragedy in the church, and, for those who knew—whoever and however many they were—the coming rebellion. Nate did his best to follow their lead.

At the cemetery, the crowd funneled through an arched entrance now wreathed with golden cempasuchitl. In the embrace of the cemetery's stucco walls, families nested at the graves of their loved ones to commence an all-night vigil. Candles burned everywhere. Low candles in small glass holders outlined the graves, and taller candles, the length of a man's arm, lined and illuminated the gravel paths. All white, pure and flickering. To souls looking down from above, Nate thought, if any were watching, the little cemetery would look like an earthbound constellation of twinkling stars.

At the graves of Amador and Jorge Cárdenas del Río, now laden with flowers, Teresa took the blanket out of the basket and spread it on the ground. Alegra sat down, retrieved her tablet and pencil and began drawing. Nate and Quina sat with her as Teresa busied herself lighting candles and incense and tidying up the graves. All around them, Nate saw other families settling themselves in the same way. Women kneeling, whispering prayers. Men talking, smoking, drinking. There was a steady low murmur of conversation overlaid with soft, melancholy music from a distant guitar and an occasional spike of children's laughter or dull report of another rocket fired into the sky. Rainbow-colored paper streamers—white, pink, lavender, blue— hung from tree branches and billowed in the breeze.

Nate waited for Quina to speak of her husband. Tell a story, share a memory, something. But she remained quiet, and he knew enough to respect her silence. After watching Alegra draw for a while, Quina took her rebozo from the basket, gathered it around her shoulders, and let her gaze drift across the dreamlike scene. Teresa settled in next to her. Quina squeezed her hand, smiled at her affectionately, took in a deep breath, let it out slowly, and finally spoke.

"The dead come in groups," she said softly in an almost trancelike tone. "They stay only a short while. Then they are gone. Sometimes they do not want to leave, but they must. They cannot stay."

Teresa nodded.

"*El muerto nada se lleva y todo se acaba.*"

"*Sí,*" Quina said. She turned to Nate. "She says the dead take nothing with them and everything comes to an end. They can stay for a while, but then they must return to the world of the dead for another year. The cycle goes on."

Teresa nodded again.

Quina looked at Nate with large, tender eyes.

"Perhaps your Sarah will come, too," she said softly.

Nate felt a deep aching at the mention of Sarah's name. He looked up at Quina. Candlelight reflected in her eyes. He looked away, across the cemetery at all the other families gathered around candlelit graves, some of the graves very fresh. *Sarah.* He wanted to believe... and he didn't. He looked into Quina's eyes again, looked away and felt... what? Was he imagining it? There had been a time when he would have clung desperately to this strange feeling coming over him. Now, for however long it lasted, it was enough. For he could not deny that he felt some warm, familiar presence. He could not help sensing that Sarah was already there.

They drank the beer and ate the bread they had set out earlier in the day. They listened to music and the low murmur of other conversations wafting on the night air. They stretched out on the blanket and gazed at the night sky. After a while, Alegra lay her head in Quina's lap and fell asleep. Quina smoothed her hair, kissed her cheek and covered her daughter with her shawl. A little while later, Quina rested her head in Nate's lap and dozed. Teresa and Nate kept vigil.

At gray dawn, Quina woke as people began gathering up their blankets and what was left of the food and drink and filing out of the cemetery. She gazed up at Nate with luminous eyes, then sat up slowly, careful not to disturb her still-sleeping daughter. Gently, she shifted her daughter's head off her lap onto the blanket, then sat for a moment, looking down at Alegra and stroking her hair as Teresa rose to begin gathering their things. A heavy sense of cold reality hung in the air now. A feeling of aftermath.

"And now we go on," Quina said softly, smiling at Nate. At home, she said, the people of Mirador would finish off the food and drink they had brought to the cemetery for *los muertos*. Day of the Dead was behind them now. It was time to put away the tradition for another year.

She fell silent, watching people walking past.

"Your Sarah and my Amador," she said softly, gazing out at the fading darkness. She fell silent again. Nate waited. "We are connected, you and I. They brought us together." She looked into Nate's eyes. "Do you understand?"

Nate wanted to, but he wasn't sure he did. Quina read the uncertainty on his face.

"El Pitón," she said simply.

No. My God.

She looked down at her sleeping daughter, fell silent again. Nate wanted to reach for her then and hold her, just hold her. But he did not.

In the gray dawn, he placed his right hand gently atop her left hand and sat silent and still beside her, gazing out into the thinning dark.

El Pitón.

Nate still didn't know how, or why, or when Amador had died, and he understood that he might never know. If Quina wanted to tell him, she would. If not, that was okay, too. It didn't matter, really. She'd told him enough.

Nate helped Quina and Teresa collect their belongings. An owl called in the distance.

"Time to go home," Quina said.

She stooped to pick up Alegra, but Nate stopped her.

"No. Let me." For a second, he thought she would refuse his offer of help, as she had that day in La Libertad. But today she accepted willingly, gratefully.

Nate gathered the sleeping child in his arms. As he adjusted his hold, Alegra stirred and woke, blinked her large, sleepy eyes at him, then wrapped her arms around his neck, lay her head against his shoulder and fell back asleep. She was warm and light, so light.

"*Ella le gusta él,*" Teresa said to Quina, nodding toward Nate, a hint of approval in her tone. "*Ya no es tan tímida.*"

"*Sí,*" Quina said, glancing at Nate as she picked up the blanket. "*Lo veo.*"

With Alegra asleep in his arms, Nate followed Quina and Teresa out of the cemetery along with other families now heading home. They passed through the gate and made their way west and north toward the square and Teresa's neighborhood farther north. They walked without speaking. All was quiet and still in the morning haze. Then Nate heard something he had not heard for a long time—so long that it didn't register at first, didn't quite make sense. He heard it again, and again, and it finally penetrated. It was a man's voice calling his name—"Nate! Nate Hunter!"—in unaccented, American-sounding English.

Nate stopped and turned. Quina and Teresa stopped, too. In the dim light, Nate saw two light-skinned men crossing the square toward them, one smaller, slighter, moving rapidly, the other heavier, slower, following behind. The smaller man waved a hand and called to him again.

"Nate! Nate!"

Who are you? Nate thought. *Do I—*

And then it hit him like a fist to the stomach. It was Tom Butler, Pastor Tom, the minister who had first brought Nate, Sarah, and the other missioners to Mirador so many months before.

What? Why? Nate suddenly felt uneasy. *What's he doing here? And who's that with him?*

Quina gently took her sleeping daughter from Nate's arms.

"Where are you going?" Nate said.

"We will wait for you," she answered calmly, walking off a short distance with Teresa.

Nate nodded and turned back toward the man rushing toward him.

"Nate! Nate! We've been looking for you!" Pastor Tom said, breathless and excited, when he reached Nate, taking Nate's hand in both of his and shaking it vigorously. I can't believe we found you. How are you? Are you all right? Is Mateo with you?"

Nate did not speak, only gawped at this sudden, impossible visitation from his former life. The second man drew nearer, and now Nate recognized him, too—from his walk and build even before he could make out the man's face. It was Trevor Blake, Sarah's father.

Still grasping Nate's hand in both of his, Pastor Tom looked over at Teresa and Quina. Nate saw a storm of unspoken questions break across the minister's face and remembered that the minister knew Quina from his many visits to Mirador. Pastor Tom nodded his head slightly toward the two women. With quiet dignity, they nodded back.

A few awkward moments passed before Pastor Tom spoke again.

"Nate... I've been worried about you. We've all been worried. When you didn't come back.... And then I couldn't reach Mateo. I finally reached Tatic. He said not to worry, that the two of you had gone off together. But it's been months now."

The pastor stepped closer and grasped Nate's upper arm.

"It's time to come home, Nate," he said. "You need to come home."

Trevor Brake now appeared at the minister's side, breathing hard, a pained expression on his face, whether from exertion or something else, Nate didn't know.

"Nate," he said gruffly, nodding once.

Nate stared at the man.

Trevor Blake stared at the ground. "I'm glad we found you."

Nate said nothing.

Trevor Blake inhaled and exhaled hard through his nose and glanced up at Nate from beneath his bushy white brows.

"I was wrong to blame you, son," he said.

Son?

Sarah's father frowned and looked down at the ground again, struggling for words. "Sarah... It wasn't your fault. I know that. Katherine and I, we both know that. It was just... when she died...." He paused, then looked up at Nate again, his eyes shining, lower lids wet. "She was our baby, Nate," he said, his voice breaking. "Can you understand that? She was our only child."

Nate stared at the man. Trevor Blake was waiting for Nate to say something. But what was Nate supposed to say? *Oh, that's okay, Dad. I understand. Don't give it another thought. I was ready to kill myself anyway. You didn't accuse me of anything I haven't condemned myself for a thousand times.*

"You've been gone a long time, Nate," the minister said, breaking another awkward silence. "We've missed you."

He was still holding Nate's arm. Nate removed his hand. He took a step back and stared at first one man, then the other.

"No," Nate said finally. He narrowed his eyes at the minister, this man of God who had deceived him, deceived Sarah. "You know about Tatic?"

The pastor's face reddened, caved. "Yes," he said.

"Who's Tatic?" Trevor Blake asked.

"He killed Tatic, too," Nate said to the minister, ignoring Sarah's father. The minister nodded.

"And twenty-two other people. Mostly women and children."

The minister hung his head.

"Who did?" Sarah's father asked. "Who killed twenty-two people?"

"Twenty-three counting Tatic," Nate said, still staring at the minister. The minister said nothing.

"What?" Trevor Blake said. "What are you—"

"Twenty-four counting Amador Cárdenas del Río," Nate said, extending an arm toward Quina, Alegra, and Teresa. "Husband, son, and father of this child."

"Stop right there," Trevor Blake commanded. "Answer my question. Who are you talking about? Who killed all these people?"

"Twenty-five," Nate said slowly, finally turning to the older man. "Counting Sarah."

Trevor Blake squinted at Nate. "What are you saying? The man who killed Sarah? He killed all these people? The same man?"

"El Pitón," Nate said. "Yes. The thug who murdered your daughter."

Trevor Blake screwed up his face, trying to make sense of what he was hearing.

"When? When did this happen?"

"You didn't know?" Nate said. He turned his gaze back on the minister. "You haven't told him?" Nate gave the minister a scathing look. "You're good at that, aren't you?"

The minister winced. "So you know, then."

"About your little deception? Yes, I know."

The minister nodded. "And how *is* Mateo?"

"*Ocupado.*"

"Is he here?"

"No."

"Haven't told me what, Tom?" Trevor Blake said.

"I just found out myself, Nate," the minister said quietly. "We got in late last night. There were no lights on at the rectory, so we drove to Mateo's. He always leaves a key. I went back to the rectory this morning, but nobody was there, so I went to the church...." The minister looked down, took a ragged breath. "That's where they told me."

"Told you what?" Trevor Blake demanded again, looking ready to explode.

"I'm sorry, Trevor," the minister said. "I was about to tell you." He looked at Nate. "Trevor wasn't with me. I'm an early riser, so I told him to meet me here in the square. I was just leaving the church when I saw you."

The minister turned now to Trevor Blake, took a deep breath.

"There was a massacre in the church," he said slowly. "Just a week ago."

"Four days," Nate said coldly.

"Four days," the minister repeated.

Trevor Blake wore the expression of a man who was certain he must have misheard. He looked from the minister to Nate. Tried to speak, couldn't. Tried again.

"The same man?"

"Yes," Nate said calmly.

Trevor Blake looked down and away, frowning, confused. "No.

That can't be." He sought Nate's eyes. "How can that be? They said they couldn't find him. Everyone I called, every time I called, everyone I spoke to, up and down the line. They didn't know where he was, they said. Off somewhere in the mountains, they said."

"He was," Nate said. "He came back."

Trevor Blake's eyes lit up. "And they caught him. This time, they caught him, right?"

"No."

"No?" Again, Sarah's father wore the expression of a man being addressed in a language he didn't understand. "What do you mean, no?"

"No. They didn't catch him. And they won't. He's in the mountains again now. But he'll be back, and he'll kill more people, and they won't catch him next time, either. Or the time after that. Or the time after that."

"So come home, Nate," the minister said as Trevor Blake struggled for words. "It's not safe here. You know that. Come home while you can."

Nate shook his head. "No. I can't do that. Not yet. Maybe after he's dead. Maybe not. I don't know."

"Nate, be reasonable. You can't stay here."

"I can't? Why not?"

"Because your home is in Dallas."

Nate shook his head again. "No, it's not." He looked from the minister to Trevor Blake. "There's nothing there for me anymore. Can't you see that?"

Trevor Blake looked over at Quina, standing next to Teresa, holding her daughter in her arms. He let his eyes rest on her for a moment, taking her in. He looked back at Nate, his expression changed.

"Yes," he said quietly. "I think I do."

Nate turned to go.

"Nate, wait," the minister said, putting a hand on his arm again. He looked at Trevor Blake, and the older man nodded and walked off as if going for a stroll. The pastor watched him go, turned back to Nate. "What you know now... what... what Mateo told you," he said. "Trevor knows, too."

"You don't say. And how did he find out?"

"I told him. When you didn't come back, he called me to ask if I'd heard from you."

That surprised Nate.

"I'd been doing a lot of thinking...and praying," the minister continued. "And I knew I had to tell him." He looked down. "I had to confess and ask his forgiveness." He looked up at Nate. "And now I'm asking for yours."

Nate stared at the minister. "You told him everything? And he forgave you?"

The minister shook his head. "I wouldn't say that, no. Someday. Perhaps. Perhaps not. But he's the reason we're here, Nate. He insisted we come. He said he'd already lost a daughter. He'd be dam— He didn't want to lose a son, too."

Son, again. Nate looked past the minister to Trevor Blake, walking slowly around the square a short distance away, meandering in no particular direction, head down, hands in pockets, frowning, glancing up occasionally to see where he was going, eyes mainly on the ground. *Our only child.* Nate had never really thought about that, he realized—how much this man had suffered, how much Sarah's parents had both lost.

The minister looked down again. "I'm sorry, Nate. I'm so deeply sorry. I don't expect you to forgive me. There's no reason you should. I just want you to know how sorry I am. I never thought anyone would be hurt. Please believe me. If you believe nothing else, please believe that."

Nate nodded. The truth was he did believe it. He didn't forgive the minister, wasn't sure he ever would, but he didn't feel angry anymore.

"None of that matters now," Nate said.

"Nate," the preacher said. "I know you want justice, or revenge, or something. But at what price? Are you really ready to kill someone? Think about it, Nate. Are you really ready to do that?"

Yes, Nate thought. *I am.* He didn't answer.

"And even if you are, Nate, what good will it do? It won't bring Sarah back. Or Tatic. Or..." The minister looked at Quina, standing next to Teresa with her daughter in her arms.

"Amador," Nate said.

"Or Amador. Or any of the other poor souls that man has killed. It will just lead to more deaths, more killing."

Nate felt anger rising. "It's a little late for that, don't you think? You're the one who got me into this, remember? Me and Sarah, both. There's a war coming. You knew that. And you brought us down here anyway. Now you're against killing? Since when?"

"Since always, Nate," the minister said, his gaze steady. "I didn't bring you down here to fight. That was never my intention. The Zapatistas needed someone to help them get their message out. I thought if we could help them do that, make the world listen, maybe there wouldn't have to be a war and people wouldn't have to die."

"People have already died. Twenty-five people and counting."

"Yes," the minister said softly, looking down and nodding his head. He looked up again. "But do you want to be part of that, Nate? Do you really? Do you want people to die by your hand?" The minister stepped closer, looked deep into Nate's eyes. "Nate, you can't win this fight. You must know that. You can't. It's not possible." The minister glanced at Quina again, then turned back to Nate. "Nate, this isn't your cause. It's not your fight. Don't throw your life away on it. Come home with us."

Nate found himself nodding, almost smiling. The minister's words were so familiar. *Not my fight. Can't win this fight.* It was exactly what Nate had told Mateo over and over when Mateo had first asked for his help. When was that? How long ago now? It felt like years. Lifetimes. *Not my cause. Not my fight. Not my country. Not my people.* Nate turned toward Quina, just as she turned toward Teresa, touched Teresa's arm and the two women walked away, heading back to Teresa's hut. Nate watched them round a corner and disappear. He turned back to the preacher.

"Okay," he said, nodding. "I understand what you're saying."

"You do?" The pastor's face flooded with relief.

"Yeah, I do."

"That's great. That's wonderful. So we can head back?"

Nate nodded.

"Good man! Good man!" the preacher said, slapping Nate on the back and turning to look for Sarah's father. "Trevor!" he called, spotting the older man and waving to him. "It's okay! Nate says we can go!"

Arriving back at Teresa's hut, Nate pushed open the door to find Teresa and Alegra at the table bundling corn cakes in a bandana as Quina stuffed Alegra's nightdress and a few other belongings into a knapsack. Teresa had changed into a plain dark dress. Quina was in jeans and a muslin blouse, and Alegra was in light cotton pants and a t-shirt. Teresa and Quina looked surprised to see Nate. Alegra smiled and got up to give him a hug. Nate squatted and lifted the girl in his arms.

"Good," he said, seeing that Quina's knapsack looked already packed. "We should get going."

Quina looked confused.

"But what about—"

"They left. They went home. Back to *their* home." He put Alegra down and looked around the hut as she went back to helping Teresa tie up the corn cakes. "Do you have everything?" he asked, taking his gun and holster from the nail on the wall and strapping it around his waist. "Alegra, did you pack your pad and pencil?"

Nate saw Quina watching him, tears welling in her eyes.

"Quina, what?"

She looked down and shook her head hard, didn't answer.

"You didn't think—"

She waved away his question and wiped at her eyes.

"Teresa refuses to come with us," she said, nodding toward the old woman sitting at the table, tying up a second bundle of cakes.

"Ach!" Teresa said, scowling and waving a hand at Quina.

"*Teresa, por favor,*" Quina said, going to the table and sitting down next to her, across from Alegra. "It is not safe here anymore."

"No," Teresa said, squeezing and patting Quina's hand. "*Soy demasiado vieja.*"

"No, you are not!" Quina insisted. "You are strong. I have seen your strength. Others older than you have gone. Lourdes has gone. And Alegra needs you. I need you."

"*Basta!*" Teresa said finally, batting away Quina's pleas with a decisive wave of a hand and swiping a tear from her eye. "*Soy vieja. Esta es mi casa. Nadie molestará a una anciana. Me quedaré.*"

Quina opened her mouth to argue, then closed it firmly and leaned forward and gathered Teresa in her arms. The old woman hugged Quina hard and kissed her on each cheek and on the forehead.

"We will come back soon," Quina whispered, holding Teresa's face in her hands. "*Lo prometo.*"

Teresa nodded and turned to Alegra.

"*Alegra, da a tu abuela un abrazo.*"

Alegra hopped off her chair, came to her grandmother and reached up her arms. Teresa leaned down and held the child close. "*Mi querida,*" she whispered, taking the child's face in her hands and smothering her with kisses. "*Sé buena,*" she said, releasing the child. "*Escucha a tu madre.*"

"*Sí, yaya,*" Alegra said, nodding.

"*Dame un beso,*" Teresa said, tapping her cheek. The child kissed her grandmother's cheek.

"*No me olvides,*" the old woman said, smiling, clasping the child's hands tenderly in hers, eyes shining with love.

"*No, yaya.*"

"*No seas tonta!*" Quina said sternly to Teresa. "We will see you soon."

Teresa nodded, rose from her chair, walked over to Nate, and put a wrinkled hand to his left cheek. Nate laid his hand over hers.

"*Protegelos, El Cazador. Prometeme.*"

Nate nodded. "I promise."

"*Gracias,*" Teresa said. "*Gracias. Vaya con Dios.*"

Quina kissed Teresa again, hugged her hard, then slung her knapsack over one shoulder and her daughter's over the other.

"*Listo?*" she said to Nate, moving to the door.

Nate reached a hand to Alegra. The girl came to him, and he lifted her onto his back, the way he often carried Rafael.

"*Listo,*" Nate said, standing and hitching the child higher.

Quina stepped through the doorway. Nate followed her out. 🔺

CHAPTER 29

The Quiet Before

Mirador looked like a ghost town in the still hours of early morning. Remnants of the preceding night's fandango littered the streets. Burned bits of sky rockets, empty paper cups, a child's skeleton mask. No more gaiety, no more music. The smells of fresh bread and pine incense had faded. Back home from the cemetery, the people of Mirador seemed to be resting, regrouping, delaying as long as possible the resumption of their labors, the return to the reality of what had happened only a few days before in their village.

Quina and Nate's plan was to make their way out of town along back streets and alleyways, then head south, keeping to the side of the road, hitch a ride as far as possible and get back to the drop-off point on the river in time for the afternoon boat run—if there was one today. If not, they had a tarp, corn cakes, water. They'd wait.

With Alegra clinging silently to his back, arms around his neck, legs gripping his waist, Nate followed Quina down a narrow cobbled passageway. When they reached the corner, they paused, looked, listened. No people. No vehicles. No movement. No sound.

They rounded the corner onto a wider lane and began moving down the street quickly but quietly, senses alert. They made it safely to the next turn, and the next. The roads widened as they neared the outskirts of the village, but luck and timing seemed to be with them. Each road they turned onto was clear and quiet, and it appeared they would make it out of town without difficulty.

"There," Quina whispered, pointing as they turned onto yet another street. Nate saw that the street opened out onto the eastern loop road

just two intersections ahead. They made it safely across the first intersection and were nearing the outlet when they heard the grumbling
engine of a truck approaching on the loop road from the south. They
halted. Quina pointed to a rusted car parked or abandoned against
a building just ahead of them, and they hurried to it and crouched
behind it, even Alegra knowing to remain still and silent. A moment
later, a pickup turned onto their street and rumbled past, belching
dark clouds of exhaust, carrying a small squad of sullen-looking men
in the bed of the truck, swearing, shoving each other, foul tempered
and hungover, it seemed, from a night of drinking.

Quina and Nate exchanged a look. They waited, crouched behind
the car, as the truck rumbled west, toward the center of town. When
they could no longer hear it and the street was empty and quiet again,
Nate signaled for Quina to stay with Alegra while he scouted ahead to
see if the turn onto the loop road was now clear. Quina nodded, put an
arm protectively around her daughter and a finger to her lips. Alegra
nodded, and Nate moved swiftly to the end of the street. Pressed against
a south wall, he could see that the loop road to the north was clear. He
edged forward to peer south, the direction they needed to go... and
immediately pulled back, suddenly dizzy and sweating, heart slamming in his chest. It was his living nightmare all over again. The road
to the south was blocked by two more trucks parked nose to nose across
the road no more than sixty feet away. Another dozen or so armed and
scruffy-looking men were lounging in the backs of the trucks, wandering the road, sitting along the roadside. And there among them, leaning against the cab of one of the trucks, neatly groomed and dressed,
legs crossed casually at the ankles, puffing on a cheroot, was El Pitón
himself. It was the first time Nate had seen the man's face since the day
of Sarah's murder, and one glimpse brought it all back—the horror, the
grief, the rage, the guilt... and the cold hatred.

I could kill him now, Nate thought. El Pitón hadn't seen him. Nate
had a gun. But then, he remembered Itzel. If he missed or even if he
killed the bastard, El Pitón's men would come after him. He didn't care
if they killed him. But they'd find Quina. And Alegra. *No.*

Quickly, silently, Nate returned to their hiding place, crouched
down beside Quina. She searched his eyes and knew.

"Where?" she whispered.

"South, not far. Blocking the road."

Quina's eyes went wild for a moment. Then she took a deep breath, collected herself and nodded.

"We are too late," Quina murmured. "We must go back. Wait for dark."

Nate nodded. He signaled for Alegra to climb onto his back, and, with Quina in the lead again, they began retracing their steps. This time, as they stole down side roads and alleys, the village began to stir, awakening from its slumber and the sweet interlude of Día de Muertos to a harsh confrontation with reality. As Nate and Quina neared the center of town, they found the last few turns in the route they had taken blocked by the paramilitary—men in trucks parked in the middle of intersections, thugs with guns wandering the streets, patrolling with angry stares. Each time, Quina found another way, looping back and around until Nate was completely disoriented. But he trusted her completely, he realized. Trusted her with his life.

Leading the way up another unfamiliar alley, keeping close to a low wall running along the street side of a courtyard, Quina stopped suddenly just short of the courtyard's entranceway, crouched down, pressed her back against the wall and signaled for Nate to get down quickly, quickly! He dropped to a crouch with Alegra on his back and scrambled to Quina, who immediately spun behind him and pressed herself against Alegra, shielding the child with her body.

Now Nate heard what Quina had heard: a rising commotion coming from deep inside the courtyard. The scuffling and dragging of heavy feet. Men shouting, cursing, begging for mercy. Then bone-jarring gunshots—a series of them, four, five, maybe more—so rapid and close, right on the other side of the wall, that Nate spun and threw his arms around Alegra and Quina, felt their bodies jerk with each report.

When the shooting stopped, Alegra whimpered and squirmed.

"*Shh. Shh. Quieto. No te muevas*," Quina whispered.

Alegra immediately went quiet and still.

Nate eased forward on his knees to the courtyard entranceway, peered around the ragged edge. Inside, against a far wall, he saw five men standing ashen-faced, hands bound, over three bloody bodies crumpled on the ground. On the wall behind them, someone had scrawled *¡Tierra y Libertad!* and *¡Muerto al asesino!* in red paint.

Nate heard rifles being reloaded inside the courtyard to his right. He couldn't see the shooters, but he thought he recognized the bound men. They had walked with Nate and Quina in the procession to the cemetery, spent the night with them in a forest of candles. He had watched them spread blankets at nearby graves and sit with their families and friends, eating, drinking, talking, laughing. *For God's sake, they were having a party just last night.*

"*Viva Zapata!*" one of the bound men called out. "*Tierra y Libertad! Viva México! Muerte a El Pitón!*"

Another volley of shots exploded, the bound men fell, and Nate jerked back. The acrid smell of gunsmoke filled the air.

Nate did not realize he had squeezed his eyes shut until Quina shook his arm and he opened them again. Clutching her daughter to her chest, Quina set her jaw, wiped tears from her face and signaled with one hand for Nate to follow quickly. Together, they rose and, keeping low, retreated back down the alley and around to Teresa's neighborhood by another, more circuitous route.

Teresa welcomed them back with kisses and soft cries of "*Gracias. Gracias. Gracias a Dios.*" She had heard the gunfire, she told them, and had been frightened. Alegra climbed onto Teresa's cot with her pad and pencil, shrank back into a corner, and lost herself in drawing.

"*Pobrecita,*" Teresa murmured, snugging a thin quilt around the child and stroking her cheek.

The rest of the day and into the night Nate and Quina waited. They ate when Teresa insisted they eat, then sat side by side on the floor against a wall of the hut, hugging their knees. They smiled reassuringly when Teresa looked at them with a worried expression as she went about her chores.

As they sat, Nate thought. El Pitón was back, sooner than Nate or Quina or probably anyone in Mirador had expected. With more trucks, men and guns at his disposal than ever before. Nate had spotted six trucks along their route back—just along the route back. There had to be more. He was sure of it. Probably not only paramilitary. Probably military, too. Like an occupying force, the paramilitary seemed to have spread everywhere, all through the village and beyond. He sat with that realization.

"We're not going to be able to get back, are we?" he said in a hushed voice, glancing at Quina.

Quina did not answer immediately.

"We will try again tonight," she finally said in a low voice, not looking at him. "After dark, we can slip out of the village and into the *campo*. We will be all right then."

"Maybe."

Quina nodded.

"*Sí. Tal vez.* But we cannot stay here. Alegra will be safer now at La Libertad."

Nate's eyes went to Alegra again. She was kneeling on a chair at the table, pencil in hand, bent over her sketch pad, her great mass of dark hair falling forward, framing her face.

"She's beautiful," Nate said.

Quina nodded. "She looks like her father," she said softly.

Nate disagreed but remained quiet, hoping Quina would say more.

Quina leaned her head against the wall and closed her eyes. She sighed.

"He was a good man, a very brave man," she said softly. "We could have stayed in the city and had a comfortable life. But he wanted to come back to his village to help *los pobres*. There was no clinic until he came. No school."

"And now there is no clinic and no school."

"No."

Nate was beginning to understand.

"Mateo's wife Elba worked in the clinic."

Quina nodded.

"Your husband's clinic."

Another nod. A silence. "They were very brave," Quina said. "After Amador died, I could not go back. But, Elba and Xoc, they went back."

"You were teaching there."

"Yes. We were living there, too."

"And the clinic gave care to everyone."

Quina looked at him in surprise.

"Mateo told me. When he told me about Elba."

Quina nodded. "Yes. The colonel and El Pitón did not like that. They told Amador, 'No medicine for troublemakers or sympathizers. No lessons. Nothing.' What he meant was, no medicine for *los pobres*. *Soldados y los paramilitaristas solamente.* No one else. But Amador refused to do that. We carried on as always. And everything was fine for a while. Then El Pitón came to warn him again. 'If you do not stop,' he said, 'I will have to stop you, do you understand?' Amador said he understood. But he did not stop. So...."

"So they killed him."

Quina nodded. "Two men came. Amador heard the truck. He told me to take Alegra and hide in the closet. Then he went out onto the porch. I could not hear them. But I heard the shots. He ran into the jungle. They chased him and shot him there."

Quina took a breath, rested her head back against the wall again and closed her eyes. Tears slid down her cheeks.

"He died alone in the jungle," she whispered, "while I hid in a closet."

"Quina, you couldn't have saved him, you know that," Nate said, suppressing a strong desire to hold her. "And you had to protect Alegra. If you had gone after him, they would have killed you, too. And then what would have happened to her?"

Quina nodded. "I know. But knowing does not help. I still feel the guilt." She put a fist to her chest, closed her eyes in pain, opened them and turned to Nate. "Can you understand?"

Nate nodded. He wasn't sure how much Quina knew about the details of Sarah's death. Perhaps one day he would tell her. It would only be fair, he thought, looking at her now and seeing his own loss, his own pain, his own shame and guilt reflected in her eyes.

Nate crossed his arms on his knees and rested his forehead on his forearms. *Too much sadness. Too much suffering. Too much senseless death.* He lifted his head and sighed.

"We aren't going to win this, you know." He turned to Quina. "You know that, don't you? We can't. How can we possibly win?"

Quina gave him a look of granite resolve.

"Perhaps we will not win, but we will mark them with our blood. The world will know who they are, and who we are, and why we fight."

"And if they kill us all?"

"Others will rise up. Like *maíz*. *La lucha continua*. We will keep fighting for as long as it takes, even if it takes another five hundred years." ⛰

CHAPTER 30

The Four Sisters

Quina and Nate waited a day before attempting a night escape, but even at night, they found their routes blocked. They tried again the next night with the same results. A time of waiting followed. Nate thought that maybe after making a big show of their presence in Mirador for a day or two, El Pitón and his men might return to the mountains, the army might stand down, and he, Quina, and Alegra would be able to leave. But that didn't happen. Each time Teresa went to the market or cemetery or church, she returned with reports of soldiers and paramilitaristas patrolling the streets in even greater numbers. Their absence during Día de Muertos had fooled Nate. But not even El Pitón or el comandante would dare interfere with that celebration, Quina said. Nobody disrupted Día de Muertos. Nobody.

The more Nate thought about it, the more he realized that the soldiers and paramilitary would have to be pretty stupid not to be on high alert after the massacre, not to expect some kind of trouble. Maybe it would come. Maybe the people of Mirador would rise up again. Not wait for the big uprising. Just rise up on their own. *And get slaughtered again,* Nate thought. Or maybe they'd try to wait out the occupation, lull the soldiers and paramilitary into thinking they were too frightened to try anything now, so the occupiers would lose interest and leave. Nate had no way of knowing, and the waiting, not knowing, and not being able to get Quina and Alegra out of Mirador started taking a toll.

Nate reasoned with Quina. "You should go," he said. "You and Alegra could probably slip out if I'm not with you."

"No," Quina said. "Teresa says they're not letting anyone in or out.

And we're not going without you."

So they waited, not knowing for what.

Not long after dusk on the evening of the fifth day in Mirador, waiting for full dark when Nate and Quina could at least go out into the yard and breathe some fresh air, Nate sat in his customary spot against the wall of Teresa's hut. He put his head back and fell into a shallow, troubled sleep that spawned a disturbing dream. He saw a man running through the jungle, being chased by two other men with guns. To survive, the man had to make it across a river. The river wasn't far. He was almost there. But the armed men were closing in.

Fleeing for his life, the man fought his way through thickets of thin-stalked saplings, around outcroppings of volcanic rock, through ligatures of climbing briars and coils of thick, thorny vines, ruthless as barbed wire, ready to lacerate and ensnare him. He leaped over fallen branches, hoisted himself over rotting tree trunks crawling with insects. The mucky jungle floor sucked at his feet, fighting every step, draining his strength. Slippery ground allowed him little purchase, sometimes sent him scrambling for handholds as he skidded and slid across jungle slime.

Nate could not see the fleeing man's face. But somehow he knew him. Knew what the man was thinking and feeling. Exhausted, depleted, again and again the man was tempted to give up, surrender, turn and face death head-on. But, no, he couldn't do that. He had to survive. He had to get home. Sides heaving, lungs burning, heart hammering in his chest, sweat drenching his face and stinging his eyes, he commanded his tremulous limbs to keep moving. "*El río*," he told himself. "If I can only make the river."

The man began descending into an abyss. *Where am I? What's happening? Where's the trail?* Like a hunted animal, he slogged on through the darkening morass, grunting, flailing, sinking ankle deep in mud. Losing his footing, he pitched forward, tumbled head over heels, clambered to his hands and knees. On all fours, he scrabbled along like some ungainly jungle critter, finally righted himself. He stood, panting, wiped the sweat from his eyes with a shirt sleeve, touched a medal he was wearing around his neck. A patron saint. He crossed himself and pushed on.

The killers were gaining on him. He could hear them shouting, thrashing behind him. He could feel their closeness. Glancing back as he ran, he caught a glimpse of them. One was older, tall and thin, dark with angular features. A scar on his right cheek. The other was younger, shorter, more muscular, with a shaved head.

"*Por allá!*" he heard one of the men shout. "*Por allá!*" They had spotted him. "*Cógelo! Mátalo!*" And then a shot split the air. A bullet ripped through jungle vegetation and struck the fleeing man in the back of his left shoulder. The impact spun him around and put him down.

The man struggled to his feet and kept moving, clutching his shoulder. He didn't try to run. He couldn't. And he didn't care. The bullet had delivered him from fear. His fate certain now, he ambled through the jungle like a man on a Sunday stroll, admiring the verdant beauty of the world around him, breathing in its sweet fragrance. His senses heightened, he heard every bird call, felt every breath of wind, saw every leaf and vine, every shrub and thorn, in vivid color and intricate detail, each one brilliant and distinct, a miracle of complex creation. The jungle was transformed by the nearness of death from an alien and hostile environment to a magnificent cathedral filled with Nature's works of art.

Feeling weak and unsteady, the man halted and lifted his face to the sky. Through the jungle canopy, he saw broken patches of brilliant blue. He gazed up in mute wonder, then noticed that the air around him had turned cool. *The river must be close,* he thought. *Or death.* It no longer mattered. He listened and heard the rumble of rushing water. He remembered what his mother had told him when he was a boy, "That is the voice of God," she had said. "Hear its power."

The river, the man thought. *I'm almost there.* He stumbled on, homing in on the sound, his body growing heavier with every step, his spirit lighter. He felt it lifting inside him, trying to break free. He didn't hear his pursuers anymore. The roar of rushing water intensified, canceled all other sounds. The man struggled toward it. *Just a few more steps. Just a few.* He touched the medal around his neck again, crossed himself. And then he was there.

The man was standing on a rocky promontory looking down at a roiling blue-green river far below. The turbulent water swirled and churned. Currents converged and convulsed. Like a living thing, the river bucked and thrashed against its cutbanks, curling and rolling, wrapping over and around itself, rising and falling. Percussive waves crested and collapsed, colliding with other waves, crashing into jagged rocks, sending up spray. The man gazed down at the roaring maelstrom. The river was beautiful, but impassable. He could not cross it. It would not deliver him from death.

The man gazed off downriver. Not far away, rock walls of the canyon closed in, choking the rushing water, heightening its fury, forcing the foaming, thrashing torrent through a narrow chute. Past the chute, the rock walls retreated, gave way to low rolling banks, and the exhausted river calmed. The tailwater widened and flattened out, settling into an emerald pool spanned by a narrow rope-and-board footbridge. *Ahh*, the wounded man thought. *There. That's where I should be.* But he was not there, and he could not get there. He could go no farther. He had made it to the river. But the water would not be his salvation. It would be his grave.

The man accepted his fate. He felt serene, at peace, even forgiving of his pursuers.

Knowing death was near, the man reached into the breast pocket of his shirt and removed a photograph of a young woman. Blond hair, green eyes, brilliant smile. She had told him when she gave him the photo that at the instant it was taken she had been thinking of him, her heart filled with love. "This," she had said, "is what love looks like." But she was dead now. He couldn't remember how she died, or when. He knew only that she was gone.

The men with guns were closing in. He could hear them. They had found him, and he had nowhere to go. He gazed at the picture of the smiling woman. *This is what love looks like.* He held the picture to his heart and sighed. He turned toward his pursuers. He opened his arms and lifted his face to the sky. He closed his eyes. *God, if you're—*

The man heard a dull crack, a faint noise smothered by the rant of whitewater. A bullet slammed into his chest. He stumbled, kept his feet, turned back toward the river. He took a last labored breath of sweet air and tumbled headlong over the edge of the cliff toward the raging water below. Falling, turning, looking up, he saw the tall man with the scar above him, peering over the precipice, grinning, holding the photograph of the smiling green-eyed woman in his hand.

Nate woke with a start. Jerking upright, gasping for air, sweating, heart pounding, he sat staring into gathering darkness, bewildered and disoriented. He felt a gentle hand on his arm. Quina sitting beside him.

"*Fue un sueño,*" she whispered. "*Sólo un sueño.*"

Nate nodded, coming back to himself, looked around. The hut was dark. Teresa was napping on her cot. Alegra was sleeping on her pallet on the floor. Nate massaged his eyes with the heels of his hands, rubbed his cheeks with his palms, patted them. He rose and shuffled to the front door, peeked out through a gap in the weathered planks. Almost full dark. Not yet, but soon.

And then movement caught his eye. A shadow figure darted like a nighthawk across the yard. He went rigid.

"Someone's out there," he whispered to Quina. He extended his arm, keeping a sharp eye. "Give me the gun."

Quina came silently to Nate's side, handed him the pistol.

"Where?" she whispered, pressing an eye to the gap.

"Behind the tree."

Quina pressed herself against the door. "I see him," she whispered.

Nate stepped back, checked to make sure the gun was loaded, glanced up to see Teresa awake now, standing by the bureau in the dark, eyes wide.

"No, wait, wait!" Quina hissed, eye still at the door, waving a hand at Nate to put the gun away. "*Está bien! Está bien!*"

She stepped back and pulled open the door, and Nate recognized Sebastiano standing in the doorway, hand raised as if about to knock. Quina pulled him inside and closed the door behind him.

Nate took a series of slow, deep breaths and returned his gun to the holster hanging on the wall.

"*Buenas noches, Señora,*" Sebastiano said, nodding to Teresa.

Teresa returned the nod.

"*Sebastiano, nos asustaste,*" Quina said as Teresa lit the lamp. "*Es bueno verte.* I am glad you made it here safely. *Pero por qué estás aquí?*"

The young man shrugged. "*Oh, estaba caminando y pensé en decirte hola.*"

Quina slapped his shoulder in mock reproof.

"*Ser grave!*"

Sebastiano feigned pain in his arm, then grinned, and Quina laughed, and Nate was astounded again by their ability, their determination, to find levity even in moments of fear and suffering.

"*Siéntate, por favor,*" Teresa said, bringing the lamp to the table and motioning for Sebastiano to sit. Quina checked on Alegra as Teresa put water and bread on the table. Then everyone sat and Quina turned serious.

"Tatic," Quina said softly.

Sebastiano nodded. "He rests in peace," he said, crossing himself. Quina and Teresa did the same. "We buried him high on the ridge, facing Mirador."

"*Está con Dios,*" Teresa said softly.

"*Sí,*" Sebastiano said, nodding.

"Why are you here, Sebastiano?" Nate asked.

Sebastiano turned to Nate. "Mateo thought you would be back by now. When you did not come, he sent me."

"But how did you get through? We've been trying to get out for days."

Sebastiano gave Nate a level look. "*Este es mi pueblo,*" he said. "*Yo nací aquí.*"

Nate nodded, feeling properly put in his place.

"So you've come to take us back," Nate said.

"*Sí.* No. You, yes. I have come to take you back."

Nate felt confused. "What do you mean, 'me'?"

"*Tengo ordenes de Mateo.*" He needs you back in La Libertad.

"*Por qué?*"

Sebastiano gave him another level look.

"*Porque te necesita,*" he said calmly.

Nate got the message. If Sebastiano knew why Mateo needed him back, which he might not, he wasn't about to say in front of Quina and, especially, Teresa. Nate had a hunch, though. He remembered Mateo saying they might need his help with computer and satellite phone hookups at some of the other camps when the time came.

"Is it starting?" he asked Sebastiano.

"*No ahorita.*"

"Soon, though."

Sebastiano did not respond.

Nate nodded. "When do we leave?"

"*Esta noche. Ahora.*"

Nate turned to Quina, who had drawn herself up and was sitting calm, composed, hands folded in her lap, watching him.

He looked over his shoulder at Alegra, curled up asleep on her pallet, and turned back to Sebastiano.

"We go together. Quina and Alegra, too."

Sebastiano frowned. "No." He addressed Quina. "*Lo siento, Quina,* but Mateo said he needs Nate and that it is better if you remain here with Teresa."

"No," Quina said, ice in her tone. "It is too dangerous here now."

"The journey is dangerous, too," Sebastiano said.

"We are not staying," Quina said. "We are going."

Sebastiano sighed, shook his head and raised his hands, palms up, in surrender.

Quina turned to Teresa.

"*Teresa, mamá, por favor.* Come with us."

Teresa shook her head, took Quina's hands in hers.

"*No, mi niña.* I am too old."

"But—"

Teresa put a finger to Quina's lips.

"Shh. *No más.* You and Alegra must go."

"*Pero—*"

"*No, mi hija. Esta es mi casa. Mi esposo y mi hijo están enterrados aquí, yo nací aquí y moriré aquí.*"

Quina fell silent. She nodded, lay a hand tenderly against Teresa's cheek, then rose and went to wake Alegra and prepare her, again, for the journey.

"There will be moonlight tonight," Sebastiano told Nate as Teresa wrapped bread and corn cakes in a cloth and filled a canteen with water. "We must stay low and move fast, move from shadow to shadow. No talking. That means Alegra, too."

Nate nodded. "She knows how to keep silent."

"*Bueno.* We will work our way to *La Soga,* cross the road, go east, then south. A boat will meet us at the river. It is arranged."

Quina returned with two knapsacks slung over her shoulder and Alegra in her arms. Sebastiano patted the sleepy child on the head and smiled. She smiled shyly back. Then he removed the glass chimney from the unlit kerosene lamp, ran a fingertip around the sooty rim, and blackened his cheeks. He ran his finger through the lampblack again and smudged Alegra's face. She giggled. Nate and Quina darkened their faces, too.

Nate retrieved his holster, turned to Teresa and took her hand in both of his. "*Gracias,*" he said. "Thank you for everything."

Teresa nodded and squeezed his hand. Quina transferred Alegra onto Nate's back and stuffed the bread into her knapsack. Teresa handed the canteen to Sebastiano, then moved to the door.

"You must be silent, my daughter," Quina whispered to Alegra. "Not a sound, *entiendes?*"

Alegra nodded, and Quina kissed her cheek.

Teresa opened the door quietly, just wide enough for a person to pass through. Quina embraced her again—"*Te amo*," Nate heard Quina whisper—and the travelers slipped out.

Staying low, moving fast, they cut through Teresa's front yard and snaked north along a narrow alley, keeping to shadows, avoiding pockets of light. At the first cross alley, they turned west, then north, then east through a network of lightless alleys and lanes, turning and turning again until Nate lost track of direction. Three times, Sebastiano held up a hand at the sound of men's voices ahead, a truck engine idling, boots scuffing on cobblestone, rifles clattering. Each time, he slipped silently behind them, signaled for them to follow and found another route.

When they struck el camino principal at the eastern outskirts of the village, they ducked into a dry drainage ditch on the near side of the road and waited, watching and listening. It seemed to Nate that they were somewhere near where he'd seen El Pitón's trucks when he and Quina had made their first escape attempt. Now peering up and down the road until it bent out of sight in each direction, they saw and heard nothing. No cars, no trucks, no people. A black-and-white world, still and dark as a child's charcoal sketch. Razor-edged silence.

Sebastiano nodded and they started to climb out of the ditch to gain the brush on the far side of the road when they heard a vehicle approaching from the north and beams from a pair of headlights swept down the road toward them. Ducking back into the ditch, the travelers pressed themselves low and hard against the fetid earth as the vehicle came nearer. Nate hazarded one glimpse, then flattened himself against the earth again. An army jeep carrying two soldiers, one driving, the other raking the road and surrounding countryside with a spotlight mounted on the hood. The jeep slowed and stopped. Nate and his companions shrank deeper into the ditch as the probing beam played over the top of it and slightly down the far side. They waited, not breathing, as the beam came back the other way. A shifting of gears, and then the jeep drove on.

They stayed where they were, not moving, until they couldn't hear the jeep anymore and all was still and silent again. Sebastiano raised a finger. "Fast and low," he whispered. Nate and Quina nodded. Sebastiano rose to a crouch, scouted up and down the road again and signaled to move out. As quietly and quickly as possible, they climbed out of the ditch and stole across the road and into the cover of dense underbrush on the other side. Sebastiano signaled for Nate and Quina to sit and wait as he disappeared deeper into the brush. They waited, surrounded by the soothing night sounds of breeze rustling the grasses, and chirping, buzzing insects.

"*Ven,*" Sebastiano called softly. They rose, Nate with Alegra clinging awake and silent to his back, and made their way through the brush to where Sebastiano waited. Looking down, Nate saw that they were now on a vague footpath that only someone born to the land could possibly know was there.

They walked through the night, Nate and Quina taking turns carrying Alegra, and arrived at the meeting place on the river just before daybreak. The motorcraft and driver were there. Quina climbed in first. Nate handed Alegra to her and stepped in as Sebastiano held the boat steady. Then Sebastiano let go and stepped back onto the bank as the helmsman poled the craft into the current.

"You're not coming?" Nate said.

Sebastiano shook his head. "Mateo needs you. I will come soon."

Almost twenty-four hours after leaving Teresa's hut, Nate and Quina, carrying Alegra, walked back through the gates of La Libertad. The evening meal was just ending. Mateo and Oscar were sitting at Lourdes's cookfire, deep in conversation. Glancing up and seeing them approach, Mateo came to his feet with the agility that always surprised Nate and walked toward them. Oscar also stood but did not approach.

"Ah, my sweet Alegra," Mateo said, smiling and opening his arms wide. "It does an old man's heart good to see you." He took the girl's face gently in his hands and kissed her forehead. Alegra smiled shyly, then buried her face in her mother's neck.

Mateo took a step back, hands on hips, and gave Nate and Quina a once-over. He nodded, satisfied.

"Sebastiano found you?"

"*Sí,*" Quina said.

Mateo looked past them toward the gate.

"He said he will come soon," Quina said, her guard up as if ready for an argument.

Mateo nodded again. If he was unhappy to see Quina there instead of Sebastiano, he kept it to himself.

"Teresa *está bien?*"

Quina nodded, relaxing slightly. "*Sí, gracias.* She is well." Quina sighed. "But she will not leave Mirador."

Mateo nodded. "It is not easy for her, I know."

Nate unbuckled the gunbelt and handed it back to Mateo. "Thanks for the loan."

Mateo weighed the holster in his hands, brought the gun's muzzle to his nose.

"You did not use it."

"No, but it was good to have it."

"Alegra," Quina whispered to her daughter, tapping her lightly on the arm. "Look who is here. *Mira.*"

Alegra lifted her head and peered in the direction Quina was pointing. She was pointing toward Lourdes, who had turned toward them, and was sitting back on her knees, smiling.

"Loulou!" Alegra cried.

The old woman broke into a grin. Quina put Alegra down, and the little girl ran into the curandera's arms.

"They know each other," Nate said, watching the two embrace. "Obviously."

Quina nodded. "Lourdes delivered her. She has been a second grandmother to her all her life. Alegra couldn't say Lourdes when she was very young, so she calls her Loulou."

Then, to Nate's surprise, Oscar crouched down, tapped Alegra lightly on the shoulder, and the girl came into his arms, too.

"Alegra has many friends here," Nate said, aware of sounding slightly jealous.

"Yes," Quina said. "Oscar has been a good friend to us."

"Come, you must be hungry," Mateo said, putting a hand on Nate's shoulder and gesturing toward the cookfire.

Nate looked around the camp in the gathering darkness.

"Behind you," Mateo said.

Nate turned and saw Rafael standing behind him on his crutches.

"Ah, there you are," Nate said. "How'd it go while I was gone? Any problems?"

Rafael shook his head no.

"Everything under control?"

The boy nodded.

"Good. Good work," Nate said, patting the boy's shoulder. "Want to keep me company while I eat? You can give me a full report."

Rafael nodded again, and Nate tousled his hair.

"Good, I'm starving."

Nate slept soundly in his small room that night, with Rafael on his cot beside him, and awoke before daybreak the next morning to the smell of coffee already on the fire. He breathed in the aroma and allowed himself a contented smile. *Home,* he thought. That's what La Libertad had become for him, and it felt good to be back.

Emerging barefoot from the room to take in the early quiet, Nate saw Lourdes and Quina already at the cookfire and Mateo at his favorite table with a mug of coffee. Mateo waved him over. He headed to Lourdes's cookfire first. Lourdes saw him coming and held up a mug as he approached.

"Gracias, Lourdes."

The old woman nodded and went back to her cooking.

"Good morning," Quina said, glancing and smiling. "Sleep well?"

"Sí, muy bien, gracias. You?"

"Sí, gracias. Alegra is still asleep."

Nate smiled, "Rafael, too."

Nate walked over and took his usual seat across from Mateo, who seemed to be in a contemplative mood. He sat silent for a while, leaning back in his chair, coffee in hand, gazing out at nothing. He took a sip of coffee, grunted.

"Shoot, move, communicate," Mateo said. He leaned toward Nate, elbows on the table, and lifted a fist. "Shoot," he said, raising an instructive finger. "Move," he said, raising a second finger. "Communicate." He raised a third. "Shoot, move, communicate," he repeated, his expression serious. "Say it with me. 'Shoot, move, communicate. Shoot—"

"—move, communicate," Nate recited, nodding. "I know, Mateo. We've been over this before, remember?"

"Sí, I remember," Mateo said, frowning. "But I need to know that *you* remember."

"I remember. I had a good teacher. Do you want to tell me what this is about? Sebastiano said you needed me back right away."

Mateo nodded. "We have acquired four more satellite phones," he said.

"Really? How? When?"

"*No importa*," Mateo said, waving a hand. "They have been delivered to four of our sister camps—*nuestras hermanas*—but our people need help setting them up, getting them working, learning how to use them."

Mateo looked at Nate. "Can you do this?"

Nate sat back in his chair. "I had a hunch it might be something like this."

"Well?"

"Well, what?"

"Can you do this?

"Can I? Or will I?"

"Both."

Nate frowned. "I can. Yes, I think so. But. . . . " He cocked his head, considering.

"Sebastiano will be back soon," Mateo said. "He has volunteered to go with you. He is a good man, a good guide. He can be trusted."

"I know he can," Nate said sincerely. "That's not the issue."

Mateo hunched forward across the table toward Nate. "You said before that you would think about it. That I should ask you again when the time came. Well, the time has come, my friend, and I am asking. I need to know. Will you do this for us?"

"Do what for us?" Quina asked, walking over to the table with her own mug of coffee. She pulled a chair over and sat down, looked from one man to the other.

"Do what for us?" she asked again.

"It does not concern you," Mateo said gruffly.

Quina gazed at him. "What does not concern me?"

"Mateo, could you give us a moment, please?"

Mateo growled, stood and examined the contents of his mug. "*Necesito más café*," he said and walked off.

When he was gone, Nate told Quina what they had been discussing.

"No one else can do this?" Quina asked.

"I'm not sure, but I don't think so. Mateo doesn't seem to think so."

Quina nodded. "Then you must go," she said. "That is why you are here. To help us, no?"

Nate hunched forward over his mug, twirled it in his hand. "Yes. . .

and no." He fell silent for a while. Quina waited. "It's one of the reasons, yes," he said. "But there are others."

"El Pitón," Quina said.

"Yes... and now...."

"Now?" Quina asked, puzzled.

Nate looked at her, held her gaze, fell into her eyes. *Don't you know, Quina? Can't you see?*

Quina reddened slightly, looked down. She and Nate sat in silence for a moment. Then she looked up at him.

"You must do this, Nate Hunter," Quina said. "You must go. And I will go with you."

"No, Quina, you—"

"No, listen to me," she said, holding up a hand to silence him. "This must be done, and it must be done right. Your Spanish is improving but it is not that good yet, and your Tzotzil is still weak. You will need an interpreter. We cannot afford mistakes. I will go with you. Alegra will stay here with Lourdes."

Quina sat back and looked at Nate, her expression resolute. It was a look Nate was coming to know well, a look that reminded him of Sarah. The two women looked nothing alike. But they were very much alike.

"I will get Mateo," Quina said. She stood and took Nate's mug. "*Y más café.*"

Nate watched Quina and Mateo talking, saw Mateo put his hands on his hips, look down and frown, shake his head, say something, saw Quina shake her head and say something back. Back and forth they went, as Nate watched and wondered. Was Quina doing this out of a desire to be with him? Support him? Or was she doing it for the cause? He laughed, knowing the answer: Does it matter?

Finally, Mateo nodded. Quina smiled and patted his arm, and they returned to the table.

"Okay," Mateo said. "Be ready to go when Sebastiano returns, *sí?*"

"I need at least one day with Alegra," Quina said.

Mateo nodded. "Sebastiano will not return until tomorrow, I do not think. You can leave the day after."

"How long do you think this will take?" Nate asked.

"It is hard to say," Mateo said. "A month. Maybe more. *Las Hermanas* are spread out. It will depend on how fast you travel, if you encounter any delays, how much time you need at each camp." Mateo looked at Nate, his expression grave. *"Por favor,* do not rush this," he said. "Work quickly, but do not cut corners, as you Americans say. Please do not leave a camp until you are sure everything is in order. Much depends on it."

Nate nodded. Mateo's comment about "you Americans" sort of irked him, but he let it pass.

Mateo said to Quina, "Sebastiano will take you from camp to camp, but he will not stay with you. He is needed here and other places, so he will travel back and forth. If you decide at any point that you are not needed and want to return. . . . "

Quina nodded.

"How much time do we have?" Nate asked. "Is there a deadline? Has the date been set?"

"It will be soon," Mateo said. "You have time, but not too much time."

"You're not going to tell us."

Mateo shook his head.

"Not when or where," Nate pressed.

"No. Not yet. It is not time yet."

"Okay. Just tell me this. What about Mirador?"

"What do you mean, 'What about Mirador?'" Mateo asked impatiently.

"What do you mean, what do I mean?" Nate retorted. "Is Mirador part of the plan?" He leaned across the table toward Mateo. "I mean, will we have revenge?"

Mateo nodded slowly. "Ahh, yes, that. *Revancha. Venganza. Justicia.*" He looked up at Nate. "Do not worry, my friend. Your time will come. You will have your revenge." He turned to Quina. "And you will have yours. And I will have mine." He put a hand on his heart. *"Tomo un juramento.* I take an oath on it."

Nate gave him a long, level, silent look.

"I will hold you to that promise," Nate said.

Mateo nodded. "I know."

Quina spent that day and the next taking Alegra around camp, reintroducing her to Mirasol and Rafael and other adults and children she had known or met in Mirador, getting her comfortable and settled, watching her with Lourdes, making sure she minded the old woman and helped with chores. Nate spent as much time as he could with Rafael, who was not happy that Nate was going away again so soon.

"I want to come with you," Rafael said as they sat side by side in the computer room, going over a list of tasks Nate was assigning to Rafael during his absence, a few last items that needed reviewing and double-checking before the website went live.

"I know, and I wish you could come," Nate said. "But I need you to stay here and watch over things while I'm gone. And I need you to help take care of Alegra, like a big brother. Will you do that for me?"

Rafael nodded sullenly. "You will be gone a long time," he said, not looking at Nate.

Nate pushed his chair back and turned Rafael's chair toward him so they were now sitting face to face.

"I'll be gone for a while, yes. But I'll be back. I said I'd come back last time, and I did, didn't I?"

"*Sí*, but you were not gone so many days."

"*Eso es verdad*," Nate admitted. "But you will be busy, and the time will go fast, and then I will be back..." He gestured toward the computer. "And we will launch the website together, you and I." He looked around the computer hut as if making sure they were alone, leaned closer to the boy and gave him a conspiratorial look. "Now I will tell you something, Rafael, and you must not tell anyone. It will be our surprise, okay?"

The boy nodded slowly, suspicious and intrigued.

"Okay. Just between you and me. When I come back and it is time to launch the website, you will be the one to launch it."

The boy sat up, surprised and confused. "*Yo?*"

Nate nodded. "*Sí. Tu.* You are very smart, Rafael. *Muy intelligente.* And you are very, very good at computers. As good as me. Maybe better. You have learned well, and I am proud of you. So when the time comes, you will launch the website. I will be here with you, but you will do it. Not me. You."

The boy's eyes went wide and a slow smile spread across his face.

Nate held up a hand for the high five he had taught Rafael the first time they had solved a sticky computer problem together.

"Okay?" he said, raising his eyebrows.

Rafael grinned and slapped his palm. "Okay," he said, grinning.

And then Rafael laughed. Which started Nate laughing. And they sat together in the computer hut, laughing together for a long time.

On their third morning in La Libertad, Quina smoothed back her daughter's hair and kissed her cheek while she slept, and Nate and

Quina hoisted their packs and crossed the square to the gate, where Sebastiano, Mateo, Oscar, Lourdes, and Rafael stood waiting.

"You have your gun?" Mateo asked Nate.

Nate patted his gunbelt.

"Be careful, and remember your training."

"I will."

"Do not worry about Alegra," Oscar said to Quina, ignoring Nate. "Lourdes and I will protect her with our lives. You know we will."

"I know," Quina said, smiling at Oscar and kissing him lightly on the cheek. "*Gracias, mi amigo. Muchas gracias.*"

Quina embraced Lourdes.

"*Vaya con Dios, mi hija,*" the old woman whispered in Quina's ear.

Nate squatted in front of Rafael.

"Remember what we talked about," he said, giving the boy a serious look.

Rafael smiled and nodded.

Nate put his hand up, and they exchanged another high five.

"Okay, *listo?*" Sebastiano asked.

Nate and Quina nodded. "*Listo,*" they answered in unison, and, hitching up their packs, they followed Sebastiano out the gate and down the ridge, heading toward the first of the four sisters. They walked in silence—Sebastiano in front, Quina in the middle, Nate in back. Watching where he stepped, Nate fell into a rhythm, Mateo's instructions and pledge echoing in his ears. "Shoot, move, communicate. Shoot, move, communicate. You will have your revenge, and I will have mine." Mateo would not say when it would be, but Nate sensed that the day of reckoning was approaching.

At about dusk on the second day of travel, Sebastiano, Nate, and Quina arrived at the first of the four outposts. It was another, smaller abandoned hacienda high up on a ridge, so hidden by thick vegetation that Nate and Quina would have continued right past it if Sebastiano hadn't turned them onto a faint trail winding up through the brush to the front gate.

The rebels had seen them, though.

Nate and Quina were startled when they came around a bend to see Sebastiano stopped a few feet from a heavyset man standing in front of them, blocking the path, legs apart, hands on hips. Nate moved his hand slowly toward his gun, but then the man grinned, opened his arms, and he and Sebastiano embraced, laughing and slapping each other on the back. The man looked vaguely familiar to Nate. Had he also been in the procession to the cemetery in Mirador? Nate couldn't be sure.

Sebastiano introduced the man. "This is Santiago," he said. "We call him Santi. Santi, this is Quina and Nate. They have come to help us with *el teléfono*."

Santi gave Nate a long, guarded look.

"*Es un amigo,*" Sebastiano assured him. "*Nos ha estado ayudando durante muchas meses. Puedes confiar en él.*"

"*Gracias,* Sebastiano," Nate said. "*Con mucho gusto,*" he said, nodding to Santi.

Santi nodded back, looked from Nate to Sebastiano, then stepped forward and extended his hand to Nate.

"Welcome to *El Grito de Justicia*," he said, shaking Nate's hand

"Cry of Justice," Nate said.

"*Sí,*" Santi said, looking impressed. "Come," he said, turning and gesturing up the trail. "You have traveled far. You must be tired and hungry."

El Grito was a different outpost, and yet it felt familiar. The people were different, and yet they seemed familiar, too. There was a newness and yet a sameness to this first of the four *hermanas* they would be visiting—the same high walls and central square and cookfires, the same mix of adults and children casting him curious but not unfriendly glances as they went about their chores. It made Nate feel almost instantly at home.

Santi led them to a cookfire being tended by an elderly woman named Carmen, who offered them a warm, gap-toothed smile, motioned for them to sit, and passed them mugs of water and plates of tortillas and beans.

"We will begin early tomorrow," Santi said to Nate and Quina as they ate and drank. "Thank you for coming. Tonight you must rest."

After they had finished eating, Santi showed them to a small hut nestled under a shade tree at the back of the cantonment. It reminded Nate of the computer hut at La Libertad, even down to the blue-green door.

"Sebastiano will share my quarters," Santi said. "You two can sleep here." He opened the door to a small room with two pallets made up side by side on the floor. A packing crate turned upside down to serve as a table was pushed up against the wall, under a small, high window facing onto the square. An unlit kerosene lamp and box of matches sat atop the crate. What looked like a large briefcase sat in a corner. The satellite phone, Nate realized.

Nate and Quina exchanged a sideways glance. *Well, this is awkward,* Nate thought. He turned to Santi. "I'm sorry—"

"*Gracias,* Santi," Quina said, smiling, cutting him off. "We will be very comfortable here." She stepped inside and dropped her pack against the wall, reached for Nate's and dropped it next to hers. "*Buenas noches.* Sleep well."

"*Hasta mañana,*" Santi said, nodding politely, and he and Sebastiano walked away.

It was the first time Nate and Quina had been alone together since their visit to the temple, which felt to Nate like a very long time ago. He had wanted her every night since. He wanted her now. He stood in the doorway, unsure what to do, as Quina sat down on one of the pallets, loosened her hair and shook it out.

"Ah, there is a breeze coming in through the window," she said. "Do you feel it?" She turned her dark eyes on him.

Nate didn't answer, didn't move. She was so ravishing sitting there. He wanted her so much.

Quina began unbuttoning her shirt.

"Close the door, Nate."

Nate stepped into the room and closed the door behind him.

Quina reached out a hand, and he came to her. And there was no more questioning. No more doubt. Yes, she wanted him as much as he wanted her.

At Carmen's cookfire the next morning, Santi introduced Nate and Quina to the three other camp residents—two men and one woman—who would share responsibility with Santi for satellite phone operations. After everyone had eaten, Nate retrieved the case from his room, set it up on a shaded table and opened it for inspection. Coffee mugs in hand, Santi and the rest of his team immediately began peppering Nate with questions he could only half understand.

Quina laughed and held up a hand. "*Una pregunta a la vez, por favor.*" The team members laughed with her, and they started again with Quina translating questions and answers fluidly back and forth in English, Spanish, Tzotzil, and at least one other indigenous tongue Nate didn't recognize. Nate was in awe. How many languages did she speak?

Sebastiano stayed through the initial orientation. When the group took a break before moving on to setup and testing, he told Nate and Quina that he'd be leaving.

"You will be fine," Sebastiano said to Nate, eyes twinkling, a smile playing at the corners of his mouth. He glanced at Quina. "You are in good hands, I think."

Nate chuckled and nodded. "I think you are right."

"I will be back in five days," Sebastiano told them. He waggled a hand. "Maybe more, maybe less. *Veremos.*"

"That should give us plenty of time," Nate said. "Are you heading back to La Libertad?"

"*Sí.*"

"What day is today, Wednesday?"

"Thursday," Quina said.

Nate nodded. "Tell Mateo that if the weather is clear, we will try to reach him at midday on Sunday."

Sebastiano nodded.

"And give Alegra a hug for me," Quina added. "Tell her that *Mamí* loves her and is well. Will you do that, Sebastiano?"

"*Sí, claro,*" Sebastiano said, nodding.

"*Gracias,*" Quina said, giving him a quick hug.

Sebastiano and Nate shook hands.

"Thank you again, Sebastiano," Nate said. "I am in your debt."

"No, no," Sebastiano said, frowning. "You are helping us. *Hasta luego.*" And he turned and headed out the gate.

The work went well at El Grito. Santi and the rest of the team caught on quickly, the setup and testing went smoothly, and the Sunday call to La Libertad went through without a hitch. When it ended, grins, whoops, and applause broke out and everyone hugged and patted one another on the back.

"*Muy bien, muy bien,*" Santi said, slapping Nate on the shoulder. "*Gracias, amigo.* Now we will be ready."

Ready for what? Nate wanted to ask. *What is about to happen? When? Where?* He smiled and said nothing. He had spent enough time with Santi now to note the similarities to Mateo. Santi wouldn't answer Nate's questions, either. They would only make him uncomfortable. So Nate didn't ask.

With their main mission accomplished and no other pressing tasks to fill their time as they waited for Sebastiano to return, Nate and Quina immersed themselves in the rhythms and routines of camp life, helping with many of the same chores and tasks that kept them busy at La Libertad. Quina helped Carmen and another woman named Beatriz cook and deliver food to the old ones. Nate helped tend the livestock, hauled water, carried wood. In the afternoon, they sometimes grabbed a canteen and explored outside El Grito. In the evening, they strolled the square, chatted with other camp residents, sat by the cookfires late into the night as campesinos brought out their instruments to play and sing under the stars. They talked, they laughed. They sat together in easy silence. At night, in their hut, they made love.

And so it went, from camp to camp, as Sebastiano came and went, bringing news from La Libertad and drawings from Alegra, guiding them to the second outpost, then the third, and finally to the fourth, leaving them longer each time before returning, apologetic and, each time, a little more distracted and tense.

It's coming, Nate thought, studying Sebastiano's changing demeanor. *Whatever it is, it's coming soon.*

"I will try to return for you in seven days," Sebastiano said, shouldering his pack to leave after delivering them to the last of the four sisters, an outpost the residents had christened *Ojos Sonrientes.* "It may be longer. I cannot say. I am sorry. I will return as soon as I can."

"Do not apologize," Quina said mock sternly, giving Sebastiano a hard look. "You have much to do, we know. We will be fine here until you return."

The name of the camp puzzled Nate at first—a rebel outpost called Smiling Eyes? But after spending one day there, it made sense. Unlike the other compounds, which were contained within high walls, this camp consisted of a number of small huts and buildings scattered along the slope of a sparkling clearwater tributary of *El Río Lacanjá.* It was a beautiful place. Remote. Serene. Being there with Quina felt almost like being on a vacation. Or a honeymoon.

At the gloaming of a day toward the end of December, their daily chores complete, Nate and Quina strolled hand in hand along a narrow foot trail that traced the clearwater stream, watching the land and water darken beneath a lowering sky. Pausing in the shelter of a grotto of trees, they turned toward each other. Nate took Quina in his arms and kissed her tenderly. She sighed and lay her head on his chest. Neither spoke. Nate tried to fix the moment in his memory, everything about it. The falling dark, the sound of the water, the rustle of the trees. Standing there, in that idyllic spot, with his arms around this woman, holding her, breathing in her scent. He wanted the moment to last forever. He knew it could not. They both knew time was running out.

A fine evening rain began to fall. Muted thunder rolled in the distance. Quina took Nate's hand again and led him back up the slope to their small hut. She struck a match and lit the candle on the vegetable crate that served as their table, then reached into her pack and took out what looked like a small black cassette player.

"What the... Is that a—"

"Shh," she shushed him, smiling and holding up a finger. She stood the cassette player upright on the crate, pushed a button and waited.

Against the patter of a gentle rain, music began to play. A slow, wistful, tinkling piano melody accompanied by a rhythmic whisk of a melancholy guitar. "It's Not for Me to Say." Nate recognized the classic recording before the mellifluous-voiced crooner even began to sing.

"Johnny Mathis?" Nate said, smiling. "You're a Johnny Mathis fan?"

Quina nodded. "Big time," she said softly, smiling seductively and holding her arms out, inviting Nate to dance.

He shook his head, smiling.

"I didn't know," he said, taking her in his arms and holding her close. He was no dancer, but he could manage this.

"There are many things you do not know about me," she murmured in his ear.

"But I'm learning," he murmured back.

And then they danced, pressed against each other, cheek to cheek, lost in the music, lost to the world. And Nate knew, during those near-perfect minutes, that the love he felt for this woman, at this time, in this place, was deeper in many ways than any he had ever felt before. A whisper of sadness and guilt passed through him as he admitted this to himself. There... then gone. He held Quina closer, and they danced.

The song ended. The dancing stopped. Nate gazed into the dark, shining eyes of the woman in his arms. He had sincerely wanted to die once. He didn't anymore. He wanted a life with this woman. When it was over. If they survived it. Whatever was to come.

Nate's eyes misted. Quina looked up, raised her hands to his cheeks.

"*El pequeño perdido,*" she said.

"The little lost one?"

"*Sí.*"

"Me?"

Quina didn't answer. She kissed him gently.

"Merry Christmas, *mi amor.*"

Mi amor? Quina had never called him that before. *And, wait. Christmas?*

"Today is Christmas?"

Quina smiled and nodded. Nate had lost track of the days.

Quina stepped out of his embrace, turned and began unbraiding her long ebon-hued hair, shook it out and let it fall down her back like a shower of warm, black rain.

She lifted her blouse over her head and laid it on the chair by the bed, unbuttoned her skirt, let it billow to the floor, gathered it up and laid it atop her blouse. She turned and smiled at him as she slipped out of her underwear. In the candlelight, her skin was golden, her eyes glistened. She sat and stretched out on their double pallets and watched, smiling, as Nate undressed and hung his clothes on the back of the chair, and stretched out naked beside her, arms behind his head. He sighed.

"I wish we could just stay here. Bring Alegra and Teresa here. Build a house. Forget about everyone and everything else."

Quina sighed. "*Yo también,*" she said softly, shifting closer, putting an arm around him and laying her head on his chest.

They were silent for a while, listening to the soft patter of rain.

"Sebastiano will be back soon," Nate said.

"Yes."

"Maybe even tomorrow."

"Yes."

Another silence.

Nate looked down into Quina's upturned face, turned toward her and held her close. And then they made love with the urgency and passion of knowing that tomorrow would bring a return to the harsh realities that had brought them together—and a night like this might never come again. ▲

CHAPTER 31

Viewpoint

Sebastiano returned the next morning to take Nate and Quina back to La Libertad. Mateo was waiting to greet them with Alegra and Rafael at his side when they came through the gate thirty-six hours later.

"*Mamí!*" Alegra cried, running to Quina.

"*Ah, mi hija,* how I have missed you," Quina crooned, lifting Alegra in her arms and smothering her with kisses. "Were you good? Did you mind Loulou? Did you miss your *mamí?*"

"*Sí, sí, sí,*" Alegra answered, nodding emphatically, arms wrapped around her mother's neck.

Quina laughed. "*Mi corazón, mi querida.* Thank you for the beautiful drawings."

"You are welcome," Alegra said formally, and Quina laughed again.

Nate gave Rafael a serious look. "Well, lieutenant? Everything under control?"

Rafael grinned and nodded.

"Very good," he said, tousling the boy's hair.

"Welcome back," Mateo said, putting a hand on Nate's shoulder. "Thank you. Thank you, my friend. *Y tu también,* Quina. *Gracias a* both of you. You have done good work. Important work." He patted Nate's shoulder. "And now, soon, we will launch the website." Mateo nodded at Rafael. "Your lieutenant here says all is ready. *Verdad,* Rafael?"

"*Sí,*" Rafael said, all seriousness. He looked to Nate. "*Somos listos.*"

Nate nodded and patted his shoulder. "If Rafael says we're ready, then we're ready," he said to Mateo. "Rafael is my second-in-command. He could launch the website himself if he had to." Nate winked at the boy. "Isn't that so, Rafael?"

Rafael grinned and nodded. "*Sí. Es verdad.*"

"So when do we launch?" Nate asked Mateo.

"Soon," Mateo said. "Very soon." He pointed to Lourdes's cookfire, where Sebastiano was already sitting cross-legged on the ground with a plate of food. "Eat, and then rest. We will talk in the morning. I will tell you then."

Quina and Nate returned to their respective quarters that night, Quina with Alegra, Nate with Rafael. Nate fell asleep working out the plan for the house he was going to build in Los Ojos Sonrientes, so Rafael could live there, too.

Mateo was at his usual table with his usual mug of coffee when Nate emerged from his room the next morning.

"*Buenos días, Lourdes,*" Nate said, coming up behind her at the cookfire.

"*Buenos días, El Cazador,*" Lourdes said, handing him two mugs. Nate glanced up and saw Quina crossing toward them dressed in olive drab fatigues. He handed her a mug and they sat down with Mateo.

"So when do we launch?" Nate asked. *And if he says "soon" again, I'll—*

"Four days."

"What?"

Nate fell back against his chair, looked at Quina, saw that she was as surprised as he was.

Mateo hunched forward, put his mug on the table. "Four days," he repeated, turning his mug in his hands. "At the stroke of midnight on *La Nochevieja.*"

"*La nochevieja.* The old night."

"New Year's Eve," Quina translated.

Mateo nodded. "*Sí.* At the stroke of midnight, when the old year passes and the new year begins. That is when NAFTA goes into effect." He looked from Nate to Quina. "That is when we rise up. That is when it begins." He turned back to Nate. "*Estamos listos?*"

"The website, you mean? Yes, we're ready."

"*Estás seguro? Esto es muy importante.* We cannot have any problems. No delays."

Nate nodded. "I understand, Mateo. We're ready. Trust me. Rafael could do it himself if he had to. I'm serious."

Mateo nodded, mollified if not completely reassured.

"Where will it be?" Nate asked.

"Different towns and villages."

"Coordinated."

Mateo nodded.

"By phone."

"Some of them. Yes."

"Which villages?" Quina asked.

"I cannot tell you," Mateo said. "I do not know all of them."

"I do not need to know all of them, Mateo," Quina said coolly. "I just need to know one."

Mateo frowned, turned his mug in his hands. He didn't answer.

"Mateo."

Silence. And then, "*Sí*" Mateo said. "Mirador. *Sí.*"

Nate's spirit quickened. Quina leaned across the table, put a hand on Mateo's arm.

"You are going?"

Mateo frowned. "No. I will remain here with my own squad." He glanced at Nate. "We must guard our investment. It is key to our success."

"Who then?" Quina asked.

"From here, Sebastiano. He leaves today. Maybe Oscar tomorrow or the day after. That is undecided. Fulgencio went yesterday. Many others have already gone."

Quina withdrew her arm, sat up. Nate knew what was coming.

"I am going," Quina told Mateo.

"No, Quina," Mateo said. "You are needed here. To help with communications. We need your language skills."

Quina shook her head. "No. Mirasol speaks Tzotzil. Lourdes, too. She speaks Tzotzil, Tzeltal, Chol. She can help."

"No, Quina, *por favor, escúcheme*," Mateo said. "You are needed here. And Alegra is here, *recuerdas?* What about her? Will you leave her again?"

Quina jerked back as if struck, and Mateo immediately held up his hands and bowed his head in apology.

"*Lo siento, lo siento.* I should not have said that. *Perdóname.*"

Quina narrowed her eyes at Mateo. "Do... not... ever..." she said slowly, "try to tell me what is best for my child." She glared at Mateo. He nodded. Quina took a deep breath, calmed herself.

"Alegra is safer here," she said. "You know that. That is why I brought her here." She extended her hand again, rested it on Mateo's arm. "But Teresa is still in Mirador, Mateo. She is old, and she is alone."

"And El Pitón is still in Mirador," Nate said calmly. "And you made us a promise."

Mateo looked confused.

"You don't remember? Before we left, you said we would have our revenge, that our time would come. You swore it. Remember?"

Mateo nodded. "*Sí.* I remember."

"Well, this is that time."

"What do you mean?"

"I mean, I'm going, too."

"No!" Mateo exploded, slamming the table with the flat of his hand. "No! You also made a promise! Are you forgetting that? You promised to help us bring our struggle to the attention of the world."

"And I have, and I will," Nate said calmly. "The website is ready, Mateo. I told you that. I'll go over everything again with you and Rafael before we leave. Rafael can launch the website. He and I already discussed it. He knows what to do, and he can show you. You already know most of it. It's not that hard."

"No!"

"Yes. You two can keep it going while I'm gone, and I'll take over again when we return."

Mateo sat back in his chair. "When you return," he repeated, his tone mocking. He leaned forward again, glowered at Nate. "*If* you return."

Nate nodded. "Okay. If. You're right. If I don't return, don't worry, the website is in good hands." He gave Mateo a sly smile, waved a hand in the air. "No problem, no problem." Mateo shook his head. "And if I do return," Nate continued, raising his mug, "we will drink to the death of El Pitón." He put down his mug, leaned forward, and looked Mateo straight in the eye. "Because now I make another promise to you, my friend. I will not return until El Pitón is dead."

After the morning meal, Nate, Rafael, and Mateo went over things again in the computer hut until Mateo was satisfied that he and the boy both knew exactly what to do.

"But Rafael is in charge, Mateo," Nate said in the boy's presence. "I'm serious. You're in charge of the satellite phone, but he's in charge of the computer. You can trust him. He knows exactly what to do."

Nate put a hand on the boy's shoulder. "Right, Rafael?"

The boy nodded. "*Sí.*"

Out in the courtyard, Quina was sitting at a table with Lourdes, holding Alegra on her lap. Seeing Nate, Mateo, and Rafael approach, Quina hugged and kissed her daughter hard, then stood and put her down. "Walk me to the gate, *querida,*" Quina said, holding out her hand to Alegra. Lourdes stood and took Alegra's other hand, and the two men and women, one boy and one girl, moved to the gate where Sebastiano was waiting.

Mateo handed Nate the gunbelt again. "Shoot, move, communicate," he reminded him once more.

"I know," Nate said, cinching the belt around his waist. "Thank you, Mateo."

"I will be back soon, my darling," Quina said, kneeling to hug and kiss Alegra.

"*Te amo, mamí,*" Alegra said, hugging her back.

"I'm counting on you," Nate said, putting a hand on Rafael's shoulder. "You're in charge until I return."

Rafael nodded. Nate knelt and folded the boy in his arms. Then he stood, tousled his hair and decamped for Mirador.

They made the journey in good time, arriving at the outskirts of Mirador in the early evening and taking cover in the bush to wait until full dark before slipping into the village and making their way to Teresa's home.

"Where do you go after you leave us?" Nate asked Sebastiano as they sat cross-legged on the ground, waiting.

"*El ejército* is assembling farther south," Sebastiano said. "I go there." He looked at Quina. "Teresa should be safe if she stays inside. But you must keep her inside until it is over, *entiendes?* Bring what you need into the hut. Water. Everything. And then bolt the door and stay inside. Do not go out until one of us comes to tell you it is safe."

Quina nodded. "It begins at midnight, at the stroke of the new year?"

"Yes, I think so."

"How long will it last?" Nate asked.

"*No sé,*" Sebastiano said, hunching over and pulling up blades of grass. "Perhaps a day, perhaps more. They do not know we are coming. That is good." He looked up at Nate. "You want El Pitón."

Nate nodded.

"He is there. He and his men. In the old barracks. But you must wait until it begins. You cannot move until then. They cannot know you have returned. They cannot know we are coming."

"I understand."

Quina knocked on the door of Teresa's hut and called softly to her when they arrived, not wanting to frighten her this time by pushing the door open.

"*Gracias a Dios, gracias a Dios,*" the old woman whispered, tears spilling down her cheeks, embracing first Quina, then Nate and pulling them inside. Nate looked around for Sebastiano, but he was already gone.

Teresa was well, she assured Nate and Quina. El Pitón and his men were still in Mirador. But things seemed to have calmed down some. Not so many paramilitaristas and soldados in the streets. Not so many patrols.

"So things have been quiet," Quina said, as they sat at the table eating pinole.

"*Sí,*" Teresa said, pouring them cups of water. "But that will change now."

"*Por qué dices eso?*" Quina asked, surprised. She and Nate exchanged a look.

"*Porque estás aquí,*" Teresa said simply. She put the water pitcher down on the table, sat and took Quina's hand in hers, looked at her with clear eyes. "It comes now. *Lo sé. La lucha comienza por fin.*"

"Does anyone else know?" Quina asked.

Teresa shrugged. "The people wait. They hope. Some may know." She smiled gently and patted Quina's hand. "I know because you are here."

All the next day, Teresa and Quina prepared. Going to market under the watchful eyes of the occasional army patrol, both dressed in traditional garb, like ordinary villagers on an ordinary day. Making bread, tortillas, and corn cakes, beans and pinole. Filling the water jugs. Nate stayed inside, out of sight, waiting again for darkness, when he and Quina could slip out into the yard, breathe the night air, gaze up at the night sky, the just-past-full moon. Under cover of darkness, they lay together beneath the low-hanging branches of the cedar tree. Being careful to draw no attention to themselves and to make no sound—not a moan, not a sigh—they made love. Afterward, they held each other. Then they rose silently and went back inside and tried to sleep.

The next day was *La Nochevieja*. Through the long, slow hours of the last day of the year, knowing they were edging toward the brink of war, Nate and Quina waited. The apprehension and the tedium set off in Nate a stampede of emotions—fear, anger, sadness, guilt, love. When he dozed, he faced a parade of ghosts—Jack, his mother, Sarah, the soldier in the jungle, the running man in his dream.

Night finally fell. They stayed inside now, with the lamp turned low. Ate in the semidark. Talked in whispers. After the evening meal, Teresa lay down on her cot, doused the lamp and was soon asleep. Nate and Quina took their usual positions side by side on the floor, backs against the wall, Nate's gunbelt on the floor next to him within easy reach.

Nate closed his eyes and began to doze. All was still. And then a faint creak, the sound of Teresa's front gate slowly opening, brought him awake. He looked at Quina. She nodded. She'd heard it, too.

Sebastiano? Or someone else? Nate reached for his gunbelt and unholstered the .45. He and Quina came quickly and silently to their feet and moved toward the table, watching the door. Nate cocked the gun and held it in his right hand, supporting it with his left. The door began opening slowly, and Nate saw what looked like the brim of an army cap appear. His pulse raced. He eased his finger toward the trigger, lowered the muzzle, remained acutely focused, silent, still.

"*Quina?*" the intruder whispered. "*Teresa? Está aquí?*"

Quina put a reassuring hand on Nate's arm. "*Oscar?*" she whispered back.

"*Sí, soy yo.*"

Nate uncocked and lowered the gun and took a series of slow breaths to calm himself as Quina went to the door, opened it a little wider and pulled Oscar inside. He was wearing fatigues and an army cap and carried a bulky, heavy-looking black canvas duffel slung over his shoulder.

"*Oscar! Tu nos has asustado!*" Quina said, her tone scolding, still whispering, closing the door quickly behind him.

"*Lo siento,*" Oscar said, breathing heavily, lowering the bag he was carrying slowly and carefully to the floor. He wiped his brow with the back of his hand. "*Puedo tomar un poco de agua, por favor?*"

Teresa stirred and woke.

"*Quién es?*" she whispered from her cot, sounding alarmed.

"*Está bien, Teresa,*" Quina reassured her, pouring Oscar a mug of water. "*Es Oscar.*"

"*Ah, Oscar,*" Teresa said, sounding relieved.

Oscar took the cup of water from Quina and drank deeply, draining it, sighed in satisfaction and wiped his mouth with his sleeve. "*Buenas noches, Teresa,*" he called softly to the old woman. "*Lo siento por despertarte.*"

Awake now, Teresa sat up, lit the kerosene lamp on the bureau, turned the wick down low and brought the lamp to the table. In the dim light, Oscar saw the gun in Nate's hand. He snickered, water dripping from his chin.

"You going to shoot me, *cabrón*?" He gave Nate a scornful look. "I do not think so."

Nate didn't respond. He stood silent and still, holding the gun in both hands, and returned Oscar's cold gaze. The two men stood like that, neither one blinking or looking away.

"*Basta,*" Quina said, annoyed, waving a hand. "Oscar, sit, please," she said, pointing to the chair nearest him. "Nate, you, too," she said, indicating the chair across from Oscar. Nate sat and put the gun on the table. Oscar sat down heavily, clearly spent. Quina took the chair between them. "*Teresa, más agua, para Oscar, por favor?*" Teresa refilled Oscar's mug, set the pitcher and two more cups on the table and sat down.

"*Gracias, Teresa,*" Oscar said. He took another long drink.

Nate and Quina waited. Oscar had traveled hard and fast to get there, just hours before the uprising was to begin. Whatever he had come to tell them had to be important. But what was it?

Quina suddenly jolted, grasped the edge of the table, her eyes wide. "Oscar, is it Alegra? Did something—"

"*No, no, no te preocupes,*" Oscar said, reaching and covering her hand with his. "*Alegra está bien.* She is safe."

Quina sighed in relief and sat back in her chair. Oscar removed his cap and set it on the table, wiping sweat from his forehead with the palm of a hand. He slowly pulled the bag over and carefully propped it against his right leg.

"*Mañana,*" he said, looking from Quina to Nate and back to Quina. "It begins tomorrow."

"*Sí*" Quina said.

Oscar nodded.

"You have a job for us," Nate said calmly.

Oscar did not answer immediately. He drank more water, put down the cup, stared across at Nate.

"You want El Pitón," he said finally.

Nate nodded.

"So do we."

Nate raised an eyebrow. "And who's we?"

"Who is we?" Oscar repeated, curling his lip in disgust. "You need me to tell you, *cabrón?*"

Nate shook his head. "No."

"Okay. You want El Pitón. We want him and his men. All of them. *Todos los paramilitaristas.*" He let that sink in for a moment. "So . . ." He looked from Nate to Quina. "We are going to firebomb the barracks."

"His headquarters?" Quina said.

"*Sí. La sede.* At dawn."

"*Madre de Dios,*" Teresa said, bowing her head and crossing herself. "*Más muerte. Más muerte.*"

Oscar gave Quina a look, and Quina nodded.

"Teresa," Quina said gently. "*Quizás es mejor que no escuchas.*"

Teresa nodded sadly. "*Quizás.*" She rose slowly and returned to her cot, pulled a thin quilt over her shoulders and lay down facing the wall.

Quina watched her settle in, then nodded to Oscar, and he began again.

"We firebomb the barracks at dawn," he repeated, keeping his voice low. The others will be hiding in the jungle. That will be their signal. When they hear the explosion and see the fire, they will attack." He looked from Quina to Nate. "We will fire the shot that begins the battle to free Mirador."

"We," Nate said again.

Oscar looked directly at Nate.

"*No te preocupes, El Cazador,*" he said in a mocking tone. "You do not have to come if you are afraid. I will go alone. *Creo que es mejor.* But Mateo knows you are here. He says to ask if you will help. He makes me promise." Oscar shrugged. "So I am asking."

Oscar turned serious again, locked eyes with Nate.

Nate returned Oscar's gaze, waiting him out.

"Well," Oscar said finally. "Yes or no?"

Nate dropped his gaze to the gun on the table between them. It wasn't his ideal scenario. If he could do things his way, he'd get El Pitón on the loop road, just the two of them, near where Sarah died, get him down on his knees, make him beg for his life and then put a bullet in his brain. But that was a fantasy. In reality, Nate knew, he'd be lucky to get a shot at the man from a distance, if El Pitón or one of his men didn't see and shoot Nate first. Slipping back into old habits, Nate did a quick analysis of objectives, options, and potential outcomes. The goal was to kill El Pitón. It didn't matter how he died, really, as long as he died. Oscar was a good fighter. Teaming up and adding explosives to the mix vastly increased the odds of achieving the primary objective.

Nate looked at Oscar, nodded once.

"Yes," he said.

Oscar squinted at him, scrutinizing him coldly. *"Estás seguro."*

"Yes."

"It will be dangerous."

Nate nodded. "I know."

"And you can do it?"

"Yes."

Oscar turned to Quina.

She nodded. *"Sí.* It must be done."

Nate's stomach dropped.

"No. Wait... You're not.... "

Quina and Oscar turned to him, matching expressions of calm determination on their faces. Nate looked from one to the other.

"No, Quina, you can't... "

"Yes, Nate," Quina said quietly. "This is our time. *Este momento.* This is what we've trained for. We must rise up together. All of us. Men and women both."

No! Nate wanted to argue back. *You can't! I won't let you! I've already lost Sarah. I can't risk losing you, too.*

But Quina was not his to command, anymore than Sarah had been. Nate had made a vow to die for Sarah. He had broken that vow. He made another vow now: his life for Quina's. If one of them had to die, it would be Nate. It had to be. Or he'd have no reason to go on living at all.

"*B*ueno," Oscar said. *"Estámos de acuerdo.* Now, we must prepare." He pulled the lantern closer, rubbed his hands together with what struck Nate as an intentionally dramatic flourish, leaned down and unzipped the bag. As Nate and Quina watched, he reached in and withdrew a woolen bundle and set it carefully on the table. It was long and slender, rolled and bound with a leather thong, like a scroll. He held his hands up near his chest, stretched and clenched them, rubbed the thumb and fingertips of each hand together as if limbering them up, then delicately untied the knot and unfurled the fabric to reveal the disassembled components of a rifle.

Oscar arranged the rifle parts on the table, laying them out one by one. When he was finished, he went over them, pointing to each freshly oiled part and muttering to himself, taking inventory.

"*Bueno*," he said, nodding. "*Todos están aquí.*"

Quina examined the display.

"M1?" she asked.

"M1 Garand," Oscar grumbled. "Semi-automatic. Gas-operated. Clip-fed."

Quina nodded. Nate said nothing, embarrassed by how much more she knew about guns than he did. He doubted he could have identified the rifle even fully assembled. She knew it from its parts.

Teresa stirred again on her cot, sat up.

"*Ach,*" she muttered to herself. "*No puedo dormir.*" She rose with a sigh. "*Voy a preparar café.*"

Oscar, Nate, and Quina exchanged looks, waited for Teresa to react to what was spread out on her table. She paused on the way to the cookstove, took a long look and shook her head, but said nothing, allowing herself quick, anxious glances in Oscar's direction as she brewed the café.

With that, Oscar started assembling the rifle in what Nate recognized as a well-practiced routine that Oscar clearly knew by heart and could probably do blindfolded. Nate and Quina watched intently as Oscar worked, naming each component as he reached for it and slid or snapped it swiftly in place. Nate watched him lower the barrel and receiver group into the wooden stock, raise the trigger housing group to the underside of the stock and lock it into position. It was clear to Nate that Oscar was trying to impress Quina with his proficiency. That was okay. Nate was impressed, too.

When Oscar had the rifle fully assembled and the parts tightened down, he pointed the muzzle at the ceiling, pulled back the bolt and let it fly forward with a jarring clang of steel slamming against steel that made Nate and Quina jerk and made Teresa spill some of the coffee she was pouring into her mug.

"Oscar, we must be quiet!" Quina reprimanded him in a harsh whisper.

"*Sí, Sí,*" Oscar said, making a placatory patting motion with his hand. He stood, pulled the bolt back again and eased it forward, then put the stock to his shoulder and pointed the rifle at a clay pot filled with wildflowers sitting on the shelf above Teresa's cookstove. Holding the rifle in firing position, Oscar adjusted the rear sight with thumb and forefinger. Then, slowly, deliberately, he brought the barrel around toward Nate, letting the muzzle settle not eighteen inches from a spot just above the bridge of his nose.

Nate froze. Sitting across from each other at the table, Teresa and Quina exchanged anxious looks. The two men stared at each other over the rifle's sights. Then Oscar pulled the trigger and the firing pin clicked. Nate, Quina, and Teresa jerked as one. Oscar smiled and lowered the rifle to his hip, still aimed at Nate, this time at his chest.

"*Basta!*" Quina hissed at Oscar, jumping up and pushing the rifle away. "*No más!*"

Teresa lowered and shook her head.

Still smiling, Oscar lifted the rifle and held it in front of him in the two-handed grasp Nate recognized as port arms, pulled back the bolt and locked it down. He sat down again, cradling the rifle in the crook of his left arm, and took an olive drab bandolier of ammunition from the canvas bag. He put it on the table and removed one clip holding eight brass cartridges. Keeping his eyes on Nate, he pressed the clip into the rifle's receiver with a thumb and released the bolt. It lurched forward with another clang, driving a round into the chamber. He engaged the safety and stood the rifle upright against the wall.

Now Oscar stood again, moved to the front door and cracked it open. He reached outside, retrieved two five-gallon plastic gasoline containers, both empty, and set them on the floor.

"Where did you find those?" Quina said.

"*No importa.*"

Oscar set the canvas bag carefully on his chair and began removing other tools and equipment and setting them on the table. A pair of eighteen inch bolt cutters. A U.S. Army bayonet. A four-inch folding knife. A roll of gray duct tape and a coil of thin nylon cord. Finally, he reached into the bag and brought out a brown drawstring pouch. He placed it gently on the table, untied the knot at the top, loosened the string, opened the pouch, and removed a cloth-wrapped bundle the size of a small gourd. He slowly unwrapped it to reveal a hand grenade.

"*Madre de Dios*," Teresa whispered, covering her mouth with her hand. She stood and moved back from the table, eyes wide with fright. Quina and Nate stood and backed off a few steps, too.

Oscar reached into the bag and produced five more grenades, placed them carefully on the table and unwrapped them. When he was satisfied with the arrangement, he looked up at Quina and Nate, brandishing a boastful smile.

"*Bueno. No?*"

Teresa looked pleadingly at Nate and Quina.

"You are frightening Teresa," Nate said calmly.

Oscar glanced at the old woman and saw that it was true.

"*Perdóname, Señora*," Oscar said softly. "*No quisé asustarte.*" One by one, he wrapped five of the grenades, returned them to his bag, and set the bag on the floor, leaving only one grenade on the table.

Teresa lowered and shook her head, walked around to Nate and Quina, patted Nate's arm in passing, and returned to her cot.

Oscar watched her go, then nodded toward the table, and the three co-conspirators sat. Keeping his voice low and speaking in a rapid-fire mix of Spanish and English with Quina translating where necessary, Oscar went over the plan.

"Before sunrise, we make our way to *la sede*," he said. The *paramilitaristas* keep the gasoline for their vehicles in fifty-five-gallon steel drums locked in a small cage behind the building." Oscar and Nate would cut the chain and fill their two containers with gasoline. "Quina, you will cover us."

Quina nodded.

They would empty one container all over the old wooden front porch of the barracks and tie the other container to a wooden post, tape a grenade to the second container, tie a cord to the pin, and retreat. Oscar mimed paying out the cord in front of him as he backed away. "We take cover..." Oscar mimed crouching. "We pull the cord... " He mimed giving it a yank. "*Entonces...*" He looked from Nate to Quina, eyes electric with anticipation. "*Entonces... boom!*" he whispered, throwing his hands in the air, fingers spread.

He clapped his hands softly for emphasis and grinned.

Quina gave Nate a dubious look.

"Then what?" Nate said.

Oscar shrugged.

"We burn the place down. Kill everyone."

Nate stared at the man sitting across from him, taken aback by how casually he had uttered those words, how eager he seemed to be to carry out the bloody enterprise. Nate tried to envision it step by step— stealing the gasoline, dousing the porch, detonating the grenade.

"We burn the place down, kill everyone," Nate repeated in a monotone, checking to see how it felt to hear the words coming out of his own mouth. It didn't feel real.

Oscar sat silent across from him, watching him, waiting.

Nate shrugged.

"We burn the place down," he said again, this time with cold resolve.

Oscar hunched forward, leaning on his palms, and glared at Nate across the table, his face tight, his look hard.

"If you cannot do it, *gringo*, tell me now."

Nate met Oscar's gaze, felt Quina watching him. Could he? Could he kill? The image of the dead soldier in the jungle still dogged him. He liked the fantasy of putting a bullet in El Pitón's brain, but could he actually do it? Could he blow up a building with people inside?

Nate remained silent, calmly holding Oscar's gaze, and Oscar sat back, calming himself.

"We will take them by surprise," Oscar said. They will not be expecting us." Mirador had been quiet since the massacre in the church. The soldados and paramilitaristas had relaxed their guard. "They do not think we have the courage to attack," he growled. "But we do." He ground a fist into his palm. "We do."

Oscar picked up the grenade he had left on the table. Any paramilitaristas who were not killed in the firebombing, he said, if they tried to escape, "when they start coming out... the ones who are left... we throw these."

Oscar juggled the grenade in one hand, making Quina gasp.

"Oscar, *por favor*."

Oscar stopped juggling. He lowered his head and peered up at Nate with a cold glint in his eye. Keeping his gaze fixed on Nate, he grasped the grenade in his right hand, keeping the safety lever pressed down, put his left index finger through the steel ring, and pulled the pin.

Nate jerked and grunted involuntarily. Quina let out a soft cry.

"Oscar! Qué haces? Estás loco?"

Oscar ignored her, all his senses focused on Nate, relishing the power to cause him to feel fear.

Nate studied the grenade in Oscar's hand, then looked calmly into Oscar's eyes.

"Okay. You've made your point. You want to put the pin back in the grenade now?"

Oscar stared at Nate a moment longer, then gave up a low, bitter laugh. He returned the pin to the grenade and set it on the table.

Quina stared at Oscar in cold silence. "I thought you were my friend, Oscar," she said calmly.

Oscar looked confused. *"Sí,* I am your friend."

Quina shook her head. "No." She leaned toward him. "You do this thing in this house? In Teresa's house?" She sat back, shook her head again. "No, Oscar. You are not my friend."

The stupidity of what Oscar had done seemed to hit him then.

"Quina, no," Oscar said, cajoling, reaching across the table for her hand.

Quina kept her hands in her lap.

Oscar frowned, withdrew his hand and nodded. "I should not have done it," he said gruffly. "You are right." He looked at Quina. "But there was no danger. *Nunca haría nada que te hiciera daño a ti o a Teresa. Tú lo sabes."*

Quina sat like a stone for another few moments. Then she pulled her chair closer to the table. "We have a mission," she said coolly. "We must prepare."

Oscar nodded and sat back heavily. His manner became business-like again.

"When our troops hear the first explosion, they will attack. Some will come to us to help us take the barracks. Others will attack the garrison. *Con suerte,* Mirador will be liberated by noon."

Oscar looked from Quina to Nate. *"Okay? Estámos claros?"*

Quina sat silent, staring at the grenade, still disgusted at Oscar's recklessness. Nate said nothing.

"All we have to do," Oscar said, leaning forward again, "is firebomb the headquarters. *Nada más. Entiendes?"*

Quina nodded coldly, glanced at Nate. Nate didn't answer, didn't move.

"*Cuál es el problema, gringo?*" Oscar sneered. "Afraid?"

Nate gave Oscar a steely look. "Aren't you?"

Oscar's face darkened. He leaned toward Nate, forearms on the table, hands clenched into fists. His eyes were bloodshot, his breath sour.

"*Mira, gringo.* I do not like you. You do not like me, eh? But you are part of this now. So I ask you again. Do you understand? Are we clear?"

Staring calmly back into Oscar's bloodshot eyes, refusing to be intimidated, Nate did not answer immediately. He raised a hand and rubbed his chin. Enraged, Oscar grabbed his arm.

"I asked you a question, *cabrón*," he growled, eyes searing. "Do you understand? Are we clear?"

To Nate's own surprise, he didn't react, didn't pull back. Instead, fixing Oscar with a look of pure contempt, he peeled Oscar's fingers from his arm and shoved his hand away.

"Yes. We're clear."

He leaned in, anger churning his belly. "And don't ever touch me like that again," he said slowly. He leaned in closer, stared hard into Oscar's eyes. "Ever." He took a breath, anger still roiling. "Are we clear?"

Oscar sat back.

"*No jodas, gringo,*" he said, seething. "*Si lo haces, no tienes que tener miedo de que El Pitón te mata. Lo haré yo mismo.*"

Nate nodded.

"Not if I kill you first."

Oscar chuckled derisively. "*No tienes el coraje.*"

"*Basta!*" Quina hissed at both men. "*No más!*"

Nate and Oscar stared at each other across the table for a few moments. Then Oscar turned to repacking the grenades and other equipment, and the tension eased. Oscar glanced at his watch.

"Two hours," he said, raising two fingers. "I will return in two hours. Be ready."

"*A donde vas?*" Quina whispered.

"*Mirar alrededor.*"

Oscar set the repacked bag carefully against the wall, opened the door just wide enough to slip through and disappeared. Nate turned to Quina, took a deep breath and let it out slowly.

"That man is dangerous," he said.

Quina frowned. "He has a temper. But he is a good man."

Nate was surprised.

"You're defending him? After what he pulled?"

Quina nodded. "*Sí*. And he will have to live with that, *pobrecito*. But he would not have hurt us."

"I don't know about that. I think he might enjoy hurting me."

Quina nodded again. "Perhaps. But he would never hurt me, or Teresa, or Alegra." She looked down at her mug of coffee. "He knew Amador, you know."

Nate jolted in surprise.

"No. I didn't know."

"Yes," Quina said. "They were good friends." She looked up at Nate. "My husband knew his life was in danger. Before he died, he made Oscar promise that if anything happened to him, Oscar would watch out for us."

"How do you know that?"

"Amador told me."

"And he promised," Nate said.

Quina nodded. "Yes."

Nate sighed.

"What was that he said just before he left?"

"That he was going to look around."

"No. Before that."

"He was threatening you."

Nate nodded. "Threatening to kill me. Yeah, I got that part. The first part. What exactly did he say?"

"He said do not fuck up. If you do, he will kill you."

Nate took that in, let it settle.

"I guess I better not fuck up, then," he said, smiling a half-smile, trying for a moment of levity, in the Mexican way.

But it was not that simple. The prospect of the mission he had taken on and the battle it would ignite filled him with fear. Not that he would die. That didn't frighten him. If he was fated to die in Mirador while trying to avenge Sarah's murder or fighting for the Zapatista cause, so be it. It would be an honorable death. That's all Nate cared about now. His fear, his dread, was that he would fail, yet again. The way he had failed to protect Sarah. The way he had frozen in the jungle. His greatest fear was that Oscar was right. That when the moment came and he was called upon to kill, he would lack the courage. That he would be the embodiment of the mathematical concept devised by the ancient Mayans—zero.

In the jungle, beneath the light of a waning gibbous moon, groups of rebels emerged from concealment in various remote precincts of the Lacandon and followed a web of trails and routes to their assigned gathering spots. They had started amassing days before. Moving north, they carried rifles and pistols, backpacks clattering with handmade Molotov cocktails, hoes and machetes, heavy clubs and sharpened sticks. Some came armed only with their courage, their willingness to fight and die. They traveled on foot, on horseback, on bicycles. Some rode in vans and in cars along rutted roads, in the beds of pickup trucks along muddy trails, concealed beneath blankets and tarpaulins, among sacks of coffee beans and loads of sugar cane. They climbed into row boats, canoes, and small outboard craft and pushed up *El Río de la Revancha*, sitting quietly with rifles across their laps, determined looks on their faces. Some wore blue jeans, t-shirts, baseball caps. Others wore the black fatigue pants and handstitched brown shirts of the army of insurrection. Women wore dresses of homespun fabric, straw hats with ragged brims, bandoliers slung across their chests. The fighters wore rubber farmer boots, tennis shoes, huaraches. Some walked barefoot. Many, both men and women, wore red bandanas tied around their necks.

On the last leg of their approach, the fighters heading to Mirador moved along their line of march, sometimes two abreast, with Sebastiano and Fulgencio in the lead, following a muddy jungle trail north toward the village. They traveled with two horses carrying food and provisions, and two mules pulling rickety wagons laden with munitions.

Sebastiano and Fulgencio marched in silence, solemn expressions on their young faces, senses alert, studying the jungle to their flanks, glancing back or pausing on a promontory to survey the landscape ahead. Sebastiano consulted his watch, checked the position of the moon in the sky, looked to the east, watching for the first subtle suggestion of sunrise. He and Fulgencio urged the others on, patting their backs, whispering encouragement.

"*Vámonos. Vámonos. No se cansen. Hoy es el día de la liberación. Hoy es el día.*"

Los insurgentes nodded and stepped up the pace—men and women, old and young—never flagging, never halting. Rest would come later—after the liberation of Mirador. The death of El Pitón.

The rebels reached the southern outskirts of Mirador under cover of darkness and fanned out just below the crest of a ridge overlooking the village. The fighters along the front line concealed themselves and checked their weapons and equipment, said their prayers, readied themselves for battle. To the rear, other men and women held the nervous horses and burros on short leads, calming them with gentling hands and soothing words. Together, they waited for sunrise, the sound of an explosion, flash of fire, billow of smoke.

Teresa lay on her cot, tossing in a troubled sleep, snoring, snorting awake, shifting, falling asleep again, muttering. Nate and Quina carried their quilts outside and stretched out next to each other under the concealing branches of the cedar tree, dozing, waking, gazing into each other's eyes, holding hands.

Waking from a brief sleep, Nate opened his eyes to see the moon shining like a spotlight through the tree branches.

"It is beautiful, isn't it?" Quina murmured beside him.

"It's the same moon," Nate whispered. "The same moon everywhere. But here it looks so different. Bigger. Brighter." He smiled. "Better."

He squinted.

"Is it closer? Is that it?"

"It is how you are seeing it," Quina said softly. "It is not the moon that changes. It is you. Teresa says, *Todo en el color del cristal trans qué se mira*. Everything is the color of the crystal you look through."

Nate thought about that.

"And the moon is more beautiful to me now because...?"

He turned to Quina, put out an arm, and she came closer, laying her head on his chest.

"I guess you could say that about almost everything," he said. "It's not what you're looking at, it's how you look at it. It's all in your point of view."

"You know, that is what Mirador means," Quina said. "It means vantage point or viewpoint."

Nate smiled to himself.

"I didn't know that. All this time, and I never thought to ask."

He raised his other arm and pointed to the brilliant celestial orb, narrowed his eyes and sighted along the line of his arm and rigid index finger. He held his aim for a few seconds, then lowered his arm and sighed.

"You see that dark splotch on the moon? That must be the Sea of Tranquility. It's where the astronauts landed."

He raised his arm again, splayed his fingers.

"I can almost touch it."

Quina shifted closer, sighting along the line of his arm. "I see it."

And suddenly Nate remembered another night, standing on a museum terrace with Sarah, holding her close, letting her sight along his arm as he pointed out something in the sky to her, just as he was doing with Quina now. He dropped his hand, let it rest on his heart. When had that been, that night with Sarah? A year ago. A year ago last month. And where had he been on the anniversary of that night? At one of Las Hermanas, Nate realized. With Quina. Preparing for this night.

Nate closed his eyes and sighed, felt Quina's hand on his cheek. He opened his eyes and smiled at her. She knew. Somehow she always knew. Whenever painful memories hit him, she saw it, sensed it, and he would feel her gentle touch on his cheek. He covered her hand with his own.

"The Sea of Tranquility," he whispered. "Imagine that. An entire sea."

"It sounds lovely," Quina murmured. "We should go there some time."

Nate looked down into her dark eyes. He was aware at that moment of wanting to live as much as he had ever wanted to live in his entire life. More, he realized. Yes, more. He wanted to share a life with this woman, a peaceful, simple life. The life of a man who had little, but wanted and needed little. Nate felt contented at that moment, like a man who had found his way to the life he was meant to live. And it was loss that had led him to it. Tragedy and loss, not fame and success. He wondered if the same might be true for other men. Perhaps for all men.

"Strange," he said. "Strange how things happen, how we end up somewhere we never expected to be. I can't help but wonder . . . "

He stopped himself.

"I can't help but wonder . . . if we'd met sooner, before . . . "

He caught himself again. He closed his eyes, took a deep breath.

"If we'd met before Sarah. Before Amador. Do you think we'd have fallen in love? Or is it just because of what happened? Because they were killed?"

He turned to Quina. She lowered her eyes and looked away.

It was the first time Nate had spoken to her of love. They had felt love. He was sure of that. They had shown it, acted on it. Quina had called him *mi amor* that night at Los Ojos. But they had never spoken of love to each other, never professed their feelings out loud.

He waited.

Quina looked up at him and smiled tenderly. But she did not answer.

"I know," Nate said. "Does it matter? It's impossible to say, anyway. I was a different man then. You were a different woman." He gazed up at the moon. "But the man I am now does know one thing for sure."

He looked into Quina's eyes, stroked her hair.

"I do love you, Quina. God help me, but I do."

There. He'd said it.

Quina turned her face away, laid it on Nate's chest. They held each other in the predawn dark, neither speaking. Nate was at peace. Quina didn't have to respond. He didn't ask that. He just wanted her to know, needed her to know before the dawn broke, in case he didn't have another chance to tell her. He felt a great sense of relief. Now, what would be would be.

Then Quina stirred, looked up and met his eyes. She put a hand to his cheek again.

"*Y te quiero, tambien, Señor Nate Hunter.* I love you, too. I do. *Con todo mi corazón.*"

Quina lifted her face to his and kissed him. Nate turned and pulled her close. Remaining mostly clothed, they made love, silently, tenderly, and fell asleep in each other's arms.

It was still dark when Nate was startled awake by someone kicking the bottom of his right foot. He opened his eyes to find Oscar standing over him.

"*Es la hora*," Oscar said.

Oscar headed inside to collect his equipment. Nate and Quina came to their feet. Nate took Quina's face in his hands and kissed her—first on the forehead, then on the lips. She wrapped her arms around his neck and returned his kiss. Quick, deep, passionate. And then Nate broke away and bent to gather up the quilts, fearing that the intense desire to live that his love for Quina had stirred up in him might give him second thoughts about his involvement in the deadly mission that lay ahead, might cause him to hesitate or pull back at a critical moment and prove Oscar's assessment of him and his worst fears about himself right.

Quina and Nate followed Oscar inside. Quina went to Teresa's cot to wake her and bid her farewell as Nate retrieved his gunbelt and adjusted it around his waist.

The old woman sat up slowly, wrapped a rebozo around herself, then came to her feet. She took Quina's hand and enfolded it in both of hers, put it to her lips. Tears shimmering in her eyes, she made the sign of the cross over Quina and Nate, and embraced each in turn.

"Vayan con Dios, mis hijos," she said softly, putting one hand to Quina's cheek, the other to Nate's. *"Vayan con Dios."*

Then Teresa went to the table, where Oscar was sitting, zipping up his bag, took his head in her hands, kissed his forehead, and made the sign of the cross over him.

"Gracias, Teresa," Oscar said softly. He took the old woman's hand in his. *"Quédate dentro hoy, okay? Cierra la puerta y no la abra para nadie hasta que regresamos. Nadie. Entiendes?"*

Teresa nodded.

"Prometes?"

Teresa nodded again, tears now spilling down her cheeks. *"Te prometo."*

"Bueno."

Oscar patted and kissed Teresa's hand. Then he stood, shouldered his bag, and picked up his rifle. Cradling it in the crook of his arm, he handed one five gallon container to Nate, the other to Quina.

"Listos?"

They nodded.

"Vámonos."

Oscar, Quina, and Nate slipped out the door. Teresa closed and bolted it behind them, and without another word, the three co-conspirators moved out in darkness—the tip of a spear aimed at the heart of El Pitón. 🔺

CHAPTER 32

The War Against Forgetting

L ike predators of the Lacandon, Oscar, Quina, and Nate made their way in stealth to the barracks, staying low and hidden, moving silently, doubling back and circling around to avoid the occasional patrol. When they neared their objective, approaching from the south at the first faint thinning of dark, they slipped down into a gutted ravine that furrowed parallel to the north-south road in front of the old building. Long-stepping over a rivulet running along the bottom, they crept to a position just south of the barracks, stopped at Oscar's signal, and pressed themselves against the ravine's eastern slope.

Peering up over the rim, Nate saw that the barracks looked exactly as it had when he and Sarah and the other missioners had spent their one night there some eleven months before. Simple, two-story, wood-frame construction, cinderblock foundation, weed-filled crawlspace beneath. Four concrete steps leading to a small latticework wood porch. Sunbaked, the whole structure. Splintered boards. Paint peeling and curling. It would burn like kindling, Nate thought.

On the porch, beneath the sallow light of the single overhead bulb in the green metal shade, a sentry slumped in a ladder-back chair tilted against the wall. He was asleep, rifle across his lap. After watching the man for some minutes, Oscar handed his M1 to Quina, then motioned for Nate to follow him. Oscar hefted the munitions bag carefully over a shoulder and picked up one of the empty five-gallon containers. Nate took the other. The two men doubled back about ten yards down the ravine, climbed out over the eastern rim and, moving in a crouch, crossed the road and continued east beyond the sentry's line of vision, then angled north toward the cover of a row of two pickup trucks and a jeep parked on the south side of the barracks. The predawn sky was turning gunmetal gray. The air was still, the silence so thick that each footfall, each brush of fabric, jostle of equipment played loud in Nate's ears. Following Oscar, Nate kept scanning the barracks's south-facing windows, checking for signs of movement, someone awake and watching inside. He saw nothing.

Nate and Oscar crossed swiftly from the line of vehicles to the building's southeastern corner. The gasoline drums were located on a rise about fifteen feet behind the building—a half-dozen black and rust-colored fifty-five-gallon drums standing upright on an elevated concrete pad, enclosed in a locked chain-link cage, each drum emblazoned with the warning *Gasolina! Peligrosa!* in large stenciled letters across its girth.

They moved as quietly as possible to the cage. Oscar set down his bag, pulled out the bolt cutters and went to work cutting the padlocked chain that secured the gate while Nate held it to keep it from clanking noisily to the ground. Removing it carefully from the fence, Nate turned to lay it aside and heard the gate squeal as Oscar began to open it. Both men froze. The squeal had sounded loud to Nate—loud enough to carry into the barracks through opened and screened windows. The two men waited. Nothing. They shared a warning glance. Oscar held up a closed hand, did a silent count, extending his finger—one, two, three—and swung the gate wide with one quick movement. He slipped inside, and Nate handed him the canisters. On his knees at the closest drum, Oscar pulled out his knife, cut the end of the rubber hose coming off the spigot to a manageable length, opened the spigot and began filling the first container. Nate stood guard, eyes on the barracks, hand on his pistol grip, gut twisting, perspiration streaming down his face. It seemed to take Oscar forever.

When both cans were finally full, Oscar passed them to Nate, draped the gasoline hose over the edge of the concrete pad, aiming it toward the barracks, and opened the spigot wide. Working swiftly, he cut the ends off the hoses attached to the other five drums, aimed them in the same direction, opened all the spigots and sprang out of the cage. Nate watched a river of gasoline form, widen, and begin flowing downhill toward the barracks.

"You knew?" Nate whispered to Oscar, watching the shimmering river gather momentum as it headed downhill.

Oscar shook his head. "Luck."

Oscar knelt and slipped the strap of the black bag over his head, shifted the bag onto his back and took hold of one of the now-filled gasoline cans. Nate took the other and the two men crossed back to the building's south wall. Moving as quietly as they could, they hauled the sloshing containers of gasoline back toward the front porch. Glancing up toward the ravine, Nate could just make out Quina's head and arms above the rim, Oscar's rifle snug against her shoulder, her eye to the sights, ready to shoot if necessary. She would do it, too, Nate thought. He had no doubt. If she thought their lives were in danger, she'd shoot to kill without hesitation.

Just as Nate and Oscar were nearing the front corner of the barracks, they heard the sound of chair legs scraping on wood, boots thumping and shuffling on the porch. The sentry was awake. Oscar and Nate skittered back, stashed the containers in the weeds under the crawlspace and made for the cover of the three vehicles parked a short distance away. Crouching behind one of the pickups, Oscar and Nate watched the sentry come around the front corner of the building and begin strolling along the south side toward the back, apparently making his rounds. Reaching into his shirt pocket, he pulled out a cigarette and stuck it in his mouth. Unaware of the river of gasoline flowing under the building, he lay his rifle on his left shoulder, muzzle pointed rearward, gripping it by the stock, and reached back into his shirt pocket for a match.

Nate fought an impulse to shout a warning. He tapped Oscar on the shoulder, pointed at the sentry, put two fingers to his lips to mime smoking, and made the "boom" gesture with his fingers that Oscar had used in Teresa's hut. Oscar paid him no attention. He went back to studying the sentry, keeping his eyes fixed on the man like a predator tracking its prey as he felt around in his bag and pulled out his bayonet. Nate's stomach dropped. He thought of the soldier in the jungle. He knew what was coming, and it could jeopardize the whole mission. He gripped Oscar's arm. Oscar yanked it away, gave Nate a vituperative look of savage fury. There was no stopping him.

Oscar turned back to his target. He and Nate watched the sentry pat his other breast pocket for matches, burrow in his right-side pants pockets, then stop, shift his rifle to his right shoulder and dig in his left-side pockets without success. He wagged his head, seemed to swear something under his breath, turned and began walking slowly back the other way, searching the ground. Oscar dashed across to the side of the building before Nate knew he was making his move and was stealing up behind the sentry with his bayonet in his right hand when the sentry turned. Oscar jumped him. He took the sentry down, covered his mouth with his left hand, buried the bayonet blade in the man's belly. On his back in the dirt with Oscar on top of him, the sentry bucked and kicked, arms grabbing at his assailant, as Oscar fought to keep him pinned and keep his mouth gagged.

Glancing over again to check quickly on Quina, Nate saw another figure in the distance, a man coming up the road from the south. He was walking slowly and unsteadily, rifle slung on his back. One of El Pitón's men returning from a night of drinking and whoring, it looked like. Nate grabbed Oscar's bag and shifted to a position in the shadows between the two trucks. Quina hadn't seen the man yet. Heart racing, mouth dry, Nate unfastened his holster and drew his pistol.

Come on, come on, Oscar! he willed his co-conspirator, breaking into a sweat, watching Oscar still struggling with the sentry, watching the other man amble up the road. *Kill him, dammit! Finish it and get up! Get up!*

But the sentry had a hold on Oscar now and Oscar was fighting just to keep a hand over his mouth.

Inside Nate's head, a shrill voice screamed, *Get the hell out of here! Run! Don't be a damn fool!* His thigh muscles twitched in response to his mind's command. And then, *No!* came an instant, stronger counter-command. *No! Not again! Not this time! This time you fight!*

For a moment that stretched an eternity, Nate was frozen in place. He grimaced, squeezed his eyes shut, saw Sarah's face, then El Pitón's face. He thought of Tatic and Itzel, Elba and Amador. He remembered what Mateo had said when Nate had insisted the rebels couldn't win this fight. *It is better to die on your feet than live on your knees.* Nate knew the scalding humiliation, the waking hell of living on his knees. *No more! Never again!*

Nate opened his eyes, steadied his breath, hardened his resolve, set his jaw. Oscar was still wrestling with the sentry on the ground, but he had a grip on his throat, and the sentry was weakening. Quina had a bead on the paramilitarista coming up the road, but she knew not to shoot unless she had to. *Stealth,* Nate reminded himself. *Silence. Sur-*

prise. He looked down at the pistol in his hand, reholstered it, fastened the flap, and grubbed in a pocket for his folding knife. Working quickly, keeping an eye on the paramilitarista, he pulled the nylon cord out of Oscar's bag and cut off a length of it, put his knife back in his pocket, and twined the ends of the cord three times around each hand. *I can do this. I can do this.* He'd refused Mateo's offer to teach him how to do it, but he'd watched trainees practice it during drills. *Step. Loop. Pull. Pivot.* Nate never imagined needing to know how to do it himself. Until now.

Oscar was coming to his feet, smeared with blood and dirt, his struggle with the sentry over, when the other paramilitarista angled off the road toward the barracks. Bending over the sentry to retrieve his bayonet and strip the dead man of his rifle and ammunition, Oscar didn't see the other man approaching from behind, but Nate knew that as soon as the man passed the jeep parked nearest the road, he'd see Oscar—and the dead sentry at Oscar's feet. Steeled and ready, Nate slipped around to the south side of the row of vehicles and over to the jeep just as the man passed it, and fell in silently behind him. At that moment, the paramilitarista saw Oscar standing over the dead sentry, holding his bloody bayonet. The paramilitarista stopped. He reached up and clumsily unslung his rifle.

Oh no you don't! No you don't.

In one swift, silent move, Nate surged forward and threw the garrote over the man's head. He yanked it tight at the base of his neck, pivoted sideways to twist and pull the loop down hard over his right shoulder. The leashed man dropped his rifle and clawed frantically at his throat. Unable to loosen the cord, he threw himself backward on top of Nate, slamming him to the ground, knocking the wind out of him and sending a bolt of pain shooting through Nate's right arm and shoulder. Nate began blacking out, but marshaled himself—*No! Not this time!*—kept his grip on the cord and yanked. He felt the man kicking and bucking on top of him, pulled harder, holding fast until the man's body jerked and went slack. Nate kept pulling and holding, making sure. And then Nate loosened his grip, and it was over. That simple. That final. That quick. Nate had killed a man.

Nate shoved the dead man off his chest, sent him sliding face up to the ground. He rolled over, sat up and looked down at the man whose life he had just taken. An ordinary-looking young man wearing a green t-shirt and black pants. Dark hair, brown skin, dark sightless eyes. Nothing evil or malevolent-looking about him. Someone's brother. Someone's son. What was the man now? Not a man anymore. Just a husk. Lifeless remains. A body. Another dead body.

The man's rifle was lying on the ground. Nate reached for it, picked it up, got to his feet. Should he go for the bandolier? Out of the corner of his eye, he saw Oscar pressed against the wall of the barracks, holding the sentry's rifle, furiously waving Nate over. Nate scuttled to his side. "*Vámonos*," Oscar rasped, seizing Nate's arm. Nate jerked back violently, rage exploding inside him.

"Get your hands off me!" he snarled, baring his teeth, leveling the rifle at Oscar's chest, eyes burning with hatred.

"Okay, okay," Oscar hissed, yanking his hands back and holding them palms up. The two men locked eyes. Oscar waited, breathing heavily, hands in the air until Nate finally lowered the gun.

Oscar eyed him warily, lowered his hands and checked his watch.

"We must hurry," he said in a harsh whisper.

Refocusing on their mission, Nate retrieved the containers of gasoline from the crawlspace as Oscar retrieved his bag from between the parked trucks. Working together again, the two men moved silently around to the front of the barracks. Nate carried one container up the concrete steps and quietly poured the gasoline all over the front porch and door, then went to Oscar and held the second container in position against a corner post while Oscar lashed it with duct tape, wrapping it securely once, then again.

As Nate crouched beside him, rifle in hand, watching the barracks door, Oscar took a grenade from his bag, unwrapped it and taped it to the gasoline container, routing the tape carefully under the safety lever and wrapping it three times. He removed the container's cap and set it on the porch, tied the cord to the ring attached to the grenade pin, checked the knot, gave Nate a thumbs-up, and the two men backed away, Oscar paying out cordage as he went, Nate covering him and carrying his bag until they reached the ravine.

Oscar handed Quina the cord and dropped in next to her. Nate handed Oscar the bag and dropped in next to him. Oscar switched rifles with Quina, took back his M1 and the cord, and gave Nate an approving nod. Nate ignored it. He moved to Quina's left side and flattened himself against the dirt beside her. From his position, Nate could see the bodies of the two dead paramilitaristas, one of whom he had killed.

I just killed a man, Nate told himself. *That man lying right there. I killed that man with my own hands.*

How was he supposed to feel about that? How *did* he feel? He didn't hate himself for it, the way he thought he would. But he wasn't proud of it, either. The truth was, he didn't feel anything. The shock to him was how easy it had been. If he'd known it could be so easy, El Pitón might have been dead a long time ago. . . and Sarah might still be alive.

Oscar looked at his watch, checked the sky. The three Zapatista fighters raised their rifles, Nate and Quina each armed with a dead man's gun, and watched the barracks. The gasoline drums had been opened, one cannister had been emptied, the other secured with tape to a post, the explosive had been set. Oscar held the detonating cord lightly in his right hand. Daybreak neared.

When the cathedral light of the coming day, the first day of the new year, flared over the eastern horizon, Oscar glanced at Nate and Quina. *"Ahora,"* he whispered. Nate and Quina ducked down, chests against the forward wall of the ravine, put fingers to their ears. Oscar took the cord in both hands, tautened it, counted aloud—"One, two, *three"*—and gave it a quick, hard jerk. It went slack from the far end—the grenade's pin had come free, allowing the striker to slam down on the primer. Oscar dropped down, arms over his head. And then the stark morning silence of Mirador, swollen with expectation, exploded. Mirador was at war.

The blast launched a concussive shock wave that quaked the ground beneath the bombers. Rising again after the tremor passed, peering over the brow of the ravine, shielding their faces from the heat, they watched a monstrous orange fireball blossom skyward, chased by a billowing cloud of black smoke flashing lightning, swirling with bits of splintered wood and flaming debris. After a few moments, the fireball subsided into a ravenous blaze. Through the fire and smoke, Nate saw that the whole front of the barracks had been blown to matchwood and what was left was being devoured by flames.

Immediately, amidst the whoosh of fire and the crackling of burning lumber, Nate and his two comrades heard yelling and screaming inside the barracks, saw men jumping out windows, rushing out of the flames. Following Oscar's lead, Nate and Quina shouldered their rifles and opened fire.

Then Nate heard shouts, glass shattering, and caught movement at the back three first- and second-story south-facing windows, screens being knocked out in the only section of the barracks not consumed by flames. Heads and arms appeared, rifles and pistols, and the men still alive inside started firing furiously in any direction they could point a gun. *Stealth and surprise,* Nate thought. *It had worked. They don't know where we are.* Nate and Quina opened up on them as Oscar grabbed a second grenade out of his bag, got to his knees, pulled the pin, drew back his arm and hurled the missile at one of the windows. It landed under the nearest ground-floor window and another explosion rocked Mirador. Two rifles in one of the second-story windows jerked up and fell to the ground.

Nate and Quina kept firing as Oscar pulled the remaining grenades from his bag. Oscar held a grenade out to Nate, gave him a fiercely commanding look. Nate put down his rifle and took the grenade, weighed it in his hand. Oscar picked up another grenade. "Together," he said, holding the grenade in his right hand and reaching for the pin with his left. Nate copied him and at Oscar's three-count command both men pulled the pins and heaved the grenades. Two near-simultaneous flashes and explosions followed, an intense rain of hot shards of steel, piercing screams, and, when the smoke cleared, two windows that had been filled with rifles were destroyed. Quina kept firing. Oscar handed Nate another grenade, took the last one for himself, and, in unison, they pulled the pins and let fly. Two more explosions, more screams, the last windows blown to oblivion.

Now more men came leaping and running, crawling and scrambling out of the inferno, screaming, shouting, shrieking in anguish, torn and bleeding, faces marked with powder black, clutching themselves, stumbling and shoving, shooting blindly, running for cover. *Stealth and surprise.* Oscar raised his M1 and commenced methodically cutting them down one by one. Quina and Nate opened fire again. As he was shooting, Nate scrutinized the frenzied paramilitaristas, searching for one man.

But now, the escaping men began zeroing in on the shooters' position, and they began taking fire. Paramilitaristas still able to fight hit the ground, ducked into tall grass, took cover behind vehicles parked near the barracks and turned their rifles and pistols toward the ravine. Bullets whizzed past Nate's left ear. He ducked, returned fire, heard the snaps and cracks of more gunfire. The ground in front of the conspirators began coughing up little clouds of dust where bullets struck—too close to Quina, all too close to Quina.

"*Donde están?*" Oscar muttered, snapping a fresh clip into his M1. "*Donde están?*"

The reinforcements, Nate thought. *That's right.* The first explosion was supposed to be their signal. Where were they? Why weren't they there?

The snap and crack of rifle fire coming at them was now joined by the staccato rat-a-tat-tat of machine-gun fire, the scream and whine of ricochets. Nate, Quina, and Oscar kept reloading and shooting, but the fusillade was becoming more intense, and it was getting harder to see the men shooting at them through the dust and smoke.

Shoot, move, communicate. They'd forgotten their training completely.

Nate ducked and was reaching for Quina to signal that they should relocate farther down the ravine when he heard gunfire coming from the south, horses whinnying, burrows braying, the clatter of wagons and equipment, men and women running, ululating and yelling battle cries. "*Ataque! Ataque! Adelante! Adelante! Viva Zapata! Viva México! Viva Mirador!*"

Two armed men on horseback led the charge up the north-south road, followed by what looked to Nate like two hundred or so fighting men and women advancing swiftly in a swelling wave. Some with guns, some wielding machetes, some carrying homemade pikes and sharpened sticks, some waving banners.

"*Ataque! Adelante! Viva Zapata! Viva Mirador!*"

In the village to the north, Nate heard the church bells ringing.

The paramilitaristas trained their heaviest fire on the approaching rebels, who answered with a volley of well-hurled Molotov cocktails that landed and exploded into fireballs in their midst. Through the gunfire and explosions, the clouds of smoke and hail of debris, Nate heard more and louder cries of anguish. Curses, shouts, screams of pain. Still the paramilitaristas kept firing, and still the rebels kept coming, running, shooting, yelling, never faltering despite the firepower bearing down on them.

As the rebels closed in, the paramilitaristas suddenly stopped shooting. What was happening? It was hard to see through the smoke and flames. And then the shooting started again, but not from the same position south of the barracks. Now it came from farther north, on the far side of the burning building, from up the road toward the village. The paramilitaristas were pulling back. The rebels began streaming past the barracks in pursuit. At Oscar's signal, the three firebombers clambered out of the ditch and fell in with them, heading north into the village, where the paramilitaristas disappeared down lanes and alleys and the rebels split up and pursued them in what was now a moving firefight being played out street to street, house to house. *Shoot, move, communicate. Shoot, move, communicate.*

Main mission accomplished, Oscar peeled off down an alleyway with a contingent of other rebel fighters. Sticking together, Nate and Quina advanced toward the heart of the village with a smaller group, crouching against buildings, rifles in hand, keeping low. Nate was a killer now. He had murdered one man and perhaps had killed others who'd been trying to kill him. But he had no appetite for random killing. He wanted only one life and cared now about only two things— getting Quina back to Teresa's hut to protect the old woman, and killing the man who had murdered his wife. Nate's gut told him El Pitón was still alive. And that had to change.

The rebels seemed to be everywhere now, swarming through Mirador. Nate heard pistol shots, an occasional burst of rifle fire as he and Quina made their way toward the square, but no sustained firing. It seemed Oscar might have been right. The army had reduced patrols during the months of quiet, and there didn't seem to be enough of El Pitón's men left alive to put up real resistance.

But then Nate and Quina heard trucks roaring in from the east, men shouting, guns rattling. And then more trucks from the west. And the north. Soldiers. Troops from Colonel Delgado's garrison.

Ducking into an alleyway with their fellow fighters, Nate and Quina saw six trucks loaded with soldiers converge on the north side of the square, watched the regulars dismount the trucks, and saw a group of paramilitaristas appear out of nowhere and run over to them. The soldados and paramilitaristas quickly conferred, arguing and gesturing, and then three of the soldiers reached into the truck bed and began distributing rifles, ammunition, grenades to the paramilitaristas. Nate and Quina watched the combined forces fan out in all directions— north toward Teresa's neighborhood, west and east, south toward them. They heard more trucks approaching. More soldiers. More guns. The tide of battle was beginning to turn.

Out-gunned and soon to be outnumbered, the rebels fought on, pressing the attack. Sticking together, staying low, moving in shadows, Nate and Quina advanced with their companions. Gunfire and explosions rang out incessantly in every direction. Buildings and cars burst into flames, windows shattered, walls collapsed into rubble. Everywhere, people were running and screaming. Men and women lay bleeding in the streets, crying out in pain, as a few brave souls tried to pull them to safety or bind their wounds where they lay. Bodies were everywhere.

Pinned down by a spray of automatic rifle fire, crouching against a low wall, Nate heard a bullet bury itself into the flesh of a man ahead of him. It sounded like the flat of a hand slapping freshly butchered meat. The man grunted and went down on his back, legs folded awkwardly beneath him. With bullets still zinging past his head, Nate scrambled forward on all fours and bent over the man to see where he'd been hit. A pink froth bubbled from a hole in his chest. His eyes were open but unseeing. His body quivered, then went still.

Nate closed the man's eyes, folded his hands over the hole in his chest. He wanted to do more but he couldn't. And then the shooting seemed to let up. Nate felt Quina's hand on his arm. Their comrades in arms were moving. They had to move, too.

Back on their feet, Nate and Quina broke from the other rebels and began working their way around to the north of the square toward Teresa's hut, dodging wave after wave of gunfire, not knowing where the bullets were coming from. *We're sitting ducks out in the open like this*, Nate thought. *We have to get off the street.* Another burst of gunfire. Nate pulled Quina down in a doorway and tried to force the door open but it wouldn't budge. Bullets found them again, began spraying the walls around them, splintering the door above their heads. Nate pushed Quina against the door, shielding her with his body and covered his head with an arm.

Make it stop! Make it stop!

And then something—a hand grenade, Molotov cocktail, rocket-propelled grenade—something, exploded in the street behind them with enough deafening, concussive force to knock Nate sideways to the ground under a hail of debris. A suffocating blanket of thick, black smoke engulfed him, choking him, burning his eyes and throat, filling his nose and mouth with the smell and taste of gunpowder. He couldn't think, couldn't see or hear, couldn't speak or breathe. He thought he might be dying.

No! Not yet! Nate demanded of himself, gasping for air. *Not yet!*

Slowly, his breathing returned, the blackness thinned, and Nate saw Quina bending over him, calling his name. He could see her lips move but couldn't hear her through the ringing and throbbing in his ears. Nate struggled to bring himself upright, propped his back against the doorway, massaged his ears and looked out at the street. Through the smoke, he saw a riderless horse galloping toward him, pale gray, saddle askew, reins streaming in the wind. ▲

CHAPTER 33

Atonement

Nate rubbed his eyes, still dazed.

Quina was kneeling beside him, shaking him gently. "Nate, Nate. *Estás bien?*"

Nate nodded, able to hear again. He looked around. The pale horse was gone. A fresh wind swirled and thinned the smoke.

And then Nate saw him. A thin, dark-haired, solitary figure, hazy at first, across the road, about a hundred yards away, standing with his back pressed against a whitewashed wall scrawled with the words *No hay guerilla* in black paint, pistol in hand, looking the other way. His hair was disheveled, his white shirt covered with blood and soot, his trousers dirty and torn, his boots caked with mud. Nate couldn't make out the scar on his cheek, but there was no mistaking who it was.

Nate reached up and pulled Quina back down in the doorway behind him.

"What?"

Nate put a finger to his lips and pointed. Quina saw him, too.

As the smoke thinned more, Nate was able to make out the man more clearly. His instinct had been right. El Pitón had survived the firebombing, but things were not going well for him. His men were dead or scattered. There were no soldiers in sight. He seemed to have lost his sidekick. He was alone, on foot, and on the run.

El Pitón turned to look in Nate and Quina's direction. They pressed back into the doorway. He turned away. Nate checked his rifle. It was empty. He laid it aside and went for his pistol. Before he could unholster it, two shots rang out from somewhere close ahead and two bullets struck just behind El Pitón and ricocheted off the wall in a shower of stucco chips.

Nate expected him to run. But he didn't. Instead, with lightning reflexes, he spun, spotted the shooter, raised his pistol, fired two shots, and the shooter went down, tumbling out of an alleyway into the street.

It was Oscar.

Now El Pitón fled as gunfire erupted again all around them.

Nate and Quina rushed to Oscar, who lay curled on his left side, clutching a bloody wound to his left shoulder, wincing and gritting his teeth.

"Oscar, *soy yo*," Quina said, dropping to her knees and pulling Oscar's hand away to check the wound. He was losing a lot of blood.

Oscar opened his eyes, saw Nate.

"Go after him!" Oscar demanded. "Go! Go!"

Nate checked his .45. A round in the chamber. Three in the magazine. Four altogether.

Quina looked up at Nate.

"I will go with you," she said matter-of-factly, reaching for her rifle.

"No," Nate said, blocking her reach. "Get Oscar to Teresa's."

"No, I am coming."

"No, Quina," Nate insisted. "Teresa needs you. Alegra needs you."

Nate saw warring emotions do battle in Quina's eyes. She wanted to argue, but knew she couldn't, and that distressed her even more.

Nate leaned across Oscar and kissed Quina quickly, deeply.

"I love you."

She put a hand to his left cheek, his scarred cheek, and kissed him back.

"Be safe, my love."

Nate allowed himself one more moment of looking deep into her eyes, then rose, crossed to the far side of the road and began moving swiftly up the street in pursuit of his quarry. Those few moments of delay had given El Pitón enough time to slip down a side alley if he wanted to. But they were on the north side of the village now, near the outskirts. Nate's gut told him El Pitón would continue north and try to make it to the jungle. Nate had to find him before he did.

Ducking bullets, skirting crumbled walls and burning cars, squinting through the smoke of smoldering debris, Nate continued north, pistol in hand. He hadn't gone far when, through the lingering smoke, he saw someone moving in a low crouch a short distance ahead. A younger man, thickset, built low to the ground, muscular, shaven-head. He was wearing a black t-shirt and carrying an assault rifle. Chuy. So he'd survived, too. Nate considered following him. He might lead him to El Pitón. But Chuy didn't look like he'd just come through a firebombing. He wasn't disheveled and dirty. His clothes weren't torn, his boots weren't caked with mud. Nate suspected he hadn't been in the barracks. Maybe he'd spent the night in the village and was searching for his jefe, too.

Chuy disappeared around a corner. *Let him go*, Nate thought, working his way carefully up the street, away from the heaviest fighting, searching every doorway, every niche and shadow. With every step, the sound of gunfire behind him faded and Nate felt himself moving away from the main battle, leaving it behind. He was on his own quest now. His alone.

This is how it should be, he thought. *Him and me. Just him and me. He doesn't know it yet, but he's going to die today. I'm going to kill him or die trying. Maybe we'll both die. That's okay. As long as I—*

A sudden presence to his left startled him. He whirled and found himself facing his own indistinct reflection in a small circular sheet of tin that had been nailed over a recessed doorway. He could make out his form, but not his face. *Just as well.* Nate didn't want to see himself. He was a killer now. A murderer out to kill again. He moved on.

He approached an entrance to a courtyard, pressed his back against the stucco wall, pistol ready, peered around the corner. Nothing. He moved on.

He came to an alleyway. A short cul-de-sac. Empty. He kept moving.

Farther ahead, he caught another distant glimpse of white shirt. Too far ahead. They were nearing the edge of the village now and Nate started to run, trying to close the distance without being seen, knowing that if El Pitón disappeared into the maze of streets and alleys now, he'd make his way out into the jungle and get away.

Unaware he was being followed, in this remote part of the village, his destination almost in reach, El Pitón relaxed his guard, came out from the shadows and began walking swiftly up the middle of the empty street, checking back over his shoulder just often enough to prevent any pursuer from running up the middle of the street after him. Nate had to get closer before he took a shot. He didn't want to give himself away, and he didn't have bullets to spare.

Then, in an unexpected twist, a grizzled old campesino carrying a machete and wearing the trademark rebel-red bandana around his neck came shuffling out of an alley a few yards ahead of El Pitón. He assumed a wide-legged stance and gripped his machete in both hands, as if determined to strike the butcher of Mirador down.

"*Viva Zapata!*" the old graybeard wheezed, bringing his arms back as El Pitón lunged toward him.

El Pitón shoved the old man aside without breaking stride, sending him tottering backward, continued on a few paces, then stopped. He turned, sauntered back, hands on hips, and stopped in front of the old man. When the campesino drew back his machete again, El Pitón wrested it easily from his hands, tested its sharpness with a thumb, nodded approvingly, then raised the blade and sank it into the man's torso at the base of his neck. The old man crumbled, gushing blood. El Pitón dropped the machete and stood over him, watching his body jerk in the dirt. Then, he took out his pistol and shot him.

Nate heard the shot. He moved toward it. He had halved the distance between himself and El Pitón, and he knew he could take him now. He was close enough. He moved out of the shadows into the street, wanting El Pitón to see him, wanting Sarah's murderer to know who his murderer would be. But instead of looking up, El Pitón wedged his pistol back in his waistband, turned away, raced up the street and disappeared into an alleyway.

Nate ran past the old man lying in a spreading lake of his own blood and turned into the narrow alley just as El Pitón reached the far end and turned around to come back out. It was another cul-de-sac, a short, walled, graveled alleyway with no outlet. The only exit was past the tall man who'd come into the alley after him and now stood blocking his path.

The two men faced each other, about thirty feet apart. Nate's pistol was in his hand, pointed down at his side. El Piton's was in his waistband. Nate could shoot him down now like the dog he was. But now that he had his wife's killer cornered, he didn't want to do that. Nate didn't just want El Pitón to die. He wanted him to die knowing who his killer was.

El Pitón squinted at Nate, arms down and held slightly away from his body, as if getting ready to go for his gun. He furrowed his brow and narrowed his eyes, and the beginning of a smirk formed on his face.

"*Ah, sí,*" he said. "*Te recuerdo. El norteamericano.* They say you are here."

Someone had told El Pitón he was there? That shouldn't have surprised Nate. But it did.

El Pitón flicked his tongue over his lips. "*Maté a tu esposa. La puta rubia. Y ahora tu vas a matarme?*" He chuckled, then tilted his head to his left, distracted by something behind Nate. Nate heard the slow crunch of footsteps. They stopped just behind him. El Pitón raised his eyebrows in surprise.

Chuy. It had to be.

El Pitón grinned at Nate. "Now you have a new whore, eh?" he said in heavily accented English.

What? Who—And then it hit him. *No. No. It can't be. She can't be here.* He glanced quickly over his right shoulder. *No, no, no, no.*

Quina was standing just behind Nate, carrying Oscar's M1 in front of her, muzzle pointing down, eyes fixed on El Pitón.

Nate wanted to howl in anguish. He wanted to grab Quina and shake her, yell at her to get out of there. *Get out! Get out! Get out!* But it was too late. Nate felt his courage drain away. *Not again. Not again.*

"Quina," Nate whispered. "Why? Why?"

El Pitón eyed Quina up and down, assessing, calculating. The corner of his mouth turned up again.

"*Ah, sí,*" he said. He lifted his left hand slowly to his head, tapped a finger to his left temple. "*El Pitón nunca olvida.*" He smiled. "*Yo maté a tu esposo también, eh?*"

Quina did not answer.

El Pitón nodded. "*Sí, sí. El médico.*" He took a step forward, brought his hands to his hips. His smile turned to a sneer. "*Bastardo estúpido,*" he said, his eyes cold and hard. "I tell him, but he does not listen."

Nate's heart banged inside his chest. That look. He knew that look. He knew the voice. Nate tightened his grip on the .45 hanging loosely in his right hand. *Kill him now. Kill him now.* He slowly thumbed back the hammer, searched out the trigger with his finger, closed his fist.

El Pitón's eyes slid to Nate's gun hand, then up to his face. The two men locked eyes.

"Your wife, too," El Pitón growled. He took another step, spat at Nate's feet. "She deserve to die."

Faster than Nate could raise his gun, El Pitón pulled out his pistol and pointed it... not at Nate but at Quina. Reacting instinctively, Nate threw himself at Quina, knocking her aside before the muzzle flashed and he heard the crack and felt the bullet whiz past his neck. He landed hard on the ground, rolled onto his belly, raised the .45, locked eyes with El Pitón, and squeezed off all four rounds.

El Pitón dropped where he stood. Through a haze of gunsmoke, Nate watched him go down, twitch once, twice, utter a low gurgling groan, and fall still. And that was it. That quick. That final. El Pitón lay on his back in the gravel, head turned toward Nate, eyes open, arms flung out, legs splayed, red blood seeping across his shirt front. Sarah Hunter's murderer, the man who had killed Tatic and Itzel, Elba and Amador, was finally dead. Nate had killed him.

Nate tossed the .45 aside and scrambled on all fours to where Quina lay on her back, the M1 on the ground next to her. Her eyes were closed. She wasn't moving. But she was breathing. He grabbed her by the shoulders and looked her over frantically. She opened her eyes.

Thank God.

"Quina, are you all right?"

She smiled weakly, came to her elbows, winced, put a hand to the back of her head.

"You're hurt."

"No, no. I am fine."

Nate helped her to her feet, took her in his arms and held her, pressed her head against his chest, awash in anger and relief. He let her go, picked up the M1.

"He could have killed you, Quina," Nate said, handing the rifle back to her.

She nodded. "*Sí,*" she said softly. She looked up at him, eyes flashing. "But he did not."

Nate shook his head.

Quina looked past him at the crumpled body of El Pitón.

"*Está muerto?*" Quina asked.

Nate walked over to where El Pitón lay and stood over his lifeless form. "Yes," he said. "He's dead." He looked down into El Pitón's slitted, milky, unseeing eyes. "He looks so... insignificant now," Nate said, turning to Quina. "So—"

He didn't hear the shot. When the bullet struck, it felt like someone had whacked him across the chest with a two-by-four. He stumbled backward a step, coughed, and time slowed. He began collapsing where he stood, saw Quina's stricken expression, saw her turn and look up, drop to one knee, raise the rifle to her shoulder, and fire. One, two, three, four shots. Nate was able to count them. Falling slowly to the ground, sighting along Quina's line of fire, Nate saw the short, bald, muscular man in the black t-shirt crouched on a pitched roof overlooking the alleyway, pointing a rifle at Nate, watched him double over, drop his rifle, and somersault slowly off the roof into the alley, heard his body hit with a dull thud, kicking up a cloud of dust.

Now, Nate felt a searing pain in his chest. He tried to right himself, but couldn't. Couldn't move at all. *Hmh. That's interesting.*

Quina was there, kneeling over him, gently lifting his head and shoulders onto her lap, gazing down at him with frightened, loving eyes. *So beautiful. Such a strong, beautiful face.* He had to tell her. She needed to know.

"You... are... so... "

Quina put her fingers to his lips. "*No, mi amor,*" she whispered, smiling, eyes glistening. "*Tranquilo. Tranquilo.*"

He laid a hand on his chest, felt something wet and warm, lifted it to where he could see it. It was covered in blood. He felt a jolt of fear. But then it passed and he felt calm. His chest hurt, but that was okay. *No problem, no problem.* Nate wanted to laugh, but it hurt too much. And that was all right, too.

He looked up into Quina's beautiful face. Her cheeks were wet. He reached up, touched a tear.

"Don't... cry. Don't cry, Adelita."

She smiled, wiped her cheek, leaned close and kissed him tenderly on the lips.

Nate closed his eyes. He felt sleepy. Suddenly so sleepy. He opened his eyes again and caught a glimpse of the blue sky overhead. Brilliant blue. *Maya blue.* It began to fade and dim. All the light was dimming. The light above, and the light within.

A pain unlike any he'd ever known tore through him, shaking him. Quina gathered him more tightly in her arms.

"It's all right," he whispered. "*De veras. Está bien.* I don't mind."

The pain left him, and he felt at peace, serene. Felt something loosen inside him. Something not of flesh, blood, or bone. Felt his spirit lighten, become airy with the shedding of burdens, hopes, and desires.

He could go now. He saw that. He had a sense of completion.

Nate looked into Quina's eyes again.

"Rafael...."

"*Sí, mi amor.* I will tell him. I will keep him safe."

Darkness engulfed him.

"Are you there?" Nate whispered.

"*Sí, querido.* I am here."

"Will you remember?"

"Yes, I will remember. Everything. *Siempre.*"

Nate shivered.

"Are you cold, my love?" Quina said.

"Yes... yes... I am." ▲

Día de Muertos

*M*onday. *November 1, 1999. Mirador, State of Chiapas, Mexico.* The church bells began ringing at dawn, beckoning the spirits of the dead and rousing the villagers to begin preparing for their annual festival of communion with departed souls.

Women and girls busied themselves baking round loaves of bread and wrapping them in cloth. They packed baskets with rags and scrub brushes, photos and mementos, then went to the market to purchase flowers and candles, beer and cakes. At midday, grandmothers and mothers, daughters and sons gathered at the cemetery to prepare the graves, pulling weeds and sweeping away leaves, scrubbing away dirt and moss, pushing back against the jungle's unrelenting drive to reclaim the small patch of cleared ground. They set out food and drink for returning loved ones, draped tree branches with multicolored paper streamers, scattered flowers along the paths, and lined the walkways with candles. Then they returned home and rested for the celebration to come.

At dusk, the townspeople returned to the square—adults in their finery, children in masks and face paint—to join the evening's celebration and procession. Minstrels wandered through the crowd, singing and playing their instruments. Youngsters ran and danced. Mummers costumed as death itself led the procession through streets lined with stalls, past windows and doorways lit with jack-o'-lanterns, beneath strings of paper skeletons overhead.

At the cemetery, families gathered in small clusters at gravesides, spread out blankets, and settled in for their all-night vigil. A haunting calm set in as the light of day began surrendering to the amber radiance of candles. Soft prayers and whispered conversations mixed with warm laughter rose to Heaven on the evening air.

A group of seven people—two women, two men, two young adults, and a young child—stopped and stood at the foot of three graves identified with simple white stone markers, one older, one newer, one newer still. Teresa, Quina, and Alegra, twelve years old and on the threshold of womanhood, stood together, at the foot of the graves. They were dressed almost identically in fresh white folklorico blouses with ribbon and lace bibs, and matching skirts, scarlet sashes tied around their waists, woolen rebozos the color of midnight around their shoulders. Their hair hung in long braids plaited with blue-green ribbons. The first whisps of gray were appearing at Quina's temples.

Mateo, Oscar, and Rafael, a young man of eighteen standing without crutches on a prosthetic leg, positioned themselves a few steps behind the women, dressed in clean white shirts and freshly pressed black trousers, their hair neatly cropped and combed. A five-year-old boy held Rafael's hand—not white, not Indian, but a striking mestizo with chestnut hair, hazel eyes, tawny skin, and a cleft in his chin.

Teresa, Quina, and Alegra crossed themselves and stood silent for a moment, then spread two blankets on the ground in front of the graves and sat down and began unpacking their baskets. Mateo, Oscar, and Rafael settled against the high stone base of a neighboring grave marker. Rafael set the boy next to him. The men could not stay. They also had vigils to keep. Mateo would spend the night at Elba's grave.

For a while, no one spoke. Soothing music of guitars and flutes wafted over the cemetery. Thin strains of children's laughter laced through the evening air. A whisper of wind carried a veil of smoke from small fires people were building to warm themselves through the night.

Teresa took round loaves of pan de muerto and bottles of beer from her basket and passed them to Alegra and Quina to arrange around the three graves. Alegra took a framed picture out of her basket and placed it on the middle grave marker—a photograph of a handsome young couple and their laughing baby girl. The three women gazed at it for a moment, then Alegra took a second framed picture out of her basket and handed it to Quina to set atop the newest stone—a faded child's drawing of a jaguar with a black flower between its teeth. Mother and daughter gazed at the drawing and exchanged tender smiles.

Quina turned and put out a hand to the boy sitting with Rafael.

"*Nataniel, ven,*" she said.

Rafael lowered the boy to the ground and he went to Quina and climbed into her lap. Quina held him close.

"Do you know who that is?" she whispered in his ear, pointing at the drawing.

The boy nodded and smiled. "*Sí.*"

"*Quien? Quien es?*"

"*Es mi papá.*"

Quina laughed and kissed his cheek.

"*Sí, mi querido. Es tu papá.*"

"Your father was a very brave man," Mateo said to the boy. "A strong man." He put a fist to his heart. "*Un hombre verdadero.*"

The boy looked from Mateo to Rafael, hazel eyes wide.

"*Es verdad,*" Rafael said.

Oscar nodded.

Quina smiled, wrapped her rebozo around her son and folded him in her arms. In the west, the sun was slipping below the horizon. Night was coming. Soon, the dead would return. ▲

Historical Note

On Friday, February 16, 1996, after two years of negotiations, the Ejército Zapatista Nacional de la Liberación (EZLN) and the Mexican government signed a peace agreement, now known as the San Andrés Accords, that officially recognized the rights of the indigenous people of Mexico and granted them autonomy. Hopes for a better future ran high among los indígenas. But, since then, although the people have established a number of autonomous communities complete with clinics and schools in some remote parts of Chiapas, the Mexican government has largely ignored the agreement and has passed laws to undercut its promises. The military presence in Chiapas has not decreased since; it has increased. The paramilitaries returned almost immediately after the Accords were signed, and on Monday, December 22, 1997, a government-backed paramilitary group called Mascara Roja (Red Mask) attacked a church in the Zapatista-friendly Tzotzil village of Acteal, slaughtering 45 people, mostly women and children, and injuring 25 more.

The Acteal massacre is commonly considered one of the worst crimes committed against the indigenous people of Chiapas since the Zapatista uprising, but it is by no means the only one. From the day of the uprising, the Mexican government through numerous administrations has sought to brand the EZLN as a terrorist group and crush the Zapatista movement and spirit. But it has failed.

The EZLN was the organizing force behind the creation of the National Indigenous Congress (CNI) in October 1996 and worked with CNI to create the Indigenous Governing Council (CIG)— an initiative launched in January 2017 to be an independent voice for the indigenous peoples of Mexico and support community-organizing "from below and to the left," with the ultimate goal of establishing a new collective form of national self-government.

CIG's oath: "Never Again a Mexico Without Us."

As the group's founders warned in a Declaration issued at the close of its October 2018 Second National Assembly, "the path will be neither easy nor fast...." A quarter century after the Zapatista uprising, NAFTA is being replaced by a new United States-Mexico-Canada Agreement (USMCA) that does nothing for los indígenas of Chiapas—Mexico's poorest state—and time will tell if the country's new left-leaning President Andrés Manuel López Obrador (AMLO) will do anything to help them.

The War Against Forgetting is not over. The struggle that has gone on for more than five centuries continues. *La lucha continua.* The Zapatista website is still up and running.

Visit *ezln.org* and *chiapas-support.org* to learn more. 🔺

Selected Bibliography

The writing of *Mirador* consumed the better part of a decade and a half. The works I consulted during that process are too numerous to list. A selection follows for readers interested in learning more about Mexico, Chiapas, and the Zapatista Movement.

Barry, Tom. *Zapata's Revenge: Free Trade and the Farm Crisis in Mexico.* Boston: South End Press, 1999.

Garcini, Ricardo Rendón. *Haciendas de México.* Mexico City: Banamex-Accivla,1994.

Garfias, Luis M. *The Mexican Revolution: A Historic Politico-Military Compendium.* Mexico: Panorama/Ediciones Lara S.A., 1979.

Greene, Graham. *The Lawless Roads.* New York: Penguin Books, 1982.

Hayden, Judith Cooper. Introduction by Phil Borges. Text by Matthew Jaffe. *Oaxaca: The Spirit of Mexico.* New York: Artisan, a Division of Workman Publishing, Inc., 2002.

Kemper, Robert V., and Anya Peterson Royce, editors. *Chronicling Cultures: Long-Term Field Research in Anthropology.* Walnut Creek, CA: AltaMira Press, A Division of Rowman & Littlefield Publishers, Inc., 2002.

Mauldin, Barbara. Field photography by Ruth D. Lechuga. Studio photography by Blair Clark. *Masks of Mexico: Tigers, Devils, and the Dance of Life.* Santa Fe, NM: Museum of New Mexico Press, 1999.

Morris, Walter F., Jr. Photographs by Jeffrey Jay Foxx. *Living Maya.* New York: Henry M. Abrams, 1987.

Nierman, Daniel, and Ernesto H. Vallejo. Translation by Mardith Schuetz-Miller. *The Hacienda in Mexico*. Austin, TX: University of Texas Press, 2003.

Perry, Richard D. *More Mayan Missions: Exploring Colonial Chiapas*. Santa Barbara: Espadaña Press, 1995.

Poniatowska, Elena. Translated by Helen R. Lane. Introduction by Octavio Paz. *Massacre in Mexico*. New York: Viking, 1975.

Ramírez, Gloria Muñoz. *The Fire and the Word: A History of the Zapatista Movement*. San Francisco: City Lights Books, 2008.

Ross, John. *Rebellion from the Roots: Indian Uprising in Chiapas*. Monroe, ME: Common Courage Press, 1994.

Ross, John. *The War Against Oblivion: The Zapatista Chronicles, 1994-2000*. Monroe, ME: Common Courage Press, 2002.

Vogt, Evon Z. *Zinacantan: A Mayan Community in the Highlands of Chiapas*. Cambridge: Belknap, Harvard University Press, 1969.

Vogt, Evon Z. *Fieldwork Among the Maya: Reflections on the Harvard Chiapas Project*. Albuquerque: University of New Mexico Press, 1994.

Wild, Nettie (Director). *A Place Called Chiapas: Inside the World's First Postmodern Revolution* (documentary, 93 minutes). Vancouver: Canada Wild Productions, 1998.

Witynski, Karen, and Joe P. Carr. Foreword by Eugen Logan Wagner. *The New Hacienda*. Layton, UT: Gibbs Smith, 1999.

Womack, John, Jr. (Editor). *Rebellion in Chiapas: An Historical Reader*. New York: The New Press, 1999. ▲

Acknowledgments

I would like to express my appreciation to Universidad Iberoamericana, Museo Nacional de Antropología, Museo Nacional, and Museo de Historia Natural, all in Mexico City, for the incredible work these institutions do in preserving and educating about Mexico's history—its lands and peoples, politics and culture—and for nurturing the desire to learn more and delve deeper that led to the writing of this book. My thanks also to Señora Carmen de Carrillo, wherever she may be, for her hospitality and kindness during my initial stay in Mexico as an undergraduate student at La Ibero, and for being the first to sprinkle the dust of Mexico on my heart. Thanks to my late parents, Jim and Betty Jennings, for more gifts and blessings than I can count—among them, sending me to school in Mexico City at a time when I thought I was hearing the call of loftier pursuits in the north, then insisting I come home despite my reluctance and the post-sojourn murmur of a broken heart. Thank God for unanswered prayers.

I am grateful to Sara Orwig, an extraordinary novelist and teacher, for being the first to set me on the road to authorship in earnest; to the late Dr. Clif' Warren for being a visionary, for loving *Mirador* when it was little more than a fanciful notion, and for fanning the flames of creativity through the years; to my lifelong friends and fellow travelers, Ron Perry, Tim Kline, Bill Field, and the late Richard Ingham for their loyalty, their spirit of adventure, their love of exploration, and their willingness to go and see.

I would like to thank my friends at New York Writers Workshop, Ducts.org, and Greenpoint Press for giving *Mirador* a longer life in print. Thank you to Ross Klavan, Tim Tomlinson, and Charles Salzberg for their early feedback and encouragement. Thank you also to Charles Salzberg for adding *Mirador* to Greenpoint's select list. Thank you to Bob Lascaro for his wonderful cover and page design. And heartfelt thanks to my editor, Gini Kopecky Wallace, for her friendship, wisdom, sage advice, tireless labor, excellent work, and for caring so much about *Mirador*.

I thank my children, Devon, Drew, and Julie, for giving me clear focus and purpose, and for carrying the fire. Finally, most of all, thank you to my wife, Vicky, for all things good and true. Without you, there would have been no dance. ▲

About the Author

James Jennings is a writer and trial lawyer who lives with his wife, Vicky, in Edmond, Oklahoma. He is a fifth-generation Oklahoman and a citizen of the Chickasaw Nation. His ancestors came to what is now called the Sooner State on the Trail of Tears in 1837. He is descended from tribal chiefs, warriors, horse breeders, scholars, judges, and men of the cloth. A great-uncle was a Rough Rider and an aide to Theodore Roosevelt.

A founder of the law firm of Jennings Teague, Jim is admitted to practice in Oklahoma and before the U.S. Supreme Court. He is a fellow of numerous professional organizations including the prestigious American College of Trial Lawyers, and is a director of Bank2, a $200 million community bank owned by the Chickasaw Nation.

During his undergraduate years, Jim studied Latin American history and politics at Universidad Iberoamericana in Mexico City, where he fell in love with Mexico: the people and their history. He has traveled extensively throughout the country and has seen the poverty in the state of Chiapas, the site of the Zapatista uprising in 1994 and the setting for *Mirador.* He has felt the tension between *los indígenas* and the army, and knows that, for the locals, the Zapatista slogan still applies: *La lucha continua!* The struggle goes on!

Mirador is Jim's second novel. His first, *The Light Most Favorable*, was published in 2012. His third, *Blue Wild Indigo*, is nearing completion, and his fourth, *Travertine Rim*, is in progress.